RUDOLFO A. ANAYA: FOCUS ON CRITICISM

RUDOLFO A. ANAYA: FOCUS ON CRITICISM

Ed. CÉSAR A. GONZÁLEZ-T.

LALO PRESS
LA JOLLA, CALIFORNIA

Rudolfo A. Anaya: Focus on Criticism

Lalo Press
P.O. Box 12086
La Jolla, California 92039

Cover Photo by Barbara Urrea, Copyright © 1990

Layout by Mayela Padilla

ISBN: 0-9616941-4-9

Library of Congress Catalog Card Number: 89-64446

The editor thanks the following authors and/or publications for permission to reprint materials which appear in this volume:

Rudolfo A. Anaya and the *Gale Research Company*, for permission to reprint his autobiography, "Rudolfo A. Anaya," which appeared in **CONTEMPORARY AUTHORS: AUTOBIOGRAPHY SERIES**, Vol. 4, edited by Adele Sarkissan (copyright © 1986 by Gale Research Company; reprinted by permission of the publisher, all rights reserved), Gale Research, 1986, pp. 15-28.

Critica: A Journal of Critical Essays, for Héctor Calderón, "Rudolfo Anaya's *Bless Me, Ultima.* A Chicano Romance of the Southwest," 1.3 (Fall 1986): 21-47.

Hispania, for Enrique Lamadrid, "Myth as the Cognitive Process of Popular Culture in Rudolfo Anaya's *Bless me Ultima*: The Dialectics of Knowledge," 68.3 (Sept. 1985): 496-501.

Imagine: International Chicano Poetry Journal, for "Interview with Rudolfo A. Anaya," 2.2 (Winter 1985): 1-9. Interviewed by César A González-T.

David Johnson, for permission to reprint "Myth and the Writer: A Conversation with Rudolfo Anaya," *New America* 3.3 (Spring 1979): 76-85. Interviewed by David Johnson and David Apodaca.

Maize: Xicano Art and Literature Notebooks, for "Mesa Redonda con Alurista, R. Anaya, M. Herrera-Sobek, A. Morales y H. Viramontes," 4.3-4 (Spring-Summer 1981): 6-23. [Note: José Monleón chaired the *Mesa redonda*.]

[Some editorial adjustments have been made in reprinted materials, principally in accents and punctuation.]

Dedicated to
DON LUIS LEAL
pionero ejemplar
el que abre caminos

TABLE OF CONTENTS

ACKNOWLEDGEMENTS

My first thanks are to the contributors for their generous cooperation, scholarship, and patience. A special word of appreciation to Don Luis Leal, to whom this work is dedicated, for his friendship, encouragment, and counsel. To my beloved spouse, Bette Beattie González, my grateful thanks for the precious gift of time.

Erlinda Gonzales-Berry first suggested the idea of this collection, during my sabbatical at the University of New Mexico in the spring of 1986. *Gracias.*

A special word of thanks to the many librarians and professional researchers who gave so generously of their time in assisting me in background research and confirmation of sources. María Teresa Huerta Márquez of the Zimmerman Library at the University of New Mexico deserves a special word of gratitude. I am also indebted to Iliana L. Sonntag, Latin American Bibliographer of the University Library, San Diego State University; Lillian Castillo-Speed, and the staff of the Chicano Periodical Index at the University of California, Berkeley; Salvador Güereña and Raquel Quiroz González of La Colección Tloque Nahuaque, the University of California, Santa Barbara; Barbara G. Valk, Editor of the Hispanic American Peiodicals Index; and Warren Heyer and the staff of the San Diego Mesa College Library.

Others from Mesa College whose encouragement and cooperation I am pleased to acknowledge, include first and principally Betty Jo Tucker, Dean of Humanities; then Dean Ray Ramírez and the members of the A.B. 1725 Committee; also *mi colega* Michael R. Ornelas who carried the chairmanship of the Chicano Studies Department beyond his tenure, allowing me time to work on this project; Larry Atherton, Director of the Independent Learning Center and his staff, for computer and technical advice, including John Tessin,

Melissa Nyiri, Mike Gast, and Nam Dang.   Sra. Araceli Fisk and the members of MEChA helped with the copyings and mailings of the manuscript.

A very special word of thanks to my dear friends Robert Hollis Watrous and his wife, Susan A. Mercure, for their sustained, generous, and invaluable technical advice; also to Margaret Siderius for her continued encouragement.

To my publisher, Ernesto Padilla of Lalo Press, my thanks for your caring, for your loyal support, and for your friendship.   To Dana Jackson, thanks for your patient, professional technical support with the final computer editing of the manuscript.

To Rudolfo A. Anaya and Patricia, thank you for your trust, for your *aprecio*, and for your abiding *amistad*.

INTRODUCTION

Rudolfo A. Anaya is a founder of the canon of the contemporary Chicano literary movement. Together with the late Tomás Rivera, Rolando Hinojosa, and Estella Portillo Trambley, he was among the first winners of the Quinto Sol Prize, awarded by Quinto Sol Publications of Berkeley, California, under the editorship of Herminio Rios C. and Octavio Ignacio Romano-V.[1]

The writings of Anaya, especially *Bless Me, Ultima,* have generated more substantive critical response than the *opera* of any other Chicano author. Future students of the history of Chicano literary criticism will study this body of texts as a paradigm of the evolution of approaches, emphases, and trends which characterized the beginnings of our critical analyses. They will raise the question of how Chicano literary critics developed their own perspectives, and to what extent they reflected established European schools, especially French and historicist schools of thought, filtered through mainstream American schools of literary criticism.[2]

If, as the editor of *The Americas Review* has pointed out, "the culture bearers of American literature have been somewhat tardy in confirming [Latinos'] existence, the Europeans have not" ("Latinos" 8).[3] A series of biennial conferences organized by Juan Bruce-Novoa and others are in progress in Europe: the first symposium was held at the University of Mainz in July, 1984,[4] followed by another at the University of Paris (March 1986),[5] then at the University of Barcelona (June 1988), with the most recent scheduled to be held at the Johannes Gutenberg University Mainz at Germersheim, July 3-6, 1990.

This international interest is represented in our collection by the contributions of three outstanding European scholars. **Jean Cazemajou** of the University of Bordeaux brings the audience of the writer into play in his treatment of mediation. He tells us, in his essay--"The Search for a Center: The Shamanic Journey of Mediators in Anaya's Trilogy, *Bless Me, Ultima*; *Heart of Aztlán*, and *Tortuga*"--that "the central problem of mediation for a writer has to do with the very instrumentality and scope of literary communication," which for Anaya transcends the limits of a New Mexican or Chicano audience. Cazemajou identifies mythic, textural, and semi-religious dimensions of mediation brought into play by Anaya to communicate with this world-wide audience. Anaya's work, therefore, "cannot be described with the reductive phrase 'minority literature'" (256, 258). As an authority on Stephen Crane, Cazemajou also sees textual interplay between Crane and Anaya.

Heiner Bus, of the Johannes Gutenberg-Universität in Mainz, compares Sherwood Anderson's Beaut in *Marching Men*, with Anaya's Clemente in *Heart of Aztlán*,[6] "giving special emphasis to the emergence of the leader, his interaction with the group, and the function of change as depicted in physical and mental movement"(114). He includes Freudian/Jungian oppositions which have also been commented on by Anaya in his interview with David Johnson and David Apodaca.[7]

Horst Tonn of the University of Duisburg, West Germany, is the translator of *Bless Me, Ultima*; *Segne mich, Ultima* (Frankfurt/M., 1984). Both his master's thesis and his doctoral dissertation include work on Anaya. Tonn develops the theme of "Fictional Response to Times of Transition." The "extraliterary context" of the novel, he tells us, "adds an important dimension. . . . The novel constitutes a significant response to relevant [community] issues . . . identity formation, mediation of conflict and utilization of the past for the exigencies of the present" (1-2). Nostalgia gives way to "a sense of anticipation for the future whereby the past serves as a storehouse of valuable experience, not as an object for retrogressive fantasies" (9).

This abundance of critical comment reflects the significance of Anaya in the expanding history of Chicano literature. Antonio Márquez, in his analysis of Anaya's place in Chicano letters, has stated that Anaya's work liberates "Chicano literature from the confines of 'ethnic' or 'regionalism' literature" (33). Márquez adds that "mythopoesis and the art of myth making--is the crux of Anaya's philosophical and artistic vision. . . . informed by the conviction that myth is an eternal reservoir that nourishes the most creative and the most universal art" (45-46). Ironically, these very strengths have raised a tempest of heuristic controversy over the "relevance" of Anaya within the context of certain definitions of Chicano literature, while others favor opening the frames of our literature to preclude "the politics of exclusion," as Bruce-Novoa expressed it (4/14/88) at the National Association of Chicano Studies Conference (NACS XVI), celebrated at the University of Colorado, Boulder.

The mythico-mystical heartland of Anaya's writing concerns some critics who question the relevance of myth and cosmic purposefulness in the world. This historicism would interpret the problem of evil in terms of social evils seen as a consequence of class exploitation. Hence, human suffering, which is a concern in all of Anaya's works, especially in *Tortuga*, should be alleviated through concrete social action and strategies available to all people, rather than through cosmic insights available only to shamans and their proteges. Poets and writers who would transcend these parameters of analysis and structure, it is sometimes suggested, are revisionists.

The underlying philosophical assumption is that being is not analogical nor composite in any sense, but is rather univocal--matter pure and simple. Spiritual problems, spiritual solutions (including magic, religion, and myth) are anathema and belong to the naifs of ages past. José Monleón, for example, characterizes Anaya as a medieval anachronism in a twentieth-century technologically sophisticated society, whose ultimate solutions are for the shamans, the elect, the *selecti quidem* (187). Elsewhere, he tells us that we must set aside the universalist perception of myth as an eternally abiding essence once-and-for-all revealed by the classic writers of antiquity, for from the point of view of historicism, myth is a political stance, an ideological de-affirmation of reality.[8]

Yet, Anaya would address the problem of evil on another scale, not of human creation. Deformed children are not necessarily resultants of social exploitation. Human suffering, death and change, beginnings and ends confront the human spirit seeking comprehension, raising larger questions, requiring other answers. **Vernon Lattin** first addressed these concerns in his article "The Horror of Darkness," in which he discussed Antonio's loss of innocence and the construction of a new faith in *Bless Me, Ultima.*[9] Now, Lattin offers us a mythopoetic view of evil in his "Chaos and Evil in Anaya's Trilogy." He argues that Anaya sees evil as more than "a social/political reality" (350). Hence "a spiritual transformation is essential to a meaningful confrontation with evil and chaos" in the spirit of Martin Luther King who "led his people into a *real* confrontation with injustice and was successful because he was able to move them spiritually" (355).

And **Roberto Cantú** in his "Apocalypse as an Ideological Construct: The Storyteller's Art in *Bless Me, Ultima*" studies the complex metaphor of apocalypse seen as revelation, disclosure, and the end of the world, looking to a new creation. Cantú, typically is eclectic in his use of critical approaches. Although some find this dismaying, I find it liberating and refreshing. He draws from the work of Fredric Jameson, Derrida, Lacan, Lévi-Strauss, and others. Here he see literature not so much as mimetic of reality, but rather as giving symbolic resolution to a given problem. He uses the rhetoric of *adynaton* or of the "world upsidedown" to demonstrate how, ideologically and formally, "the apocalyptic conventions that 'speak through' *Bless Me, Ultima* are ancient and of diverse sources, in character with Anaya's propensity towards syncretism, variants, and the transgression of static cultural structures" (47). *Ultima* then reflects the political unconscious of Anaya, who is a pacifist, contemplating the continuous violence of our Hobbesian world. And in exploring the deconstruction which Cantú finds at the core of the novel, he considers the ultimate irony of the Judas motif in which Antonio discovers that it is his fate to be instrumental in the undoing of his mentor as part of a larger cosmic design. Throughout his life, he is blind to his destined role in the physical dissolution of Ultima.

Anaya, moreover, questions the responses of the nihilists and of the existentialists as well. In this regard, **Bruce-Novoa** points out that Anaya will not settle for Mike's position in *Tortuga*: "Things just happen," (47) and there is no God. Bruce-Novoa adds that "although [Mike] represents a positive pole of thought, and despite his apparent closeness to Solomon, [he] limits his goals to the mere material level" (190). For Anaya, negation is endemic, inherent in process, in change. Evil is part of the order of good. Hence he will not settle for the archetypal existential hero of Musil's young Torless, who accepts the world as a place where things are as they are in a flow of arbitrary non-sense-nor-order (186). Nor will Anaya accept a world where the "gods" roll us about like marbles in the palms of their hands for their amusement (León-Portilla 121). "Anaya's belief in essentialistic truth and transcendent order," Bruce-Novoa tells us, "demands a different type of hero, one who, while passing through the questioning phase when necessary for the communal good, eventually transcends it in order to lead the community into a higher realm of existence, one in which the essential, transcendent order of being can be recognized and followed in daily life." In essence then, Anaya's break with the past is relative. If there is no divine Word infleshed, no purpose nor divine plan, yet there is an essential plan, truth, and transcendental order. Tortuga "is rewarded with a faith in the ordering and signifying power of a new creative principle based in the regenerative power of the word" (193).

Anaya, then, sees beyond the matter of the world to a spiritual context, just as he portrays people, society, and human contexts, embedded in a larger psycho-moral space. The mythic level is that of universality, but for the post-structuralists, the deconstructionists, and the materialists, universality and universals do not exist. And in a sense they are correct. Existence does not exist *in se*; only existents exist. Existence is an abstraction, just as Anaya's realities of myths are abstractions. However, when he writes of myths, of the spirit, he is addressing real affirmative *potentials* within existents, within people, centers of human energy who can affirm constantly.

Ernesto Padilla, in his sensitive commentary on the Dantesque journey of *Tortuga*, wrestles with the problem of physical and moral evil. He values Anaya's revelation of the height of human affirmation through the experience of the depths of evil, and discovers that the protagonist "is destined to achieve the only thing that is not expendable for humanity: a simple love that asks for no reward other than to love" (232). Padilla, along with Monleón, objects to the "ideological defect" of magic and cosmic mysticism as solutions for suffering humankind. These critics reject myth as a response out of tune with the times, which demand communal social action. However, as I have reiterated, for Anaya there is within historicity a real creative potential for affirmation, order, and life which will not be overcome, and which will prevail within individuals and within society. And this creative potential transcends matter and any given historical society, state, or system.

The dynamics of this process are perceived differently by **Enrique Lamadrid** and **Roberto Cantú**. Lamadrid avoids ideological analysis by taking a structuralist approach. He sees myth as "an ongoing process of interpreting and mediating the contradictions in the everyday historical experience of the people" (103). He finds embedded in *Bless Me, Ultima* "the process which generates social and historical consciousness. . . . [which] a Marxist-Structuralist perspective defines . . . as myth, the collective interpretation and mediation of the contradictions in the historical and ecological experience of a people" (101). Cantú, as mentioned earlier, sees the search for synthesis ruled by an inner principle which perpetuates, aside from brief intervals of apparent harmony, a process of continuous fragmentation and disjunction.

These discussions propel us toward philosophical-theological considerations. However, for those who eschew faith and reason, much of this is vanity. For them, reality is better explicated in a univocal, materialistic sense, rather than in an analogical sense; just as the deconstructionists see reality in an equivocal, forever indeterminate sense. However, for Anaya, it appears that "there is little to choose between the soulless materialism of the West and the militant materialism of the East," (Malik 30) and the skepticism of both. Neither addresses the hunger of the spirit. Anaya stubbornly insists that there is something more. And, although I may not agree with him as to what that something more is, I heartily agree that the very work of art is an analogy, a witness to the something more that can be made a reality as a result of the infinite potential of the human spirit for affirmation--for immaterial truth and for immaterial love.

In this regard, **Luis Leal** comments, on "Anaya's ability to write about universal themes as they are interpreted through the perspective of a Chicano who sees reality as it has been seen by the people whose culture he has inherited." Don Luis presents us with a new study of Anaya's short fiction, while pointing to thematic textualities with Latin American literature. Anaya, Leal tells us, even as "Miguel Ángel Asturias (Nobel Prize, 1967), Alejo Carpentier, Juan Rulfo, and Gabriel García Márquez (Nobel Prize, 1982). . . . has been able to create new visions out of old realities" (335). We might add to Don Luis's list the name of Jorge Luis Borges (1899-1986). For what Octavio Paz has said of Borges' stories and poems is relevant here. They are, Paz tells us, "the inventions of a poet and a metaphysician. . . . [satisfying] two of mankind's central faculties: reason and fantasy." For in the end it may be that "perhaps literature has only two themes--one, man among men, his fellows and his adversaries; the other, man alone against the universe and against himself" (34). These themes and these discussions engage the critics who have contributed to this collection, and also appear in Anaya's autobiography which appears at the end of this collection.

The book, then, presents a cross-section of important contemporary critical thought, including essays by many well-known American and European critics. Almost all of the works are new, reflecting a variety of critical approaches. The essays deal, moreover, with four significant areas in Anaya's work: (1) self-definition, (2) the sacred and the profane, (3) mediation and mediators, and (4) the oneiric. And, at the risk of redundancy, I add four transcendental concerns which consistently engage Anaya: (1) the search for a center, (2) the search for a balance of dialectic tensions, (3) the search for continuity in reality, (4) transcendence.

The closing essays look across the works of Anaya from intertextual, semiotic, and comparative points of view. Besides the works of Cazemajou and Lattin, we find in **Roberto Cantú's** "The Surname, the Corpus, and the Body in Rudolfo A. Anaya's Narrative Trilogy," a breaking away from traditional readings and critiques of Anaya's canon. In what I believe to be the most comprehensive reading made to date of all of Anaya's writings, Cantú looks across the trilogy, seeing Anaya as coyote, transgressor, and ecstatic, searching for the integration of the individual within nature, and a brotherhood of community and humankind. Extending a Freudian term, he approaches the texts, from a deconstructive/semiotic point of view, as auto(psycho)grapy. Anaya, he tells us, penetrates and explores cosmological levels--heaven (*Bless Me, Ultima*), earth (*Heart of Aztlán*), and hell (*Tortuga*)--using a rhetoric "of disclosure and concealment" (277). Hence, as a Border coyote himself, Cantú leads us into Anaya's trilogy through "a transgression of limits and undocumented entries" in search of reconciliations (275).

Margarita Nieto presents us with "The Writer as Shaman: A reading of Rudolfo A. Anaya through the works of Carlos Castaneda." Her work enhances our understanding of the power and creative potential of the text and confronts us with comprehensive alternatives. She gives insight into the significance of shamanism and another approach to the grasping of dimensional reality, which we have discarded and ignore in the Western world. Her essay provides a point of comparison for understanding the margins of shamanism as expressed in the canon of Anaya. I understand her to say that both texts (Castaneda's and Anaya's) open to us other potentialities within ourselves through which we can read and be extended by the text. However, Castaneda's way of moving us through the text into a non-Western sense of other-than-linear-Cartesian reality is more in tune with "the world of meso-American myth and prophecy," than Anaya's fictional approach (330).

It should be noted that in the course of her study, Nieto acknowledges the controversy questioning whether Castaneda's popular works are those of a fiction writer or of a scientist. She does not present him as someone to whom we should turn first as a principal exponent of Native American spirituality, something to which Native Americans take serious exception.

The opening essays address, in turn, each novel of the trilogy: *Bless Me, Ultima*; *Heart of Aztlán*, and *Tortuga*. The studies on *Ultima* included in this collection reflect the centrality of that work to the first period of Anaya and to his canon. Beside the authors already mentioned addressing *Ultima*, **Héctor Calderón** seeks to refine the attribution of novel, suggesting that the work is better read as a romance, following Northrop Frye's critical sense of *romance*:[10] "It is the romance whose formal possibilities and stylistic features can accommodate mythic and religious materials, as well as folk beliefs, and then project them in almost any age as ideals and wish-fulfillment fantasies, that will give us greater insights into *Bless Me, Ultima*" (66). For in its pristine sense, the novel deals with the real rather than the fabulous. Calderón, however, sees Anaya's use of myth as a flight from history.

Along with Heiner Bus, **María Herrera-Sobek** and **César A. González-T.** address *Heart of Aztlán*. Herrera-Sobek looks at "Women as Metaphor in the Patriarchal Structure of *Heart of Aztlán*." She asserts that "the construction of the female characters in the novel's universe is that of metaphoric entities representing the loss of Chicano (male) power in the Anglo capitalist system depicted in the novel. . . . [Women] serve the larger interests of the structure of the novel which is to present the plight of the dispossessed, disenfranchised, and marginalized Chicano population" (166). Anaya would agree that his universe is a male universe. González, after first discussing Anaya's use of myth with reference to the social responsibility of the writer, considers "the function, structure, and movement of *Heart*, . . . with reference to the theories of myth proposed by Lévi-Strauss, Carl J. Jung and, Northrop Frye"(133). González sees *Heart* as moving "through a quest myth that escapes from romantic irony into the revolutionary dimensions of myth" (155).

María Elena López sees *Tortuga* as a novel of initiation and of physical and psychological *renovatio*: from the depths of the unconscious, through a series of hierophantic dreams, to individuation and shamanic initation. She further illumines our reading of the novel through her extrapolations from José A. Arguelles' *Transformative Vision* in which he argues for a redress of the imbalance brought about by rationalism and linear evolution. A merging of the insight of the scientist and the vision of the artist, he tells us, will return us to the more natural cyclical order of the universe. López's Jungian analysis of mythic symbolism sees Salomón as the mystic child and the personification of the self, and Ismelda as Tortuga's anima.

María Teresa Huerta Márquez updates her on-going comprehensive bibliographic research on Anaya, begun in *The Magic of Words*, edited by Paul Vassallo (1982), in which she graciously acknowledged the pioneering work of Ernestina Eger. Márquez' outstanding selected crtical bibliography, which, for the sake of completeness includes the titles in this text, is a major and valued contribution.

The book closes with an appendix which includes Anaya's autobiography, written with poetic sensitivity, candor, and economy of style, reprinted here with the kind permission of the author and of the Gale Research Company. It might, otherwise, remain relatively inaccessible to the broader public who will find in it the balance and strength of the polished writer who gives rich bio-textuality to his works. The interview with **David Johnson** and **David Apodaca** and another with **César A. González-T.**, along with the "Mesa Redonda con **Alurista, R. Anaya, M. Herrera-Sobek, A. Morales y H. Viramontes**," were selected because of the forum which they give to the voice of the author, Rudolfo A. Anaya, dealing with a number of themes central to his search for center. These articles also serve as a historical review for students new to the field.

It is hoped that this introduction will interest the reader in turning to this collection of critical studies and especially to the texts of Rudolfo A. Anaya. Like all significant writers, he is damned, patronized, and lionized. Some indulgently say that "he is teachable," while others say that "he is writing at a depth that is not fully appreciated." Anaya does not respond to critics. They will continue to do what they must, and he will continue to do what he must. He will continue to be read as a Chicano writer who speaks to that something more within that can help us make ourselves human. He is comprehended by the resonances, continuities, and analogies between the heart of matter and the heart of spirit, which we divine only from a distance. For human space and time too are curved, and in the end it is literature which reflects the uniqueness of all human experience as it flows into the communality of unity in diversity.

César A. González-T.
San Diego Mesa College
December 12, 1989

NOTES

[1] Bruce-Novoa has commented on the role of Quinto Sol Publications in establishing the canon of Chicano literature (122).   See his essay on "Canonical and Noncanonical Texts."   *The Americas Review* 14.3-4 (Fall-Winter 1986):   119-35.

For collections of critical articles on two of these authors, see the following:

Saldivar, José David, ed.   *The Rolando Hinojosa Reader: Essays Historical and Critical.*   Houston: Arte Publico,   1985.   [*Revista Chicano-Riqueña* 12, 3-4 (Fall-Winter 1984).]

Olivares, Julián, ed.   *International Studies in Honor of Tomás Rivera.*   Houston: Arte Publico, 1986.   [*Revista Chicano-Riqueña* 13. 3-4 (1985).]

[2] Roberto Cantú raised this concern on December 14, 1986, at a workshop of the Stanford Program for Faculty Renewal, December 12-14, 1986, "Chicano Studies: Theories and Methods," in Pasadena, California.   He also suggested that Gustavo Segade, in his landmark article of 1973, which perhaps deserves more attention than it has received, laid the foundation for future theories of space, dialectics, difference, and otherness.   ["Toward a Dialectic of Chicano Literature."   Mester 4.1 (Nov. 1973): 4-5.]   Carmen Salazar called attention to Segade's work in her article: "Current Trends in Chicano Literary Criticism."   *The Identification and Analysis of Chicano Literature.* Ed. Francisco Jiménez.   New York: Bilingual Press, 1979.   134-42.

[3] Referring to "minority" writers as strangers in their own land among academics and publishers, Leslie Marmon Silko, in a dialogue with Rolando Hinojosa, remarks: "America might be one of the few countries where some of the best writers have to have *international* recognition before our own nation recognizes us" (117).   *Puerto del Sol* 22.2 (Spring 1987):   112-27. The biases of mainstream publishers are an oft-repeated concern of Anaya, as

a cursory review of María Teresa Huerta Márquez's forthcoming annotated bibliography (Greenwood Press) on Anaya will reveal.

[4] Twenty-six papers presented at the Mainz conference have been published by the Johannes Gutenberg-Universität Mainz, cosponsored by UC MEXUS Center for Chicano Studies of the University of California at Santa Barbara: See Renate von Bardeleben, Dietrich Briesemeister, and Juan Bruce-Novoa, eds. *Missions in Conflict: Essays on U.S.-Mexican Relations and Chicano Culture.* Tubingen: Gunter Narr Verlag, 1986. The collection includes an essay on Anaya: See Alfred Jung. "Regionalist Motifs in Rudolfo A. Anaya's Fiction (1972-82)." 159-67.

[5] See *European Perspectives on Hispanic Literature of the United States.* Ed. Genvieve Fabre. Houston: Arte Publico, 1988.

[6] Both *Marching Men* (1917) and *Heart of Aztlán* (1976) were the second novels written by each author; neither was well received.

[7] See David Johnson and David Apodaca. "Myth and the Writer: A conversation with Rudolfo Anaya." *New America* 3.3 (Spring 1979):   84. **Reprinted as an appendix in this volume.**

[8] See Monleón's prefatory remarks to the UC Irvine round table: "Mesa redonda con Alurista, R. Anaya, M. Herrera Sobek, A. Morales y H. Viramontes." *Maize* 4.3-4 (Spring-Summer 1981), 6. **Reprinted as an appendix in this volume.**

[9] "The 'Horror of Darkness': Meaning and Structure in Anaya's *Bless Me, Ultima. Revista Chicano-Riqueña* 6.2 (Spring 1978):   50-57.

[10] Calderón expresses his belief that Anaya derives from Frye "his plot structures of romance and key terms in his literary vocabulary, such as archetype, mythos, inscape and epiphany" [See Héctor Calderón. "Rudolfo Anaya's *Bless Me, Ultima. A Chicano Romance of the Southwest." Critica: A Journal of Critical Essays* 1.3 (Fall 1986): 23.] Calderón footnotes this

statement as follows: "Other influences aside, the similarities between Anaya and Frye are beyond mere coincidence. Márquez reaches a similar conclusion" (See Antonio Márquez. "The Achievement of Rudolfo A. Anaya." *The Magic of Words: Rudolfo A. Anaya and His Writings.* Ed. Paul Vasallo. Albuquerque: U of New Mexico P, 1982, 46).

In the place cited by Calderón in "The Achievement of Rudolfo A. Anaya," Márquez expresses himself as follows: "Anaya's aesthetic credo is in accord with Northrop Frye's distinction that 'myth is a form of verbal art, and belongs to the world of art. Unlike science, it deals, not with the world that man contemplates, but with the world that man creates' [Northrop Frye, "Myth, Fiction and Displacement," *Myth and Myth Making,* ed. Henry A. Murray (New York: George Braziller, 1960), p. 164.]."

In an interview which I had with Anaya in San Diego, on March 31, 1985--before Calderón's article appeared--I asked Anaya: "Do you sometimes use Northrop Frye's 'Structure of Literary Types' as a map, as it were, for developing your novels?" Anaya, without hesitation, categorically answered: "No, never." See special prose issue of Tino Villanueva's *Imagine,* edited by Luis Alberto Urrea: "Interview with Rudolfo A. Anaya." 2.2 (Winter 1985): 1-9. **Reprinted as an appendix in this volume.**

WORKS CITED

Anaya, Rudolfo A. *Tortuga.* Berkeley: Justa, 1979.

"Latinos at PEN and Paris: The U.S. Hispanic Esthetic." *The Americas Review.* 14.3-4 (Fall-Winter 1986): 8-10.

León-Portilla, Miguel. *Aztec Thought and Culture: A Study of the Ancient Nahuatl Mind.* Trans. Jack Emory Davis. First pub. 1956. Norman: U of Oklahoma P, 1963.

Malik, Charles. *War and Peace.* A statement made before the Political Committee of the General Assembly, November 23, 1949. New York: The National Committee for Free Europe, Inc., 1950.

Márquez, Antonio. "The Achievement of Rudolfo A. Anaya." *The Magic of Words: Rudolfo A. Anaya and his Writings.* Ed. Paul Vassallo. Albuquerque: U of New Mexico P, 1982. 33-52.

Monleón, José. "Ilusión y realidad en la obra de Rudolfo Anaya." *Contemporary Chicano Fiction: A Critical Survey.* Ed. Vernon E. Lattin. Binghamton, New York: Bilingual Press, 1986. 171-99.

Paz, Octavio. "In Time's Labyrinth." *The New Republic,* 3 Nov. 1986: 30-34.

Bless Me Ultima: Fictional Response to Times of Transition

Horst Tonn
University of Duisburg
West Germany

In a recently published autobiographical statement, Rudolfo Anaya talks about the circumstances surrounding the publication of his first novel *Bless Me, Ultima.* After the manuscript had been repeatedly rejected by New York publishers, Anaya sent the book to the small Chicano press Quinto Sol in Berkeley. Herminio Ríos and Octavio Romano, then editors of Quinto Sol, accepted it almost instantly, and *Bless Me, Ultima* was first published in 1972.[1] Since its first appearance, the novel has continuously sold well. Sales figures are well beyond the 250,000 mark. The novel has generated the largest body of review, interpretation and analysis of any work of contemporary Chicano literature; *Bless Me, Ultima* has been called a "classic" by some.[2] While that assessment may be disputed, hardly anyone would deny that the book must be viewed as a key text in the development of the Chicano novel. The acclaim it has received both nationally and internationally is well justified. In sum, *Bless Me, Ultima* seems to have been "the right book at the right time."

This catchy phrase, however, carries little explanatory value, especially since the novel does not seem to harmonize with the historical context, the militant and disruptive political climate of the late 1960s and early 1970s. Enrique R. Lamadrid has pointed out how the novel stands in contrast to the dominant mood of that period: "*Ultima* was serene in the face of this turmoil, full of conflict, yet non-combative, a portrait of the developing consciousness of the young protagonist, Antonio" (496). Despite this apparent contradiction, the nexus between the work of fiction and its extraliterary context adds an important dimension.

Bless Me, Ultima is certainly more than a New Mexican variant on the universal theme of adolescence and apprenticeship which, if told well, will always find its audience. Apart from the mythical, psychological, regional, and supernatural elements there is another layer where the novel constitutes a significant response to relevant issues in the community. In broad terms, these issues are identity formation, mediation of conflict, and utilization of the past for the exigencies of the present. Both the narrated time and moment of the novel's first appearance can be called periods of transition. Both United States society at large during the 1960s and early 1970s and the rural New Mexican community of the mid-1940s portrayed in the text were undergoing major changes. Traditional lifestyles had become obsolete; newly emerging patterns of meaning were competing to replace them. Values and identities were seriously questioned and required adaptation or replacement.

In the novel, the pressures of change are most cogently dramatized in folk responses to the detonation of the first atomic test bomb near Alamogordo, New Mexico, on July 16, 1945. There is nothing to match the distress caused by the enormity of the event. Apocalyptic fantasies featuring a revengeful God are the only communal resources which provide some measure of relief:

> "The atomic bomb," they whispered, "a ball of white heat beyond the imagination, beyond hell--" And they pointed south, beyond the green valley of El Puerto. "Man was not made to know so much," the old ladies cried in hushed, hoarse voices, "they compete with God, they disturb the seasons, they seek to know more than God Himself. In the end, that knowledge they seek will destroy us all--" (183)

This sense of being aghast in the face of the incomprehensible was shared by many Americans in the 1960s. Major upheavals posed a serious challenge to the dominant self-image of United States society at the time. Widespread dissent on internal and external affairs led to fundamental shifts in societal values and mores. The overall consensus was modified, or categorically rejected by some and even destroyed beyond repair. Various marginal groups presented their cases and at least gained visibility:

> The Civil Rights Movement, Vietnam, the assassination of John and Robert Kennedy and of Martin Luther King, urban renewal à la Watts and Detroit, shattered the dominant self-image of many Americans. The tacit hierarchical definition of culture came under severe questioning by the American youth culture. Proportionate to the decline of the dominant macho-ideology the other cultural alternatives and traditions in America--most of whom had not been victorious rose into visibility: Blacks, Native Americans, Chicanos, Appalachians, and Women. (Ostendorf 6)

Chicanos participated in the general movement for societal change. If one is willing to accept landmark events as parameters of an essentially continuous social process, then the most active part of the recent Chicano political movement extends roughly from the first Delano grapepickers' strike in 1965 to the "Chicano Moratorium" in Los Angeles in 1970.[3] In the fall of 1965 Filipino and Chicano fieldworkers in the Delano area staged a major strike which was to last five years before union contracts were finally signed. This strike sparked the farm labor movement which then spread throughout the country. While fieldworkers in California were radically challenging their inferior status, Chicanos in New Mexico rallied almost simultaneously under Reies Tijerina to confront the authorities with claims to land ownership. In addition, Chicanos elsewhere participated in protests against the war in Indochina and vehemently fought for civil rights at home. In March of 1968, Chicano high school students in Los Angeles organized massive school-walkouts which inspired similar political actions in other parts of the country. On August 29, 1970, the "Chicano Moratorium" took place: an estimated 20,000 to 30,000 Chicanos from all over the United States gathered in Los Angeles to voice their protest against the war.[4]

Concomitant with heightened social protest there was also increased artistic productivity in the group.[5] For the Chicano novel, which is of prime importance in this context, Charles Tatum sees a first stage of maturation in the period from 1971 to 1975. During this period several novels appeared which were well received and readily accepted into the gradually emerging canon of Chicano literature. *Bless Me, Ultima* was one of the novels in this group. While it is clear that these works of fiction are related to the political issues and social concerns of the movement, it is difficult to state in more precise terms the exact nature of that relationship. Rudolfo Anaya himself has commented on this point. According to him, his novel relates to the Chicano reader's common experience and allows for identification:

> *Bless Me, Ultima* had touched a chord of recognition in the Mexican-American community. . . . Most of the Chicanos who had lived the small town, rural experience easily identified with it. Everybody had stories of *curanderas* they had known in their communities. The novel was unique for its time; it had gone to the Mexican-American people as the source of literary nourishment. It became a mirror in which to reflect on the stable world of the past, a measure by which to view the future. (*Contemporary Authors* 24)

Bless Me, Ultima, no doubt contributes to an ongoing dialogue about revised group identity which was most forcefully articulated at the time. Set in a rural New Mexican environment which is subject to dramatic transformations, the novel explores various responses to the deterioration of a traditional life-style exposed to the pressures of conquest and assimilation. Cultural conflict calls for mediation and reconciliation; elements vanishing from a tradition must be replaced by others. Influences disruptive to the collective self-image require either adequate defense mechanisms or a rearrangement of that image into a new order.

The formation of an identity is inconceivable without sound knowledge of the past. In such moments of transition or crisis, fictional texts can help to explore potentially successful strategies for the group. It has been pointed out that Antonio and Ultima, the two protagonists, function as mediators within the plot structure of the novel.[6] Their task is to heal and reconcile when the community is faced with cultural strife and disruptive outside influences. On another level, the novel itself can be said to share in and contribute . mediation process at work in the Chicano community during the 1960s and early 1970s.

One explanation for the success of *Bless Me, Ultima* may be the fact that the novel responds to a pressing need for adaptation in the vision of the collective identity. To be sure, the text does not speak for the whole group, and it does not cover the entire complexity of the identity formation process at hand. The scope of the narration, with its focus on rural New Mexico in the 1940s, is, in fact, rather limited. Apart from curiosity about that particular environment, what may appeal to a broader audience is the probing and truly exploratory character of the text. *Bless Me, Ultima* does not present a finished version of adapted identity, but rather prefigures the process of identity formation itself.

Anaya refuses to give easy answers nor does he offer ready-made concepts. His novel cannot be read as being complementary with any particular variant of the ideologies available at the time, regardless of whether they are nationalistic or assimilatory, militant or conciliatory in outlook. The reader is allowed insight into the labor that is involved in coming to terms with the complexities of cultural conflict. The impetus in the narration explores avenues of comprehension in a shifting world rather than a static "nailed down," world, to borrow a phrase here from the autobiographical protagonist in Ralph Ellison's *Invisible Man* (560).

Antonio's development in the novel can be viewed as the groping discovery of potentially useful strategies that will enable him to confront the challenges of present and future. He starts out by searching for a model to be imitated or at least closely followed. As all accessible models, upon closer inspection, display grave defects, he comes to reject, under Ultima's guidance, the very idea of aligning his destiny with any preconceived pattern. Parental authority, Catholic dogma, and folk belief suffer a severe loss of credibility while Antonio gains in self-assurance and critical intelligence. His probing investigation of traditional patterns of meaning is the foremost concern of the novel.

The claim that *Bless Me, Ultima* contributes successfully to a revision of group identity must lead to the question of how history is presented in the novel, an issue which continues to be disputed among critics. Anaya has been repeatedly criticized for a nostalgic world view or for inadequate treatment of the historical in his novel. Joseph Sommers' judgment is obvious when he talks about "the harking back with sadness and nostalgia to a forgotten, idealized and unobtainable past, as is true of *Bless Me, Ultima*, by Rudolfo Anaya" (61). Héctor Calderón interprets Anaya's narrative strategy as "a flight from history" (39). However, it is my contention that the representation of history must be seen in connection with the narrative voice employed in the novel.

Although *Bless Me, Ultima* is a novel with a first-person narrator, that designation tends to blur the real issue. The narrative voice is neither that of the child-protagonist nor that of the matured author-narrator. It has to be located somewhere in between. If we follow Franz K. Stanzel's theory of narrative, then *Bless Me, Ultima* belongs to the category of "quasi-autobiographical novels." These texts are characterized by a structural tension between the older, matured, insightful "I" as narrator and the younger "I" as protagonist for whom the plot is existential reality.[7] Anaya handles this tension in the narrative voice extremely well. The retrospective narrator asserts himself on the very first page of the novel. It is his task to determine beginning and end, to transform memory into a cohesive story: "Let me begin at the beginning. I do not mean the beginning that was in my dreams and the stories they whispered to me about my birth, and the people of my father and mother, and my three brothers--but the beginning that came with Ultima" (1).

The presence of this narrator who adds order to the otherwise unintelligible flow of memories remains, of course, noticeable throughout, and it is his linguistic and intellectual competence which "writes" the text. The fictional world created, however, is essentially that of the child-protagonist.

With few exceptions, the narrative voice successfully manages to recreate the perceptual and intellectual limitations of a six-to-eight-year-old boy. Accordingly, the sum total of historical "sophistication" acquired by the boy in the course of the novel remains more or less on the level of hearsay, random pieces of information and rumors infused with folk belief. In Antonio's perception, World War II occurs vaguely as "the far-off war of the Japanese and the Germans" (30). The period of Anglo-American conquest is equally reduced to what seems manageable for a child:

> Then the railroad came. The barbed wire came. The songs, the corridos became sad, and the meeting of the people from Texas with my forefathers was full of blood, murder, and tragedy. The people were uprooted. They looked around one day and found themselves closed in. The freedom of land and sky they had known was gone. (119)

Childlike naiveté, curiosity and eagerness are utilized to set the pace and direction of the narrative. Diction and style contribute to the same purpose. As a result, the novel closely approximates the world of childlike perception and conceptualization and, more importantly, the tension inherent in the narrative voice is maintained. The "I" as narrator and the "I" as protagonist do not supersede nor interfere with one another. The narrative impulse is generally towards re-creation of the past event rather than towards retrospective assessment from a privileged, that is to say, matured and more knowledgeable, point of view.

Within this scheme the major social and political issues such as conquest, racial discrimination, or exploitation of labor do not figure prominently, but the lack of historical context should not be regarded as a flaw of the novel. Instead, it can be seen as an inherent limitation in the choice of a narrative voice which is highly effective in recreating an approximation of the protagonist's world. The perceptual limitations of the young boy restrict the use of historical material in the text. To call for a more extensive representation of history in *Bless Me, Ultima* is to call for a change in the narrative voice, which is almost to imply that Anaya should have written another novel. This hardly seems a legitimate claim.

Historical allusions extend from early Spanish colonization to the first atomic explosion in New Mexico in 1945. While their quantity is certainly negligible, it should be noted that a historical dimension is structurally embedded in the narration. The Spanish period and the Mexican period are aligned with opposing strains in the genealogy of Antonio's family. On his father's side, the family sees itself as directly descending from the first Spanish conquerors. Their identity is based on an idealized, highly nostalgic vision of the past. In their collective memory, the early Spanish colonizers figure as restless adventurers who crossed the seas and roamed the American continent. Continuing that life-style, the father's family remained rootless. They turned to the occupations of shepherd and cattleman in which they could satisfy their restlessness. Antonio's father has to suffer the final break with that family tradition when a rural existence will not sustain the family. He must accept employment in railroad and highway construction and move his family closer to the ways of the town. After the nostalgically revered life as a *vaquero* has vanished, he finds himself entwined in the schemes of Anglo-American takeover of the region.

Family roots on the mother's side are closely related to the brief Mexican period in the history of the Southwest. After Mexico had gained independence from Spain in 1821, the Mexican government distributed land grants in order to facilitate the settlement of its Northern provinces. Ancestors on the mother's side had taken advantage of this opportunity. Among their early leaders was a priest whom Anaya has obviously patterned after Father José A. Martínez, an influential New Mexican clergyman in the 19th century, who is said to have played a key role in the organization of the Taos Revolt of 1846.[8] The followers of this priest had settled in a fertile river valley. As opposed to the father's family, they struck roots in the land and favored a stable, earthbound existence. Their ideal was that of a small rural community inspired by the Catholic faith and led by a priest.

While visions and aspirations on the father's and mother's side are diametrically opposed, both parents share an equally nostalgic outlook on their respective ancestry. Their orientation is clearly personally historical. The deficiencies of the present are compensated by turning to the consoling wholeness of an idealized past. Antonio's father responds to the widening gap between an inadequate present and an allegedly happy past, with resignation. The mother attempts to rescue her ideal by placing expectations on her youngest son. Her hope is that he will continue the tradition of the family. Nostalgia, which is frequently evoked in the novel, occurs always in alignment with certain characters. It does not account for the overall narrative stance in *Bless Me, Ultima*. The protagonist Antonio does not share this attitude. In the course of the narration, the distance between his parents and his own concerns increases, and it becomes clear that nostalgia is an inadequate strategy for coping with the intricacies of the present predicament. No doubt, the elements of nostalgia in the text may well contribute to the reader's enjoyment. A vision that emanates serenity, peace, and wholeness will not fail to exert its attraction, regardless of whether that perfect state stems from verifiable fact or idealization. The reader, however, should not be absorbed by this. There is another level of significance in which the ramifications of historical nostalgia are explored and found wanting. The narration does not so much accentuate a sense of sorrow for what is irredeemably lost, as it thrives on a sense of anticipation for the future, a future in which the past serves as a storehouse of valuable experience, not as an object for retrogressive fantasies.

NOTES

[1] See *Contemporary Authors*, 24.

[2] For a more comprehensive and up-dated compilation of Anaya criticism see María Teresa Huerta Márquez's bibliography in this volume. Also see RUDOLFO A. ANAYA A Bio-Bibliography as a title in the Series Bio-Bibliographies in American Literature; forthcoming publication of the Greenwood Press, eds. María Teresa Huerta Márquez, and César A. González-T.

[3] To illustrate the problems involved in assigning beginning and end to an essentially continuous social process: it was the Filipino fieldworkers who had initiated the strike in Delano. The Chicanos followed at first reluctantly. César Chávez would have preferred to wait. See Levy, 182-86.

[4] See Acuña, chapters 9 and 10; Meier/Rivera, chapters 14 and 15.

[5] This is not to imply that the political movement clearly predates or even generates the cultural movement or vice versa. Again, the problem is that of establishing beginning and end. Both movements are dynamically interrelated: they may echo each other and help each other along; they can move jointly or separately, or they can be fiercely at odds.

[6] See Calderón, 29, and Lamadrid, 498.

[7] See Stanzel, especially 267-72.

[8] See McWilliams, 118 and following.

WORKS CITED

Acuña, Rodolfo. *Occupied America.* 2nd ed. New York: Harper, 1981.

Anaya, Rudolfo A. *Bless Me, Ultima.* Berkeley: Quinto Sol, 1972.

___. "Rudolfo A. Anaya." *Contemporary Authors Autobiography Series,* 4 (1986): 15-28. **Reprinted in this volume**.

Calderón, Héctor. "Rudolfo Anaya's *Bless Me, Ultima.* A Chicano Romance of the Southwest." *Critica* 1 (Fall 1986): 21-47. **Reprinted in this Volume.**

Ellison, Ralph. *Invisible Man.* New York: Vintage, 1972.

Lamadrid, Enrique R. "Myth as the Cognitive Process of Popular Culture in Rudolfo Anaya's *Bless Me, Ultima*: The Dialectics of Knowledge." *Hispania* 68 (1985): 496-501. **Reprinted in this Volume.**

Levy, Jacques. *César Chávez.* New York: Norton, 1975.

McWilliams, Carey. *North From Mexico.* First pub. 1949. New York: Greenwood, 1968.

Meier, Matt S., and Feliciano Rivera. *The Chicanos.* New York: Hill, 1972.

Ostendorf, Berndt. *Black Literature in White America.* Brighton, Sussex: Harvester, 1982.

Sommers, Joseph. "From the Critical Premise to the Product." *New Scholar* 6 (1977): 51-80.

Stanzel, Franz K. *Theorie des Erzählens.* Göttingen: Vandenhoeck & Ruprecht, 1979.

Tatum, Charles M. *Chicano Literature.* Boston: Twayne, 1982.

Vassallo, Paul, ed. *The Magic of Words: Rudolfo Anaya and His Writings.* Albuquerque: U of New Mexico P, 1982.

Apocalypse as an Ideological Construct: The Storyteller's Art in *Bless Me, Ultima*

Roberto Cantú
California State University, Los Angeles

> *All come true, all burst to light!*
> *O light--now let me look my last*
> *on you! I stand revealed at last.*
> --Oedipus[1]

I. Anaya Criticism and the Homeric Battlefield

Recent Anaya criticism--represented by Thomas A. Bauder,[2] Héctor Calderón,[3] Cordelia Candelaria,[4] Enrique Lamadrid,[5] and José Monleón[6]-- continues to struggle over the meaning (literary, cultural, or political) of *Bless Me, Ultima* (BMU). Putting aside minor differences of opinion, the prevailing commentaries are based on conceptual models meant to prove BMU's alleged Chicano worldview (with its ahistorical "Aztec" perspective), its rich magical legacy as portrayed by shamanic figures, or its "flight from history," true to its generic make-up as the Chicano romance of the Southwest. In other words, Anaya criticism is still disputing whether BMU, at an ideological level, is Chicano or not Chicano enough. It is in this sense that Anaya criticism, like most Chicano literary criticism, becomes easily entrapped in essentialist notions of an assumed Chicano ontology which would determine the structural limits of our "experience" and of our expressive culture.

Another tendency of such criticism is its fixed emphasis on the problem of meaning as it is presumed resolved at the surface logic of the narrative (the "story" being told), overlooking the narrative's structuring principles and the logical connections that constitute the complexities of narrative discourse. The result for Anaya criticism has been a propensity towards allegorization or random thematic closures based on isolated passages often read as Anaya's assumed coded "message." An example of the first is readings that transform Antonio Márez Luna into an allegory of a new cultural dominant; of the other, readings that ascribe to Antonio the role of *curandero* (as Ultima's "apprentice"), or of *writer* (for his selection of birth tokens). Anaya criticism, consequently, has produced a medley of impressionistic readings claiming, for instance, that Antonio is a *curandero*, trickster, or activist;[7] that he writes a novel (i.e., BMU) to keep a promise made to Ultima (therefore, she "lives" in the novel).[8] In addition, such criticism argues that Antonio is a poet (which somehow explains to some critics Anaya's political "ambivalence"), with gifts of prophecy much like Anaya's for, as everybody knows, one is the literary "double" of the other.[9]

My argument is that Chicano political discourse has become ideologically more complex and theoretically more sophisticated than Chicano literary criticism which, along with Anaya studies, appears to be unwilling to rethink its historical grounds. Besieged or flattered by his critics, is it a wonder that Anaya has chosen to "legitimize," so to speak, not those who represent what he calls the Chicano Gang of Four,[10] but the critics who have made of Antonio a prophet and a young Chicano subject to epiphanies? The critical work to be undertaken in this study will be to challenge Anaya criticism on its own ideological premises, while avoiding its metaphysical arguments regarding what Chicano literature is or is not. This study proposes a rereading of BMU based on the logic of its plot structure, its narrative conventions (the storyteller and the typology of the audience), and its subsumptive ideological construct: apocalypse (understood both as a mode of perception, i.e., as *revelation,* and as an *event,* namely the end of a world). Notwithstanding the importance of apocalyptic imagery in BMU, and its constant rhetorical transmutations throughout the narrative, Anaya criticism has overlooked this structural construct which I consider ideological both in its compositional arrangement and in its discourse. The apocalyptic imagery surfaces mostly in landscape descriptions, often praised by Anaya criticism for their idyllic, pastoral features, for their poetic style, and for being faithful descriptions of the New Mexican landscape--a topographical source of epiphanies and mystical raptures in Anaya's narrative. Ironically, these same features are frequently used for contrary ends: to brandish as proof of Anaya's imperviousness to history and politics. Clearly, the disparities of such views, and the theoretical conflicts present in the reading of Chicano narrative, more than pointing to textual problems, are the result of a criticism still metaphysically divided over the issue of what is *Chicano* literature. The positive side of this critical condition is that the quarrels--academic, but with diverse political concerns--ultimately create a critical setting which could be defined, borrowing Jameson's learned and pugnacious image, as a "Homeric battlefield."[11] And such is precisely my perception of Anaya criticism as being theoretically vulnerable and "soft" in its reading methods. This points to the negative side of the critical condition in Chicano literature. I refer to its relative ideological confinement and apparent inability to create grounds for strong, substantial polemical discussions which would allow, as well, for critical incursions and dialogue with kindred theoretical fields, such as feminist, Native American, and Afro-American literary criticism. The growing attention given to Chicano literature by European critics poses, therefore, promising theoretical and ideological challenges to Chicano literary criticism.

Since BMU is only a fragment of a larger historical and cultural framework, the critical act is herein understood to be one of reconstruction, building on the narrative's structuring principles as well as on what the narrative fails to articulate by itself. The proposed rereading, therefore, follows a method of analysis which is empirical (it's time to go back to the "thing itself"), with the apparently paradoxical resolve to "defamiliarize" the text (thus rescuing it from conventional readings), and to build an archeological matrix suggestive enough to generate future readings, at least of my own making.

II. The Storyteller's Art

A study of BMU's narrative demonstrates, first of all, that Antonio is *telling a story* (hence, he is not writing a novel) to a live audience; second, and contrary to critical consensus, that Antonio admits frequently to having ordinary, non-prophetic faculties. He claims to have had prophetic dreams while a child of seven to nine years old, but he also allows his audience to know that those dreams remained *incomprehensible* to him, therefore ineffective as prophecies. Obviously, such dreams have no impact on Antonio, but elsewhere: on BMU's plot structure, that is, on Antonio's "story." More important, however, is Antonio's repeated references to his incapacity to comprehend the unfolding of events that lead to Ultima's death. BMU, under this light, is a simulacrum of a story-telling situation revealed through (1) direct references to the narrator's limited perspective and faulty memory;[12] (2) modal expressions;[13] (3) passages of narrated monologue with direct audience contact;[14] and (4) an implied ethnic audience.[15] Antonio's audience appears to be *distanced* from the folk customs represented by the narrator ("It *was* the custom. . . . There *was* always room"; emphasis added), insinuating that the narrator is addressing an "urbanized" audience listening to a story about "the old days," but with more in the story than just nostalgia.

As narrator, however, Antonio not only admits to his limited perspective and memory, but also, at times he becomes an unreliable narrator by not fully developing some of the narrative's motifs, such as discrimination experienced by Antonio on his first day at school; his "maturation" after Ultima's death, shown by the example of a son ordering his mother ("[S]he nodded and obeyed" 246), etc., thereby tricking, so to speak, the unsuspecting reader with a *false* moment of recognition (e.g., Antonio and the discovery of his true identity and destiny), or by giving his audience conflicting information. For example, in chapter one there is a reference to Jasón's Indian who "was the only Indian of the town, and he talked only to Jasón" (9). Jasón's father tries to keep his son from such friendship, even punishes him, but "Jasón persisted." This friendship, in its close intimacy, almost parallels the one between Ultima and Antonio (and Anaya himself creates this illusion in *Heart of Aztlán*); therefore secrets between them are not expected. Yet Antonio declares later, through Samuel, that the legend of the golden carp was told to Samuel's father "by Jasón's Indian" (73). The audience is lead to assume, consequently, not only that Jasón knows about the legend, but that he is obviously not the only one who communicates with "his" Indian. So, Samuel learns about the legend through his father, who got it from Jasón's Indian, etc. However, as the narration progresses, Cico makes the following disclosure: "The Indian told Samuel the story; Narciso told me; now we tell you" (102). This becomes problematic, for does the Indian talk only to Jasón? Obviously not. Did Samuel learn about the legend through his father or directly from Jasón's Indian? How did Narciso know? It gets worse. Almost at the end of the narrative the audience finds that Jasón's Indian tells other persons about the golden carp, but keeps Jasón in the dark--does not tell him about it ("Perhaps later Jasón would know, and then maybe others" 228). If Jasón was so close to his Indian, why is he kept ignorant about the golden carp? Why does Antonio affirm that the Indian talks "only to Jasón" (9), when obviously that is not the truth? This self-contradictory information has, nonetheless, created an illusion of congruence. Candelaria, for example, notes that Jasón is "the friend who introduces Antonio to the mystical wonders of nature which he learned from his reclusive Indian friend."[16] With the publication of *Heart of Aztlán*, Anaya adds to the confusion when he "forgets" that Jasón's father-- Clemente Chávez--did not want his son associating with an Indian (at least with "his"), or the fact that Jasón was ignorant of the carp's legend. In *Heart of Aztlán*, Clemente Chávez sympathizes with Jasón's grief over the Indian's death (7), and Jasón, very much in the manner of Antonio as the shaman's apprentice, suddenly appears as a character with mystical tendencies (14). By this time, more than an unreliable narrator (Antonio), one has a probable example of a writer who rewrites his past work after having read his critics who celebrate Anaya's *brujos*, apprentices, and epiphanies as essential to the Chicano experience.

It might be worthwhile in this context to examine other dimensions of BMU's narrative pragmatics, for any comprehensive study must discuss eventually the literary conventions found in Anaya's narrative system. In an article based on reader-oriented criticism, Rabinowitz proposes a model composed of four audiences; applied to BMU, one would have the following:

1) The *actual audience*: readers who constitute Anaya's only "real" audience, i.e., those who purchase the book.

2) The *authorial audience*: readers who constitute Anaya's "hypothetical" audience and for whom he writes, considering their "beliefs, knowledge, and familiarity with conventions."[17]

3) The *narrative audience*: the narrator's "imitation" audience.

4) The *ideal narrative audience*: readers who accept "uncritically" what the narrator has to say.

Let us evaluate Rabinowitz's audience model using BMU as the object of analysis. Anaya's actual audience, not surprisingly, seems to be his favorite, just as most Chicano writers whose favorite audience (so they claim) is the "working class." (Regarding BMU's reception, Anaya says that "teachers and professors were reading [BMU], but most rewarding of all, the working people were reading it."[18]) Second, the authorial audience is formed by Anaya's targeted reader (not necessarily Chicano, at least in BMU); and while the narrative audience is the one who "listens" to Antonio's storytelling, and who may or may not believe in magic or in Antonio's visionary powers, the ideal narrative audience believes uncritically in everything Antonio says-- and some critics definitely belong in this category. Although this model is far from being complete (as Rabinowitz agrees), it does clarify the differences between the authorial audience (who read the fictional account written by Anaya), and the narrative audience (who listen to the story being told by Antonio). The differences are as follows:

1) Anaya: addressing an authorial audience familiar with his usage of "literary" (storytelling) traditions.

2) Antonio: addressing a narrative audience who, although distanced from their cultural background, can still understand him.

3) Antonio: the "hero" in a story rhetoricized according to "folk" conventions.

In Anaya criticism, it is increasingly difficult to distinguish between the "author" (Anaya) and the "hero" (Antonio), who are commonly held to be prophets or *brujos*. As a result, Antonio's role as storyteller has been ignored, in spite of the role's importance in Anaya's narrative.[19] Yet to understand the storyteller (what he is as an adult), one must first grasp the essential features of the story's hero: first, he is unable to interpret the nature of *events*, particularly those leading to Ultima's death; second, he is incapable of understanding his own *dreams* (which lead to Ultima's undoing); third, he plays an unwitting participatory *role* in Ultima's death. The first two (events, dreams) redefine the narrative as the story of a hero who is more the instrument of fate (thus serving its purposes) than one who is the fulfillment of exemplary character virtues (e.g., maturity, diligence, wisdom, etc.). The third feature (Antonio's role) introduces an ethical element which surfaces traditionally through the themes of remorse, sense of guilt, and sacrifice, with the victim as scapegoat. It follows then that BMU cannot be read as a *Bildungsroman*, nor as the tale of an extraordinary hero (shaman, prophet, etc.). Upon further scrutiny, BMU appears to be a mixed generic construct (tragic, pastoral, and apocalyptic), with tragedy as the main thread of the plot, beginning with a *violation of a law* (Ultima's interference in the destinies of Antonio, Lucas Luna, and Téllez), and concluding with a *nemesis* (Ultima's death). Antonio's role as an instrument of fate in Ultima's death, consequently, becomes an essential plot feature and the *telos* of the narrative itself. Antonio, in other words, is certainly a "man of destiny," but in ways he never suspected, for he is invested with a Judas-like function, namely, to be a central figure in the master's undoing. In sum, to argue that Antonio becomes a *curandero*, novelist, or prophet in his adult years, is the result of careless or ventriloquist readings.

III. Judas as an Instrument of Fate

Antonio's "blindness" to events around him is presented through a process one could define as a progressive acquisition of awareness leading to what is conventionally identified as the hero's *anagnorisis* or moment of recognition, when the hero stands "revealed at last." This feature of the Aristotelian canon is *inverted* in BMU, for the moment of recognition, instead of disclosing the hero's true identity (to himself), reveals both his role and the identity of *someone else*: Ultima.[20] Antonio's inability to interpret everyday contingencies is made clear in three instances (111, 156, 241) all connected by the metaphor of the puzzle and its pieces falling into place. The first instance refers to the thematics of sin, i.e., to the legend of the golden carp, and the end of the world. Immediately after Cico reveals to Antonio the carp's prophecy to return when "the sins of the people would weigh so heavy upon the land that in the end the whole town of Guadalupe would collapse and be swallowed by water" (110), Antonio (storyteller) exclaims: "It was unbelievable, and yet it made a wild kind of sense! *All the pieces fitted*!" (111; emphasis added)

In the second instance, Antonio is following Narciso who is on his way to warn Ultima about Tenorio's expressed intentions to kill her (Tenorio's second daughter is dying). There is a storm, so Narciso decides to stop at Rosie's place to ask Andrew, Antonio's brother and frequent patron of Rosie's brothel, to run to Ultima with the warning. Antonio, who has been following Narciso, sees Andrew in the brothel ("A single red light bulb. . . . His face was . . . bloody. . . . Her face was painted red . . . " 155) and makes this comment: "My brother. . . . *all seemed to fit. And I remembered my dream*. . . . Andrew had said that he would not enter the house of the naked women until I had lost my innocence" (156; emphasis added). According to Antonio, everything seems to "fit," although he ignores what is essential to the puzzle: the red bulb (emblematic of a brothel), and the two faces (as if covered with blood, like two "red bulbs"); his loss of innocence and the imminent death of Narciso, all symbolized by a storm and the violence of a color, represented by a bulb, blood, and a young woman's rouge.

Lastly, Tenorio's second daughter has died ("the town is in an uproar"), and Tenorio is now about to look for Ultima with far from neighborly intentions ("the man has been drinking all day and howling out his vengeance on la curandera, Ultima" 239). Word of this reaches Antonio *through his uncle Juan* (in itself an apocalyptic name); he is told to go to his grandfather's house, but instead Antonio walks "carelessly up the road, unaware of what the coming darkness would reveal to [him]" (241). As he is about to cross a bridge, Antonio almost bumps into Tenorio who is riding a horse and on his way to kill Ultima. Tenorio, in a moment of drunken euphoria, tells Antonio about his knowledge regarding the relationship between Ultima and her owl. Antonio (storyteller) then makes the following comment before he continues with his story: "It was when he said that the owl was the spirit of Ultima that *everything I had ever known about Ultima and her bird seemed to make sense*" (242; emphasis added).

A summary view indicates that the moment of recognition is not at all related to Antonio's self-discovery (conventionally found on page 236), but to his sudden recognition of Ultima's true identity (242) and, most important, of his role in her imminent death. Therefore, the allegorical readings of BMU which transform Antonio into a mestizo (or a "new man"), claiming that he combines the best of both cultural worlds (e.g., Spanish and Indian ancestries), are also flawed readings or, at best, "Chicano" readings made in the heyday of the Movimiento, which ignore what is essential to BMU, namely: Antonio's remorse. The "pieces" of Antonio's puzzle, consequently, are ominous indications foreshadowing Ultima's death, also pointing to Antonio's loss of innocence--a major theme in the narrative--as being caused by "the sins of the people," that is, by a process of violence and murder which contains the deaths of Lupito (i.e., Guadalupe), Narciso, and Ultima, but with remote origins in the regional conflicts between Mexicans and Native Americans, and between the former and Anglo-Americans ("the meeting of the people from Texas with my forefathers was full of blood, murder, and tragedy" 119). If we backtrack to the moment when Antonio begins to notice the surrounding puzzle ("All the pieces fitted!" 111), the irony of Antonio's understanding of the world around him will become obvious: when Cico declares that the golden carp will return when the land sinks with its own sins, Antonio begins, like a novice *bricoleur*, to "put things together" ("it made a wild kind of sense!"), arriving at the following stage of the puzzle: "My own mother had said that losing your innocence and becoming a man was learning to sin. *I felt weak and powerless in the knowledge of the impending doom*" (111; emphasis added). The irony of this remark is that Antonio does not yet understand the nature of the *real* impending doom: Ultima's death. His wisdom, however, is visceral ("I felt weak and powerless"); his response, candid and naively hortatory ("I thought about telling everyone in town to stop their sinning, or drown and die" 111).

The narrative process which leads to the moment of recognition, then, begins in chapter 11 (exactly at the center of the narrative, and only one chapter away from Ultima's confrontation with Tenorio and his lynch mob) and concludes in chapter 22, just before the "story" ends. Antonio's progressive "enlightenment"--ranging from the loss of innocence (Rosie's place) to the prophecy of the golden carp (the "end of the world"), and Ultima's death (the beginning of Antonio's remorse and, one assumes, his compulsive storytelling)--must be somehow related to the town of Guadalupe, to the virgin known by the same name, and to apocalypse, which the virgin symbolizes in Mexican history and culture. The analysis of this structural "knot," being BMU's overall ideological construct, shall reclaim out attention shortly. For the moment, however, one could hold that Ultima's "sacrifice" at the hands of Tenorio is a negation of her promise made to Antonio (" . . . good is always stronger than evil" 91), but a *fulfillment of her destiny*. It is in this sense that one must reread Ultima's initial words to Antonio ("I knew there would be something between us" 11), for more than an anticipation of her death at Guadalupe ("I have come to spend the last days of my life here, Antonio" 11), Ultima also appears to know Antonio's role in her own death. Seen under this light, Antonio's last farewell to Ultima acquires an ominous meaning: "Then *I did something I had never done before.* I reached up and *kissed Ultima*" (234; emphasis added).[21] By modifying the traditional version of Judas, the storyteller is proceeding consistently with his didactic plan, namely, to carry his culturally distanced and urbanized narrative audience from past traditional folkways ("It was the custom. . . . There was always room . . ." 4) to a situation belonging to cultural insiders and transformers.[22] On the other hand, between the beginning and conclusion of the narrative, there is a perfect correspondence of tokens of birth and death: just before Ultima's *arrival* at Guadalupe, Antonio dreams about his birth and hears Ultima declare, "I will *bury the afterbirth . . . Only I will know his destiny*" (6; emphasis added). Just before her *departure* (i.e., her death), Antonio runs to *bury Ultima's owl*, but now a lot wiser as to the nature of *his own destiny*. This narrative juncture marks a decisive turn in our reading of BMU, for the recognition of this structural feature replaces Antonio as the hero, with Ultima now as the heroine who holds the reins of the plot's principal actions. In retrospect, every narrative detail seems to point in this direction, for Ultima is the one to engage in actions, while Antonio, unable to understand, much less to control, the "world" surrounding him, remains a passive spectator of events whose unfolding he comprehends only too late.

IV. Juan's Revelations on a Metaphorical Island

Antonio and the nature of his dreams are also best understood through his instrumental role with Ultima. In three dreams (VII, 132; VIII, 167; and X, 233) he has clear indications not only of Ultima's death, but also of the cause and the agent. But Antonio's dreams remain incomprehensible; his dreams are prophetic, yet he remains blind to the significance of the dream narratives. Tenorio's threat to kill both Narciso and Ultima occurs at a fateful moment in the narrative (chapter 12, 127), right after having an eye gouged out by Ultima's owl. Though the link between the owl and Ultima should have then been clear to both Tenorio and Antonio, it is not. In chapter 16, just when Antonio (distracted as usual) is thinking of the Virgin of Guadalupe, day-dreaming that he is Juan Diego's "double" (and, indeed, Juan is Antonio's middle name), he runs into Tenorio and, in his attempt to intimidate him, threatens the former with Ultima's owl: "the owl will scratch out your other eye" (181). This is the result of Antonio's threat:

> He crouched as if to pounce on me, but he remained motionless, thinking. I braced to ward off his blow, but it did not come. Instead he straightened up and smiled, as if a thought had crossed his mind, and he said, "ay cabroncito, *your curse is that you know too much!*" (181; emphasis added)

Antonio is definitely under a "curse," but Tenorio is wrong: Antonio does not "know." Does Antonio reach then a similar conclusion, discovering the link between the owl and Ultima? He doesn't, even though by chapter 16 Antonio has had previous disclosures of Ultima's death (132), and of her relationship with the owl (167). That same night Antonio dreams again of Ultima's death ("But often at night I awoke from nightmares in which I saw Tenorio shooting Ultima as he had shot Narciso" 182. The "often at night" obviously compounds the futile warnings given to Antonio regarding the manner and agent of Ultima's downfall). As noted earlier, Tenorio gloats over Ultima's vulnerability (as suggested by Antonio) on page 242; three pages later (and as Antonio "closes" his storytelling), Ultima dies just as foretold in Antonio's dreams, but with one important variance: Ultima dies to save Antonio's life:

> I froze as Tenorio turned and pointed his rifle at me."
> --¡Espíritu de mi alma!" I heard Ultima's command ring in the still night air, and a swirling of wings engulfed Tenorio. He cursed and fired. . . . That shot destroyed the quiet, moonlit peace of the hill, and it shattered my childhood into a thousand fragments that long ago stopped falling and are now dusty relics gathered in distant memories. (245)

It is instructive to observe that at the precise moment when Antonio's childhood bursts into fragments, the event is in perfect synchrony with Tenorio's shooting of Ultima's owl ("a swirling of wings"), marking, as well, the climactic moment reached by Antonio's narration. The "dusty relics" and "distant memories," as a result, constitute the narrative that is BMU, but, more important, they form a symbolic concentration composed of three motif elements: the end of Antonio's innocence ("shattered my childhood"); the end of Ultima's life; and the dénouement or unravelling of the plot's fabric. Consequently, the motifs weaving their way throughout BMU, such as the end of the world (the sinking of the "island" of Guadalupe, a town "surrounded by water"); Antonio's dreams and "destiny"; and the bond between Ultima, the owl, and Antonio, all converge at this narrative locus, revealing both the art of BMU's *raconteur* (Antonio), and the riddle-like structure of Antonio's story. If one follows the sequence of warnings received by Antonio regarding Ultima's death, and arranges them graphically, the following is the result:

PORTENTS OF ULTIMA'S DEATH

Dreams			VII	VIII		X
Chapters	11	12	13	14	16	22
Clues (Ultima-owl)		127	132	167	181-2	233
Antonio's "puzzle"	111		156		242	
Antonio's discovery						242
Antonio's remorse						248

In this graph, Antonio's discovery of Ultima's true identity becomes a climactic moment in the narrative, linking dream prophecies, incidental clues, and puzzle-like situations which allow Antonio to become aware of his *destiny* at a decisive moment (242), while all along the narration has been moving and advancing towards Ultima's death. If one compares the thematic consistency of the three "prophetic" dreams (VII, VIII, and X) with the three instances when Antonio sees that "all of the pieces" are falling into place, there will be a direct correspondence: the prophecy of the golden carp and the sins of Guadalupe (chapter 11, 111) form the *beginning* of the process which leads to Ultima's downfall, anticipating the confrontation between good and evil in Guadalupe (Ultima and Tenorio, chapter 12). The process continues then to two dream revelations (dreams VII, VIII) and three clues (127, 132, 167) which should have formed part of the second puzzle situation (but do not). It then proceeds with Antonio following Narciso (chapter 14, 156) who, on his way to warn Ultima of Tenorio's intentions, stops at Rosie's place and is killed shortly afterwards by Tenorio (thus fulfilling his threat made on page 127). The process then advances to clues and dreams (chapter 16, 181-182) where Antonio is still in the dark (!) about Ultima's identity, something to be revealed six chapters later (chapter 22, 242), right after another moment of "distraction":

> I walked carelessly up the road, unaware of what the coming darkness would reveal to me. . . . As I walked I gathered ripe mesquite pods and chewed them for the sweet juice. . . . And so it was not until the horseman was almost upon me that I was aware of him. (241)

This scene becomes the repetition of a preceding encounter between Antonio and Tenorio, with Antonio also distracted, thinking about the Virgin of Guadalupe (chapter 16, 181). It is also homologous to the scene in which Narciso attempts to warn Ultima of Tenorio's plans (chapter 14, 154). Both scenes, as a result, contain and foreshadow the *third* scene (chapter 22, 242) in which Antonio comes across Tenorio in the *bosque* between El Puerto de los Luna and Guadalupe (in a south-north direction), and runs to warn Ultima of Tenorio's vengeful plans (repeating Narciso's former actions). These figural "doubling" of scenes, or narrative telescoping, is a signpost technique that carries the reading to the final conflict between Ultima and Tenorio (read according to page sequence, from bottom):

Tenorio vs. Ultima
(chapter 22, 246)

Encounter between Antonio and Tenorio; Antonio discovers Ultima's vulnerability (242) and attempts to warn Ultima of Tenorio's plans.

Encounter between Antonio and Tenorio; Tenorio discovers Ultima's vulnerability (the owl, 181).

Encounter between Narciso and Tenorio, as Narciso
attempts to warn Ultima of Tenorio's plans (154).

Every reader of BMU knows the aftermath: Tenorio fulfills his
promise to kill Narciso and Ultima, and so does Pedro Luna--he kills Tenorio.
Antonio's despair and remorse are evident right after the passage in which he
becomes aware of Ultima's true identity:

> A long time afterwards I thought that if I had waited and gone to
> my uncles, or somehow sneaked across the bridge and warned my
> grandfather that *things would have turned out differently*. (243;
> emphasis added)

One paragraph prior to the conclusion of BMU, Antonio reflects again
on the result of his "dream-fate" (132), and states: "perhaps if we had come
earlier we would have saved Ultima. *But it was better not to think that way*"
(248; emphasis added). This statement is almost an identical response to
Narciso's death: "Perhaps if I had been closer to Narciso what happened would
not have happened" (159). As Antonio "relives" the deaths of Narciso and
Ultima, he reveals in his narration his incapacity to understand the forces of
destiny that threw him into the unfolding of events in which he functioned as
an *instrument* (Ultima deploys him as a "Juan"; fate makes use of him to bring
Ultima to her doom, etc.). His feeling of impotence and remorse is expressed
through phrases such as "if I had waited," "perhaps if we had." Conversely,
the "instrumentality" of Antonio as a hero in the narrative appears to be the
inversion of Antonio the storyteller, who displays full command (at least most
of the time), playing with his audience through storytelling devices such as
delayed (and false) information, strategic equivocality, and scene correlation or
"doubling." Is Antonio really over his despair, or does Ultima's death haunt
him in his adult years as a storyteller? Ultima seems to sense the probable
impact that her death might have on Antonio, so at the close of her third and
last blessing, she adds: "if despair enters your heart look for me . . . I shall

be with you" (247). This closing passage recalls another found at the beginning of the narrative where the despair of the adult Antonio is implied:

> As Ultima walked past me I smelled for the first time a trace of the sweet fragrance of herbs that always lingered in her wake. *Many years later*, long after Ultima was gone and I had grown to be a man, *I would awaken sometimes at night* and think I caught a scent of her fragrance in the cool-night breeze. (11; emphasis added)

In the pursuit of his destiny, Antonio learns that he plays a role in the fulfillment of Ultima's destiny, that he is a part of a larger "scheme of things" that he does not understand, but that somehow his subsidiary role has been part of events having metaphysical resonances. And this is Antonio's greatness, and his tragedy. How might the narrative audience view Antonio? One is lead to speculate that as it follows Antonio's "autobiographical" account, the impression moves from an initial presentation of the hero as being *exceptional* (prophecies, visions of his birth, etc.), to one of dramatic irony where the narrative audience is allowed to know more than the narrator's remote self (the hero), but not more than the storyteller. Continuing with our speculation, how would the narrative audience understand Antonio's role? What folk traditions are available that allow the narrative audience to recognize and comprehend Antonio's narration? Undoubtedly, Ultima and Antonio would be understood as biblical variants of the Jesus and Judas story, with Antonio as the "disciple" who learns, to his anguish and dread, that his "destiny" (Antonio's quest throughout BMU) is to be instrumental in the master's downfall.

The narrative audience has been alerted all along about this variant (rewritten in a matriarchal mode): the relationship between the Virgin of Guadalupe, Ultima, and the owl as variants of the Father, the Son, and the Holy Spirit, respectively; Ultima's "saintly" bearing amid the people of Guadalupe and El Puerto ("She knelt by Ultima's path and touched the hem of her dress as she passed by" 96); Ultima's function as the "woman" in Revelation (12:1) in her encounter with the "red dragon" (Tenorio) precisely in chapter 12 (123-128); Ultima's payment after the clearing of the curse in

Téllez house (a sacrificial lamb 224), which foreshadows her own "sacrifice"; Ultima's "work" on earth ("to heal the sick and show them the path of goodness" 247); her acts of thaumaturgy (the "resurrection of the dead," curing of "diseases," etc.); and her death, so that others may live (Antonio). And, of course, Antonio's farewell kiss to Ultima, a symbolic parallel to the Judas' kiss. The matriarchal modality of the life of Jesus (= Ultima) and the Hellenized version of the Judas story (Antonio's preordained fate) can be conceptually schematized as follows:

	Christianity	BMU
Christ's Parentage:	Divinity + Virgin	Divinity + Virgin
Symbolic Inter-mediaries:	Dove	Owl
Sacrificial Lamb:	Christ	Ultima
Instrument of Fate:	Judas	Antonio

The Jesus/Judas story is not at all uncommon in regions close to the Mexico-United States Border. In fact, it is one of the best known biblical passages throughout Christendom, for centuries having stimulated the imagination of Christians and given them a human paradigm of treason, hypocrisy, and remorse. Mexicans of the border regions close to the Río Bravo share in this tradition, and know well of the "kiss of Judas." For instance, Américo Paredes' *bricolage* of the Gregorio Cortez legend contains elements taken from Christian iconography, encoded numerologically and with fragments of the Jesus/Judas story, all subsumed under a legend dealing with border conflict where loyalty is prized highly. In the legend, Gregorio Cortez is "the seventh son of a seventh son";[23] he has prophetic powers (39); is a man of peace but is also a man of "destiny" (35, 36); he has the gift of tongues (communicates with rangers as well as with mares, 35, 45, 46); encounters "eleven" Mexicans upon his return to Goliad, and among them meets "El Teco" (*El Tecolote* = the owl), of whom the legend says "Judas should have been his name" (49): he delivers Gregorio and receives a reward in silver, and is forever driven by a sense of guilt, etc. Paredes' version of the Judas story, although molded in the traditional version, has been rewritten in an ethnic mode:

> But El Teco did not enjoy the reward. . . . because he could not spend it anywhere. If he went to buy a taco at he market place, the taco vender would tell him that tacos were worth two thousand dollars gold that day. People cursed him in the streets. . . . [H]e never knew peace until he died. (49)

But Antonio's role suggests another, "estranged" version of the Judas story. This Judas is the disciple who loves Jesus, who is his faithful follower (never to deny him), but who eventually learns of his destiny, namely: to be a crucial part in the apprehension of Jesus.[24] The Judas variant, then, is culturally the obvious "reading," but the wrong one if such a variant produces the "traitor" and not the man whose fate has plotted against him. In sum, Ultima and Antonio do not necessarily fit into only one "variant," for they appropriate different signifieds in the narrative (e.g., Antonio as Juan Diego and as John of Patmos), all consistent with an overall plan: the apocalyptic moment in an "old" cultural world (such world being "upside down"), and the emergence of a New World. The narrative homology between BMU and John's Apocalypse, revealed in their common stylistic features, their use of symbolic numbers, and their syncretic amalgam--all embedded in an apocalyptic construct with dense ideological detail--can also be sustained due to a cultural continuum characteristic of the West, a continuum to which Mexicans belong.[25] As I will propose in what follows, echoes of this continuum resonate in BMU through Mexican cultural motifs.

V. The Ideal Landscape in BMU

BMU's initial paragraph contains a symbolic condensation of the major features of apocalyptic literature: an advent, a revelation, and the "creation" of a new entity risen from its former, less conscious antecedent.[26] Marking the fateful encounter between Antonio and Ultima, this passage clearly divides Antonio's life into two periods with Ultima as the vital partition. As the second paragraph indicates, the *true* beginning of Antonio's story, and of his fateful destiny for that matter, begins with Ultima's arrival. Logically, the connotation of a *double birth* is textually implicit, as well as the notion of Antonio's *double parentage*: the mother, María, is the uterine origin of his biological life; Ultima, on the other hand, is the cause of Antonio's spiritual awakening to his dramatic role in life, creating bonds that transcend biological ties ("I felt more attached to Ultima than to my own mother," acknowledges Antonio 115). The initial passage reads as follows:

> Ultima came to stay with us the summer I was almost seven. When she came the beauty of the llano unfolded before my eyes, and the gurgling waters of the river sang to the hum of the turning earth. The magical time of childhood stood still, and the pulse of the living earth pressed its mystery into my living blood. She took my hand, and the silent, magic powers she possessed made beauty from the raw, sun-baked llano, the green river valley, and the blue bowl which was the white sun's home. My bare feet felt the throbbing earth and my body trembled with excitement. Time stood still, and it shared with me all that had been, and all that was to come. . . . (1)

To say with Anaya criticism that such landscape descriptions are poetic, mystical, or epiphanic would be merely to postpone indefinitely the analysis of the rhetoric being deployed. In BMU, the landscape has no referential, mimetic function, and it is integrally rhetorized in an apocalyptic mode according to the ideal landscape literary tradition. The revelatory experience undergone by Antonio is extraordinary in the sense that he reaches a peculiar level of cognition better known in apocalyptic literature as a vision trance.[27] This initial scene resembles a slow-motion take, allowing for the progressive, cumulative description of exterior details and mental processes, of physical distances, approximations, and the moment of contact (a hand, the earth, a trembling body). Noticeable also is the repetition of an advent

("Ultima came . . . When she came") and the "freezing" of time's flow ("the magical time . . . stood still . . . Time stood still"), narrated in the context of an encounter which generates a semiotic continuum ranging from Michelangelo's pictorial depiction of Adam's creation (the approaching, "flying" deity, the nude body reclined against the earth, hand contact about to occur), to the sublimated, spiritualized eroticism of mystical raptures. This encounter between Ultima and Antonio is described again a few pages later, but with important modifications:

> She took my hand and I felt the power of a whirlwind sweep around me. Her eyes swept the surrounding hills and through them I saw for the first time the wild beauty of our hills and the magic of the green river. My nostrils quivered as I felt the song of the mockingbirds and the drone of the grasshoppers mingle with the pulse of the earth. The four directions of the llano met in me, and the white sun shone on my soul. The granules of sand at my feet and the sun and sky above me seemed to dissolve into one strange, complete being. (10-11)

The differences between the first and second descriptions of this initial encounter are evident: in the first, the stress is on tactile contact ("She took my hand . . . My bare feet felt . . . My body trembled"); in the second, although repeating the hand motif, the emphasis is transferred to the visual ("Her eyes . . . through them I saw for the first time"), and to a synesthetic merging of the olfactory, tactile, and auditory senses ("My *nostrils* quivered as I felt the song of the mockingbirds . . . the drone of the grasshoppers . . . the *pulse* of the earth"). This sudden activation of Antonio's sensorium is apocalyptic in the sense that it is the unveiling of a surrounding world manifested through emblems of *air dominion* (mockingbirds, grasshoppers), cardinal points ("four directions of the llano"), and a concluding narrative principle, the *adynaton*, which "strings together" cosmic dissolution ("seemed to dissolve into") with anthropomorphic transformations ("into one strange, complete being").[28] In addition, these two passages introduce (1) a schematization of BMU's rhetorized landscape (e.g., the llano, the river valley); (2) the classical motif of the elements, with earth, fire, and water as dominants in the first passage, and wind in the second; (3) the thematics of flying ("her eyes swept"), suggesting the perception of an owl in flight while confirming an affinity between a "flying woman" and a "flying boy" ("*in my dream I* **flew** *over the rolling hills*" 4; **emphasis added**); and (4) the apocalypsis of a cosmic cataclysm and the emergence of new forms of life.

Ultima's owl-like sensorium (peripheral vision, powerful tactility) exhibits the presence of a more acute and unified sensory system than its human analog. Therefore, Antonio's synesthetic experience, which transforms him metaphorically into a fledgling owl, would appear to be the confirmation of the relationship existing between a master and an apprentice ("I knew there would be something between us"); nonetheless, the plot structure of the narrative precludes such reading, as I have shown in the first part of this study. These apocalyptic passages are best read as revelations of the sites (the llano, the river valley) *in which Ultima will perform thaumaturgical acts*, with Antonio acting alongside Ultima and, simultaneously, "against" her as an instrument of fate (after all, she does intervene in the destinies of Antonio, Lucas Luna, and Téllez). While Anaya criticism has repeatedly interpreted these passages as paradigmatic of Anaya's epiphanic landscapes and of Antonio's exceptional prophetic faculties (mislead, no doubt, by Antonio's remark: "Time stood still, and it shared with me all that had been, and all that was to come"), my reading proposes that Ultima, as of her first encounter with Antonio, reveals to him (1) her link to the owl, (2) the sites of her forthcoming "interferences" (a man from Las Pasturas, another from El Puerto de los Luna), and (3) a "cataclysm": her own death as the sacrificial victim which *reintegrates* the communal body. Antonio will not comprehend the magnitude of her revelation at first contact. When Antonio finally understands Ultima's "riddle," it will be too late.[29]

Ultima's self-disclosure to Antonio, subtly enacted in their first encounter, occurs again the day after Lupito is slain, and while Antonio remembers the tragedy ("I felt a soft hand on my head . . . her eyes held me spellbound" 28); it is repeated just before Antonio's departure to his first day in school:

> I felt Ultima's hand on my head and at the same time I felt a great force, like a whirlwind, swirl about me. I looked up in fright, thinking the wind would knock me off my knees. Ultima's bright eyes held me still. . . . But how could the blessing of Ultima be like the whirlwind? Was the power of good and evil the same? (51-52)

The description of the first encounter occurs twice (1, 10-11), followed by two more instances of self-disclosure (28, 51); there are, therefore, *three* revelations of Ultima's identity, with the third being also the occasion of Ultima's first blessing, followed by two more: one, before Antonio departs to El Puerto to spend a summer learning the lifework of the Lunas (234); and, second, just before Ultima's death (247), when Antonio has finally understood the nature of his real lifework. It is this third blessing, after all, that gives the novel its title.

The three blessings also progressively manifest Ultima's heterodoxy in matters related to institutionalized Catholic sacraments, moving from an orthodox blessing (51), to two others which are heterodox and given at crucial moments in the narrative, but which are, according to Antonio, just "as holy" (234). Chapter 6, consequently, becomes a narrative "turning point," with *three apocalypses* (1, 10; 28, 51; the first is repeated), and *three blessings* (51, 234, 247). The design formed by the three revelations poses an inherent contradiction in cognitive modes; concomitantly, Ultima's blessings are introduced in a progressively heterodox mode (with the deletion of the Trinity), hence in a contradictory relationship in regards to institutionalized religion (i.e., Catholicism). The blessings, nonetheless, lead directly into the Luna side of the family, suggesting that once Antonio's "destiny" is fulfilled (Ultima's death), he is free to return to the *matrilocal* part of his kinship network. But Antonio does not turn into a Luna (a farmer); he becomes a storyteller in an urban setting, that is, away from El Puerto and Las Pasturas. And yet, this detachment from his community (Luna or Márez)--a "metanoic experience" in its own right--is a fact foregrounded as of their fateful first meeting, when Ultima receives Antonio into this world and decides, amid the noise and quarrels of the hostile family clans, Antonio's destiny.[30]

VI. **The Rhetorization of Demonic Landscapes**

Ideal landscape descriptions have their demonic parodies in BMU, appearing on six narrative settings: (1) the slaying of Lupito (20); (2) the curing of Lucas Luna (84, 87-88); (3) Tenorio's aggression against Narciso (151-152), against Antonio (180, 241), and agair st Ultima (244-245); (4) the meteorological eff ... ... atomic bomb (183-184); (5) the clearing of the curse on Téllez house (213, 221); and (6) Ultima's death (248). Consistent with its narrative organization, BMU begins at daylight and concludes, in a "forked" mode, with night both as the tin. ˘ *the narrative* ("Around me the moonlight glittered . . . in the night a million s. ¬arkled" 248), and as the time of the *narration* ("Ultima was really buried here. ¯night" 248). Does this mean that Antonio's "compulsive" storytelling ends that evening at the conclusion of his story? The narrative itself discloses no suggestion, much less any evidence that would produce an answer to this question.

Ideal landscapes, not surprisingly, are described with sunlight, whereas their demonic parodies are presented with storms, "eclipsed" suns, and whirlwinds. The first instance of a demonic landscape is introduced just after Lupito is slain:

> The dark shadows of the river enveloped me as I raced for the safety of home. Branches whipped at my face and cut it, and vines and tree trunks caught at my feet and tripped me. In my headlong rush I disturbed sleeping birds and their shrill cries and slapping wings hit at my face. The horror of darkness had never been so complete as it was for me that night. (20)

Beginning and ending with metaphors of night, this passage abour δ_{b} with demonic reversals of apocalyptic imagery ("The panoramic apoc $_{y}$ se ends with the restoration of the tree and water of life, the two elemer of the original creation," notes Frye),[31] and with natural features conspicu in their intended assault on Antonio. The portrayal of an inverted Garden of Eden is seen through splintered trees (branches, trunks) with anthropomorphic attributes associated with *error* ("tripped me"), unyielding *constraint* ("caught at my feet"), and infernal *suffering* ("whipped"): in other words, the reason and condition of the damned. Other motifs associated with Christ are also parodies, such as the vine that gives everlasting life, and the path that leads to it; the "disturbed sleeping birds" as an inversion of the Holy Spirit (dove), and as an analog of the inverted tree of life; both birds and branches attack Antonio's face, as if to stress his "blindness," while attempting to destroy the site of his social identity. The terror and physical damage caused by this experience will be the occasion for Ultima's first thaumaturgical act ("There was a strange power in Ultima's medicine" 25). Lupito is killed by the river, close to a juniper tree which will continuously be a place of death or burial; in his mind, Lupito is in the Pacific Ocean, at war with Japan. His death, consequently, links two violences, two forms of madness: one, global; the other, local. Where's God? Where's his Justice? These will soon become Antonio's recurring questions.

The unnatural meteorological changes which take place during daylight, on the other hand, involve the presence of Tenorio Trementina and are described in four narrative passages. The first is introduced when Ultima and Antonio are approaching El Puerto with plans of curing Lucas Luna; the second, when Ultima is inside Tenorio's bar "reasoning" with him ("tell your daughters to lift the curse" 87), and also as she leaves the bar, accompanied by Antonio. These passages, consequently, form a semantic unit: Ultima's acceptance to "interfere" in the destiny of Lucas Luna; her offensive strategy (goes straight to Tenorio's bar); and her direct threat ("I thought I could reason with you" 88); the following are two of such passages:

> The drive to El Puerto was always a pleasant one, but today it was filled with strange portents. . . . whirlwinds and dust devils darkened the horizon. I had never seen anything like it . . . all around the sky darkened. . . . A strange, dark whirlwind swept through the dusty street and cried mournfully . . . The storm broke . . . and the rising dust seemed to shut off the light of the sun. . . . so concerned was I with finding some direction in the strange duststorm. . . . The rider

. . . disappeared into the swirling dust . . . The sky remained dark around us. (84, 87-89)

If Ultima's arrival at Guadalupe is described as a "whirlwind," her destination to El Puerto, on the contrary, is portrayed as a progressive meteorological violence produced by the conjunction of two sharply opposed rivals: a healer and a destroyer. Anaya criticism has emphasized Ultima's qualities as a *curandera*, viewing her as a benefactress whose world is one of "harmony" and whose magic is in opposition to the black arts of the Trementina sisters; but are they ever a match for Ultima? She openly scorns them, considering them mere "amateurs" (92). The reading of BMU must be conducted at different levels, hence to limit one's critical focus to the ideologeme (in Jameson's sense) of good and evil, or of "white" versus black magic, is to be satisfied with mere narrative commentary.[32] The thematic cluster related to thaumaturgy should be analyzed using Native American and Mexican-European cultural sources as constituents of an intertextual setting; this task, obviously, falls outside the limits of this study, but the outlines can be sketched briefly. For example, the cosmic correlation between Ultima (born in Las Pasturas) and Tenorio (from El Puerto) is made clearer when one remembers that the governing astral body, for each village, is the sun and moon, respectively. Ultima's *conjunction* with Tenorio, seen in cosmic terms, can be viewed virtually as an *eclipse*, with the correlative atmospheric disturbances that are associated with dangerous cosmic unions: darkened suns, strange portents, whirlwinds, and duststorms.[33] At yet another level, one hears mythical echoes of the origin of fire, cooking and a *burned world*; for example, Ultima *cooks* her remedies (90, 93), *burns* the Trementina sisters' "evil load" (97); burns the three bundles of evergreen branches, which are symbolic replacements of the hanged Comanche Indians (223); she asks Gabriel that her body be *cremated* after her death (224); and orders Antonio, just before her death, to burn all her medicines and herbs "somewhere along the river" (247). Associated with *fire*, Ultima--who is already linked to a bird and, in regards to knowledge, to "el hombre volador," who is a metaphorical master of the air--becomes a mixed metaphorical construct of the *phoenix*, a variant of the resurrection of the body, the tree of life, and apocalypse. In this regard Frye tells us that

> on metaphorical principles all the categories of apocalyptic existence can be thought of as burning in the fire of life. The bird is an image of the Holy Spirit, and the burning bird is the phoenix, whose story was regarded later as a type of the Resurrection . . . the tree of life . . . in Greek is also called phoinix.[34]

Contrary to the disjunction that as a rule should prevail between Ultima and Tenorio, the golden carp and Ultima are homologous: both are periodic and seasonal, both produce vision trances in Antonio, both cause his body to "tremble," etc. The following is the passage where this homology is evident:

> "The golden carp," I whispered in awe. I could not have been more entranced if I had seen the Virgin, or God Himself. . . . I felt my body trembling as I saw the bright golden form disappear. I knew I had witnessed a miraculous thing . . . a thing as miraculous as the curing of my uncle Lucas. And I thought, the power of God failed where Ultima's worked; and then a sudden illumination of beauty and understanding flashed through my mind. (105)

Strong examples of *adynata*, both Ultima and the golden carp represent the world's end manifested as a world upside down: he is an Empyrean god transformed (and demoted) into a *chthonic beast*; she, a "demonic" woman (as sorceress) who is converted (and promoted) into a *Christological figure*. The golden carp, originally master of the air (as a god and prior to his metamorphosis into a carp), is now master of water (hence the expected end of the world through a deluge). Ultima's thaumaturgy connects her at times to the *underworld* (as "destroyer", making *clay* dolls), and at others, she is a mediator with the *upperworld* (she is master of air, her teacher was "el hombre volador," etc.). Her triumph over the Trementina sisters results in a proof of her healing powers. The women of El Puerto, nonetheless, have mixed feelings, and some call her a witch, while others think of her as a *curandera* or a virgin ("una mujer que no ha pecado" 96). The ambiguity of the last term is clarified when one reads it as follows: in its metaphorical sense, Ultima is a construct of son and mother, Christ and the (Mexican) Virgin (of Guadalupe), a microsystem which encloses an ancient mystery, namely, the conjunction of different cosmic levels. And the triune aspect of Ultima *combines* three cosmic levels: as a witch, *curandera*, and virgin, she is the underworld, the earth, and the sky, respectively. At this critical moment, we can affirm that the dispersal of signifieds in BMU is the result of its decentered universe and an upside down world which generate a continuum of variants, parodies, and cultural transgressions: for example, an owl associated with beauty and goodness; a *curandera* whose face "was old and wrinkled, but [whose] eyes were clear and sparkling, like the eyes of a young child" (10); youths--like Samuel, Cico, and Antonio--who seem "wise and old" (71), have eyes which are "clear and bright, like Ultima's" but already show "lines of age" (109), and who generally feel "older" than the rest of the local boys (156); and, lastly, a Catholic priest (the Luna ancestor) who is the founding father of a numerous clan. These code violations--e.g., an old woman with eyes of a child, youth with signs of old age, a Catholic priest and his progeny, etc.--are *adynata* associated with paradox, transgressions of the logical order, apocalypses of a *renovatio mundi*.

The distribution of evil surfaces in the forms of Tenorio, the Trementina sisters, static cultural structures (the Márez, the Luna); and Anglo-American signifiers, such as the railroad, barbed wire, and the atomic bomb. In a fashion similar to the ancient fear of uttering God's name, or of invoking the devil, Gabriel--through Antonio, the storyteller--encodes the Anglo-American conquest of 1848 through *technical metaphors* (the railroad network), or as *meteorological analogies* of violence ("it was like a bad wave of the ocean covering all that was good" 51). BMU's demonic landscapes, in sum, are recontainments of evil seen through manifestations of destruction, disturbances of cosmic harmony (interferences, reprehensible conjunctions, etc.), and threats of a return to chaos.

VII. **Mulier fugit in solitudinem** (*Apocalypse* 12:6)

Anaya criticism has brought thematic closure to BMU's landscape either as the cause of Antonio's epiphanies or as the symbol of his ethnic synthesis (Luna + Márez), thus interpreting Antonio's metanoic trance as the direct anticipation of the unity of his conflictive genealogy, generally understood to be Spanish and Indian. This type of analysis, which gave BMU a *political* reading in the 1970's (including my own), has an ideological basis which can be retained, but without former "ethnic" or "oppositional" overtones. As every reader of BMU knows, Antonio is a *pacifist*, and his reactions to violence are visceral (he is always feeling nausea, throwing up, falling sick, etc., when confronted by violence, as illustrated on pages 103, 154, 156, 202, and 231). Could a close reading suggest that Antonio, in his adult years and as a storyteller, becomes an apostle-like member of an Ultima cult (against war as well as against any form of violence), with an ecumenical scope not necessarily limited to U.S. Mexicans? Antonio's "proclamation" or kerygmatic discourse makes sense only in this evangelical context.

In general terms, however, the emblematic topography in BMU has been polarized in two categories: the llano (by referential contiguity, Las Pasturas), and the river valley (associated with El Puerto de los Luna); the liminal post is the *hill* (adjacent to the town of Guadalupe), site of Antonio's home and boundary of the llano. Because of BMU's meta-linguistic landscape descriptions, the ideal topography triggers a number of possible readings; for example, in the first passage, a first reading may not transcend the aesthetic level, and one may close the book assuming an implied ecological harmony of man with the forces of creation; second, it may be read through a cultural code in which the llano and the river valley, associated now to Las Pasturas and El Puerto de los Luna, respectively, appear as inherent features of a cultural conflict *resolved* in Antonio who, thanks to Ultima's intervention in his destiny, is able to synthesize the contradiction of a historical dialectic (Márez versus Luna), becoming the logical counterpart to a racist ideology and an allegory of New World miscegenation, with the constituent elements being Native Mexico and Spain (i.e., the mestizo). The polysemic dimension of the initial landscape description, as a result, can generate a number of readings which easily bring ideological closure to the narrative at an *aesthetic* or *cultural nationalist* level (i.e., an "ethnic" reading). In this study I am proposing a reading of BMU that incorporates the notion of pharmakos (scapegoat), a role belonging primordially to Ultima. Ultima's function as *pharmakos* (suggested to Antonio in BMU's initial paragraph) allows for logical connections to be made not with Antonio's alleged dual ancestry (Spanish/Indian), but with the two sites where the thaumaturgical works are to be performed, one in the *river valley* (Lucas Luna, chapter 10), the other in the *llano* (Téllez, chapter 20). The "beauty" of both threshold symbols ("When she came, the beauty of the llano . . . ")--which for years have been the governing lifestyles and economies of two hostile villages of farmers and sheepherders--signifies the prospect of their *unification* through Ultima's sacrifice (therefore, the narrative process being one from disjunction to conjunction, from *conflicting members* to a *reintegrated body*). Anaya's ideal "body," consequently, is none other than the conciliation of dissimilar and feuding "members," a notion which would require a reconceptualization of BMU according to the "political unconscious" of the text, which diverts our attention towards a resolved conflict between two Mexican villages, while it represses the real contention between members of a social body, namely, Mexicans and Anglo-Americans.[35] I will return to this issue later in this study.

The disharmony between feuding "Mexican" clans is bridged, at one level, by the marriage of a Márez and a Luna (Gabriel and María); at yet another level, by Ultima's interference in three destinies (Antonio's, 6; Lucas's, 80; and Téllez's, 217), although she "was not to interfere in the destiny of any man" (247). Ultima accepts functioning as a benefactress in the last two cases after making the following cautionary remarks:

> "You must understand that when anybody, bruja or curandera . . . tampers with the fate of a man that sometimes a chain of events is set into motion over which no one will have ultimate control. You must be willing to accept this responsibility." (80)

This warning is given to members of the Luna clan--María and Pedro--who accept the responsibility. By simple deduction this is connected to Ultima's interference in Antonio's destiny, resulting in a richer reading beginning to unfold which produces a different set of expectations. This reading is strengthened in subsequent chapters (when Antonio begins to acquire features of a Judas variant), particularly during Ultima's last thaumaturgical intervention (Téllez). The question becomes, then, why did Ultima interfere in Antonio's destiny to begin with? Surely not to turn Antonio into a *curandero*.

When Ultima arrives at Antonio's house, he gazes at Ultima and remembers his dream. He holds hands with her, and everybody expects him to show his good manners and welcome Ultima properly--but Antonio is under a vision trance and hardly hears his father and mother, who are prompting him to follow customary rules (11). Meanwhile, Ultima's owl-like sensorium has confirmed a relationship; Antonio has, as well, just transgressed a customary law of etiquette, eliciting from Ultima the phrase "I knew there would be something between us" (11). And thus the bond is cemented. A rereading, however, indicates that such a bond had already been established at Antonio's birth. And when the Luna and Márez clans argue over Antonio's destiny, it is Ultima who intervenes and changes Antonio's future life. Although only a dream, the reader assumes that Antonio's birth occurs as described (7-8). Ultima's interference in Antonio's destiny, consequently, brings along a responsibility that, given Ultima's prophetic powers, she must have accepted before Antonio's birth. This is clearly disclosed when she offers the umbilical cord and the afterbirth to the Virgin of Guadalupe, while the Márez and Luna clans are arguing over the fate of the newborn. The strife between both clans forms a microcosm of a regional discord, apparently the result of a momentum carried over from the wars against Native Americans; the regional history is, therefore, a history of devastation and displaced aggression. It is in this context that the *llano* reveals itself as a demonic waste land.

Besides being the youngest of María's offspring, Antonio is also the sixth child, with a diffusive numerical symbolism: the days of Creation and God's sixth covenant with Moses; John's Apocalypse, with the number six linked to the name of the beast (= Nero), the New Babylon (= Roman Empire), and war (e.g., persecution of Christians). Viewed as code terms, and commutable to other texts, the beast finds a remote but direct association with Tenorio Trementina; the New Babylon, with the town of Guadalupe; and war, to the local history of hostility and persecution: Mexicans against Native Americans; Anglo-Americans against Mexicans (a history "full of blood, murder, and tragedy" 119); and men in general against witches ("Under the old law there was no penalty for killing a witch" 82), an aggression that is described in the mob scene against Ultima (chapter 12) and which reveals that such law is not "old" at all (125-126). Ultima's status in the region, consequently, is delicate and vulnerable to *male* aggression, which explains the uneasiness with which she is admitted into Gabriel's household. Ultima's frequent association with Native Americans would seem to apply more to their *fate* (i.e., "the only good witch is a dead witch") than to their *folklore*. Her role as *pharmakos* or sacrificial lamb becomes, then, a required figure in this setting, for it discloses the violence of the region and the absence of the law--two motifs in the apocalyptic tradition whose demonic emblems are found in the Four Horsemen and the New Babylon.

In the historical references found in BMU, one reads that Antonio's ancestor, the priest Luna, was sent by the Mexican government to colonize New Mexico (27, 49), where he founded El Puerto de los Luna between the years 1821-1848 (years when the land belonged to Mexico), close to the town of Guadalupe. Although never stated, Guadalupe must have been a Native American settlement overrun by Mexicans from El Puerto, who then changed the name of the town to Guadalupe. (The town's *ethnic sedimentation*, in other words, would be a parallel to the Tepeyac hill in Mexico, where the Virgin of Guadalupe is superposed over a preceding native deity, Tonantzín). Besides Mexicans from El Puerto and Las Pasturas, however, Anglo-Americans also live in Guadalupe; this town, therefore, represents a slice of regional history (golden carp, Jasón's Indian, wars, etc.), as well as the prototype of the *city*, with peoples of diverse racial and cultural backgrounds.[36] Whereas Las Pasturas is now a desolate town (2), and although El Puerto continues to be the stronghold of the Luna clan, Guadalupe is the only town with a mixed and growing population. Furthermore, of the three towns of the region, Guadalupe is the *original site* of the "settlements" and the place where the "people" communicated with the gods (110), where communication was lost, and where the prophecy of the golden carp is expected to be fulfilled. Hence, Guadalupe is at once Babel as well as where the Paraclete is awaited. Interwoven into the various settlements of Guadalupe, one finds the following periodization of a multilayered history of violence and conflict:

Diachronic Construct of History in BMU[37]

Settlement	"Worlds" or Eras	Phases of Revelation	Time
6) Sixth (dream, 168)	Fulfillment of prophecy	Apocalypse	Future
5) Fifth (119)	Anglo-American	Gospel of Metanoia	Present
4) Fourth (27, 49)	Mexican	(Western) Law	Past
3) Third	Native American	Wisdom	Legend
2) Second (110)	Second "Fall"	Prophecy	Myth
1) First (74)	The *People*	Fall of Man	Myth

In a narrative such as BMU, the representation of history is logically encoded in a pre-modern, Manichean master narrative where the destiny of mankind hangs in the midst of an inexorable struggle between the forces of creation and chaos, harmony and violence, disintegration and reintegration. The result is a historical emplotment presented in the form of *myth* (e.g., the golden carp), and *legend* (the heroic past of the Luna and the Márez clans);

with *history*, in its modern sense, as a subtheme embedded in the narrative: first, the 1846 war between the United States and Mexico; second, World War II, almost a century later. If Antonio is seven years old in 1945, the adult storyteller would be addressing his narrative audience during the 1960s--therefore at the time of the Vietnam war--with a message of peace and against notions of *terrestrial* empires.[38]

Present also in BMU is a "historical" construct that connects the narrative to the tradition of *celestial* empires, with its own versions of the Millenium, the Second Advent, and Apocalypse (a tradition best portrayed by the *penitentes* of New Mexico who act as "doubles" of medieval flagellants). The "textual" sources are the Bible and Mexican history. It is also at this level that BMU establishes a synchronic unity composed of the Roman Empire, the Spain of the sixteenth century, and modern United States; all three signified by an *island* (literal or metaphorical), a man of revelations whose name is "Juan," and an era of "world" conflict.

Antonio's reference to the story of "Diego" rewrites legend in the interests of the narrative's "ideology of form" (in Jameson's sense). As is widely known, the Virgin of Guadalupe does not appear to a "Mexican boy" (as claimed by the storyteller), but rather to an adult Christianized Aztec whose name was not Diego, but *Juan Diego* (a "double" entity, since they are the names of two apostles).[39] Second, analogies are made between Antonio's hill and the hill of the Tepeyac ("much like ours"), where the Virgin appeared to Juan Diego. This, logically, only serves to affirm the homology between the infant Antonio (whose middle name is Juan) and "Diego" (whose other name is also Juan). Third, since the town of Guadalupe is surrounded by water, it is the equivalent of a *metaphorical island*, just as the hill of the Tepeyac is a *metonymical island* (due to its contiguity to a lake). In sum, the narrative develops a diachronic construct composed of three *Juanes*, three *islands*, and three *apocalypses* or revelations, which in turn coincide with an empire, with the historical conflict of peoples of different "nationalities," and with a New World foretold in each apocalypse.

Apocalyptic History in BMU

Site	Recipient of Vision	Era	Empire
Storyteller's	Narrative Audience	1960s	United States
Guadalupe's Hill	Juan (young Antonio)	1945	Axis Powers
Tepeyac Hill	Juan Diego	1531	Spain
Island of Patmos	John	1st century A.D.	Rome

The diachronic construct formed by the three apocalyptic "Juanes" obviously refers to a New Jerusalem, the New Church, or to the New World rising, frequently expected to last a millenium. BMU's ideology of form, therefore, is achieved *ideologically* (as this study has attempted to illustrate) as well as *formally*: John's Apocalypse has 22 chapters, and so does BMU; in Revelation 12:3-6, the Beast attempts to devour the woman's child (who, by the way, "is destined to rule all nations with an iron rod"), while in BMU (also in chapter 12) Tenorio organizes a mob with the purpose of lynching Ultima (to avenge the death of his "child," the Trementina witch). The importance of number 22 is explained by Curtius in a brief study given to "literary trifling with numbers," as he calls it. Raban Mauer, according to Curtius, made a compilation of his *De rerum naturis* in 22 books; the Old Testament, "in conformity with the 22 letters of the Hebrew alphabet," has 22 books; St. Augustine's *City of God* is also divided into 22 books. "This fact," Curtius writes, "justifies us in seeing a stimulus to medieval numerical composition in 'Biblical poetics' . . . Here number is no longer an outer framework, but a symbol of the cosmic *ordo*."[40]

VIII. The Horse, The Hanged Man, and Forbidden Marriages

The apocalyptic conventions that "speak through" BMU are ancient and of diverse sources, in character with Anaya's propensity towards syncretism, variants, and the transgression of static cultural structures. Viewed in this light, the best icon for BMU is that of the *hanged man*, represented numerologically by the number 12, and rhetorically by the *adynaton* or "world upsidedown." Through these inversions, BMU nonetheless recontains Mexican historical constructs, autobiographical traces, along with the anti-war advocacy of the 1960's. BMU, in other words, achieves its truth in its inner coherence and not in a misunderstood representational intent. Its truth points towards a world-historical horizon and what could be referred to as a contradiction. Since Ultima, as an apocalyptic figure, represents a *method of cognition*, her revelations will stand in direct opposition to secularized, modern science. In this contradiction, then, one finds the locus where the initial passage of ideal landscape description acquires a more profound meaning, revealing a lexicon and a cluster of signifiers in opposition to Ultima, either in the form of *technical* (e.g., the railroad), or *scientific* knowledge (e.g., the atomic bomb). Whereas Ultima's knowledge uplifts and "unfolds" the truth of creation (based on the principle of destruction and renewal), and blesses in the name of health, goodness, and beauty (all in the name of body unity), modern man's science has an opposite effect: madness (Lupito), disintegration, confusion. The analogy between modern science and the Tower of Babel becomes at this point an implicit mental operation.

Ultima's apocalypsis, consequently, could appear as a symbolic resolution to two contradictions: one, social; the other, scientific. As already proposed, her death corresponds to the paradigmatic sacrifice of the *pharmakos* whose function, in the case of BMU, is to reunite a society splintered by a history of conquest and violence. In addition, Ultima's cognitive powers may be read as a symbolic resolution to a local contradiction between traditional and scientific knowledge. While this may suggest the availability of a "naive" resolution (and, in more than one respect, it is Anaya's form of representing a "catastrophe" or apocalyptic closure to a historical period), one should remember that science's dismissal of traditional knowledge is known for its "perversity," as Lyotard well illustrates:

> The scientist questions the validity of narrative statements and concludes that they are never subject to argumentation or proof. He classifies them as belonging to a different mentality: savage, primitive, underdeveloped, backward. . . . At best, attempts are made to throw some rays of light into this obscurantism, to civilize, educate, develop. . . . It is the entire history of cultural imperialism from the dawn of Western civilization.[41]

The notion of a historico-cultural world that has reached its end is elaborated explicitly by Anaya in *Tortuga*, a novel where apocalypse finds its clearest thematic representation.

In BMU, the regional contradiction in epistemological modalities finds its emblematic expression in the *horse* and in its cultural correlates according to Native American, Mexican (Márez), and Anglo-American variants. Although brought to the New World by Spaniards, the horse soon became (from a Western point of view) an intricate part of the cultural fabric of Native Americans and a symbol of their freedom and nomadic way of life. In turn, the Márez, who consider themselves descendants of Spanish *conquistadores*, appropriate this Native American "lifestyle" as their own, thereby distinguishing themselves from the sedentary and agricultural Luna clan. Anglo-Americans, conversely, achieve their cultural expression through the railroad (an *iron horse*), which radically transforms both the economy and the regional culture. Besides being a cultural emblem, and a symbol of war, this iron horse also represents a new epistemological development, namely, the metamorphosis of a *natural* horse into its *unnatural double* which, like the Trojan antecedent, carries the forces of empire in its belly.

In his role as storyteller, Antonio refers to the Anglo-American arrival not directly (i.e., through racial categories), but as a *technical modality* (railroad), a *land tenure system* (barbed wire, i.e., individual property as opposed to the traditional communal land holdings), and a *regional origin* (Texas), with its own history of strife and cultural upheaval.   Antonio's rhetorical strategy is revealed in the thematic cluster organized with variations of the theme of metamorphosis or zoomorphic transformations introduced as a *faculty* (when linked to cognition), as *punishment* (when associated with transgression), or as *entropy* (when the result of war, such as madness, cultural regression, etc.).[42] The metamorphoses are revealed through an owl, carps, and "wild" boys, respectively.   Horse, for example, is given the following "horselike" description:

> The Horse came up to me very slowly until his face was close to mine.   His dark, wild eyes held me hypnotically, and I could hear the deep sounds a horse makes inside his chest when he is ready to buck.   Saliva curled around the edges of his mouth and spittle threads hung down and glistened like spider threads in the sun.   He chomped his teeth and I could smell his bad breath. . . . "Whagggggggg!"   He brayed.   (34)

If one compares this passage with the initial encounter between Antonio and Ultima, the parody will be evident: instead of the unfolding of cosmic forces, gurgling waters, and the "hum of the turning earth," Antonio witnesses the unfolding of a face (mouth, saliva, spittle, wild eyes), and hears "deep sounds" originating in Horse's chest; instead of being "spellbound" under Utima's gaze, Antonio is held "hypnotically" under Horse's "dark, wild eyes." Through a rhetorical operation, Horse has acquired equine traits expressive of an arrested cultural development and suggestive of the regional babel of tongues in which English has become the *lingua franca*, while Spanish is becoming, among the local youth, a fragmented language.   Compared to Horse and Bones, the "spirituals" (Samuel, Cico, and Antonio) are the ideal counterparts and the mode of "cultural power" introduced by the narrative. The names alone are symbolical reductions of their significance: to *war* (horse) and *death* (bones)--the two historical signifiers of the llano.   The members of the cult, on the contrary, are figural representations (if not fulfillments) of the

Biblical priest (Samuel, with the barren mother and double parentage), the *apocalyptic prophet* (Cico = Ezequiel), and a *saint* (Antonio) associated with temptations and visions of Hell. In sum, the rhetorical process organized around the horse motif ranges from a *metaphor* (the youth called Horse), and a *metonymy* (the Márez horsemen, "horselike" by contiguity), to a *synecdoche* (a cultural "whole"--Anglo-Americans--represented by one of its parts: the *iron horse*).

Having reached this point, it appears that the reading touches on what the narrative can not utter by itself (the "unspeakable" in BMU), not because of literary decorum but because of an unwritten law regarding what may be called *forbidden marriages*. One can easily grasp the commutability of the males from Las Pasturas (e.g., Márez) and the men from Texas (e.g., Anglo-Americans): in both instances, they are related in BMU to *aggression*. "Márez" and "Anglo," in a sense, are code terms that can be interchanged, reducing the regional violence to one between Anglo-Americans and Mexicans. María, by marrying outside of her clan, has, in a way, married an "Anglo" (Gabriel), thus transgressing a local prohibition regarding interracial marriages. The commutability of code terms, such as Márez and Anglo-American, would better explain, from a historical and cultural point of view, the long-standing enmity between the Márez and the Luna clans ("We have been at odds all of our lives" 235). As it stands in the narrative, such enmity has been encoded according to a *preceding* opposition that has been resolved in Mexico, namely, the conflict between Spaniards and the Mexican native population, a conflict which resulted in *mestizo* offspring. In New Mexico, the offspring of Anglo-Mexican unions are still called *coyotes*; could BMU be "talking," in its own muffled way, about coyotes in New Mexico, and not about Mexican mestizos? Antonio's dilemma (to be a Márez or a Luna) may conceal much more than a choice between being a horseman or a farmer; if so, then perhaps in this dilemma, and in its resolution, is where Antonio acquires a Judas role.

IX. Summary

BMU is a richly textured narrative which operates with culturally relevant expectations. The story line appears at times to wander over to secondary themes, turning on itself--and against itself--at key passages, advancing then to another narrative signpost, another meaningful thematic knot, at which point one discovers that the narration had been moving all along toward its climactic end. In the ontological duality established between the speaking subject (the storyteller) and his remembered self (his distant "I"), the paradoxical role of passive witness without sight corresponds to the young Antonio, registered in the narration of a consciousness which is retroactive vision, narrative memory, and remorse. Antonio's narration incorporates in its path fragments of Native American lore, Christian iconography, and Anglo-American emblems (e.g., the railroad, barbed wire, institutional hegemony). The reading of BMU, therefore, becomes a complex activity, identifying with the narrative audience ("listening" to Antonio) while, at the same time, keeping a critical distance, attentive to structuring significations and correlative mechanisms that govern the flow of the narrative.

The rethinking of BMU as an artistic fragment of a vast expressive culture which belongs to Mexicans living on both sides of the Border, has brought us to the examination of the storyteller's art and to the analysis of apocalypse as an ideological construct. The results have revealed a pattern of recurrent motifs and themes throughout BMU's discourse, such as numerology, the Judas variant to the traditional "traitor" motif, the theme of double parentage, spiritual brotherhoods, forbidden marriages, the "double" or split character, the topos of the world "upsidedown," and "the hanged man." Embedded in this pattern is a duality composed first of all by Ultima, as a woman who is a personification of regional folk wisdom (Mexican + Native American); who crosses regional and cultural frontiers (much like a coyote, and in her role as sacrificial victim); and who is a symbolic resolution to conflictive epistemological modalities (traditional versus modern knowledge). The other part of the duality is found in Antonio (Ultima's metaphorical son), who plays a decisive role in her downfall; hence his remorse and role as Judas (with the correlative signifier of the tree). This thematic construct recontains the ancient belief that someone must die so that someone else may live, a belief fundamental to Christology, as well as to Anaya's narrative.[43] This motif and thematic pattern, with its own ideological base, could be read as the intermittent, half-concealed, register of authorial self-inscription. Conventional critical approaches, deployed by most Anaya studies, find the motifs and themes of the novel instead in Anaya's "collective unconscious," or in his "epiphanies" and "flight from history." In a separate study [See "The Surname, the Corpus, and the Body in Rudolfo A. Anaya's Narrative Trilogy" **included in this volume**], I undertake a more sustained analysis of such autobiographical passages as they are written in Anaya's narrative trilogy, using this study as its foundation.[44]

NOTES

[1] From Sophocles, *The Three Theban Plays*, trans. Robert Fagles (New York: Penguin Classics, 1984), 232. In the course of writing this article, César González tactfully and wisely advised me to abbreviate where I was prolix and to clarify what often resembles critical short-hand. I could not follow his advice. There is, in my two contributions to this volume, a book-length study that I have *repressed;* hence the short-hand and the intermittent logomania. Partly for his reserved insistence that this study be completed, but mostly as a form of revenge, this article is dedicated to him.

[2] "The Triumph of White Magic in Rudolfo Anaya's *Bless Me, Ultima,*" *Mester*, Vol. XIV (Primavera 1985), No. 1, 41-54.

[3] "Rudolfo Anaya's *Bless Me, Ultima.* A Chicano Romance of the Southwest," *Crítica*, Vol. 1, No. 3 (Fall 1986), 21-47. **Reprinted in this volume.**

[4] "Anaya, Rudolfo Alfonso," *Chicano Literature: A Reference Guide*, eds. Julio A. Martínez and Francisco Lomelí (Connecticut: Greenwood Press, 1985), 34-51.

[5] "Myth as the Cognitive Process of Popular Culture in Rudolfo Anaya's *Bless Me, Ultima*: The Dialectics of Knowledge," *Hispania*, Vol. 68, No. 3 (September 1985), 496-501. **Reprinted in this volume.**

[6] "Ilusión y realidad en la obra de Rudolfo Anaya," *Contemporary Chicano Fiction*, ed. Vernon E. Lattin (New York: Bilingual Press, 1986), 171-199.

[7] In a keen attempt to "politicize" BMU, Lamadrid produces a reading which transforms Antonio into a cultural mediator, with permutations as

trickster, *curandero*, or political activist. According to Lamadrid, "After Ultima's death, her knowledge continues in Antonio and the reader feels sure that whatever his fate may be, he possesses the conceptual tools to continue to help his people and culture with their internal conflicts as well as with the oncoming struggle between a whole new set of oppositions stemming from the fast approaching aggressive proximity of the Anglo culture and way of life" (op. cit., 500). At the mere story or content level, objections to this interpretive passage could point to the idea of fulfillment of the apprentice's role ("her knowledge continues in Antonio") as being only an assumption made by Lamadrid, for there is absolutely no reference, and no valid grounds for an inference, regarding a continuation of Ultima's knowledge. On the other hand, how would Ultima's knowledge function in the "oncoming struggle" with Anglo culture? Surely, clay dolls and pins are out of the question. Second, if Ultima, as her name suggests, represents the closing of an era and the end of a cultural paradigm (as my study proposes), how can Antonio continue practicing with epistemological categories that belong to an unredeemable past? Furthermore, Anglo-Americans are not "fast approaching" New Mexico; they have been there for some years with a history not unknown to Antonio ("The meeting of the people from Texas with my forefathers was full of blood, murder, and tragedy" BMU 119). Lamadrid's passage concludes, nonetheless, a forceful, allegorical reading of BMU processed on a posited problem (two feuding families), resolved in Antonio (an alleged synthesis of the Márez and Luna ancestries), and therefore representative of *ethnic unity* through the mestizo (i.e., Spanish and Indian), a stage necessary for Antonio and the people he represents to meet another opposition (Anglo culture) in a struggle which, according to the inherent principles of the dialectic, might result in yet another synthesis, namely: Mexican + Anglo. Or could the opposition be sustained indefinitely? Lamadrid's article offers no comment on this dialectical (im)possibility. Most Chicano literary criticism, however, tends to support the simplistic notion that Chicano culture is the "synthesis" of Mexican and Anglo-American cultures. Lamadrid keeps his dialectics at a safe distance from this "best-of-both-worlds" synthesis.

[8] According to Juan Bruce-Novoa: "the space of literature is open to Antonio and he becomes the narrator of the novel. . . . He creates the novel

to keep his promise to Ultima within a space of total harmony analogous to the one she revealed to him, and ultimately the same" (quoted by José Monleón, op. cit., 192). Bruce-Novoa is right in asserting that Antonio is the narrator in BMU, but his assumption regarding Antonio's creation of a novel is unfounded, for nowhere in the narrative is there a reference to such action. Second, is the "space" revealed to Antonio by Ultima one of an alleged "total harmony"? If Ultima signifies anything to Antonio, it is, on the contrary, the *disharmony* of the world, made evident as of Ultima's arrival at Guadalupe.

[9] Bruce-Novoa's reasoning has motivated other critics, such as José Monleón and Héctor Calderón, to reach similar conclusions. Monleón, for example, proposes the following: "Ultima . . . es defendida y ensalzada en la medida en que es vista como antecedente directo del escritor moderno . . . El poeta--en eso se convierten Antonio y Tortuga . . . --reemplaza al curandero. BMU es el proceso de iniciación de Antonio no sólo como persona sino como escritor" (Monleón, op. cit., 190). Is Ultima really defended and dignified inasmuch as she is seen as the "direct antecedent" of the modern writer, or is this another example of ventriloquist criticism? Monleón sees in BMU the replacement of the *curandero* by the modern writer (a poet now, not a novelist). Beginning with Bruce-Novoa's assumption (Antonio = novelist), Monleón then proceeds to base his argument on the political views of Christopher Caudwell, resulting in a most interesting syllogism: Antonio is a poet; poets can't undermine or work against their social class; therefore the political ambivalence of Anaya the poet/writer. Basing the argument of his article on an obviously "inharmonious" foundation (Bruce-Novoa's interpretation of BMU and Caudwell's crude notions of "reality" and "illusion"), Monleón's reading will convince only the uninformed. Why has Bruce-Novoa's limited reading of BMU been so influential among Chicano critics (since it is based solely on birth tokens and a promise not kept--the former disclosed by Antonio's choice of "pen and paper" when still a child; the latter, when Antonio promises Ultima "You will never die. . . . I will take care of you," BMU, 11)? Given that Ultima dies at the conclusion of BMU, Bruce-Novoa interprets a problem (a promise not kept) resolved by an action, namely: the writing of a novel where Ultima "lives." In their readings of

BMU, Monleón remains caught in Caudwell's illusions; Bruce-Novoa, conversely, continues reading novels as if all were portraits of the novelists as young men. Notwithstanding its inherent limited scope, Bruce-Novoa's interpretation has a peculiar echo in a recent article by Calderón, who adds: "Only the visionary Antonio, who in his dreams dons the priestly robes as poet and prophet, is capable of articulating the teachings of nature. . . . Ultima is . . . superior to any realistic portrayal of a *curandera*. Her vision animates the landscape for Antonio; through her prophecy his future is determined. She is . . . the Romantic genius loci of the llano with whose guidance the future writer (and Anaya) is blessed," (op. cit., 30). What does this mean? Apparently that Antonio is a prophet ("visionary") like Ultima ("through her prophecy"), and that Antonio is also a writer ("and Anaya") who, one presumes, will write BMU. Yet immediately after raising Antonio to the prophetic heavens as well as sinking him to the less grandiose role of a writer, Calderón turns towards Antonio's "novel" (BMU) and judges it as a "flight from history": "Anaya's narrative strategies can be pressed for meaning within a wider cultural context and interpreted as a flight from history. . . . The agents of imperialism, the conquistador, and the priest, are legitimated and viewed as better alternatives to the fallen men of Guadalupe" (39). Compared to Lamadrid's political reading of BMU, Calderón's represents its direct opposite: one views Antonio as preparing for the "oncoming struggle" with Anglo culture; the other sees BMU as a "flight from history," giving legitimacy to the "agents of imperialism."

[10] See Rudolfo A. Anaya, *A Chicano in China* (Albuquerque: The University of New Mexico Press, 1986), 119-120.

[11] Fredric Jameson, *The Political Unconscious: Narrative as a Socially Symbolic Act* (New York: Cornell University Press, 1981), 13.

[12] See Rudolfo A. Anaya, *Bless Me, Ultima* (Berkeley: Quinto Sol Publications, 1972), for the following passages: "I do not know what he said because of the shouting" 118; "that is all I remember" 94; "I don't know how long I stood there thinking" 152; "I did not know why he would pause here. . . . I did not know what to do" 155; "I think I started laughing, or

crying" 163, etc. In this critical study, all references to BMU derive from this edition and pagination will be given in parenthesis.

[13] For example, "He *seemed* to be thinking" 19; "he *seemed* older than the rest" 53; "She held her head high, *as if* sniffing the wind" 121 (emphasis added).

[14] For example, "Bones might kill *you* and not care" 139; "if *you* had to stay after school it was eerie and lonely" 141 (emphasis added).

[15] For example, "It was the custom to provide for the old and the sick. There was always room in the safety and warmth of la familia" 4; "harvest time was a time for work and not for mitote" 131.

[16] Cordelia Candelaria, op. cit., 41; see also 37-38.

[17] Peter J. Rabinowitz, "Truth in Fiction: A Reexamination of Audiences," *Critical Inquiry*, Vol. 4 (Autumn 1977), No. 1, 123. See also Jonathan Culler, *On Deconstruction: Theory and Criticism after Structuralism* (New York: Cornell University Press, 1982), 1-83. It is appropriate at this time to remember the obvious, namely, that Anaya wrote BMU with an ethnically unidentified audience, that is, he did not write it specifically for a Chicano readership, and intended at first to have it published through a Boston or New York firm; this does not apply, obviously, to the narrative written by Anaya after BMU; by that time, according to Anaya, "I had made my connection to the Chicano movement. . . . Everywhere there was a feeling that the artist had to return his art to the people, to the pueblo." In Rudolfo A. Anaya, "Autobiography," *Contemporary Authors Autobiographical Series* (Detroit: Gale Research Co., 1986), 25.

[18] Anaya, *Contemporary Authors*, op. cit., 24.

[19] See the excellent short story by Anaya, "The Place of the Swallows," in *The Silence of the Llano* (Berkeley: Tonatiuh-Quinto Sol

International, 1982), which illustrates the role of the storyteller (with a reference to Salomón and the death of a turtle), and has an oblique insinuation to a "Gang of Four" and to the notion that a storyteller must *walk alone.*

[20] Most Anaya criticism locates Antonio's anagnorisis at a different narrative site (236), during Antonio's conversation with his father. The true moment, however, occurs six pages later, when Antonio discovers his "destiny" in regards to Ultima's downfall: "I was afraid for Ultima. I realized the evil Tenorio had found a way to hurt Ultima. . . . A long time afterwards I thought that if I had waited and gone to my uncles . . . that things would have turned out differently" (242-243; emphasis added).

[21] This "transgression" recalls another which occurs at the beginning of the narrative: Antonio's first greeting to Ultima when she arrives at Guadalupe; instead of calling her "la Grande," Antonio addresses her by her first name ("My mother was shocked. . . . But Ultima held up her hand. . . . I knew there would be something between us" 11). Antonio is a man of fate and Ultima, as well as his mother, express concern over his "destiny" and, as such, resemble the Fates who "weave" a man's destiny; at the beginning of BMU, when discussing Ultima's moving from Las Pasturas to Guadalupe, María's decision (and Gabriel's) to bring Ultima to their home is actually part of Antonio's destiny: María, at the moment of her decision, is *weaving,* assuming the activity associated with the Fates ("I knew her nimble fingers worked the pattern on the doily she crocheted" 2); much later, when Antonio is almost dying of pneumonia, Ultima sits by his side ("she sat crocheting . . . she did her embroidery work. She told me stories about the old people of Las Pasturas" 170). The Fates, according to Barbara G. Walker, "bear traces of the Triple Goddess as three Fates rulers of the past, present, and future in the usual *personae* of Virgin, Mother, and Crone. . . . Nearly always, they were weavers. . . . Greeks still say the Fates visit the cradle of every newborn, to determine the child's future as his fairy godmothers." In *The Woman's Encyclopedia of Myths and Secrets* (San Francisco: Harper and Row, 1983), 302-303.

[22] This narrative maneuver may be inferred in page 236, during the

conversation between Gabriel and Antonio, a situation frequently interpreted as Antonio's moment of recognition. The didactic process inherent in Antonio's account appears to range from the assumption of a U.S. Mexican audience which is *culturally*, and *historically*, distanced (with Antonio as a point of reference), to one of *cultural insiders*, and then (reaching the didactic objective) to one of *cultural transformers* ("reform the old materials, make something new" 236). Stretched enough, this apocalyptic moment, with its consciousness of the "old" and the imminence of the "new," could well mark the narrative audience's anagnorisis in an ideal situation; as it stands, it is a pedagogical feature worthy of reflection. For a similar view, although in reference to the teaching of literature, see Northrop Frye's discussion of (1)"social mythology," (2)"serious belief," and (3)"individual recreation of mythology," in *The Secular Scripture: A Study of the Structure of Romance* (Massachusetts: Harvard University Press, 1976), 167, 170, 171.

[23] Américo Paredes, *"With His Pistol in His Hand": A Border Ballad and Its Hero* (Austin: University of Texas Press, 1958), 35. The legend of Gregorio Cortez is Paredes' own bricolage or "arrangement," as he informs his readers: "It is the legend [of Gregorio Cortez] that has developed the heroic figure, which the ballad keeps alive. . . . The legend, on the other hand, has grown considerably. . . . There is no standard version of the legend and it is never, as far as I know, told complete at one sitting. . . . The legend as it appears . . . is my own creation. I have put together those parts that seemed to me the farthest removed from fact and the most revealing of folk attitudes" (108, 109).

[24] This "Hellenized" Judas is also found in the version given by Tim Rice and Andrew Lloyd Weber in the musical recording of *Jesus Christ Superstar*, released by Decca Records in 1969.

[25] The point to be made in this context is not to suggest the critical precondition of biblical exegesis for a proper analysis of BMU, but merely to emphasize the rhetorical framework that informs the narrative, and to provide for a critical ground where BMU can be analyzed as an ideological construct

built with apocalyptic notions transmitted to New Mexico, in great measure, by the Franciscans (e.g., the *penitente* tradition, the Virgin of Guadalupe, a theological sense of history with a millenarian scope, etc.). Regarding the origin of the *penitentes*, see Frances L. Swadesh, *Los primeros pobladores*, trans. Ana Zagury (México: Fondo de Cultura Económica, 1977), 79-107; also, for a parallel with the Flagellant Movement and its notion of the end of the world, consult Marjorie Reeves, *Prophecy in the Later Middle Ages: A Study in Joachimism* (Oxford: Clarendon Press, 1969), 54-55; refer to the chapter on Charles V and the prophecies linked to this emperor, 359-374. For a general overview of the Franciscans in Mexico, consult John L. Phelan, *The Millennial Kingdom of the Franciscans in the New World*, 2nd ed., rev. (Los Angeles: University of California Press, 1970), 41-58.

[26] On this subject, consult Marjorie Reeves, op. cit., 270, 447, 503; also, David E. Aune, *Prophecy in Early Christianity and the Ancient Mediterranean World* (Michigan: W. B. Eerdmans Publishing Co., 1983), 106-138; and Northrop Frye, *The Great Code: The Bible and Literature* (New York: Harcourt Brace Jovanovich, 1982), 135-137.

[27] See David E. Aune, op. cit., 19.

[28] Regarding the adynaton, see Ernst R. Curtius, *European Literature in the Latin Middle Ages*, trans. W. R. Trask (Princeton: Princeton University Press, 1973), 95.

[29] Antonio completes the "puzzle" on page 242; notice that just before chapter 12--in other words, just before the mob scene in which Tenorio attempts to lynch Ultima and ends swearing that he will kill her--Antonio has a dream in which Ultima tells him, "You have been seeing only parts . . . and not looking beyond into the great cycle that binds us all" (113). In spite of the dream, Antonio continues seeing only parts.

[30] For the notion of *metanoia*, the "new man," and the view of a person's separation from the primary community, see Frye, *The Great Code*, 130-131; also, 136, 165.

[31] Ibid., 137.

[32] See Jameson, *The Political Unconscious*, 110-119.

[33] Consult Claude Lévi-Strauss, *The Raw and the Cooked*, trans. John and Doreen Weightman (New York: Harper and Row, 1975), 298-299.

[34] Frye, *The Great Code*, 162.

[35] According to Frye, "the social relation is that of the mob, which is essentially human society looking for a *pharmakos*, and the mob is often identified with some sinister animal image as the . . . Beast," in *Anatomy of Criticism: Four Essays* (Princeton: Princeton University Press, 1971), 149. Prior to this, Frye refers to the pharmakos as the sacrificial victim "who has to be killed to strengthen the others," 148.

[36] Regarding the city and apocalyptic literature, consult Frye, *The Great Code*, 144, 154-156.

[37] Ibid., 106. The phases of Revelation, somewhat modified, have been taken from Frye. In BMU, the sources of myth are Samuel and Cico (73-74, 104-111); of legend, the sources are Ultima (37, 39, 115, 170, 216), Gabriel (27), María (49), and the people of Las Pasturas (118-119). While myth deals with the two original settlements and their transgressions, and subsequent "fall," clan legends also refer to foundations (El Puerto, Las Pasturas); transgressions (e.g., a priest's celibacy vows); a fall (the enmity between local Mexican clans), and to their subsequent uprootedness after the Mexico-U.S. war of 1846.

[38] For an exposition of the role of empires as a major theme in apocalyptic literature, see Frye, *The Great Code*, 83, 89, 160, 177.

[39] There are only three extended references to the Virgin of Guadalupe

in BMU, and they refer to the Virgin's relationship to the town of Guadalupe and to Ultima's owl (12); to the Virgin's apparition to "the little boy in Mexico," and her healing powers (42); and in the longest reference where the parallel is fully established between Juan Diego and Antonio (180). If one recalls the textual setting of each reference, the first corresponds to Ultima's arrival and takes place in Antonio's dreams; the second, to the first occasion in which Ultima begins her "history lessons," telling Antonio about his ancestral past ("Long ago . . . long before you were a dream. . . ." 37), and her lessons in herb collecting (the tree of life, by semantic expansion); the third, to Antonio's first encounter with Tenorio, exactly where Narciso was killed (the juniper tree), and corresponding to the site in which Antonio indicates to Tenorio (without himself knowing) the spiritual bond between Ultima and the owl, information which will lead eventually to Ultima's death.

[40] Curtius, *European Literature*, 508, 509.

[41] Jean-Francois Lyotard, *The Postmodern Condition: A Report on Knowledge*, trans. G. Bennington and B. Massumi (Minneapolis: University of Minnesota Press, 1984), 27. A few pages later, Lyotard adds the following comment: "Technology is therefore a game pertaining not to the true, the just, or the beautiful, etc., but to efficiency: a technical 'move' is 'good' when it does better and/or expends less energy than another" (44).

[42] The theme of entropy emerges as a narrative construct in *Heart of Aztlán*, where urbanization, gangs, war, and labor problems are developed by an Anaya who by then is writing for a Chicano readership.

[43] In BMU, Ultima dies to save Antonio; in *Heart of Aztlán*, Frankie instead of Benjie; in *Tortuga*, Salomón, once Tortuga's "destiny" is set.

[44] See my article, "The Surname, the Corpus, and the Body in Rudolfo A Anaya's Narrative Trilogy," in this volume. At this point I should add that this present study updates my previous analyses of Anaya's narrative, such as "Estructura y sentido de lo onírico en *Bless Me, Ultima*," *Mester*, Vol. V (Noviembre de 1974), Num. 1, 27-41; and "Degradación y regeneración en

Bless Me, Ultima: el Chicano y la vida nueva," *Caribe*, Vol. I (Spring 1976), Num. 1, 113-126; reprinted in *The Identification and Analysis of Chicano Literature*, ed. Francisco Jiménez (New York: The Bilingual Press, 1979). 374-388.

Bless Me, Ultima: A Chicano Romance of the Southwest

Héctor Calderón
Scripps College
Claremont, California

The latest (1986) edition of Rudolfo A. Anaya's *Bless Me, Ultima*, first published in 1972, boldly states on its cover that it has achieved the status of a best-selling novel and a Chicano literary classic. Although Anaya has written two other similar works, *Heart of Aztlán* and *Tortuga*, and recently published a collection of short stories, *The Silence of the Llano*, his fame rests on the success of his first book. As Octavio I. Romano-V., the Tonatiuh-Quinto Sol publisher, explains in a brief introduction of the seventeenth printing, no other novel written by a Chicano has received such wide reception and international acclaim.[1] The over 250,000 copies sold have been read by untutored readers, by high school and university students, as well as by professional critics. Like other books that have gained an international audience, Anaya's narrative has produced a variety of differing interpretations. The critical reception of this book in which readers refer to different cultural spaces associated with a number of oral, literary and popular narrative genres casts doubts on the monolithic classification of the Chicano novel. The practice of designating every lengthy Chicano narrative a novel is evident in every critical piece that I have read on this genre.[2] This occurs to such an extent that even autobiographies are labeled novels.[3] I would like to take this occasion to question the indiscriminate use of the term novel and pursue the intelligibility of *Bless Me, Ultima* according to the rhetoric of romance.

A brief survey of the interpretive responses to Anaya's narrative will allow us to situate it less within the realism of the novel and more within a tradition of highly symbolic fictions. The book has been read by Albert D. Treviño as a novel of maturation, a *bildungsroman*, accurately and realistically describing the mental development of a Mexican-American child, Antonio Juan Márez y Luna, in rural eastern New Mexico during the years immediately prior to and after the end of World War II. Even though the historical and geographic settings may lend this story of maturation the impression of literary realism, the reader is presented with figurative ambiences, dream visions and symbolic characterizations that heighten contrasts between heroes and villains. There is a constant struggle between good and evil forces, as in the case of Antonio's spiritual guide, the beneficent mother-figure Ultima, and the evil father Tenorio Trementina. Following these obvious contrasts, Daniel Testa refers to the book as a good, mass-media action tale resembling the "wild west" plots of popular literature and the Hollywood western. To be sure, the book contains the usual settings for evil, Rosie's house of prostitution and a Longhorn Saloon with drunken brawls, and the proverbial battles between cowboys and farmers. Jane Rogers has focused on the numerous references to archetypes of world literature, to popular beliefs and folk motifs to Native American and Mexican oral traditions, of which the best known is the apparition of "la llorona" or "wailing woman." David Carrasco, reading the book from the point of view of the history of religions, has even dared to call it a quasi-religious text because of scenes demonstrating the shamanic power of the *curandera* (folk healer) Ultima.

These interpretations offered by other readers force upon the critic the question of genre. Though the book is different for everyone, it is also the same for all have accepted that Anaya's narrative conforms to the rhetoric of the novel. After all, it is a lengthy narrative with a first-person narrator, a clear plotline, characters, settings and scenes. However, as critics of Chicano literature, we should begin to draw distinctions among all the narratives classified as Chicano novels. For example, how dissimilar Anaya's vision of nature, the mythical significance given to meteorological phenomena and the physical landscape, from Tomás Rivera's realistic description of natural events that will not allow for supernatural agency in ". . . *y no se lo tragó la tierra*" / ". . . *And the Earth Did Not Part.*" Or how different the reconstruction of historical events in Anaya's idealized world of the forties from Oscar Zeta

Acosta's rambling satire of the sixties drug culture in *The Autobiography of a Brown Buffalo*. In terms of the critical reception of a literary text, brand-name labeling will serve no useful interpretive purpose. It is the romance whose formal possibilities and stylistic features can accommodate mythic and religious materials, as well as folk beliefs, and then project them in almost any age as ideals and wish-fulfillment fantasies, that will give us greater insights into *Bless Me, Ultima*.

We can situate Anaya's romance within the literature of the Southwest as an extension of a native New Mexican literary tradition. Prior to the contemporary Chicano period, a regional romantic tradition developed out of an Anglo-American cultural hegemony and, in some instances, out of the complicitous relations of older Hispanic elites with the newly-arrived easterners. Early in the twentieth century, a whole set of discursive and cultural practices were set in motion which survived until recently in the scholarly and popular imagination. These were marked by an emphasis on a beautiful, empty landscape, folkloric customs, and an idyllic "Spanish Southwest," while refusing to represent the real social conditions of Native Americans and the large numbers of recent peasant and working-class Mexican immigrants (see Chávez 97-106). Recently, Genaro Padilla has returned to this early period of struggle through the autobiographical texts of New Mexican Hispanas. He writes:

> The site of this particular discursive struggle for ideological domination is found in what I call folkloric autobiographies composed by Hispanos in the first half of the 20th Century in New Mexico. I wish to argue that the composition of these autobiographies find their generative will in folkore and historical society development in the Southwest from the turn of the century to a pitch of activity in the 1930's during the Worker's Project Administration (WPA) programs, especially the Federal Writer's Project. Moreover, I argue that Anglo-American intellectuals, writers and artists, who came to New Mexico at the beginning of the 20th Century invented an aesthetic discourse of myth and romance that deeply inscribed itself upon the popular consciousness and provided one of the few forms through which

Hispanos could compose their lives for public view. (Padilla "Lies, Secrets, and Silence in New Mexico" 3-4)

To claim that Anaya's book is a romance, however, implies more than just situating it within a literary tradition; it also involves explaining under what cultural conditions is it possible to conceive of this literary form. As bilinguals, Chicano writers have a variety of communicative discourses at their disposal, and the language of literary expression is telling of influences. Anaya is a university instructor and holds a master's degree in English from the University of New Mexico. Thus, he knows the classics of Western literature and the English tradition, both British and American, as a scholar and writer. And although Anaya uses Native American and Chicano cultural motifs, English literary traditions by way of the Romantics, Gerard Manley Hopkins, T. S. Eliot and James Joyce have played a significant role in shaping his first book.[4] But also Northrop Frye--who has done so much to establish the legitimacy of romance as a critical concept--is an unquestionable dominant influence. From Frye, it seems to me, Anaya derives his plot structures of romance and key terms in his literary vocabulary, such as archetype, mythos, inscape and epiphany.[5]

Historically, romance is possible, using Frye's often repeated phrase, during periods of cultural transformation when myth is displaced toward the aesthetic realm.[6] As a written form, romance follows in the wake of the dissolution of a world conceived through mythic or, with reference to Lévi-Strauss, magical consciousness and whose dominant form of discourse is oral and formulaic. Displacement means that beliefs in foundation myths are depragmatized, removed from their original collective context, deprived of their truth effect and transformed into the metaphors and archetypes of imaginative literature. This was the case with the Greek and Medieval romances and a similar situation obtains with Chicano romance. Most residents of the Southwest enjoy the technological advancements of the twentieth century and belong to a literate, mass-media culture. However, because of the uneven evolution of the area, many Chicanos (like Latin Americans and other members of the Third World) still live in a world whose only discourse is oral and whose consciousness is still highly influenced by myths, folk beliefs and superstitions, the remnants of pre-Columbian life together with Hispanic folk traditions. This discourse with its world-view and lively imagination is available to Chicano writers, and in large measure accounts for similarities with contemporary Latin American fiction. Even though the displaced formulaic units of myths and folk beliefs stand out in *Bless Me, Ultima*, the book is not a folklore collection, nor is its radical of presentation oral as is the case with novels written in Spanish (". . . *And the Earth Did Not Part*," for example); this is a deliberately crafted fiction, written in lofty, often poetic style, treating of heroism and fabulous things. It approaches the level of narrative fantasy and should be interpreted accordingly.

The folk motif of "la llorona", for example, has a special function within the book and is related to the theme of misdirected responses to a calling or vocation. The "wailing woman" is transformed into an evil spirit who wanders along river banks seeking to drink the blood of men and boys, and is, therefore, a negative feminine archetype along with the siren of the Hidden Lakes and the prostitutes of Rosie's house. As in the *Odyssey* and Joyce's *Ulysses*, these three figures act as blocking agents and beckon men to their haunts to seduce them and turn them away from their heroic destiny. Along similar lines of argument, I cannot totally agree with David Carrasco who reads *Bless Me, Ultima* as a religious text because of what he terms non-Christian, authentic Chicano religious experience depicted in the scene of *curanderismo* or folk healing (206-208). This most important scene occurs in Chapter 10, near the center of the book, and is contrived to reflect mythic patterns of both Native American and Christian traditions. The young (about eight years old) Antonio and Ultima must struggle against the sorcery of the three evil daughters of Tenorio Trementina. The blood of the youngest Márez is tested to resurrect his youngest uncle, Lucas Luna, from certain death at the hands of the Trementina sisters. For three days the innocent Antonio, the son of María and Gabriel, suffers in a semi-conscious state and eventually through magical sympathy heals the bewitched Lucas. These events of the hero as donor, scapegoat and savior show up for the reader not an undisplaced religious belief, but a semantic component intrinsic to the romance when Ultima tells Antonio that life is never beyond hope because good is always stronger than evil (91).

My analysis of *Bless Me, Ultima* as a romance will benefit from two elements in the scene of *curanderismo*: one is the semantic opposition between good and evil, and the other is the messianic structure of the plot. These elements in Anaya's narrrative will lead, on one hand, to the representation of subjectivity and, on the other, to the reconstruction of historical events in the romance form.[7]

We can approach the question of the representation of subjectivity in Anaya's romance through the high level of abstraction that runs through the stylized characters, both attractive and evil, settings, scenes and almost any aspect of the physical landscape. These aspects of the narrative can be meaningfully good or evil, which is to say, that through the filtering mind of the characters they can be given the categories of subjectivity and agency. Anaya portrays more than the physical landscape of eastern New Mexico, for a romantic sense of place unfolds for the reader in the opening paragraph of the book as Antonio's consciousness is awakened by Ultima's guidance to the spirit and beauty of the *llano* (plains) in summer. In the area surrounding the small town of Guadalupe even the dark River of the Carp has a soul, can experience feelings, rising and falling emotions. For Antonio, his friends and Ultima, the river can be at times an evil *presence* that watches over people. The darkness of the river is counterbalanced by the sense of sanctity that pervades the clear pond where the golden carp, the image of a pre-Columbian god, surfaces every summer. There is a flow of agency among human, animal and vegetable worlds. The town drunk Narciso can make his garden (reminiscent of the Garden of Narcissus in the *Romance of the Rose*) grow into abundance by ritual magic, by singing, dancing and planting by moonlight. Anaya's commitment to the plots of myths and fairy tales is emphasized by the role given to Ultima's owl that carries her soul within its body. It is her bond to time and the harmony of the universe, and when her protective spirit dies at the hands of Tenorio Termentina so does Ultima. In terms of the history of the evolution of consciousness, we are clearly within an animistic landscape where transformations can occur at any moment and events are the products of cyclical patterns or magical causality, spells and curses. In sum, it is a preindividualistic world of higher and lower realms for which the magical and later religious categories of spirit and soul, not character, have served Anaya well.

The problem of good and evil is not avoided by the novel, nor is the question of the religious category of the soul excluded. They are recombined through an ideological and historically determined solution to causality furnished by the birth of modern psychology. This is the conceptualization of an individual psychological subject, the rational soul or *ánima racional* of Renaissance thought, henceforth known as the individual self. This *ánima racional* with its productive and discerning mental faculties through Classical--mainly Aristotelian and Galenic--and Renaissance sources-- especially Juan Huarte's *Examen de ingenios* (published in England in 1594 as *The Examination of Men's Wits*) and Alonso López Pinciano's *Philosophía antigua poética*--greatly influenced Cervantes' *Don Quijote*.[8] By modifying Aristotelian and Horatian precepts, Cervantes transforms the cult of hero worship of the chivalric romances into an exemplary tale of the imperfections of an all-too human nature conceived from Christian creationism and Classical thought. The psychological malady of Don Quijote allows the reader to see that the world of sixteenth and seventeenth-century Spain is ruled not by magical forces, curses, spells and enchantments, but by a system of physical and natural causes. Angus Fletcher has written some succinct remarks on mimesis distinguishing Aristotle's rational approach to the actions of human characters prescribed by what is natural and probable versus the imposed actions of magical causality determined by ritualistic necessity (147-51, 181-83). The same holds true for Cervantes. Although he ranks as one of the most imaginative writers and elicits surprise from his readers, he never wavers from Aristotelian rationalism and does not resort to supernatural events. The plot of his novel is ruled by what is logical and probable, and the world of romance is held up for scrutiny, parodied and ridiculed.

If we as critics of Chicano literature are to continue using the word novel with any validity, we should understand its common ancestry with romance within the history of narrative forms, as well as with the practice of literary criticism in English. Although at present almost every lengthy narrative is marketed as a novel, for eighteenth-century British critics who established the legitimacy of both terms, the novel was a picture of real life and manners of the times in which it was written, and the romance was an heroic fable treating of fabulous persons and things (Reeve, Pt. 1, 111). And Cervantes' distrust of fantasy and commitment to the representation of the individual subject as the locus of signification, played a major role in supplying the generic conventions for the two forms. Although I am writing about generalities, I believe these conventions to be operative depending on the particular narrative situation. For example, in Anaya's case, modern writings on magical causality, the unconscious and collective memory, and archetypes in anthropology, psychology and literary myth criticism (I am thinking specifically of such influential writers as Frazer, Jung and Frye) together with the refurbished, prenovelistic materials of myth and folktales have made for the appropriate superstructural conditions for romance.

Unlike the more secular plots of the novel, a sense of Messianic vocation governs the overall structure of *Bless Me, Ultima.* As in religion, at a privileged moment in history and in a forsaken world, there is a need for a providential hero capable of resolving the contradictions between past and future, good and evil. The hero of romance is analogous to the mythical Messiah, and such is the case with Antonio whose destiny is prophesied by dream visions and epiphanies. The events crucial to the hero's maturation are structured around a harmonious past belonging to his forefathers and Ultima and a chaotic present symbolized by the dissolution of communal existence. Here Frye's notion of the romance as an expression of desire or nostalgia for an imaginative Golden Age is foregrounded for the reader (*Anatomy* 186). Anaya's book can be described as an elegiac romance, a beautiful vision of an Hispanic Southwest that is passing out of existence set against the background of world-historical events whose repercussions are felt throughout the region surrounding Guadalupe. These events are dramatically significant because Anaya has felt the need to recall them: they are the end of World War II that disrupts the unity of the Márez family turning sons against father and older ways of life and the advent of the nuclear age that can signal the destruction of both humankind and nature.

The narrative fantasy of the Golden Age establishes on biological and historical levels an ancestral homeland for Antonio. The young protagonist is the son of Gabriel Márez and María Luna, members of patriarchal clans who have settled in Spanish New Mexico. These colonists are emblematic of two Hispanic archetypes of male leadership, the conquistador and the priest. The Márez are rough men who derive their symbolic name from seafaring conquistadors turned sheepherders and *vaqueros* who ride the virgin *llano* (actually the western edge of the *Llano Estacado* or Great Plains explored by Cabeza de Vaca in 1535 and Coronado in 1542). The Lunas derive their patronymic from a priest who founded a farming community in the valley of the moon. Two antithetical but nonetheless similar principles are operative in these bloodlines. The Márez are people of the sun and lead a life of freedom on the unspoiled sea-plain near the village of Las Pasturas; the Lunas are stable, more civilized, tied to the soil in the community of El Puerto de los Luna, and lead their life under the aegis of the moon. Though both settlements have historical antecedents in New Mexican towns with similar names, in the transformation of the area from Native American nomadic life to Spanish pastoral and agricultural stages, they represent idealized worlds better than the city life of Guadalupe. These families belong to a romantic pastoral, a village life when men lived unalienated from nature and in harmony among themselves. Visions of extreme toil and hardship have been replaced by freedom, idleness and happiness. The Márez and Lunas enjoy a communal existence of a limited number of individuals, uncorrupted by the outside world, and are reminiscent of the Golden Age and the Earthly Paradise, two motifs that have continually molded the vision of the New World as witnessed in Columbus' first accounts of Native Americans.[9]

In "The Gospel According to Mark," Borges writes: "generations of men, throughout recorded time, have always told and retold two stories--that of a lost ship which searches the Mediterranean seas for a dearly loved island, and that of a god who is crucified on Golgotha" (310). These plot summaries of two collective epics have structured many of the plots of romance including Borges' fiction. The epics tell of departure and return, a rupture with an original unity and a quest for a lost homeland by way of suffering, endurance and a perilous voyage. "Borges," writes Frye of these two plots, "is clearly suggesting that romance, as a whole, provides a parallel epic in which the themes of shipwreck, pirates, enchanted islands, magic, recognition, the loss and regaining of identity, occur constantly" (*Secular Scripture* 15). Similarly for Anaya, a patriarchal foundation myth, the ancestral homeland, provides a context for individual adventure, for what will be Antonio's difficult voyage to manhood and fulfillment of his destiny within the postlapsarian world of the twentieth century. Antonio wanders, as his restless, seafaring blood determines, through the world of romance. He crosses bodies of water, encounters evil groves, comes upon Narciso's enchanted garden within the waste land of Guadalupe and witnesses the golden carp in its sacred pool. Along the river banks he meets with sinister feminine figures: "la llorona," the siren or mermaid, and the Circe-like Rosie, the madam of the brothel. At El Puerto he faces the one-eyed (Cyclops) Tenorio Trementina and his three evil daughters. And at the Agua Negra Ranch on the sea-plain he is bewildered by the mystery of the "wandering rocks" that fall from the sky. He will suffer for three days in order to revive his uncle from certain death. In the end he will make the trip back to his spiritual homeland, to peace and contentment of mind.

Following the hero's adventure in romance which is the individual equivalent of the cyclical patterns of collective myth, Antonio will be a figure of renewal. He is destined, as Ultima prophesies and his dream visions indicate, to continue the positive elements of two bloodlines that have fallen from their historic greatness. Las Pasturas is fast disappearing and El Puerto is without the leadership of a man of learning, the priest. Having to relocate near the city of Guadalupe, the Márez father has lost the freedom of the range and is ineffectual as the patriarch of the family. No longer a *vaquero*, he now works on a highway gang and spends most of his idle time drinking. The three Márez brothers who have returned from the war in the Pacific no longer want to follow their father's dreams to go west to California as a family, nor do they want to farm like the Lunas. The shattering of the foundation myth as the context of heroic adventure is evident in the ironic gap between the brothers' actions and their names. León, the eldest, is symbolic of primogeniture, courage and leadership, and also recalls the genealogical link of the Márez family with the Spanish Empire. The second son, Andrew, derives his name from the Gr. *Andreas* and *andros* signifying male or masculine. And the youngest, Eugene, is a reference to the Gr. *Eugenios* and *eugenés* meaning well-born. Antonio's brothers should be strong male leaders of good-breeding; yet they are self-interested, alienated men, corrupted by the outside world, and succumb to the pleasures and vices that money can buy, especially to the allure of Rosie's girls. Thus, the blood of the Márez men, formerly the exuberant freedom of the *vaqueros*, is turned into aimless wandering, and the peaceful, sedentary life of the Lunas turns into inaction.

Given these historical circumstances, Antonio's destiny is to seek a reconciliation between the two bloodlines. His role as mediator between past and future is demonstrated in his first of 10 dreams that recalls both the Feast of the Nativity and of the Epiphany. At his moment of birth, the two clans converge to greet María's son, offering gifts symbolic of both life styles from which Antonio must choose one. In the wake of the loss of paternal authority, like other well-born heroes of romance--warriors, founding fathers, kings, and divine beings--Antonio must live up to his good-breeding and forge a new image of manhood. As is foreseen, he will be a man of learning and choose the pen and paper. In a new historical configuration and as an intellectual, Antonio will be restless in his search for new understanding, but tied to the traditions of his people and the land of his birth.

Since this problematic moment in the life of the Márez family is rendered in classic Romantic fashion--the dissolution of both Hispanic life styles and communal organization, and the consequent, sad transition to the free but alienated workers of capitalism, along with the disappearance of pastoral and agricultural modes of production, and the concomitant estrangement from the cyclical world of nature--Anaya will follow through with his argument and seek a resolution to these historical transformations not through the hero of epic and conquest or the priest of institutionalized religion, but through the Romantic artist-hero, here the child-man of sympathy and feeling and his relationship to the spiritual world of nature.[10]   Only the visionary Antonio, who in his dreams dons the priestly robes as poet and prophet, is capable of articulating the teachings of nature. Just as the father-centered myth of the Messiah through the archetypes of the Golden Age and the Earthly Paradise provides the background for the historical progression of events, a parallel matriarchal mythology through Ultima provides a vast panorama for the prehistory of the Southwest. Ultima is, thus, superior to any realistic portrayal of a *curandera*. Her vision animates the landscape for Antonio; through her prophecy his future is determined. She is, following Geoffrey Hartman's terminology, the Romantic genius loci of the *llano* with whose guidance the future writer Antonio (and Anaya) is blessed (314). She possesses the collective memory of the race. In her role as shaman and midwife, she knows the secret healing power of plants. She instills in Antonio a respect for the spirit of all living things and a faith in the eventual goodness of nature. As Antonio states, her protective owl is the spirit of the *llano*, night and moon, and Ultima as night sorceress is, therefore, related to lunar fertility cults and the figurative representation of the natural world as an earth goddess renewing her vitality every year. Although the events in Guadalupe (another matriarchal cult) have their historical referents in the twentieth century, they are generated out of an immemorial past through the seasonal cycle: from the harvest of the fall, to the sterility of winter, followed by the eventual rebirth in spring and summer.

Ultima is a homogeneous figuration of woman taken in part from the storehouse of images of Jung's archetypal unconscious. It is significant to recall that Antonio's first meeting with Ultima occurs in his first dream when he returns to the wilderness, to the land of his birth in Las Pasturas. Her name can be interpreted as an allusion to the anima spirit symbolizing those "feminine" tendencies in the male psyche such as intuitions, prophetic hunches, capacity for love and, above all, feelings for nature.[11] These characteristics through Ultima's teachings set off Antonio from the rest of his "crude" male friends, especially Horse and Bones, who usually assume the self-assured and aggressive behavior of machismo. Antonio's scene of heroic action will be not one of physical prowess, but thanks to his teacher recalls the chivalric knight's nobility of character, civility, courtesy and sympathy for others. In terms of a psychological fantasy, Anaya's romance evokes from the lost past the secure world of mother-infant relationships prior to the Oedipal phase and the fixing of the male ego.

Antonio's symbolic relationship to Ultima is dramatically presented in the opening lines of the book through an unmediated perception of nature which Anaya terms the "epiphany in landscape" or the "writer's inscape." According to Joyce's classic definition of the concept, epiphany is a sudden spiritual manifestation when the artist instantaneously and irrationally gains new knowledge out of proportion with the commonplace object or event which produces it.[12] The wide currency of the term, though applied to certain modern fantastic narratives, is most significantly associated with the British Romantics' use of nature imagery.[13] For Frye, as is well known, the point of epiphany describes a turn in the plot of romance, a moment of illumination when the undisplaced apocalyptic world and the cyclical world of nature come into alignment (*Anatomy* 203). Anaya has a similar interpretation:

> In speaking about landscape, I would prefer to use the Spanish work *la tierra*, simply because it conveys a deeper relationship between man and his place, and it is this kinship to the environment which creates the metaphor and the epiphany in landscape. On one pole of the metaphor stands man, on the other is the raw, majestic and awe-inspiring landscape of the southwest; the epiphany is the natural response to that landscape, a coming together of these two forces. And because I feel a close kinship with my environment I feel constantly in touch with that epiphany which opens me up to receive the power in my landscape. ("Writer's Landscape" 98-99)

Although Anaya uses *la tierra* that refers more to raw nature, the land, he interprets his moment of epiphany as a vision or recognition of the timeless spiritual forces of the Southwest. His interpretation is wholly consistent with the structures of feeling that emerged out of the Romantic movement. Thus his use of nature is not geographic, but aesthetic; it is a landscape which can inspire awe and feeling in the observer; it is a sense of place where the individual finds solace and comfort.[14] "I do not merely mean the awe and sense of good feeling which we experience in the face of grandeur and beauty," explains Anaya, "it means that there is an actual healing power which the epiphany of place provides" ("Writer's Landscape" 101). It is this sense of place that distinguishes Anaya's hero from his alienated brothers. Here Antonio describes Ultima's first touch:

> She took my hand and I felt the power of whirlwind sweep around me. Her eyes swept the surrounding hills and through them I saw for the first time the wild beauty of our hills and the magic of the green river. My nostrils quivered as I felt the song of the mockingbirds and the drone of the grasshoppers mingle with the pulse of the earth. The four directions of the llano met in me, and the white sun shone on my soul. The granules of sand at my feet and the sun and sky above me seemed to dissolve into one strange, complete being. (10-11)

And while the content of the epiphany is a spiritual return to one's ultimate origins, its representation in Romantic literature is that of inscape, a term that Anaya used and borrowed from Hopkins and which Frye associates with the concept of epiphany.[15] Inscape, as Antonio expresses above, is the underlying unity of all things, best exemplified through landscape imagery. In inscape, nature as an object of knowledge absorbs the subject, and the variety and individuality of all things become aspects of a higher cosmic unity beyond the normal functioning of the rational faculties.

The inspirational moments in Anaya's book are heightened and contrasted by imminent manifestations that are not produced by the two structures of learning that dominate the cityscape: the massive brown building that holds the Christian cross and the yellow schoolhouse with the promise of a new language. Although these institutions are for Antonio sacred in their own right, one for the mysteries of catechism, and the other for the magic in the letters, they can not equal Ultima's knowledge. Unlike the landscape, these lifeless structures offer no sense of harmony nor do they hide beneath their surface a spiritual quality that will give rise to an epiphany. As many times as Anaya forces the reader to gaze along with Antonio from the hilltop on the edge of the *llano* at the church tower and the top of the schoolhouse across the river in Guadalupe, no new spiritual understanding is forthcoming. This fact is dramatically emphasized in the Christmas play at school which is not a Nativity scene, but the Feast of Epiphany. Because of a blizzard, the girls, who had conceived along with Miss Violet the play of the wise men, are unable to attend school and participate in the performance. An important moment in Christian myth that assures all faithful the salvation of their souls turns into a satiric, topsyturvy world because of the boys' inability to feel the traditional intensity and solemnity of the play in their newly assigned roles. Someone tips over and decapitates the Christ-child; Florence, who portrays one of the wise men, questions the idea of a virgin birth; Abel urinates during the performance; Horse, Mary in the play, rebels at being called a virgin; Bones sails down from the rafters landing on Horse; a free-for-all ensues, and in the tumult stage props are destroyed.

Another similar children's drama in which Florence plays a central role leads to the culminating point of non-epiphany at Easter. On Holy Saturday, Antonio is forced into the role of religious leader and acts a priest for Horse and Bones who are preparing for their first confession. This role is a realization of his mother's wishes and one which Antonio had performed before when he recited the Act of Contrition for Lupito when he was killed in the River of the Carp and when he heard Narciso's confession prior to his death at the hands of Tenorio Trementina. Unlike these earlier solitary and fatal moments, this public gathering of children is a beginning, a rite of passage from innocence to the knowledge of sin; it is an opportunity for Horse and Bones to boast about their sins which are sexual in nature. However, what had started out as a mischievous game turns into a deadly serious ritual when the heretic Florence is chosen to go third. He is someone who seeks the same understanding as Antonio, but who has rejected the teachings of the Church. As an outsider to the Christian community, he forms a vivid symbolic triad with Ultima and the golden carp; all are bathed in light and serve as intellectual guides for Antonio. For example, as opposed to the red light bulb outside Rosie's which serves as a "beacon of warmth inviting weary travelers," a religious aura radiates from Florence giving him the appearance of angel. During the school play, "Tall angelic Florence moved under the lightbulb that was the star of the east. When the rest of the lights were turned off the lightbulb behind Florence would be the only light" (148). In church, "The Afternoon sun poured through one of the stained glass windows that lined the walls and the golden hue made Florence look like an angel" (190-191). Although Florence is a non-believer and accuses God of sinning against him, he admits to no wrong. Knowing of Florence's unfortunate life, he is an orphan and his sisters are prostitutes at Rosie's, Antonio goes against the children's evil desires, now a mob seeking death as punishment, and absolves Florence without penance. For this act of compassion, Antonio becomes the object of vengeance and the boys "engulf him like a wave." The pitiless beating and torture that Antonio receives becomes a turning point in the plot when the angel (or Apollonian messenger) tells the would-be leader that he could never be their priest.

These dramatic moments are consistent with the salvational plot and the voyage of the romance hero for they represent the fulfillment of the man of learning and sympathy. The ritual which propels the children into the world of adults through sexual and death drives is a repetition of the two earlier fatal moments recalling that Lupito's blood was shed because of a call for vengeance from a mob of armed men and that Narciso's death was in part due to Andrew who had fallen under the spell of Rosie's girls and was unable to help. At this point in the plot, however, Antonio is not a bystander; he takes the opportunity to exercise his judgment as leader and to display, according to Ultima's teachings, the courage and the sacrifice of commitment to one less fortunate. Moreover, the burden of being a priest is, in a sense, lifted from his shoulders.

On the following day after receiving the Eucharist for the first time, Antonio gains no new understanding to compete with Ultima's magic or the Native American myth of the golden carp. He recalls:

> I had just swallowed Him, He must be in there! For a moment, on the altar railing, I thought I had felt His warmth, but then everything moved so fast. There wasn't time just to sit and discover Him, like I could do when I sat on the creek bank and watched the golden carp swim in the sun-filtered waters. . . .

A thousand questions pushed through my mind, but the Voice within me did not answer. There was only silence. . . . On the altar the priest was cleaning the chalice and the platters. The [M]ass was ending, the fleeting mystery was already vanishing. (210-11)

This high moment in the Mass is not foreign to the quest-plot of romance remembering the identification in chivalric literature of the pagan graal legend with the chalice of the Last Supper containing Christ's blood. However, this is not a traditional religious romance in which the Christian soul moves toward the illumination provided by God's grace. For Antonio, unlike the Christian knight, finds no answer to the evil and chaos that besets the countryside: the alienation in his family, the deaths of Lupito and Narciso, the ill fortune of Florence and his family. The church has ceased to be a house of wonders symbolized by the absence of the traditional magic and mystery of the Mass. Antonio's experience in church is almost a non-event compared to the high and expressive style with which the spiritual forces in the landscape, the healing power of Ultima, the beauty of the golden carp, even the frightful presence of Tenorio are described. If, as Lévi-Strauss asserts that "there is no religion without magic any more than there is magic without a trace of religion," then this scene can be read as a rejection of the Christian-quest plot together with its ideological content for the magic of a prior mythical world (221). According to the rhetoric of Anaya's argument, the Church and its ritual will now appear foreign and superimposed upon a New World landscape with its new symbolic astral deities, Ultima who is associated with the moon goddess and the solar myth of the golden carp.

The weakened faith in the authority of the winter and spring rites of the liturgical calendar is counterbalanced by the knowledge that the seasonal cycle provides, and the religious book of revelations is replaced by the book of nature. As Antonio matures, he repeats similar patterns from the darkness of confusion to the clarity of vision. After he witnesses the death of Lupito-- the soldier who returned sick and crazed from the war--Antonio is troubled by the evil *presence* that surrounds the River of the Carp. As Ultima hints, the "throbbing, secret message" hidden beneath the surface of the water is not yet ready to reveal itself. Unlike the barren, hard masculine structures of the church and the schoolhouse, the river is a more animated feminine symbol with a life-supporting rhythm of its own. Although it flows south to water the fertile valley of the Lunas, during summer it can be a torrent of churning water. At the appropriate cyclical time after the summer floods have washed away all life downstream leaving only small pools of water, the hero beholds the beautiful and fatal struggle of the carp to regain their homeland in the north. Peace and tranquility may be shattered by death and struggle, yet hope remains. Like Lupito, many fish will die along the river, but others will succeed and return to their origins and assure the continuity of future generations.

"I felt I sat on the banks of an undiscovered river," narrates Antonio of the River of the Carp in summer, "whose churning, muddied waters carried many secrets" (73). These hidden messages surface to consciousness from the past of collective memory through the tale of the golden carp. This Native American myth of origins explaining the yearly struggle of the carp is told to Antonio by Samuel, a fellow fisherman and schoolmate, whose father learned it from the only Indian in Guadalupe. It tells of a tribe's search for the promised land, the rewards of faith, and the necessity of punishment because of a broken promise. The beginning and ending of a vast human cycle are evident in the transformation of the tribe into carp. There remains, however, the existence of a god so overcome by sympathy and love for his people that he chose to be a carp and rule among them as the lord of the waters. As in the chronicles of discovery whose protagonists are pressed on by strange and wondrous tales, the descendant of conquistadors follows his barefoot, Indian-like guide, Cico, across the dark waters of the river in quest of the golden carp. Through Narciso's magic garden, the modern version of the promised land, along the banks of El Rito Creek whose waters flow from the Hidden Lakes where mermaids dwell, Antonio and Cico finally arrive at the sacred pond where every summer the lord of the waters surfaces as a scenic register for a prior magical world. Under the clarity of the sun, in a pleasant environment, and as if in church where one communicates only in whispers, Antonio experiences an epiphanic moment:

> Then the golden carp swam by Cico and disappeared into the darkness
> of the pond. I felt my body trembling as I saw the bright golden
> form disappear. I knew I had witnessed a miraculous thing, the
> appearance of a pagan god, a thing as miraculous as the curing of my
> uncle Lucas. And I thought, the power of God failed where Ultima's
> worked; and then a sudden illumination of beauty and understanding
> flashed through my mind. This is what I expected God to do at my
> first holy communion! (105)

This scene represents the fulfillment of the hero's search given that Antonio
witnesses in the golden carp the Romantic affirmation of beauty and love.
This is certainly the message of goodness articulated over and over by the
plot, which, in fact, closes the book with Ultima's death when Antonio
understands that the tragic consequences of life can be overcome by the
magical strength in the heart.

However, the initiation into the secrets of the past (shared by Antonio,
Samuel, Cico, Narciso and Ultima) brings with it not only understanding, but
responsibility and conscience as well; for the hero's plot converges with a
providential masterplot. As in other instances in the narrative where objects
are coded in binaries of good and evil, love and hate, the beautiful moment
is shattered when the "waters of the pond explode" with the arrival of the
killer bass, the one who is capable of destroying his own kind:

> I turned in time to see Cico hurl his spear at the monstrous black
> bass that had broken the surface of the waters. The evil mouth of
> the black bass was open and red. Its eyes were glazed with hate as
> it hung in the air surrounded by churning water and a million
> diamond droplets of water. . . . The huge tail swished and
> contemptuously flipped it aside. Then the black form dropped into
> the foaming waters. (105)

And to underscore the unavoidable presence of evil and the sense of
impending doom, the golden carp has issued forth an apocalyptic prophecy
to haunt the fallen world of the twentieth century. As proof of the continued

moral degeneration of Guadalupe, the sins of the people will weigh so heavy upon the land that the city will be destroyed by the forces in nature. Antonio learns that the bodies of water encircling Guadalupe are united underground in a hidden lake (whose spring waters Narciso's garden) which like a nightmare breaking through from the unconscious will engulf the city and its people. Following a turn from the beautiful to the sublime, the pleasure in feeling the radiance of a natural god is converted to the terror of the future day of reckoning.

What is important at this point is not so much the confrontation of mind and nature mediated through the Romantic imagination, but the curious parallels among the messages in the landscape, the incidents in the magical world of the *llano*, the valley and Guadalupe, and the historical events chosen by Anaya as a frame of reference. The personification of the bass as hatred and contempt, together with event after event reporting injury or death can all be interpreted as commentaries on war. All these events lead back specifically to the world of men, their egos and their aggressive instincts. They are related in earlier stages of development to the excitement aroused by fighting and bloodshed among the boys. Florence's day of judgement, when the mob seeking vengeance asks for his death, serves to confirm Cico's observation that people seem to want to hurt each other, especially when they act in groups (102). In the conflictual world of adults, Antonio is unable to account for the deaths of Lupito, Narciso and Ultima, except as the result of evil and revenge. The killer bass from the world of nature certainly has his equal in the unremorseful villain, Tenorio. That fighting can lead to disorder is portrayed in the ending of the school drama when all stage props are destroyed. The annihilation of the scenic world of the play is echoed by (1) the rumors around Guadalupe that the world is going to end (69-70) and (2) the feelings among the residents that the new bomb manufactured to end the war has disturbed the seasons to such an extent that its knowledge will eventually destroy them all (184-85). Thus, it is not surprising that the providential masterplot having the sins of the people against each other as a motive force should end in the complete destruction of a city.

The interpretation of a momentous historical shift that, as I have argued, accounts for the solace in nature and the passing of an innocent, paradisiacal world (Antonio writes many years after Ultima's death), allows us to say something about the priority of a mythical code over secular history in romance. Those events which in an empirical narrative or a realistic novel could have been worked out and charged to the forces of history--ideologies, political conflicts, science and technology--are narrated along with events conceived as products of cyclical time, ritual, magic, prophecy, sin and portrayed through the myth of the hero in climactic moments as immanent moral or spiritual messages in nature.

For the most part, my interpretation of *Bless Me, Ultima* was facilitated by a methodology which beginning early in this century has been not only a critical method, but also one of the dominant aesthetics of our time, one which accounts for the book's international popularity. The reader's easy access into the Chicano world of Antonio is made possible by the archetypal or mythical method for which Eliot's *The Waste Land* and Joyce's *Ulysses* have been molding influences. In his review of *Ulysses* in 1923, Eliot took note that Joyce's book did not conform to the handling of events in the novel. And he added that while *A Portrait of the Artist* was a novel, he doubted if Joyce would ever write one again. In pursuing a parallel between the *Odyssey* and his own work through myths and archetypes, Joyce had discovered a method for others to follow. Eliot writes:

> In using myth, in manipulating a continuous parallel between contemporaneity and antiquity, Mr. Joyce is pursuing a method which others must pursue after him. . . . It is simply a way of controlling, of ordering, of giving a shape and a significance to the immense panorama of futility and anarchy which is contemporary history. It is a method already adumbrated by Mr. Yeats, and of the need for which I believe Mr. Yeats to have been the first contemporary to be conscious. It is a method for which the horoscope is auspicious. Psychology (such as it is, and whether our reaction to it be comic or serious), ethnology, and *The Golden Bough* have concurred to make what was impossible even a few years ago. Instead of narrative

method, we may now use the mythical method. It is, I seriously believe, a step toward making the modern world possible for art. (177-78)

In the light of the sixty-one years since the publication of Eliot's "Ulysses, Order, and Myth," his statements have proved prophetic. Modern psychology, Freudian but mostly Jungian, the Cambridge School of Comparative Anthropology through Frazer, Weston and others, and the general interest in "primitive" art and culture, were fruitful for some aspects of abstract art as well as for a modernist tradition of non-mimetic narrative. When we consider the enormous impact of modern psychology and anthropology upon the traditions with which I am most familiar, the Latin American and the Chicano, then family resemblances can be perceived among *The Waste Land, Ulysses,* Borges' *El jardín de senderos que se bifurcan* (1944; *The Garden of the Forking Paths*), Carpentier's *Los pasos perdidos* (1953; *The Lost Steps*), Rulfo's *Pedro Páramo* (1955), García Márquez' *Cien años de soledad* (1967; *One Hundred Years of Solitude*), Fuentes' *Terra nostra* (1975), and most recently in Chicano narrative, *Bless Me, Ultima,* Arias' *The Road to Tamazunchale* (1975) and Morales'*Reto en el paraíso* (1983; *Challenge in Paradise*). While I do not claim that all these books are romances (to *Bless Me, Ultima* we could add *The Lost Steps* and *The Road to Tamazunchale*), they are not totally representational or mimetic. Romance elements such as moments of epiphany, circular plotting, quest-motifs, the archetypes of the Waste Land, the search for the Paradise or the Golden Age are essential to all these narratives.

Eliot's comments, written in a post-war decade, are not as significant for establishing a literary tradition for *Bless Me, Ultima* as they are for suggesting the usefulness of mythical structures for controlling, ordering and giving shape to the "immense panorama and futility" of history. We are now in a better position to return to Anaya's romance and read its symbolic characterization, narrative sequences and supernatural landscape not so much as positive fulfillments of generic specifications, but, as I have tried to suggest with the man of learning and sympathy, as an occasion to express symbolic solutions to the problems posed by the uncontrollable events of history

(Jameson 79-80). Anaya's narrative strategies can be pressed for meaning within a wider cultural context and interpreted as a flight from history. The actual events of the discovery and conquest of the New World and the Southwest (the ground zero of interpretation for all Chicano narratives) are repressed and reconceptualized as a nostalgia for the heroic ideals of an earlier colonial society or as a return to the adventure and magic of the romance. The agents of imperialism, the conquistador and the priest, are legitimated and viewed as better alternatives to the fallen men of Guadalupe. And finally, the authority of a romantic rhetoric is called upon to produce an aesthetically effective and tightly-knit structure of good and evil which is then superimposed upon a region and modes of production properly belonging to Third World agrarian societies or peasant cultures yet without any worthwhile analysis or attention to the contradictions of race, class and gender which were the results of conquest.

Special attention is due to the binary structure of good and evil. It is repeated throughout the narrative by pairings and oppositions beginning with the overall pattern of 22 chapters and 10 dreams, conscious life versus semiconscious nightmares. As for characterizations, there are the abstract, phallocentric entities of male and female, María Luna versus Rosie, Ultima against Tenorio, the three sinful Márez brothers, the three Trementinas, the innocent bachelors that die, Lupito, Narciso and Florence. Rural life is contrasted with city life, Las Pasturas with El Puerto, Narciso's garden with the evil grove of the Trementinas, the dark waters of the River of the Carp with the clear water of the sacred pond, and the golden carp has for its rival the black bass. The writer utilizes a method of classification in which every narrative element appears to have its logical opposite. In addition, these binaries repeat the prophecy of redemption (Ultima's teaching that good will always triumph over evil) which functions as an alternative to history.

We should not think of this system of classification as naive or superstitious; it is one that is clear, lucid and rigorous and shares much as an ideology with another structure of thought for which a term has already been invented, Lévi-Strauss' *pensée sauvage*.[16] Although many elements of myth are present in Anaya's book, such as the ancestors in the landscape, the case of magical sympathy, I am referring instead to a very rational and purposeful system of thought that posits an all-embracing structure and leaves nothing to chance. This system does not care for natural events, for it builds inexhaustible structures of binary oppositions out of the debris of events, and then proceeds to produce events out of these structures. For Lévi-Strauss, echoing Eliot, magical thought is a way of reordering events by not permitting contingency and necessity to interfere with the human world. Myths and rituals are, therefore, by necessity of a recurrent nature allowing for the priority of synchrony over diachrony. Anaya pursues a similar course. No effort is made to focus on the psychological distance between the adult narrator and the hero Antonio. Instead, the writer constructs a plot in which the traces of history are reorganized through abstract structures, folk motifs, romance archetypes, a series of binary oppositions repeating the message of good and evil, and then a narrative is generated out of these structures. Given the nature of the oppositions and the repetition of the redemptive promise, the system is inexhaustible. Thus, what can be called the ideology of romance in *Bless Me, Ultima* is a determined effort in form and content to portray a timeless or synchronic world despite the overriding presence of history.

And yet, there remains a positive element in Anaya's romance of the Southwest. From our vantage point in 1988 with the increasing threat of nuclear destruction, the choice of the historical moment for *Bless Me, Ultima* should earn it a place in American literature. Unlike the primitive artist who internalizes timeless myths and tales and externalizes purpose and objects, the modern writer, who dwells within and is determined by history, internalizes technique and craft and externalizes myth as an aesthetic (Lévi-Strauss 29). Regardless of how the writer may want to daydream and fantasize, the events of history will loom over the horizon like an ominous dark cloud. In a crucial scene, Ultima tells Antonio that the worst evil is to tamper with someone's destiny. Perhaps this is why the real incident of the black cloud and the falling rocks that bombard the house at the Agua Negra ranch that cannot be explained by magical causality is strategically placed near the end to mark the passsing of an innocent age with Ultima's death and the coming of the nuclear age. The incident bears a resemblance to the mysterious evil--the residents of Guadalupe are aware of it--that visited the remote village of Carrizozo, New

Mexico on July 16, 1945, when its inhabitants were awakened by a roar to witness a pillar of fire six miles high just thirty miles away at point Trinity in what is now the White Sands Missile Range. Although Ultima constructs a platform to burn the three spirits which she conceives to be the cause of the wandering rocks, the reader should be aware that her magic is no match for the destructive forces that were released from a tower in the middle of the New Mexican desert in the same general vicinity as the Agua Negra ranch. The choice of this major historical turning point that is so much like sublime and apocalyptic visions in myth can be interpreted as the ultimate tampering with the destiny of the world. Now the book can be understood as a yearning for an innocent time as a response to a moment in which the future of humankind is at stake: there is no turning back from the nuclear age except through the fantasy of a Golden Age.

NOTES

[1] Although I refer to the seventeenth printing, all subsequent page references to *Bless Me, Ultima* are from the 1972 edition which received the Second Annual Quinto Sol Prize for novel.

[2] Most studies take the novel as a given and avoid the issue of genre. However, Saldívar and Calderón have applied the formulations of recent critical theory to Chicano narratives.

[3] The problem of classification is especially evident in bibliographies. Autobiographies are grouped under the heading of Biographical Novels" in *Decade of Chicano Literature* (116). This is just another indication of the "novel-centered" view of Chicano narratives. For more discussion on this topic, see Calderón (4-6).

[4] In an interview with Bruce-Novoa (*Chicano Authors* 188), Anaya has stated his debt to the Romantics. The influence of Hopkins is felt, as I will demonstrate in the essay, in landscape imagery. See also Anaya's handling of the "odyssey" motifs and in his interpretation of the concept of epiphany. Anaya's specific use of the spiritual waste land is Eliot's. See also Márquez (51). There is a moment (60) in *Bless Me, Ultima* inspired by the opening lines of *The Waste Land*.

[5] Other influences aside, the similarities between Anaya and Frye are beyond mere coincidence. Márquez reaches a similar conclusion (46).

[6] To clarify this issue, Frye conceives of displacement in two directions. It is the artistic strategems used by writers to render plausible the presence of mythical structures (*Anatomy* 136). It is also the tendency in realistic literature to conventionalize content in an idealized direction (*Anatomy*

137). Both are romantic tendencies in narrative and are anti-representational or highly symbolic (*Secular Scripture* 38).

[7] I am much indebted to Fredric Jameson. His interests in narrative not only parallel my own, but also confirm my thoughts on the subject. He conceives of the opposition between good and evil felt as magical forces and a salvational history as social messages specific to the romance form which can be resurrected as ideologemes to serve as symbolic solutions to real historical contradictions (148).

[8] The bibliography on Huarte and El Pinciano is too extensive and well-known by any Cervantista to go into any detail here. However, critics in Spanish Literature have generally failed to see the consequences of Renaissance psychology for our modern conception of character and the evolution of narrative forms. On the mythical representation of subjectivity, Jameson writes: "These [myths] are evidently preindividualistic narratives; that is, they emerge from a social world in which the psychological subject has not yet been constituted as such, and therefore in which later categories of the subject, such as the "character," are not relevant. Hence the bewildering fluidity of these narrative strings, in which human characters are ceaselessly transformed into animals or objects and back again; in which nothing like narrative "point of view," let alone "identification" or "empathy" with this or that protagonist, emerges; in which not even the position of an individualized storyteller or "sender" (*destinataire*) can be conceptualized without contradiction (124). Hurate's analysis of the individual subject endowed by nature with critical or rational faculties explains much about human intelligence, *ingenio natural*, and psychological types, and is well on the way toward characterization in mimetic literature. El Pinciano's Aristotelian treatise (indebted to Huarte's earlier formulations) is especially instructive for its understanding of representational language, linguistic signs, based on accepted conventions and the functioning of the rational soul (2:218-21). Much of Cervantes' attitude toward the representation of reality was earlier previewed by these two "left-wing" physicians when they established categories for science and the supernatural. Those phenomena •formerly explainable by miracles and the supernatural were judged by Huarte to be the products of

rational or natural causes (80-89). In addition, Huarte's (208-215) and El Pinciano's (1:170-72) interests in the affective and intellectual activities of the subject involved in the act of reading helped pave the way for Cervantes' interests in the fictional reader and his critique of the romances. Questions posed by the transformations from the medieval romances with their oral sources, mythical and religious plots, to Cervantes' highly-literate and technically-sophisticated *Don Quixote* are answerable to a large degree by the ideology of the individual subject.

[9] Harry Levin discusses the interest in the existence of the Ovidian Golden Age and the Biblical Paradise due to European reports of the cultural primitivism of New World inhabitants (58-62). A similar primitive pastoral or Arcadian world, according to Roy Gridley, has been the consistent image of the Great Plains from the narratives of Cabeza de Vaca and Coronado to the poetry of Allen Ginsberg (62, 69-70). Incidentally, the sea metaphor for the plains was first used by Coronado.

[10] Although not noticing the Romantic overtones, Bruce-Novoa was the first to suggest that Anaya's book is essentially a writer's story of apprenticeship ("Space of Chicano Literature" 35-38).

[11] Roberto Cantú, in his analysis of the 10 dream visions in *Bless Me, Ultima*, has indicated the influence of Jungian psychology (28). In various other writings, Anaya has discussed the need for a collective unconscious (Márquez 45-48).

[12] For Joyce's original statement on epiphany, see *Stephen Hero* (210-11). The bibliography on the topic is extensive, but see for two opposing views Hendry Chayes' "Joyce's Epiphanies" and Scholes' "Joyce and the Epiphany." In the writing of this essay I have been aided by Morris Beja's *Epiphany in the Modern Novel* (71-75).

[13] Although the term epiphany is a twentieth century phenomenon, Wordsworth, by all accounts, was the first to fix its typically modern version (see Langbaum). What Abrams calls Wordsworth's theodicy in landscape (97-

117) is akin to Anaya's epiphany in landscape. In opposition to positive readings of epiphanies, Jameson sees the modern fantastic from Kafka to Cortázar (we should include Borges) as those narratives where a revelation might arise, where what is an otherwise normal cityscape might release a spiritual message (134-35). Anaya oscillates between these two poles, deciding in the Romantic direction.

[14] For the historical circumstances that give rise in Romantic literature to the rhetorical distinction between corrupt city life and innocent landscape, and the consequent search for solace in nature, see Raymond Williams (127-34).

[15] In my formulations of inscape, I have been aided by Frye (*Anatomy* 121), and Hopkins scholars McCarthy (67) and Cotter (3). Hopkins supplies his own sketchy definition (289).

[16] See Lévi-Strauss (9-28) for his interpretation of myths as structures of thought. There are other relevant similarities among Lévi-Strauss, Frazer, Borges and Anaya that shed light on the evolution of narrative in the twentieth century. Borges deserves a prominent place in the history of myth criticism for having seen in "Narrative Art and Magic," published in 1932, the structural possibilities with which anthropology presented the modern artist for a lucid or magical representation of reality. Relying on Frazer, Borges studies the usefulness of magical causality for a well-constructed plot whose parts are inevitably linked by prophecies, foreshadowings, projections and ritualistic necessity (37-38). I find it interesting that in his essay, Borges chose for his models romances by William Morris and Edgar Allan Poe, gangster films and Joyce's *Ulysses* detecting in each case magical emplotment. As for Borges' role within recent critical movements, his analysis of Frazer's law of sympathy into magic by imitation and magic by contagion or contact points the way for structuralism's twin poles of language, metaphor and metonymy. The intersection of plot and subjectivity in "New Refutation of Time," when in 1928 a young Borges is pulled as if by gravitational force back to his homeland, a mythical Buenos Aires at the time of his birth, and realizes in a moment of lucidity that he is an abstract perceiver of the world, is like

Anaya's romance a synthesis of various discourses from the Romantic myth or origins of the nineteenth century to the archetypes of modern literature and anthropology, yet it also anticipates the "characterless" fiction of recent decades (184-85).

WORKS CITED

Abrams, M. H. *Natural Supernaturalism: Tradition and Revolution in Romantic Literature.* New York: W. W. Norton and Company, 1971.

Acosta, Oscar Zeta. *The Autobiography of a Brown Buffalo.* San Francisco: Straight Arrow Books, 1972.

Anaya, Rudolfo A. *Bless Me, Ultima.* Berkeley: Quinto Sol Publications, Inc., 1972.

___. *Heart of Aztlán.* Berkeley: Editorial Justa Publications, 1976.

___. *The Silence of the Llano.* Tonatiuh-Quinto Sol International, 1982.

___. *Tortuga.* Berkeley: Editorial Justa Publications, 1979.

___. "The Writer's Inscape." Paper presented at the Rocky Mountain MLA, Santa Fe, NM, 22 Oct. 1976. Abstract in *Rocky Mountain Review of Language and Literature* 30.3 (1976):161-62.

___. "The Writer's Landscape: Epiphany in Landscape." *Latin American Literary Review* 5.10 (1977):98-102.

Arias, Ron. *The Road to Tamazunchale.* Reno, Nevada: West Coast Poetry Review, 1975.

Beja, Morris. *Epiphany in the Modern Novel.* London: Peter Owen Limited, 1971.

Borges, Jorge Luis. "The Gospel According to Mark." In *Borges, A Reader: A Selection From the Writings of Jorge Luis Borges.* Ed. Emir Rodríguez Monegal and Alastair Reid. New York: E. P. Dutton, 1981, 308-11.

___. *El jardín de senderos que se bifurcan.* In *Ficciones.* Buenos Aires: Ediciones SUR, 1944.

___. "Narrative Art and Magic." In *Borges, A Reader,* 34-38.

___. "New Refutation of Time." In *Borges, A Reader,* 179-91.

Bruce-Novoa, Juan. *Chicano Authors: Inquiry by Interview.* Austin: University of Texas Press, 1980.

___. "The Space of Chicano Literature." *De Colores* 1.4 (1975):22-42.

Calderón, Héctor. "To Read Chicano Narrative: Commentary and Metacommentary." *Mester* 11.2 (1983):3-14.

Cantú, Roberto. "Estructura y sentido de lo onírico en *Bless Me, Ultima.*" *Mester* 5.1 (1974):27-41.

Carpentier, Alejo. *Los pasos perdidos.* La Habana: Editorial de Arte y Literatura, 1976.

Carrasco, David. "A Perspective for a Study of Religious Dimensions in Chicano Experience: *Bless Me, Ultima* as a Religious Text." *Aztlán* 13.1-2 (1982):195-221.

Cervantes Saavedra, Miguel de. *The Ingenious Gentleman Don Quixote de la Mancha.* Trans. Samuel Putnam. New York: Viking Press, 1949.

Chávez, John R. *The Lost Land: The Chicano Image of the Southwest.* Albuquerque: University of New Mexico Press, 1984.

Cotter, James Finn. *Inscape: The Christology and Poetry of Gerard Manley Hopkins.* Pittsburgh: University of Pittsburgh Press, 1972.

A Decade of Chicano Literature (1970-1979): Critical Essays and Bibliography. Ed. Luis Leal et al. Santa Barbara, Calif.: Editorial La Causa, 1982.

Eliot, T. S. "Ulysses, Order, and Myth." In *Selected Prose of T. S. Eliot.* Ed. Frank Kermode. New York: Harcourt, Brace, Jovanovich, 1975, 175-78.

___. *The Waste Land, and Other Poems.* New York: Harcourt, Brace, Jovanovich, 1962.

Fletcher, Angus. *Allegory: The Theory of a Symbolic Mode.* Ithaca: Cornell University Press, 1964.

Frye, Northrop. *Anatomy of Criticism: Four Essays.* Princeton: Princeton University Press, 1957.

___. *The Secular Scripture: A Study of the Structure of Romance.* Cambridge: Harvard University Press, 1976.

Fuentes, Carlos. *Terra nostra* México: Editorial Joaquín Mortiz, S. A., 1975.

García Márquez, Gabriel. *Cien años de soledad.* Buenos Aires: Editorial Sudamericana, 1967.

Gridley, Roy E. "Some Versions of the Primitive and the Pastoral on the Great Plains of America." In *Survivals of Pastoral.* Ed. Richard F. Hardin. Lawrence: University of Kansas Publications, 1979, 61-85.

Hartman, Geoffrey H. "Romantic Poetry and the Genius Loci." In *Beyond Formalism: Literary Essays, 1958-1970.* New Haven: Yale University Press, 1970, 311-36.

Hendry Chayes, Irene. "Joyce's Epiphanies." *Sewanee Review* 54 (1946):449-67.

Hopkins, Gerard Manley. *The Journals and Papers of Gerard Manley Hopkins.* Ed. Humphrey House. London: Oxford University Press, 1959.

Huarte de San Juan, Juan. *Examen de ingenios para las ciencias.* Ed. Esteban Torre. Madrid: Editora Nacional, 1976.

Jameson, Fredric. *The Political Unconscious: Narrative As a Socially Symbolic Act.* Ithaca: Cornell University Press, 1981.

Joyce, James *A Portrait of the Artist as a Young Man.* New York: Viking Press, 1964.

___. *Stephen Hero.* New York: New Directions, 1955.

___. *Ulysses.* New York: Vintage Books, 1961.

Langbaum, Robert. "The Epiphanic Mode in Wordsworth and Modern Literature." *New Literary History* 14 (1983):335-58.

Lévi-Strauss, Claude. *The Savage Mind.* Chicago: Chicago University Press, 1966.

Levin, Harry. *The Myth of the Golden Age in the Renaissance.* New York: Oxford University Press, 1969.

López Pinciano, Alonso. *Philosophía antigua poética.* Ed. A. Carballo Picazo. 3 vols. Madrid: Consejo Superior de Investigaciones Científicas, 1953.

McCarthy, Adrian J. "Toward a Definition of Hopkins' 'Inscape.'" *University of Dayton Review* 4 (1968):55-68.

Márquez, Antonio. "The Achievement of Rudolfo A. Anaya." In *The Magic of Words: Rudolfo A. Anaya and His Writings*. Ed. Paul Vassallo. Albuquerque: University of New Mexico Press, 1982, 33-52.

Morales, Alejandro. *Reto en el paraíso*. Ypsilanti, Mich.: Bilingual Press/Editorial Bilingüe, 1983.

Padilla, Genaro. "Lies, Secrest, and Silence in New Mexico: Fabiola Cabeza de Baca and Cleofas Jaramillo." Manuscript for *Chicano Literary Criticism: New Studies in Culture and Ideology*. Ed. Héctor Calderón and José David Saldívar. Forthcoming Duke UP, 1991.

Reeve, Clara. *The Progress of Romance* (1785). New York: Facsimile Text Society, 1930.

Rivera, Tomás. " . . . *y no se lo tragó la tierra* . . . *And the Earth Did Not Part*." Berkeley: Quinto Sol Publications, Inc., 1971.

Rogers, Jane. "The Function of the *La Llorona* Motif in Anaya's *Bless Me, Ultima*." *Latin American Review* 5.10 (1977):64-69.

Rulfo, Juan. *Pedro Páramo*. México: Fondo de Cultura Económica, 1955.

Saldívar, Ramón. "A Dialectic of Difference: Towards a Theory of the Chicano Novel." MELUS 6.3 (1979):73-92.

Scholes, Robert. "Joyce and the Epiphany: The Key to the Labyrinth?" *Sewanee Review* 77 (1964):65-77.

Testa, Daniel. "Extensive/Intensive Dimensionality in Anaya's *Bless Me, Ultima*." *Latin American Literary Review* 5.10 (1977):70-78.

Treviño, Albert D. "*Bless Me, Ultima*: A Critical Intrepretation." *De Colores* 3.4 (1977):30-33.

Williams, Raymond. *The Country and the City.* New York: Oxford University Press, 1973.

Myth as the Cognitive Process of Popular Culture in Rudolfo Anaya's *Bless Me, Ultima*: The Dialectics of Knowledge*

Enrique R. Lamadrid
University of New Mexico

Bless Me, Ultima by Rudolfo Anaya appeared in 1972, quickly earning a place in Chicano literary history as its first truly transcendent work of long prose fiction.[1] The novel has since captured more readers and critical attention than any other single work of Chicano literature and the debate continues concerning the implications of the author's use of what might be termed magical or even mythical realism.[2] Was the novel merely an apolitical expression of local color or *costumbrismo*, New Mexico style? And if so, how did the work fit into the overall social and creative context of *chicanismo*? As the first best seller novel of Chicano literature, it was impossible to dismiss *Ultima's* introduction of compelling mythic themes into the disjunctive context of the combative and polemical ethnic literatures of the late sixties. *Ultima* was serene in the face of this turmoil, full of conflict, yet non-combative, a portrait of the developing consciousness of the young protagonist, Antonio. The metaphysics of this emerging consciousness were so convincingly drawn that no reader doubted that the seeds of social conscience were deeply sown if yet untested in the chief character.

Rudolfo Anaya strikes a deep chord in portraying two primordial ways of relating to the earth, the pastoral and the agricultural. Bless Me,

*Reprinted from *Hispania*, 68.3 (Sept. 1985): 496-501.

Ultima (BMU), is not a quaint, ahistorical sketch of rural folkways, but rather a dialectical exploration of the contradictions between lifestyles and cultures. At the novel's heart is the process which generates social and historical consciousness. A Marxist-Structuralist perspective defines this process as myth, the collective interpretation and mediation of the contradictions in the historical and ecological experience of a people.

In his account of the relationship between a *curandera* (folk healer) and her young apprentice, Anaya deeply penetrates the mythical conscience of the reader. Despite their enthusiasm for his novel, critics have thus far been unable to define the parameters of this response nor probe the reason for its depth. Contributing elements in the narrative include: The primordial quality of the rivalry of the Luna and Márez clans, the religious conflicts and rich dream life of the boy Antonio Márez, and the power of Ultima herself which in the end is nothing more nor less than "the magical strength that resides in the human heart." (*BMU*, p. 237). From the first reviews to later articles, an increasing body of vague but glowing commentary points to a rich "mythic" or "magical" dimension that underlies the novel.[3] To those who prioritize the social relevancy of Chicano literature, this psychic plunge seemed disturbing or even reactionary in its irrationality. Despite these claims, there appeared to be something exceptional about the emerging consciousness of the boy. It was mystically harmonious with nature, yet also incorporated a dynamic, even dialectical awareness of historical forces, from the colonization of Hispanic farmers and ranchers to the coming of the Anglos and World War II. These seeming contradictions invite a reexamination of the relation of myth and social consciousness, often defined as antithetical or incompatible categories which erode and undermine each other. Since the novel apparently transcends this impasse, we are obliged to consider a critical model comprehensive enough to explain this achievement. A review of commentary on the novel is the first step in this direction.

Bless Me, Ultima has undergone extensive dream and thematic analyses which include attempts to link its "mythic" elements to pre-Columbian roots.[4] The preponderance of interest in these "irrational" aspects plus the sometimes supernatural tone of the narrative has lead politically progressive critics to characterize the novel as ahistorical, having only limited and passing value in depicting the "quaint" folkways of rural New Mexico.[5] Thematic analysis has enumerated various tendencies, especially the folkloric, but is unable to characterize the book as anything more than a local color or *costumbrista* piece.[6] Dream analysis has been more productive because of the consistency and symbolic unity of the many dream sequences.[7] Analysis of the mythic and religious systems, notably the "Legend of the Golden Carp" is unconvincing simply because Anaya's alleged allusions to Aztec or other pre-Columbian mythologies are not literal enough.[8] True, the idea of successive worlds, intervening apocalypses and the exile of Gods is common in Native American religions. The suggestion of analogical patterns achieves credibility for the Golden Carp without having to invoke Huitzilopochtli or Quetzalcóatl as other Chicano writers have done. The political analysis which deems the novel reactionary seems to be based on the assumption that Chicano novels should document only the most relevant social and political struggles. These diverse and fragmentary approaches have fallen short of estimating the overall impact and unity of the work and the structural integrity it has achieved on a number of levels.

Since the "mythic" dimension of *Bless Me, Ultima* is a point of confluence in the above commentaries, a definition of terms is now necessary. Thus far, the study of myth in Chicano literature has been scholastic. The neoclassic allusions to Aztec and other pre-Columbian mythological and religious systems is fairly common in Chicano literature, especially in poetry and theatre. Critics have been quick to point this out, elaborating only superficially by tracing the origins of the myths and speculating on how they pertain to the socio-cultural identity of the present day chicano.[9] Freud was able to tap Greek mythology for insight into the European psyche and founded the basis for Western psychology. Inspired by the work of Octavio Paz and Carlos Fuentes on the Mexican national psyche, an analogous process has been initiated in Chicano literature and criticism, although it is doubtful that an institutionalized Chicano psychotherapy will be the result. The underlying assumption that would prevent this is that these mythic or collective psychological patterns supposedly lie outside time, eternally remanifesting themselves in different epochs.[10] This same danger plagues Chicano cultural studies in general, which often tend to analyze culture and its values as something eternal and independent of history, instead of the dynamic product or actual embodiment of history, conflict and change.[11]

What is proposed here is a more dynamic critical approach to myth which goes beyond scholasticism and the tracing of classical mythologies. Myth is here considered to be an ongoing process of interpreting and mediating the contradictions in the everyday historical experience of the people. Such a structuralist approach to myth offers some analytical tools which can be applied in such a way as to avoid the ideological limitations of structuralism while opening the Chicano text to a dialectical analysis potentially much more penetrating and historically relevant than traditional thematic or culturalist approaches.

The reader of *Bless Me, Ultima* recognizes the elderly *curandera* as a kind of repository for the wisdom and knowledge invested in Indo-Hispanic culture. The novel functions well at this level, for Ultima is indeed in touch with the spirit that moves the land and is intent on conveying this knowledge to Antonio in her indirect and mysterious ways. Yet, the knowledge she commands and the role she plays go far beyond the herbs she knows, the stories she saves for the children, and her dabbling in "white" witchcraft. The crossed pins, the demon hairballs, the rocks falling from the sky, and the fireballs are "colorful" touches which are authentic enough in terms of folk legend. Anaya inserts the "witchery" only after having won the readers' trust in a clever conquest of their disbelief. However, the enumeration of the standard paraphernalia and the usual supernatural feats of a *curandera* are neither the reason for nor a barrier to the novel's success.

There is an ancient system of knowledge that Ultima exercises that in this novel does not happen to be in the herbs she uses. Anthropologists have shown that taxonomies such as those of ethnobotany actually contain the philosophical roots and perceptual conventions of the culture.[12] However, herbs and related folk knowledge are not the ultimate focus of the novel, although it is understood that Ultima is intimately familiar with them. It is her role as a cultural mediator and Antonio's natural inclination towards a similar calling that link them to their real power, which is the ability to recognize and resolve the internal contradictions of their culture. These oppositions are clearly defined in both social and symbolic terms. The rivalry of the Lunas and the Márez, the struggle of good and evil, innocence and experience, Jehovah and the Golden Carp are not simply narrative devices. If they were, then they would be merely pretexts for a combination mystery story, morality play and Hatfield-McCoy saga with a New Mexican flavor.

Something more profound is at work in *Bless Me, Ultima*, for the oppositions are dialectical, and they are mediated in such a way that has counterparts in many different cultures around the earth. In his comparative studies of origins myths, Claude Lévi-Stauss extracts the two most basic and primordial ones which occurred either elusively or in combination in every culture studied.[13] The "autochthonous" origin myth is exactly as the original meaning of the word implies: "one supposed to have risen or sprung from the ground of the region he inhabits." This version often has a vegetative model: man springs from the earth like a plant. The rival origin myth is more empirically based: man is born from woman. Then comes the task of finding the first woman. In *Bless Me, Ultima* the opposition between the agricultural Lunas and the pastoral Márez has roots that go as deep as the very foundation of human consciousness as its moves from the paleolithic into the neolithic. Each lifestyle and the world view it is based on is as compelling, soul satisfying and original as the other. The opposition as it occurs in the novel may be schematized as follows:

-pastoral economy	-agricultural economy
-the Márez family	-the Luna family
-live in Las Pasturas on the open plains	-live in El Puerto de la Luna in a fertile valley
-people of the sun	-people of the moon
-descendants of conquistadors and seafarers	-descendants of a priest
-baptized in the salt water of the sea	-baptized in the sweet water of the moon
-speak with the wind	-speak with their plants and fields
-tempestuous, anarchic freethinkers	-quiet, introspective pious people
-live free upon the earth and roam over it	-live tied to the earth and its cycles
-the horse is their totem animal	-corn is their totem plant

The earthshaking impact of the passage from hunting and gathering (paleolithic) into agricultural (neolithic) economies is recorded in mythologies the world over.[14] The crises and contradictions that history, economic change and technological innovation bring are the chief motivating factors for the collective cognitive process called myth. The settling down of humankind into the sedentary ways of the neolithic brought with it the emergence of social classes and institutionalized religion and all the economic and social contradictions that accompany the birth of civilization. Likewise, the agricultural developments of horticulture and animal husbandry are distinct enough to carry with them their own ideologies as evident above. Relating more specifically to the novel in question is the history of the colonization of New Mexico and the tremendous impact of the advent of large scale pastoralism. As grazing became more important, the communal egalitarianism of agrarian society began giving way to an emerging class system based on the *partidario* (share-cropper) grazing system and the rise of *patrones* (bosses). However, such developments are not evident in the novel, perhaps because its locale, eastern New Mexico, was the last area to be settled before American annexation.[15] The anarchic freedom enjoyed by the Márez clan was ephemeral, the basic historical irony of the story. The coming of the Texas ranchers, the railroad, and the barbed wire destroyed the freedom of the plains. As the popular saying goes, "Cuando vino el alambre, vino el hambre" (With barbed wire came hunger). When an economic system is threatened so is its ideology, which starts filling with nostalgia as its dreams are shattered.

These historical pressures intensified the oppositions listed above and made the birth of the boy Antonio Márez Luna especially portentous for the two clans whose blood coursed through his veins. Each felt the importance of having their values dominate in the boy and both vied to establish their influence at the dream scene of Antonio's birth:

> This one will be a Luna, the old man said, he will be a farmer and keep our customs and traditions. Perhaps God will bless our family and make the baby a priest.
> And to show their hope they rubbed the dark earth of the river valley on the baby's forehead, and they surrounded the bed with the fruits of their harvest so the small room smelled of fresh green chile and corn, ripe apples and peaches, pumpkins and green beans.
> Then the silence was shattered with the thunder of hoof-beats; vaqueros surrounded the small house with shouts and gunshots, and when they entered the room they were laughing and singing and drinking.
> Gabriel, they shouted, you have a fine son! He will make a fine vaquero! And they smashed the fruits and vegetables that surrounded the bed and replaced them with a saddle, horse blankets, bottles of whiskey, a new rope, bridles, chapas, and an old guitar. And they rubbed the stain of earth from the baby's forehead because man was not to be tied to the earth but free upon it. (BMU, p. 5).

The disposal of the baby's umbilical cord and placenta was also a point of contention. The Lunas wanted it buried in their fields to add to their fertility and the Márez wanted it burned to scatter the ashes to the winds of the *llano* (plain). The intervention of Ultima to settle the feud illustrates her role of mediator and demonstrates the basic mechanism of myth. As in all cultures, the thrust of mythical thought progresses from the awareness of oppositions towards their resolution.[16] Thus we see the importance in the mythic process of the mediator, which in many cultures assumes the form of powerful tricksters like the coyote and the raven in Native American mythology. In *Bless Me, Ultima*, both the *curandera* and the boy serve as mediators between the oppositions within their culture. Their intermediary functions can be traced throughout the text.

The middle ground that Ultima and Antonio occupy is evident even in spatial and geographic terms. Ultima has lived on the plain and in the valley, in Las Pasturas as well as El Puerto de la Luna, gaining the respect of the people in both places. Antonio's family lives in Guadalupe in a compromise location at mid-point between Las Pasturas and El Puerto. Through the father's insistence, the house is built at the edge of the valley where the plain begins. Antonio mediates between father and mother, trying to please the latter by scraping a garden out of the rocky hillside:

> Every day I reclaimed from the rocky soil of the hill a few more feet of earth to cultivate. The land of the llano was not good for farming, the good land was along the river. But my mother wanted a garden and I worked to make her happy. (BMU, p. 9).

Even within the town Antonio occupies a centralized neutral position: "Since I was not from across the tracks or from town, I was caught in the middle." (BMU, p. 212). This positioning made it impossible to take sides in the territorial groupings of his peers.

Anaya explains the power of the *curandera* as the power of the human heart, but in fact demonstrates that it is derived from the knowledge of mythic thought processes, the awareness and resolution of contradictions within the culture. People turn to Ultima and Antonio at crucial moments in their lives because they are instinctively aware that mediators (*curanderos*, shamans, and tricksters) possess an overview or power of synthesis that can help them resolve their problems. The multiple episodes of Antonio playing the role of priest are especially significant in this light. It is his mother's and her family's dream for Antonio to become a Luna priest and man of knowledge, a shaman. In fact he performs the role seriously, administering last rights to Lupito, a war-crazed murderer and Narciso, an ally of Ultima and Antonio's family. The blessings he bestows on his brothers and his friends are real and invested with a power they never fully realize as they taunt him. In his spiritual searching, Antonio discovers the contradictions in Christianity and realizes that the scope of his mediations would include the "pagan," animistic forces implicit in the very landscape he inhabited. In his musings, he feels the new synthesis that he will be a part of: "'Take the llano and the river valley, the moon and the sea, God and the golden carp--and make something new.' . . . That is what Ultima meant by building strength from life." (BMU, p. 236).

The dynamism of mythic thought and its power of synthesis is poignantly expressed in Antonio's description of the feelings and emotions that are aroused by contact with Ultima:

> She took my hand and I felt the power of a whirlwind sweep around me. Her eyes swept the surrounding hills and through them I saw for the first time the wild beauty of our hills and the magic of the green river. My nostrils quivered as I felt the song of the mockingbirds and the drone of the grasshoppers mingle with the pulse of the earth. The four directions of the llano met in me, and the white sun shone on my soul. The granules of sand at my feet and the sun and sky above me seemed to dissolve into one strange, complete being. (BMU, p.11).

The power invested in the mythical process is the knowledge derived from seeing the world as a totality and understanding its contradictions in a dialectical manner. There are other characters in the novel who demonstrate differing degrees of awareness of this totality, proving that it is indeed a mechanism of popular culture rather than a mystery reserved for a privileged visionary few. A good example is Narciso, a powerful man of the *llano* who nevertheless lives in the valley, having discovered its secrets. Ample evidence of this is his exuberant, drunken garden, the likes of which not many *llaneros* (plainsmen) could foster (BMU, p.101).

In perhaps the most global or cosmic synthesis of the novel, Ultima in a dream reveals to Antonio the totality which subsumes the oppositions contained in his culture at the moment when they seemed about to split into a dichotomy and create another apocalypse:

> Cease! she cried to the raging powers, and the power from the heavens and the power from the earth obeyed her. The storm abated.
>
> Stand, Antonio, she commanded, and I stood. You both know, she spoke to my father and my mother, that the sweet water of the moon which falls as rain is the same water that gathers into rivers and flows to fill the seas. Without the waters of the moon to replenish the oceans there would be no oceans. And the same salt waters of the oceans are drawn by the sun to the heavens, and in turn become again the waters of the moon. Without the sun there would be no waters formed to slake the dark earth's thirst.
>
> The waters are one, Antonio. I looked into her bright, clear eyes and understood her truth.
>
> You have been seeing only parts, she finished, and not looking beyond into the great cycle that binds us all. (BMU, p. 113).

The implied definition of apocalypse in this system of thought is the destructive result of changes which are not assimilated, of oppositions which are not mediated. The awareness of the characters of the apocalyptic threat of the atomic bomb, first tested just to the southwest of their fertile valley, demonstrates a real and historical dimension of apocalypse. They sense that the previous balance has been disturbed. The bomb seems to have changed the weather just as surely as World War II had twisted the souls of the men from the area who had fought in it. The need for a new synthesis is as urgent as ever in this new time of crisis. Ultima immediately involved herself in the healing of men who were suffering war-sickness and it would be up to Antonio to continue the tradition of mediating contradictions both old and new.

In one sense, Ultima's knowledge may seem mystical because of the way it incorporates nature as well as culture, but when applied to society and history it is just as penetratingly comprehensive and its value just as valid. After Ultima's death, her knowledge continues in Antonio and the reader feels sure that whatever his fate may be, he possesses the conceptual tools to continue to benefit his people and culture with their internal conflicts as well as with the oncoming struggle with a whole new set of oppositions stemming from the fast approaching and aggressive proximity of the Anglo culture and way of life.

In portraying power as the ability to think and understand in a dialectical way, Anaya demonstrates in *Bless Me, Ultima* the ancient collective cognitive process of mythical thought in Chicano culture and the importance of those individuals who take on the role of mediators (*curanderos*, tricksters, or activists) in pointing out and moving towards the resolution of the contradictions generated by human history and new technology.

NOTES

[1] Rudolfo A. Anaya, *Bless Me, Ultima* (Berkeley, California: Quinto Sol, 1972). All quotations are from this edition. Page numbers are noted in text.

[2] [María] Teresa [Huerta] Márquez, "Works by and about Rudolfo A. Anaya," in *The Magic of Words: Rudolfo Anaya and His Writings*, ed. Paul Vassallo, (Albuquerque: University of New Mexico Press, 1982), pp. 55-81.

[3] Among many others see Arnulfo Trejo, "Review of *Bless Me, Ultima*," *Arizona Quarterly*, 29, No. 2 (Spring 1973), pp. 95-96.

[4] Vernon E. Lattin, "The Quest for Mythic Vision in Contemporary Native American and Chicano Fiction," *American Literature*, 50, No. 4 (January 1979), pp. 625-640.

[5] Juan Rodríguez, "La búsqueda de identidad y sus motivos en la literatura chicana," in *The Identification and Analysis of Chicano Literature*, ed. Francisco Jiménez (New York: Bilingual Press/Editorial Bilingüe, 1979), pp. 170-178.

[6] Carlota Cárdenas Dwyer, "Myth and Folk Culture in Contemporary Chicano Literature," *La Luz*, (December 1974), pp. 28-29. Caroll Mitchell, "Rudolfo Anaya's *Bless Me, Ultima*: Folk Culture in Literature," *Critique* XXII, No. 1 (1980), pp. 55-64. Jane Rogers, "The Function of the La Llorona Motif in Rudolfo Anaya's *Bless Me, Ultima*," *Latin American Literary Review*, Vol. 5, No. 10 (Spring-Summer 1977), pp. 64-69.

[7] Roberto Cantú, "Estructura y sentido de lo onírico en *Bless Me, Ultima*," *Mester*, V, No. 1 (Noviembre 1974), pp. 27-41. Amy Waggoner,

"Tony's Dreams--An Important Dimension in *Bless Me, Ultima*," *Southwestern American Literature*, Vol. 4 (1974), pp. 74-79.

[8] Febe Portillo-Orozco, "Rudolfo Anaya's Use of History, Myth and Legend in His Novels: *Bless Me, Ultima* and *Heart of Aztlan*," M.A. thesis, San Francisco State University, 1981.

[9] J. Karen Ray, "Cultural and Mythical Archetypes in Rudolfo Anaya's Bless Me, Ultima," *New Mexico Humanities Review*, 1, No. 3 (September 1978), pp. 23-28.

[10] Octavio Paz, *Posdata* (México: Siglo XXI, 1970). Carlos Fuentes, *Tiempo Mexicano* (México: Joaquín Mortiz, 1971).

[11] Joseph Sommers, "From the Critical Premise to the Product: Critical Modes and Their Application to a Chicano Literary Text," in *New Directions in Chicano Scholarship*, eds. Ricardo Romo and Raymund Paredes, Chicano Studies Monograph Series (La Jolla: University of California, 1978), pp. 51-80.

[12] Claude Lévi-Strauss, *The Savage Mind* (1962; rpt. Chicago: University of Chicago Press, 1970), pp. 1-34.

[13] Claude Lévi-Strauss, *Structural Anthropology* (New York: Basic Books, 1963), pp. 210-218.

[14] Ibid, pp. 206-231.

[15] Marc Simmons, *New Mexico: A History*, (New York: W.W. Norton, 1977), pp. 107-167.

[16] Lévi-Strauss, *Structural Anthropology*, pp. 224-225.

Individual Versus Collective Identity and the Idea of Leadership in Sherwood Anderson's *Marching Men* (1917) and Rudolfo A. Anaya's *Heart of Aztlán* (1976)

Heiner Bus
Universität Bamberg
West Germany

Answering a letter in 1933 from H. S. Kraft, who had proposed a joint project, Sherwood Anderson wrote:

> Think about the figure of Hugh in *Poor White*, who has something of a Lincoln quality, and then combine him with the figure of Henry Ford. This could be worked out into the factory so that the town of Bidwell in *Poor White* became a place like Ford's Dearborn. All this contrasted with changing life out of agricultural and into industrial America, the splendor of the machines and the factories contrasted with the growing degradation of the life of the people. . . . I presume we would have to work out a definite story hung about one man or a family, and above all we must get into it the feeling that it is a transition period into some more splendid America. If we cannot get the story and the figure of one man, I am sure we can do it with a family. (Jones 279)

Anderson's reply documents his plan to concern himself with the promises of a better future emanating from the efforts of an individual or a group. He introduces the theme of leadership with his reference to Lincoln. It is quite surprising that in this context Anderson explicitly recalls *Poor White* (1902) rather than *Marching Men* (1917), his second novel, in which he struggled with the very problems discussed in the letter.[1]

In *Marching Men*, Anderson focused on the career of Beaut McGregor who tries to improve the lot of the workers through his marching-men movement. The gradual emergence of a leader and his methods of persuading the group into action are central concerns of the novel. Fifty-nine years later, Rudolfo A. Anaya's *Heart of Aztlán* again explores these phenomena, locating them in an ethnic milieu. Anaya's novel also describes a period of transition. Like Beaut McGregor, the prospective leader Clemente Chávez has to leave his home in the first part of the story eventually to gain his new status. Many of Sherwood Anderson's comments on these themes set down in his letters, his journalistic writings, and in unfinished projects can be read as an introduction to *Heart of Aztlán*. This evident kinship justifies a comparison of Anaya's novel with *Marching Men*, giving special emphasis to the emergence of the leader, his interaction with the group, and the function of change as depicted in physical and intellectual movement.

Marching Men starts with a re-christening on "an ill day for births" (9). Henceforth, "Beaut" McGregor considers himself a victim of Coal Creek society determining him as "a being, the object of an art" (12). In his article "Sherwood Anderson's *Marching Men*: Unnatural Disorder and the Art of Force," the critic John Ditsky described the impact of this introduction as follows:

> McGregor is a gargoyle of singularity in a place of dismal sameness which has thus far produced no companions to relieve the potentially tragic aloneness of the protagonist, the isolation from mankind which pre-exists the book's events. The giving of the new name to McGregor is one of those subatomic impulses, precious to Anderson, by which men are freed to act, to define themselves. The novel begins with the living tableau of its drama. (104)

The firm conviction that his parents' superior values remained unrecognized by the town generates Beaut's "intense hatred for his fellows" (10) and a strong desire for revenge. In his memory, his father "Cracked" McGregor figures as a courageous and compassionate individual dreaming of a pastoral life for his family (15-16), thus distinguishing himself from the uninspired and uninspiring miners. Beaut's hatred goes so far that during a local strike he finds himself on the side of the bosses. He can even think of using "his strength and brute courage" (36) to persuade the workers into collective action. He greatly admires the effectiveness and orderliness of the soldiers called in to restore law and order (36). Beaut deliberately sets his gospel of violence against the town socialist's dream of a meaningful life[2] and the anarchist's gentle message of "love and the destruction of evil" (38). Nevertheless, he basically shares their objectives: To "make men stop being fools. I'll make children of them" (21). In contrast to his present marginal position, this rather ambiguous reduction would guarantee him a superior status in such a re-organized society. And as Coal Creek permanently confirms his own ineffectuality by limiting his personal expressiveness and rejecting his concept of change and leadership, Beaut leaves the scene of his childhood and youth at the end of Book One to realize his full potential elsewhere:

> [A] great wave of anger passed through him. "I'll show them," he muttered. . . . The train began to move into the West. Beaut . . . wept with joy that he had seen the last of his youth. He looked back at Coal Creek full of hate. Like Nero he might have wished that all of the people of the town had but one head so that he might have cut it off with one sweep of a sword or knocked it into the gutter with one swinging blow. (42)

Beaut's interpretation of reality remains undisputed as the narrator shares his views. He even revaluates them by giving them regional and national significance (10-11).

In many ways the initial leave-taking of *Heart of Aztlán* is a totally different experience. Though Clemente, as the head of his *familia* and the person with the deepest roots receives most of the narrator's attention, this event is presented in a collective scene. Likewise, the decision to journey west from Guadalupe to Albuquerque driven by economic necessity is understood as part of a larger historical process of the dislocation of an ethnic group, thus almost entirely excluding individual guilt (5-6).

The various responses of the family members depend on their degree of attachment to the rural environment. While the daughters, Juanita and Ana, and Benjie, the youngest son, have exhausted the possibilities of Guadalupe and are glad to go, by contrast for Jason and his parents, the departure evokes a serious and painful evaluation of inherent losses and rewards. Clemente, Adelita, and their eldest son feel that they are abandoning their land-based identity (7-8). The adults take comfort in the idea that one important point of reference, the *familia*, can be saved by their move. From the beginning of the novel, fragments of legends and myths indirectly comment upon the actions and reflections of the Chávez family, foreshadowing the reinterpretation of their journey as an internal migration within a larger homeland.[3] Clemente's rather casual acknowledgement of the trip to the Rio Grande as a homecoming (9) marks the first approximation of reality and myth. In spite of such momentary glimpses of a fundamental invulnerability, the family sets out for voyage "on an unknown, uncharted ocean" (3).

In contrast to the ambiguous farewell in *Heart of Aztlán*, the hero of *Marching Men* is glad to leave behind the scene of his humiliations. Beaut McGregor's emotions resemble those of the younger Chávez children showing none of their parents' and Jason's reluctance to abandon a self-contained life style. Whereas Clemente is prepared to preserve only a minimum of his traditions, Beaut merely transfers a firm idea of himself and an equally finished vision of society to a new testing ground.

Beaut's marching-men movement was generated in his Coal Creek experience, in the miners' lack of inspiration, and in their lack of courage and solidarity. Collective physical movement as an incentive to subsequent intellectual and emotional mobility is supposed to correct some of the shortcomings of this world. Though Beaut accentuates material gain, comfort, and dumb acceptance as major vices, he and the narrator fail to produce a comprehensive cure (115, 119, 121). When they speak of reviving "the tradition of devotion" (113), they obviously deplore the isolation and uprootedness of the modern individual who has been robbed of his cultural frame of reference in order to participate in "something vast and mighty" (183).[4] This idea is frequently connected with the dream of childhood, of rural places where people live in harmony with their natural and social environment (55, 113-16). Urbanization and industrialization are blamed for the fragmentation of society. There is a distinct anti-intellectual strain in Beaut's persuasive strategies; progress cannot be achieved without appealing to instinctive, basic human wants. Hence, the narrator appropriately juxtaposes the sanity, mindlessness and nourishing quality of the cornfields in the back country with "leaderless, purposeless, slovenly, down at the heels" Chicago: "The corn grows and thinks of nothing but growth" (113). However, this preference for instinctive wisdom does not apply to Beaut's own development. He detests the "great wagging of jaws and waving of arms" (169) and the agitator "hypnotized by the wagging of his own jaw" (157); however, he himself gradually comes closer to become a "chattering puppet to the gods" (88).

As Beaut perceives the same lack of inspiration and purpose in Chicago as in Coal Creek, he does not feel obliged to make amendments. Liberated from the limitations of his family history, he mainly learns to master new techniques for influencing the city dwellers. This simple transfer is confirmed by quick successes effected by his use of his extraordinary physical powers and his readiness to use his faculties unhesitatingly. He starts an intellectual training in order to reconcile theory with practice, which will enable him to compete with the upper-class profiteers of the existing social system. Anderson here complements his triad of character determinants: heredity, environment, and education. Acquiring the strengths of more than one class further detaches him from the subjects of his reform movement without giving him a new sense of belonging. In this respect Beaut serves as a prime example of the very social fragmentation which he wanted to overcome. This becomes even more apparent when the so-called "disintegrating forces" (58)--sex, material wealth, beauty, and individual friendships--approach him, and he refuses to "be confused by little things" (90).[5]

Only for a very short period, at the death of his mother, is he able to replace his hatred of social conditions and human flaws with the idea of love (106-07). On this occasion, he criticizes the egoism of leaders (106) and their inability to identify honestly with the masses, thus formulating his own problem. After this interlude he becomes more radical, violent, and self-centered. This process blatantly contradicts his insight that some of the needs of the workers correspond with his own. He longs for an identification which his concept of leadership denies (47, 142). Hatred and revenge as his propellants force him to keep up his detachment and exclude him from the brotherhood he wants to mediate.

His character and life experience give priority to his will to power realized in traditional leadership, though the forces challenging this concept are ever-present, as in the following passage: "He was themselves become expressive . . . the things in him wanting expression and not getting expressed, made him seem like one of them . . . " (213). These preferences keep him from translating suffering, misery, and human flaws into common strength. For a time, Beaut is able to hide his own weaknesses behind his qualities, but, eventually, he fails to persuade the masses as we learn in the final chapters of the novel told from the perspective of his upper-class opponent David Ormsby. This outcome does not surprise the attentive reader who noticed that from the beginning Beaut applied not only images and rhythms,[6] but also intimidation[7] as legitimate means of persuasion of both the exploiters and the exploited. This amoral and destructive strain reaches a climax in one of his visions in which he praises as liberated individuals the Civil War soldiers who killed "with recklessness of gods" (91-92). In another chapter, he derives his ideal from the orderliness of a funeral procession (105-108). The celebration of pure action by the superior individual or mere movement totally dismisses the emotion of compassion and the idea of effecting a cure.

In *Heart of Aztlán*, a leader emerges only gradually and reluctantly after the old values have been modified and complemented by new insights. When the Chávez family arrives in Albuquerque, Clemente still makes the major decisions, but his position, not totally undisputed in Guadalupe, is very soon threatened by his children and even by his wife whose responses prove to be more appropriate to the new challenges. Clemente's dependence on *la tierra* and rituals fails to assess and counterbalance the attractions of city life; "the old earth of his valley" does not seem to mix easily with "the hard city soil" (18).

The quick accomodation of his eldest son, Jason, who bade an equally painful farewell to Guadalupe and to his mentor, the old Indian, suggests to the reader that by the change of place, leadership has been handed on to the next Chicano generation.[8] Jason demonstrates a remarkable acuteness, inquisitiveness, and alertness to interpret the phenomena of his new environment to maintain islands of human dignity and self-determination. During their first meeting, he recognizes continuities between Crispín and the old Indian of Guadalupe before actually learning that "the poet of the barrio" (13) knew the man. His pre-eminence becomes evident when his own father is about to attack his sisters and Jason is ready to interfere (34). As for himself, Jason rejects the opportunity of passing into the mainstream through Cindy, the rich Anglo girl (61). So much prudence and firmness must be rewarded: In a number of scenes he feels "composed," (28) "complete," and "calm" (95).

However, despite these virtues, in the end Jason considers himself a failure because he cannot prevent his younger brother's tragedy (199). This outcome has been prepared for: When his family discusses Sánchez's fatal accident in the railroad yards, he does not reveal himself as an eyewitness and interpreter of the scene (28-29). Later in the novel, after he faced el Super, who blamed him and his father for violating barrio conventions, he tries to redeem his irritation by a symbolic gesture which he hides from his people (187-88). These reactions set him in direct contrast with his father as depicted in the last chapters of the novel: Jason also comprehends the water tank as a symbol of human perversion, exploitation, and lost faith, (197) but he cannot deduce a larger vision. At this moment Jason, who initially proved to be the superior character, is tormented by self-reproaches, a stage his father had left behind. Yet some passages in the novel promise Jason future leadership on the basis of his barrio experience and the model of his father's slow and painful re-emergence: "Clemente looked at his son. There was something about his son that reminded him of himself when he was young. Sometimes he felt awkward when he talked with Jason, because he felt as if he was talking to himself" (34).

In stark contrast to the domineering protagonist of *Marching Men*, Anaya's troika of Jason, Crispín, and Clemente has to be interpreted in their mutual interdependence. From the outset, Crispín, the blind singer of the barrio, accompanies the efforts of the Chávez family to settle down and survive decently in Barelas. He serves them and the community by connecting their actuality to the past and the group experience; he and his guitar are "constantly reshaping things as they are" (14), striving for continuity and enlargement through memory and recognition. Though he can read the signs and make reality transparent, he is a searcher himself and merely acts at the inspiration of an authority beyond human grasp.[9] Crispín is on a quest for the missing link between past, present, and future in order to complete one cycle (126) and begin a new one. To fill in the gap, requires a leader united with his people in suffering and the desire to reform life along an ethnic myth. The message is persuasive in its simplicity as it permeates the emotions of brotherhood based on the individual *movidas* characterized by an undeserved *tristeza de la vida* (118). The myth of Aztlán as proclaimed by Crispín relates this common experience to history, as the people have been unjustly punished and the benevolent gods promised to restore life "in peace and harmony with the earth and her gods" (123). Though in many ways Crispín plays an active part in the barrio and closely ties his personal fate to that of the community, the blind seer remains detached from the daily activities of his people--just an attendant at the birth of a leader, indispensable as a transmitter of energy and knowledge, but never claiming leadership for himself.

Clemente Chávez development to such stature is not foreshadowed in the first chapters of the novel. His unproblematical integration into barrio life seems to promise an easy realization of his modest demands. So he does not feel compelled to question his role as paterfamilias or to explore the mechanics of the new place beyond the limits of random actuality and his individual horizon. Such general content even compensates his slight irritation when Crispín hints at a deeper alliance between Barelas and Guadalupe, the past and the present (13). On Clemente's momentary level of awareness, the last bond between the two places is threatened when his position in the family declines step by step. As he lacks the resources to prevent this process, he resorts to violence, (38, 43, 76) self-accusations, and alcohol. His identity is totally ruined when he becomes financially dependent after losing his job in an effort to preserve his honor in a labor dispute (78). Significantly, an individual and separate act within a collective action--by coincidence in unison--pushes him to the low point of his career and self-esteem: "Somehow he had lost command over his life and destiny" (74).

At this point, Crispín, Jason--even Father Cayo, Lalo, and el Super-- outrank him through their firmer grip on barrio affairs. Clemente's wife, Adelita, characterizes him as "a man lost in a foreign land" (78). By referring back to Guadalupe, she probes the degree of his divergence and indirectly suggests the cure--an eventual acceptance of the foreign land as part of the homeland:

> ". . . I remember watching the Chávez brothers walk on that llano-land of theirs. My God, you would have sworn that they were gods themselves the way they held themselves and walked upon that earth. . . . And there were also the people, los compadres, los vecinos, the people of the small pueblos, they understood and lent their support, so a man was never lost, never separated from his soul." (78)

In this situation, Anaya exposes Clemente to scenes in which the workers of Barelas discuss the need for leadership in their fight for self-determination. Basically, these encounters depict the various stages of Clemente's gradual growth of insight into the demands of his people, of joining his individual with the common cause.

Manuel's equating the family with the people both includes and excludes Clemente as a candidate because of his recent failures in the smaller unit. Options depend on varying definitions of leadership. At the same meeting during a wildcat strike, Crispín's storytelling and singing of the *corridos* offer relief by relating the oppressions of the present not only to the miseries but also to the heroic acts of liberation in the collective past (83). This call for identification is taken up by Clemente only reluctantly, though he asks the barrio poet to explain further the legends and the myth. His deeply-rooted llano heritage makes him particularly sensitive for Crispín's concepts and their applicability in the present situation. So his position as an uncommitted outsider is gradually undermined by his unexpectedly strong responses to the myth:

> There was something very true and very essential in the story and it kept calling to him to find its meaning. He was bound up with the people of the story, and with the legend of the eagle and the serpent, and all that related somehow to him and to the strikers who sought justice, but he didn't know how. And the place they called Aztlán was like a mysterious word, latent with power, stretching from the dark past to the present to ring in his soul and make him tremble. (85)

Clemente's physical and spiritual reverberations send him on a search for further revelations, yet without being equipped with a proper method. His unassisted individual approach to the energizing sources ends in utter disappointment. Nevertheless, he learns something about the interrelationship and continuity between larger and smaller units (89). These new insights are not yet powerful enough to sever the lifelines of his old identity. In spite of the declaration of his insolvency, there is still room for escapist acts (102). During *la fiesta del bautismo*, the blind Crispín, under strange circumstances, picks out Clemente as the future leader. One of the old men in attendance defines criteria which are met for the first time by Clemente, while they disqualify other contenders: "To be a leader a man must know the traditions of his father" (102); he must have "that spiritual attachment to the earth" (104). The following successful healing, Henry's sacrificial death, and his *velorio* demonstrate the validity of the old ways in an urban environment, and they indirectly confirm Crispín's choice without persuading Clemente to take over responsibilities. He has yet to reach the deepest point in the valley of his despair in order to connect unconditionally his own identity to the communal myth: "He reviewed his life and found that it no longer had meaning. . . . There was no reason to go on living. . . . He had lost his land and his family, and nothing else really mattered. He smiled and welcomed death" (121).

Significantly, it is Crispín who becomes his savior and interprets Clemente's experience of life in death as a rebirth (122). Crispín now has at his disposal a person in urgent need of an effective set of values and with the potential of becoming a powerful symbol of suffering and survival to persuade the barrio people to identification. By reconstructing Clemente's personality, Crispín hopes to accomplish his mission of filling the gap between the past and the present. The emergence of a leader clearly presents itself as a surrender, as a process of identification and interaction, definitely not as a solitary quest of a self-appointed candidate.

So it is appropriate that the reborn once again has to listen to the myth which reflects his own fall and Crispín's promise of wholeness restored. In the myth, the people's suffering is explained as a consequence of their refusal to fulfill the demands of the cruel gods for human sacrifice. As a reward for this philanthropic act, the good gods made a convenant with them predicting an eventual return to Aztlán and the rise of a more sane civilization. The new quality of interdependence among the myth, Crispín, and Clemente is shown in the second visit to the old woman of the barrio and *las piedras malas* which open the gates for a visionary trip to the river of human suffering and the heart of Aztlán. Clemente acknowledges *injusticia, miseria,* and *pobreza* in Barelas as a description of his own and of his people's situation (130-31). Through re-enactment and the fusion of his ego with the fate of his people, he achieves a state of heightened awareness preparing him for his leaderhip position (131-32). Like Moses, he returns from the mountain evoking feelings of awe and respect. Still, Clemente is not yet convinced of the paradoxical idea of becoming a powerful leader through defeat and surrender (139). His reluctance is quite understandable as, according to mainstream teachings, traditional leadership in the barrio is considered to be founded largely on individual achievement.[10] So, the next stage is one of self-persuasion and of extending the small group of the faithful.

Clemente temporarily feels encouraged when he is able to set his new concept of *el alma de la raza* [the spirit of the common people] and universal brotherhood against Lalo's militancy. But his persecution, for a violent strike he tried to prevent, exposes the ambiguity of his situation as an undisputed leader in terms of false criteria. At this point Clemente both suffers and benefits from outside influences because they strengthen the symbolic character of his experience. This is particularly true for his turning down the bribe money from the alliance of established leaders (170) and for his final translating of his private pains into an articulate public gesture of defiance. Both actions, denying the separation of individual and collective fate, persuade the people and Clemente himself into common action. He finally accepts the extension of his parish from his family to the people of Barelas by including himself and the barrio in the myth: "I held a fiery sword . . . and with that sword I cut down the snakes that suck the blood of our people and poison their will!" (188) In the end, pity and respect for Clemente's suffering, his persistence in identifying with the group, which in turn evokes their compassion, make them respond to his call for action. They are united in a dream of brotherly sharing, of acknowledging one's weaknesses and strengths, in "the fire of love . . . the pure fire that gushes from the soul of our people, from the foundations of our history . . . " (207):

> They could never be beaten! Never! Not as long as a single man dared to look for his humanity in the corners of his heart. That infusion of spirit into flesh which generations of wise men had described throughout the ages was the simple bond of love that gave the river its strength to surge and roar and cut its new channel into the future! (208)

In the final scene, Clemente leads the workers and their families, but the will for liberation and self-realization along the lines set by the myth has become self-propellant and no longer needs the traditional leader. In his review of *Heart of Aztlán*, Marvin A. Lewis criticizes this conclusion and incidently reminds us of *Marching Men* joining David Ormsby's and el Super's evaluations: "The final act is not convincing since the only things that can change the social order are money and power. The people of Barelas have neither and are not likely to achieve these means in the future. But there is a certain amount of strength involved in togetherness" (76).

Returning to the starting point of this comparison, we have to summarize the striking differences between the two novels within the patterns of equally conspicuous correspondences. Both begin with a departure and end with people marching to improve their situation. While Beaut McGregor activates the workers without himself participating physically, Clemente Chávez leads not only the workers but also their families in common acceptance of their immediate objectives and the basic desire for a more humane society. This collective effort is prepared for from the beginning of *Heart of Aztlán*. In the larger portion of the book, Clemente has to compete with strong individuals and forces; he is even totally excluded from a number of chapters. In contrast, with the exception of the few sections dealing with Margaret Ormsby, Beaut and his career dominate *Marching Men*. He starts as "a marked man" (20) and remains the self-appointed leader of his own movement. His departure for Chicago provides him with an appropriate stage for his self-realization. Occasional doubts about his role are quickly dispersed by his strong will to power. In the final chapters, one of his antagonists has to describe the foreseeable decline since Beaut has become blind to some aspects of reality.

Clemente's story is less straightforward as he leaves Guadalupe for an unknown future. Even the last remnants of his traditional role are very soon demolished. He has to experience various stages of reduction and extension, a dialectic process of losses and gains along the patterns of punishment and rewards, exodus and homecoming set by the ethnic myth.

Only very slowly and painfully does he emerge as a leader. He acquires strength through interaction and identification with spirtiual energies already existent in Barelas. Leadership is imposed upon Clemente, whereas Beaut imposes self-construed concepts on his environment maintaining a rather detached attitude towards the workers of Chicago. In the course of his activities, his isolation even grows, though, paradoxically, he deplores people being out of step with one another. Basically, he exploits the workers to realize his own potential and to display his achievements. The eventual failure of the traditional leader figure is explained by his monomaniacal pursuit of a single idea (qualifying him for the gallery of grotesque in *Winesburg, Ohio*), by the ever-widening gap between his own sense of mission and the effectiveness of his art of persuasion. At the end, he is as restricted as in Coal Creek because his career and his movement demonstrate "that the price of an orderly species is the loss of individual freedom" (Ditsky 114).

In *Heart of Aztlán*, the defeated, once powerful individual is reconstructed in the context of an ethnic myth, with the assistance of the tribal bard, and the co-orperation of the barrio people gradually acknowledging their common past, present, and future. The leader is exposed as a model of suffering and triumph by publicly accepting his communal identity, thus averting the temptations of isolation. The Barelas concept of brotherhood and communality is ethnic and regional, but it is also universal as an example of aspiration to social reorganization based on positive values and a meaningful reconciliation of past and present.

Beaut also traces in himself and others a longing to retrieve something lost, to live in a sane community as represented in Midwestern small town life before the disruptions of industralization and urbanization. It is the desire to extinguish ugliness and uninspiredness, to relate to something stable and whole beyond one's selfhood. In contrast to Anderson's more successful books-- *Winesburg, Ohio* and *Poor White*--this motif is not developed into a central impulse in *Marching Men* and remains secondary to the hero's egoism. Beaut cannot achieve substantial progress in realizing his more universal goals, for hatred and thirst for revenge cannot magically produce the emotion of brotherhood. With the exception of some glimpses of a rural idyll, he perceives reality as a continual power struggle between social classes and also between the outstanding individual and the group. Threats and physical movement serve as major mobilizing agents and are but poorly compensated for by a rather vague ideal. In his 1917 review of the novel, George Bernard Donlin saw "the nucleus" of Beaut's "whole philosophy" in the formula, "the 'goose-step' is the way to solidarity" (274).

Neither Beaut nor Clemente plan a return to either Coal Creek or to Guadalupe. The protagonist of *Marching Men* associates the scenery of his childhood and youth with a series of defeats that he tries to obliterate once and for all. Clemente's grief over his dislocation is only gradually eased during the reshaping process of his identity: The two places, Guadalupe and Barelas, become constituents of his restored personality and the larger homeland Aztlán. On the one hand, his instinctive and self-contained life as a farmer, but also its total loss are essentials for the deliberate surrender to his new role in Barelas. On the other hand, the diversity, denseness, and spirituality of the barrio certainly improve the chances for regeneration through a collective effort and myth. Therefore, Barelas and Guadalupe stand for necessary and complementary experiences; the intricate dialectics of loss and gain, of past and present release Clemente from replacing one with the other-- a task which the less deeply rooted Beaut accomplished quite easily.[11]

Sherwood Anderson's story of the rise and imminent fall of the self-reliant Beaut McGregor resembles Clemente Chávez's career in the first half of *Heart of Aztlán*. Rudolfo Anaya continues where the mainstream writer left off. Anderson obviously did not draw the consequences from the collapse of Beaut's rugged individualism. And he did not seriously pursue alternatives vaguely suggested in *Marching Men*: To anchor a character firmly in a distinct social class and/or a geographical region. The narrator's casual reference to Chicago's needing "a Lincoln, suffering for mankind" (46) shows a way out of the dilemma, via the Midwestern Lincoln-common-man-myth which Anderson returned to in his later writings and in the letter quoted in the introduction of this article.

Anaya makes his protagonist face the logical consequences of his individual defeat and liberates him from "the chains of isolation and loneliness" (68) and from mainstream concepts through identification with the collective experience, both ethnic and regional. To put it differently, while Anderson largely confines himself to Freudian categories, Anaya also applies the complementary findings of C. G. Jung.[12] In *Heart of Aztlán*, he even dreams of an Arcadian state making leadership obsolete because general consent on a humane social order can be reached. In spite of the familiar fervor with which it is stated, this is only partially an American dream; it is rather a spirited ethnic response to the inefficiency of mainstream myths of emancipation as generally displayed in Sherwood Anderson's *Marching Men* and summarized by his narrator: "Something is wrong with modern American life and we Americans do not want to look at it. We much prefer to call ourselves a great people and let it go at that" (71).

NOTES

[1] Quotations from and references to *Heart of Aztlán* and *Marching Men* are from the following editions: Anaya, Rudolfo A. *Heart of Aztlán*. Berkeley, CA: Justa, 1976. Anderson, Sherwood. *Marching Men: A Critical Text*. Ed. Ray Lewis White. Cleveland and London: The Press of Case Western Reserve U., 1972.

[2] ". . . of a day coming when men should march shoulder to shoulder and life in Coal Creek and everywhere should cease being aimless and become definite and full of meaning" (11).

[3] Ironically, Juanita's answer "Not a darn thing." to Adelita's question "Have we left anything behind?" will turn out to be a very perceptive comment on the situation (8).

[4] See also 67, 176, 181, and 192.

[5] See also 60 and 198.

[6] See 106, 107, 109, 128, 170, 204, 213, and 217.

[7] See 76, 92, 102, 123, and 179.

[8] "It was the first time they felt Jason take a leadership position within the gang" (51).

[9] "I had to search the past to find myself. . . . I crossed the burning desert where the sun burned away my sight . . . And so I have journeyed ever since, it was my master's wish. To travel back into time, I learned, is really only to find a spot where one can plumb the depths" (28).

[10] With the exception of Father Cayo, the barrio priest, whose attitude towards Clemente and his new ideas is, therefore, extremely disappointing.

[11] The necessity of the Guadalupe experience is indirectly proved by Jason--of about the same age as Beaut--who does not yet, perhaps, qualify as a leader. The closeness of Guadalupe and Barelas is shown in the Barelas presence of *la llorona* (25, 33, 49, and 150); the comparisons between urban and rural phenomena, e.g., the canyons of the railroad yards (22); and "a flow of energy in the barrio street, like the force of the river in Guadalupe when it rushed full with summer rain" (68).

[12] See "Some Universal Dimensions of Evolving Chicano Myth: *Heart of Aztlán*" by César A. González-T. in this volume.

WORKS CITED

Anaya, Rudolfo A. *Heart of Aztlán.* Berkeley: Justa, 1976.

Ditsky, John. "Sherwood Anderson's *Marching Men*: Unnatural Disorder and the Art of Force." *Twentieth Century Literature* 23 (1977): 102-14.

Donlin, George Bernard. Rev. of *Marching Men*, by Sherwood Anderson. *The Dial* 63 (September 27, 1977): 274-75.

Jones, Howard M., and Walter B. Rideout, eds. *Letters of Sherwood Anderson.* Boston: Little, Brown, 1953.

Lewis, Marvin A. Rev. of *Heart of Aztlán*, by Rudolfo A. Anaya. *Revista Chicano-Riquena* 9.3 (1981): 74-76.

White, Ray Lewis, ed. *Sherwood Anderson. "Marching Men."* Cleveland and London: The Press of Case Western Reserve University, 1972.

Some Universal Dimensions of Evolving Chicano Myth: *Heart of Aztlán*

César A. González-T.

San Diego Mesa College

In *Heart of Aztlán* (1976), Rudolfo A. Anaya confronts us with a syncretic work of Chicano myth that compels us to look into the nature and use of myth and its relevance to Chicano literature; otherwise, we might precipitately write off *Heart* as an anti-climax to *Bless Me, Ultima* (1972), which forms a trilogy along with *Tortuga* (1979). Anaya's understatement of horizontal story-line, characters, and setting focuses our attention on the mythical dimensions of the work. "The impact of *Heart of Aztlán*," Jane Rogers writes, " . . . lies in its rendering of legend and myth, and in this aspect Anaya has made a valuable contribution to Chicano literature" (145).

This primacy of myth in Anaya should be noted in the context of a statement by Luis Leal in which he posits myth as a *sine que non* for Chicano literature, and, indeed, by implication, for Chicanos. He tells us that

> the creation of a new image is precisely the problem that confronts the Chicano writer: for it is not easy to give universality to the regional or particular if the writer does not go beyond his immediate circumstance. The Chicano has to create a new synthesis out of history, tradition, and his everyday confrontation with the ever-changing culture in which he lives. But he cannot do so unless he creates mythical images. ("Problem" 4)

I suggest that Chicano myth will continue to evolve and be created, for in the contingencies of our Chicano experience we are children of contradiction, from the beginning--lightning rods mediating opposites. In our own way, we mirror the absolutes and the dynamics, the antithesis and unity of being and non-being interacting, finding archetypal expression in mythopoeia.

As Chicano writers such as Miguel Méndez-M., Ron Arias, Alurista, and the late Tomás Rivera--to mention some of the principal ones--express myth in their writings, some attention has been given to differing perceptions of myth and its uses and implications in Chicano literature by critics such as Sergio Elizondo, Dick Gerdes, Carlota Cárdenas de Dwyer, and Vernon E. Lattin. However, people question its prominence and relevance in the contemporary flowering of Chicano letters, especially in the novel ("Mesa" 22). These questions will continue to require our attention.

This paper will first review Anaya's use of myth with reference to the social responsibility of the writer. It will then consider the function, structure, and movement of *Heart*, as well as some of its principal imagery, with reference to the theories of myth proposed by Lévi-Strauss, Carl G. Jung, and Northrop Frye.

Our focus then is on the myth in *Heart*. Those interested in a critique of the novel from other points of view are referred to reviews by Bruce-Novoa, Karl Kopp, María López, Javier Pacheco, and others.[1] Some comments are that the novel is too brief, that it moves too quickly, and that the characters need development, especially Clemente. If *Ultima* broke with Chicano stereotypes, *Heart* did not. In a word, the critics say that the mythic statement is too big for its vehicle. Bruce-Novoa observes that "lack of space severely limits our appreciation of Clemente's mysterious pilgrimage and the brief references to the myth of the Sun-deer." He adds that *Heart* needed more work, for "what must sell the reader is not exterior reality, but the interior coherence and power of the language" (62). In spite of this criticism we believe that *Heart* makes a contribution to our understanding of Chicano myth. It will be the purpose of this study to demonstrate that fact.

First of all then, we will address the criticism concerning the use of myth and the relevance of myth to the Chicano reality which has been essentially involved from its very beginnings with the dynamics of multi-dimensional struggle in its experience with Anglo-American culture. Anaya has been endlessly challenged in this regard. "I've sat in a few campuses," he tells us, "where they told me 'You're crazy, because you're writing a myth that is not useful socially, in a social context!'" ("Mesa" 13).

Anaya has repeatedly made his position clear in this regard, taking exception to pressures put on writers to be political.[2] He tells us that he is aware of his social responsibility to the Chicano struggle. "The best writers," he tells us, "will deal with social responsibility and the welfare of the people indirectly--as opposed to a direct political statement or dogma" ("Myth" 80).

María López primarily seems to question the adequacy of the character of Clemente to "lead any form of social protest" (114). But she also implies, as I read her, not only that myth cannot be applied directly to resolve social problems in the real world, but also that perhaps it has no place in this arena. "Can insight into the existence of a spiritual bond," she asks, "destroy oppression and end exploitation? . . . Is there not some other ingredient necessary in addition to a spiritual feeling of love? Has contact with the myths provided a real tool to correct social injustice?" (114)

An extraordinary round-table discussion dealing with myth in Chicano literature took place at the University of California at Irvine, and it may help to clarify this matter. Anaya and Alurista, among others, were present. Both writers presented different approaches to myth and different perceptions of the use of myth. Alurista did not give a definition of myth, but rather emphasized its uses, speaking of it more as a *functional symbol*. He spoke in particular of the myth of Aztlán:

There was a real need for all of us to find a way, a metaphor
. . . that would serve as a unifying tool to look at each other as
brothers and sisters. . . . to forge a national consciousness . . . The
myth of Aztlán, as I saw it, in the '60s was just a way to identify
a people, a land, and a consciousness that said, "Struggle, do not be
afraid." ("Mesa" 8)

In "documenting the rebirth of the myth [of Aztlán] in Chicano
thought," Luis Leal recognizes that it was probably Alurista who first brought
it to the attention of the people in "El Plan Espiritual de Aztlán" ("Search"
20). And Aztlán has functioned very effectively as a symbol to unify us, to
give us a sense of our Indian past, and to remind us that the area in which
some of us now live was taken from Mexico to which we trace our roots. It
was also intended to give us a sense that the land belongs to those who
cultivate it. It must be noted, however, that Leal distinguishes between Aztlán
as a mythic symbol and Aztlán as a myth. He speaks of Aztlán as a Chicano
symbol with a twofold significance: First, as a representation of the land taken
by the United States; second, as a symbol of "the spiritual union of the
Chicanos, something that is carried within the heart, no matter where they may
live or where they may find themselves" (18). The latter part of this
symbolism reflects the successful and effective functional use that we have
made of the symbol of Aztlán. However, Leal does not proceed to speak of
Aztlán as a Chicano myth. He tells us of antecedents in Mexican and Chicano
literature paralleling the ancient Aztec search for Aztlán as a paradise lost. He
concludes his article speaking of Anaya's *Heart of Aztlán*, in which the
protagonist, Clemente, ends his "truly imaginary pilgrimage" discovering Aztlán
within himself. "And that is the way it must be for all Chicanos," Leal tells
us, "Whosoever wants to find Aztlán, let him look for it, not on the maps, but
in the most intimate part of his being" (22). It is here that an appropriation
of the dynamics of creating myth for functional purposes may or may not take
place.

It seems then, that whereas Alurista continues to use an increasingly
sophisticated breadth of myth in his poetic expression with a focus on its

social uses, Anaya emphasizes in his novels the structure and dynamics of myth with its individual-psychological and social implications. Anaya is not trying to develop a variant of the myth of Aztlán and use it as Alurista has already done so effectively. On the contrary, the title of his novel is clearly stating that he is going to the heart of the matter. He is frankly reaching back for archetypal expression, exploring the sources of the myth of Aztlán, and of every myth for that matter. So, *Heart* can be seen as a didactic and paradigm of mythic structure and movement. It attempts to give exemplary expression of classic mythopoesis. There seems to be greater consonance between Anaya's approach to myth and Leal's call for the creation of myth.

Anaya does not simply expose us to our cultural tradition so that we somehow establish a selfhood, as Loretta Carrillo seems to suggest (112). Anaya, invites us, rather, to return to the collective unconscious because we are human, to discover myth that leads to human integration and brings us into harmony with nature and cosmic being ("Mesa" 18-19). Whether we lived in primordial space and time or hurry today on our mad and private ways along our modern freeways, we have the ability to return to the cave, to the womb, to the water. "Mythopoesis--myth and the art of myth-making--is the crux of Anaya's philosophical and artistic vision," says Antonio Márquez (45).

Our lost sense of the relevance of myth is a matter of great concern to Anaya. "Man is a myth-making animal," Anaya tells us, "and this is one of our failures as modern man. We're not making myths anymore" (Myth" 80). In this regard, Gregory Nava, a film maker engaged with contemporary social issues (*El Norte*), observes that whereas Latin America has a strong living tradition of myth, "you don't see it in European literature and American literature where you have a repression of the mythological" (12). According to Anaya, "The mythic element in Anglo-American literature is just not there" ("Mesa" 13). That is why, he tells us, "there is a wrenching in contemporary modern man." We have cut ourselves off from our "original unity and harmony" and "have grown so perverse" that we are in peril of destroying the earth itself, a gift of the gods. "That is mind boggling," Anaya adds, "that really wrenches whatever unity anyone may have inside of him ("Mesa" 21-22).

The reason why we have come to this pass is not because we have gone back to myth, but because we have lost touch with it (22). C. Kerenyi, in his prolegomena to *Essays on a Science of Mythology* which he published with Carl G. Jung, says: "we have lost our immediate feeling for the great realities of the spirit . . . mythology . . . precisely because of our all-too-willing, helpful, and efficient science" (Jung 1). On the other hand, Lévi-Strauss tells us that myth has been replaced in good measure in modern society by politics (209).

Anaya seems to be more at home with C. G. Jung and Northrop Frye than with Lévi-Strauss in speaking of the sources, structure, and movement of myth. I believe that it is necessary to consider the work of these authors in order to establish a theoretical framework within which to consider Anaya's approach to myth. Lévi-Strauss suggests that there are sources of meaning when he remarks on the "astounding similarity between myths collected in widely different regions," unexplained by evolutionary or diffusionist theories (208). He argues that there are structural patterns of relationships in and among human phenomena including myth. Claire Jacobson, in her preface to Lévi-Strauss' *Structural Anthropology*, summarizes by saying that his emphasis is "on form, on the primacy of relationships over entities, and on the search for constant relationships among phenomena at the most abstract level. . . . Lévi-Strauss' approach is holistic and integrative" (x-xi). Lévi-Strauss himself illustrates this approach to myth in his familiar analogy with music. He points out that just as music must be read synchronically along a vertical axis, rather than diachronically along a horizontal axis, to get at harmony (212), so too the study of bundles of mythic relationships will reveal "basic logical processes [combining elements] which are at the root of mythical thought" (224). Earlier he remarks that "what gives. . . . myth an operational value is that the specific pattern described is timeless; it explains the present and the past as well as the future" (209). Hence myth has a timeless dimension and transcends space. Its meaning, he tells us, comes through, unlike poetry, even in the worst translation because its meaning lies in the story (210). This suggests that myth is epiphanic of a larger cosmic order. And I add that the larger order reflects the analogy of being in which the whole is reflected in every one of its parts. There are continuities between the anorganic and the organic, the animal and the human and the divine. There is a sense in which everything is in everything. The loss or absence of structure, most dramatically in genetic structure, is a sliding back into primal chaos--death, or the extinction of a species (Schell 112).

Lévi-Strauss, however, unequivocally rejects the psychological-affective approach to myth:

Myths are still widely interpreted in conflicting ways: as collective dreams, as the outcome of a kind of esthetic play, or as the basis of ritual. Mythological figures are considered as personified abstractions, divinized heroes, or fallen gods. Whatever the hypothesis, the choice amounts to reducing mythology either to idle play or to a crude kind of philosophic speculation. (207)

Anaya, however, as stated earlier, seems more at home in his mythopoesis with Jung, who, in his classic work *The Archetypes and the Collective Unconscious*, postulates the existence of an inherited collective unconscious, beyond our immediate consciousness and even personal unconscious, which "consists of pre-existent forms, the archetypes, which can only become conscious secondarily and which give definite form to certain psychic contents" (43).

With Jung, Anaya sees a common source from which to create myth. The well is always there for us to draw from. There is no need to go back to Aztec or any other particular myth: "How the hell do I tie in to the Aztecas? No way. I'm New Mexican Indian." In the myth of Aztlán, Anaya tells us he found rather "an archaic symbol which I don't think we have understood completely" ("Mesa" 11). He goes on to insist that myth is dynamic and "part of our evolutionary history," which, he tentatively states, has hardly been imprinted "in the human heart" in recent generations. "Primal man made myth out of given archetypes, and there's just so many of them, they're limited, and they're in all the hearts" ("Mesa" 14).

This is what Anaya means when he defines myth as "the truth in the heart ("Mesa" 11), just as Jung tells us that we do not need to go elsewhere to sew our mythic attire; we can sew our own garments, for "archetypes are complexes of experience that come upon us like fate, and their effects are felt in our most personal life" (*Archetypes* 14, 30). Lévi-Strauss too looks to a communal resource to account for the consonance of mythological motifs among people:

> From the unconscious there emanate determining influences which, independently of tradition, guarantee in every single individual a similarity and even a sameness of experience, and also of the way it is represented imaginatively. One of the main proofs of this is the almost universal parallelism between mythological motifs, which, on account of their quality as primordial images I have called archetypes. (58)

So, in *creating* a myth, as opposed to retelling it, Anaya--who lives in a New Mexican context rich in Native American myth, (Gerdes 244)--does not hesitate to take "bits and pieces" from diverse myths in fashioning or remaking a myth "with a modern meaning that says something to our lives now" ("Myth" 80). He insists that "there is no secret mythology for anyone. I think it's equal for everyone" ("Myth" 79). Hence, as we shall see, "the truth in the heart" is the source of Clemente's vision in *Heart*.

Reflecting on his work he speaks of it in classic Jungian terms. He says that he looks back at his writings "through a sense that I have about primal images. A sense that I have about the archetypal, about what we once must have known collectively. What we all share is a kind of collective memory. There was a harmony there" ("Myth" 79).

In *Heart of Aztlán*, Clemente--with his wife, his two sons (Benji and Jason) and his two daughters (the women do not figure prominently in the novel)[3]--moves some miles west from his land in the town of Guadalupe to the city of Albuquerque. Socio-economic pressures threaten the family, and he turns to drink. Through the mediation of Crispín, a blind musician with the blue guitar, which appears in Anaya's trilogy, he is taken on a mythic journey, whence he returns empowered to lead workers on strike in a march against the railroads which exploit them.

The experience of Clemente in *Heart*--who has lost control of his family, his job, and is fast losing himself in alcohol--is a Jungian experience. Its symbols and significance are literally of transcendent importance not only to Clemente in establishing a personal self, but also of overriding symbolic significance to the Chicano community in developing an identity as a group. Clemente proclaims this when, in the midst of his vision, he shouts: "I AM AZTLÁN!" (131). This pattern in hero myths, Joseph L. Henderson tells us, "has psychological meaning both for the individual who is endeavoring to discover and assert his personality, and for a whole society, which has an equal need to establish its collective identity" (101).

In this regard, I understand Jung to tell us that there is a basic, stable self and ego-consciousness that may encounter crises at critical developmental stages of personal or tribal life. These crises require the relinquishing of accepted archetypes in an earlier phase of development--for example, of the parental archetype as one moves toward autonomy, new responsibilities, and maturity. These crossroads require the resolution of the moral disjunctions created by guilt at the rejection of the familiar and the aspiration toward the development of the self in order to confront new responsibilities. These cardinal points--at which archetypal motifs from myths of initiation and myths of transcendence may appear in dreams-- include adolescence[4] as well as old age and death.[5] No external change, such as moving to a new place or taking on a new job, Henderson writes, "will serve unless there has been some inner transcendence of old values in creating, not just inventing, a new pattern of life" (151). The old patterns of integration won't work. And so, when Clemente takes a can filled with earth from the place that they are leaving in Guadalupe, "he knew he could not carry his attachment in the canful of simple, good earth. He was afraid of being separated from the rhythm of the heartbeat of the land" (7; Gerdes 242-43).

The heart of the new challenge facing Clemente and his family consists in the development of a new coherence.[6] The myths created across space and time reflect this rhythm of life, to death, to life in harmony with the rhythm of the pulse of nature. In his mythic vision, Clemente is drawn through the door of the magic rock--a symbol of continuity and synthesis, a talisman symbolic of and leading to a center--into a river whose source he seeks. This is a universal mythic symbol. Throughout the world, openings in the earth, such as caves or fountains, have been seen as sacred places because they are at the interstices of vertical and horizontal time and space. Here, reality along the vertical axis--the heavenly and the chthonian--meet with reality along the horizontal axis of present space and time. This is the centering point at which the transcendent past and future meet the contingent present. The Aztecs spoke of vertical reality in the complex of two words--a *difrasismo*: *in topan, in mictlan* (what is above, what is below); they referred to horizontal reality as *tlaltícpac* (*the here and now*) (León-Portilla 14). Clemente finds this center within himself.

His vision is a return to the collective unconscious in order to achieve transcendence. His visions of a volcano are a return to the vault, the womb of mother earth. The water swirling about him is a symbol of life and death in world myth, even as the waters that baptize the child of Roberto and Rita-- Clemente's son and daughter-in-law, for whom he and Adelita stand as godparents--symbolize death and life.[7]

Many other symbols in Clemente's journey can be seen as metaphors of his search for the crossroads and healing transcendence. Henderson speaks of animals such as snakes, birds, or fishes as universal symbols of transcendence, "denizens of the collective unconscious" which seem "to embody a kind of mediation between earth and heaven." The symbols of their healing power is reflected in the Aesculapian symbol of medicine, the non-poisonous snake on a cross (153, 155).

In this regard, Robert F. Gish, is understood to speak of "Anaya's novels as *kunstlerromans*, affirming the creative imagination, the poet as culture hero, and the novel itself as a magical instrument of healing . . . " (67). And although it may seem to be a rhapsodic exaggeration to speak of the novel and of the earth as healing, that is what Anaya is saying in leading us back to myth in his novels. Karl Kopp (63) calls attention to Anaya's essay, "The writer's Landscape," in which Anaya proposes that "just as the natural end of all art is to make us well and to cure our souls, so is our relationship to the earth and its power." Beyond the sense of well-being which we sense before the majesty of nature, he insists that "there is actual healing power which the epiphany of place provides" (101).

When Clemente leaves the land, he is not only concerned because of some Arcadian, romantic attachment to it, or only because he fears that the city will ruin the family (Rodríguez 4), but because "his soul and his heart were in the earth" ("la sagrada tierra"), and because "they would be like wandering gypsies without a homeland where they might anchor their spirit" (*Heart* 3-4). Anaya himself calls attention to a passage in *Heart* where he relates the healing process to the land ("Writers" 101). Shortly after moving into the city, Clemente's world begins to disintegrate. He has turned to alcohol, and after a climactic confrontation with his family in which he tries to reassert his control, he stumbles into his bedroom and falls into a drunken sleep. Adelita, his wife, turns to Juanita and Ana:

> "You see," she spoke earnestly to her daughters, "once there would have been the land to make him whole again. A man who met defeat could go out on the land, and the earth would make him well again. It might take weeks, or months, or years, but always the man who looked found himself in his earth and he was well again. . . . Well, things have changed, and your father, he is a man lost in a foreign land--" (78)

However, Clemente can no longer return to the land, anymore than urbanized Chicanos can. Clemente--as Anaya would have Chicanos do--will turn to the "truth in the heart," the collective unconscious, to find reintegration and transcendence. Once healed, he will soar like an eagle, representing the release of the spirit. He will become like the "flying man" of myth (*Heart* 84; Henderson 150), who "liberates the deeper psychic contents so that they can become part of our conscious equipment for understanding life more effectively. . . . But today we could as well speak of jet planes and space rockets" (Henderson 155-56). The symbol of the eagle is used by Crispín, the blind poet-singer who is Clemente's tutelary figure (Henderson 101-06) in his search for the heart of Aztlán.

Crispín is at a meeting of railroad workers trying to decide on a course of action and unsuccessfully looking for a leader after a failed wildcat strike. The men are divided in their proposed courses of action and Crispín is asked to play on his blue guitar to help bring them back together again. He speaks to them of the legend of Aztlán. Clemente asks what these stories have to do with the strike. (In much the same way that Anaya is asked what his writings have to do with political unrealities.) Crispín sings, and "in his song the winding trains were like the poisonous serpents . . . (84). He goes on to sing:

> "But oooh, there was a protector once before; a giant bird sent by the guardian Sun, a bird to mate the snake and steal its fear! So now we need a man who will rise like the eagle and melt the power of the steel snakes! The soul of the people is trapped in steel and the cry is for the man who will let them go!" (84)

In an inverse metaphor, we have a classic dualism, affirmate and negate, in balance; for the serpent comes forth from the earth whence springs life, and the eagle who can master the serpent comes from above.

After a meeting at which some of the men have tentatively looked to him for leadership, and he has refused to get involved in politics, he recalls that there were places on "the wide llano where he had once stood and felt the elation of flying! . . . Perhaps that is what Crispín meant when he said a man could fly like the guardian bird of the legend" (86). He also remembers an "old sheepherder they called *el hombre volador*," who had told him "that the dark secrets of the earth were only for those who were willing to search to the very core and essence of their being. . . . Then he remembered that the old man had said to make the trip a man should be without fear and that he needed a spiritual guide . . . " (86).

These passages, filled with explicit mythical symbolism, point to the outline of the rest of the novel. Clemente must make a classic mythical journey or quest, but not back to the land which had brought him a measure of personal and social integration, and where the sheepherder had found such inner harmony with the rhythms of life and death in nature that he could fly like an eagle. Clemente must now journey into his own heart to discover new archetypes that will bring him personal integration anew and integrate him with his people. This will make it possible for him to lead the people as a shepherd leads his flock--a reference to the shepherds of secular myth who became leaders of their people--paralleled by David and by Christ, the Good Shepherd of sacred scripture. Allusion is made once again to the need for assistance from the tutelary figure of Crispín.

With the help of Crispín, Clemente is going to break out of the ironic circle of negative repetitive human experience. If there is no way out, he is condemned to a flight into the non-life of alcohol, or he can tough it out with some kind of stoic macho *angst*. However, he does not break out with the help of the institutional church. The church, in the gross caricature of Father Cayo (who is as callous as his name) is aligned with powerful secular institutions--"the government, the banks, the military"--against the workers (143). The Church provides stability, Father Cayo tells him, so that wealth can exist. "We teach the poor how to bear their burden; they are promised the kingdom of heaven . . ." (142). But Clemente has already had another vision, another promise. He breaks out of the circle of ironic meaninglessness by turning to a secular revelation. He takes off in a literary lyric leap into the world of myth where almost anything is possible, where he can aspire toward the fullness of human potential and create meaning for himself and his people. He steps out of the microspace of everyday life into the macrospace of universal myth. This man who is in the process of disintegration, in contrast to the Apollonian stability of his son Jason--who received the story of the golden carp from an Indian in Anaya's first novel (*Ultima* 73)--undergoes a personal metamorphosis and begins to reintegrate himself at this crucial juncture of his life through a mission that unites him with the people whom he is to lead.

Ironically, Clemente, a nobody in an ordinary setting such as Barelas, a barrio in Albuquerque (Janowski; Anaya, "Barrio"), becomes a prophet (*Heart* 134, 186). To López this is outrageous. And she is right. But that is as it should be; prophets are outrageous. The entire situation and Clemente himself are paradoxes.[8] They go against the *doxa*, the opinion of the crowd. They rub us the wrong way, which they are supposed to do. With the help of Crispín, Clemente becomes an ecstatic: from "ex-stare" to stand or to be beside oneself--literally, to be "one who is out of it." The only reasonable reaction to Clemente is to say that he is out of his mind. For when the selfishness and egoism of the Hobbesian world have beaten our idealism to cynicism, for someone to come along and tell us that love is at the center of the whole "big bang," that love "is the holy sacrament of the new movement," this is outrageous (147). And this is what Clemente does when he looks into another dimension. To understand the design of this other literary dimension, we must look to Northrop Frye.

If Clemente's experience is functionally Jungian, in order to understand how Clemente's quest in *Heart* is what I have referred to as a paradigm of mythic structure and movement, we must refer to Frye's works, *Anatomy of Criticism* and *The Secular Scripture*, with which Anaya is familiar, but whose structure of literary types, he tell us he does not use as a map in developing his novels (Interviewed 20). The quest myth, according to Frye, is the one myth unifying what he calls "the four mythoi" of comedy, romance, tragedy, and irony "episodes in a total quest-myth" (*Anatomy* 192, 215).

To get at the structural elements of Western literature, Frye tells us, we should look to myth which "is the most abstract and conventionalized of all literary modes" (*Anatomy* 134). He illustrates his point with an example from art. The structural elements in a painting can be analogically expressed through geometrical shapes; however, the structural principles are not derived from the analogy of geometrical shapes, "but from the internal analogy of art itself. The structural principles of literature, similarly are to be derived from archetypal and anagogic criticism, the only kinds that assume a larger context of literature as a whole" (*Anatomy* 134). In a sense, myth is one of the frames of literature, "one extreme of literary design," with naturalism at the other, "and in between lies the whole area of romance, using that term to mean . . . to displace myth in a human direction and yet in contrast to 'realism,' to conventionalize content in an idealized direction" (*Anatomy* 136-37).

In *Heart* we find a structural cyclic movement of displaced myth. The frames of such movement, I understand Frye to tell us, are the two extremes of myth--the apocalyptic/affirmative (toward which Clemente moves) and the demonic/negative--which constitute the horizons of undisplaced myth, pure metaphor which is a universal, meta-temporal order where there is absence of process. The movement between these two frames is a dialectical movement. And between these horizons of myth is found the order of nature which is particular and temporal, the place of processional phenomena. Here, in this arena of displaced myth, movement is cyclic, the downside of the human cycle penetrating the lower horizon of demonic myth. Within this cyclic movement we have the world of realism, that Frye calls the analogy of experience which can move negatively to irony or satire. The upside of the cycle is the world of romance which he calls the analogy of innocence. Comic movement is from threatening complication to a happy ending. However, whereas in comedy, the escape solutions are social, the movement being toward reconciliation and integration in a social setting--accepting and reinforcing established society--in romance the individuals are allowed to move more freely toward independent resolutions of conflict. Romance can be "kidnapped," projected to reinforce the structures and values of a prevailing establishment. However, the real challenge of romance, its truly revolutionary character consists in its challenge to recreate a lost Eden, not to go back to a lost paradise--time being irreversible.

But before discussing the spiral movement in *Heart* toward apocalyptic myth, we must first point out correspondences of imagery. In *Heart*, this includes apocalyptic imagery proper to undisplaced myth as well as demonic imagery proper to the ironic mode of myth; and although it also includes romantic imagery, it abounds in the low mimetic imagery approaching irony associated with displaced myth. Frye, as we have seen, calls the low mimetic the analogy of experience "which bears a relation to the demonic world corresponding to the relation of the romantic world to the apocalyptic one."

Examples of the seven categories of low mimetic imagery identified by Frye, abound in *Heart*, centered about what he calls "the organizing low mimetic ideas [of] genesis and work" (Anatomy 154): (1) The *divine world* parallels the death and rebirth of the cycles of nature. Prometheus, in particular, according to Frye, is a favorite among writers of the industrial age (*Anatomy* 155). And at the end of *Heart*, Clemente longs for a new creation, the incarnation of a society which would be human, that is free, yet perfected in love with a right will, when he declares:

> "--The real fire from heaven is not the fire of violence it is the fire of love!" . . .

> "--We know that violence breeds violence, and that this fire the wayward god stole from heaven is the same fire that melts the steel and forges the chains that enslave us! What that god should have stolen for us mortal men is the pure fire that gushes from the soul of our people, from the foundations of our history-- Only that fire can burn down the temple of the false gods!" (207)

(2) Life in *human society* is common and typical, a parody of the idealized life and of the religious and esthetic experiences of romance. (3) The qualities of the *animal world* are reflected in people, as when El Super, an opportunistic, sycophantic Chicano businessman who is aligned with the establishment tells Jason that people are like dogs and then goes on to ridicule Clemente vision of brotherhood. Jason had come into El Super's store on

New Year's Eve to buy some hamburger, and El Super "tossed the package of meat at Jason . . . . " Jason does not take it home, but throws it to the dogs (187-88).⁹ (4) In the *vegetable world*, forms are the result of hard work. (5) The *mineral world* takes "the shape of the labyrinthine modern metropolis, where the main emotional stress is on loneliness and lack of communication" (*Anatomy* 155). (6) Water is destructive, reflected in *Heart* by Henry's drowning (110), about which we have spoken earlier. (7) Finally, *fire* is also destructive, as when the exasperated workers in *Heart* riot and set fire to the old boxcar that is the signalman's shack in the rail yards (150). "[T]he fire of violence" is, indeed, presented as the antipode of the Promethean "fire of love!" (207)

However, if "divine and spiritual beings have little functional place in low mimetic fiction" (*Anatomy* 154), *Heart* also contains other fundamental movements of narrative. It has beside the cyclic movement proper to the analogy of experience and the analogy of romance--reflecting the real world and the natural cycle of time and space, characterized by process and the particular--the dialectic movement between the apocalyptic and demonic order of myth: This is reflected in the contrasts between Crispín and the nameless witch, both of whom are introduced early in the novel. Both have magical powers. Crispín has the blue guitar and "magic in his fingers . . . for plants and for the strings." The old woman who lives "in one of the dark pockets of the barrio near the irrigation canal" has *la piedra mala* which, it is rumored, "contains magic" (13, 15).

But there is yet another movement in *Heart* beside the cyclic and the dialectic. There is the spiral movement from romance upward to affirmative apocalyptic myth, a point where both movements meet. "This ascent," says Frye, "is full of images of climbing, of flying, of mountains . . ." (*Secular* 151).

Even so, in his vision, Clemente seeks the source of the river to which the rock has led him. The wind answers that it is *"where the seven springs form the sacred lake! There by the desert of the white herons!"* (130)

These refer to the lost paradise of Aztlán, "Chicomostoc (seven caves)" (Leal, "Search" 19) which is also the place of the cranes or herons.

In *Heart* there are symbols of ascension and transcendence--climbing a mountain, the flying man; symbols of the search for the center, for the *axis mundi*:

> *And they traveled on, following new signs . . . moving towards the center. . . . and the mountain trails cut his feet until they bled, and still he moved forward, whispering the name Aztlán.*
>
> *High on a mountain. . . . Two forms rose from the lump of the earth. One was a man clad in shining scales and the other was a woman dressed in feathers. They mated, twisting together like snakes, forming the tree which Clemente climbed, and from which he soared like a giant bird. . . .*
>
> *It is the center, Crispín answered. . . . (130)*

In this complex of syncretic myth, Anaya (who is a reader of León-Portilla) creates an androgynous (Ometéotl-like) feathered serpent, Quetzalcóatl, who represents the attribute of the wisdom of the one god, Ometéotl--god of duality (León-Portilla 83-84, 111). Anaya considers "the Quetzalcóatl myth [as] the most basic one to the mythology of Meso-America," which is why he chose it for *Heart*. It weds the polarities of life and death, the serpent and the eagle.

> How do you wed the highest aspirations of man with the earth? How do you wed God and the snake? The eagle that represents the aspirations toward the sky-head--and the understanding of that kind of unity--with the unity that the earth itself gives you? Knowing that you are part of both, both polarities again. ("Myth" 81)

Frye states that this summit of the quest indicates that the movement is toward a point of self-recognition. The hero "finds and becomes his real self as it would have been if Adam had not fallen and man's original identity had been preserved.   This movement upward toward self-recognition is central to romance . . . (*Secular* 152).

It is the poet, symbolized by the blue guitar (*Heart* 27; "Myth" 81), who points out that if the potential for human negation is there, the potential for human affirmation is there too, specifically the potential for ultimate human affirmation in love.   Love is seen as of an individual, a self realized in a social setting.   The integration of the self and of society are then inextricably related in the great human romance.   It is the writer who challenges with this human prophecy of faith in human potential for creating meaning in an existential dialectic.   Hence Frye writes in his *Secular Scripture*: "The real hero becomes the poet, not the agent of force or cunning whom the poet may celebrate."   It is then that "the inherently revolutionary quality in romance begins to emerge" as our focus moves toward the faith inherent in the process of giving expression to the aspiration (178).

This is part of the response to the impatient questions about the relevance of myth to the harsh social realities in which might makes right and in which there seems to be no room for love.   Clemente integrates universal meaning through the contingencies of his particular Chicano experience--something which requires more development in the novel.   He then challenges the readers to integrate themselves in their social context, recreating a new society of human equality, while yet remaining faithful to reason and to love.   He challenges us to make Aztlán a reality.   This is the struggle of all humanity, hence universalism expressed through the particular Chicano experience.   However, there is an irony for Chicanos in attempting to recreate a lost paradise in the labyrinthine, alienated setting of the city.   The integration of individuality and selfhood includes relating to a historically hostile and culturally antithetical society.   Anaya is sensitive to these nuances of imagery.   For example, he has Clemente Chávez's family move from east to west, from Guadalupe to Albuquerque.   The movement between Barelas and Country Club is also east to west, which Anaya sees as the axis of European migration, basically Freudian and individually oriented, as opposed to the north-south axis of original Asiatic migration, symbolic of the search for the reconciliation of polarities represented by the eagle and the serpent, which is more Jungian and socially oriented. Both axes meet in us and in Aztlán, seeking reconciliation. Hence Anaya notes that much of Chicano literature "is talking about the reconciliation of the self within the community, within the communal self, which is exactly what Jung says. You rediscover who you are individually in your collective memory, not in your individual memory" ("Myth" 84).[10] Clemente's mythic quest-vision takes him in the four cardinal directions, but *"the signs pointed them back to the center, back to Aztlán"* (129-30).

I note further that Clemente finds integration in creation myth which, Frye tells us, comes from an older tradition, an order of nature in which "we are the creators," rather than "actors in a drama of divine creation and redemption." However he adds that "identity and self-recognition begin when we realize that this is not an either-or question, when the great twins of divine creation and human recreation have merged into one, and we can see that the same shape is upon both" (*Secular* 157, 112).

Before proceeding further with *Heart* as seen through Frye, I point out that it is beyond the scope of this study to make a complete structural analysis of the myth in *Heart* or to attempt to detail the superabundance of mythic imagery in the novel; however, a general outline is sketched. The structural movement in *Heart* proceeds from the downside of the analogy of experience and the world of realism with its attendant low mimetic imagery of the urban-industrial setting of Albuquerque, to the upward movement of the analogy of innocence, to the apocalyptic vision of Clemente. The imagery of the four seasons parallels this. The novel opens with the end of a springtime of primal closeness to the land and ends with the promise of a second spring. The romance of summer is paralleled by the tensions set up between Jason's growing attraction for Christina, whose father had been killed in an accident at the railroad yards, and the threat of their opposites--Sapo, the Chicano drug pusher, and Cindy, the Anglo from Country Club. She is attracted to Jason and tries to seduce him. Jason, however, gets away from Cindy by leaping over the cinder block fence and through the zoo that separates Barelas from Country Club to "the warm lights of the barrio" (61).

Autumn moves downward through the failure of a wildcat strike against the railroad with its steel trains which parody the feathered serpent. Clemente has his first contact with *la piedra mala* and wanders in symbolic circles through brush and thickets. All of these details--the zoo, cinder blocks, railroad, and wild brush--are, of course, typical low mimetic imagery that fills the novel. Fall ends with *ubi sunt* transitional reflections by Jason who recalls more innocent spring days in Guadalupe when "they raced to the church to have the priest hear their confessions" (94). He looks forward to the uncertainties of the future from the dissolution and isolation of the present. The Anglo cowboy stompers fight the Chicano Pachucos, and the vatos are drawn into the "raging river . . . the thundering torrent" of the clash (95). The deer, (in an Aztec/Pueblo syncretism) that symbolizes the sun (2) and the fifth sun which has yet to be reflected in a new myth (25), runs south fleeing from approaching winter.[11] Clemente's son Roberto and Roberto's wife, Rita, have their child baptized with the ritual water symbolizing life and death, "but the most meaningful part was when the baby was returned and he was baptized by the love of the people" (100). This birth is followed by the twin brother of death (107). Henry, the brother of Jason's friend, Willie, cries out like the Llorona to the "Loooooooo-nah!" (108) and follows the "*deer moon, sister of the sleeping sun*" (107) . . . into the "fish-thumping river" which pulls his body "south towards the sea (110). . . . towards the land of the sun, beyond succor, past the last blessing of las cruces, into the dissolution that lay beyond el paso de la muerte" (112; "Myth" 83-84). Henry's death is a symbolic sacrifice to the resurrection of the fifth sun and the creation of a new myth. Because of his condition, he can symbolize an innocent sacrificial lamb. And there are many other reflections of Christian symbolism here, indexes of Anaya's ongoing work of syncretism, a study of which remains to be done. Rufus, Henry's father, carries the coffin alone as Christ bore his cross, and the alabados are sung by Lazaro whose namesake in the gospel was raised from the dead by Christ (115).

We have arrived at a winter point where "the earth herself seems to forget her promise of life" (120). The stage is set for the beginning of Clemente's mythic quest vision. Clemente Chávez is drunk and collapses into the gutter. The snow that covers him is like another "veil covering the consciousness he wanted buried" (121). This is a classic mythic "break in consciousness" of a hero in a romance, mentioned by Frye (*Secular* 102). This may also be seen as a taking of the ritual wine required to initiate the "rite of passage in the Dionysiac ritual" oscillating between the forces of nature and the forces of the spirit (Henderson 135).

Clemente, like Christ bearing his cross, stumbles three times (122). But with the help of Crispín, who knows "his way through the jungle of brush, Clemente begins his journey to the heart of Aztlán with "la piedra mala" which he gets from "the old witch by the water," (125-26) who, it is said, brought it up from Mexico (49). Elsewhere, Anaya comments on this rock telling us that just as poets must reconcile myth with their realities, so too is the rock a symbol of the blending of polarities (God and earth, spirit and flesh), even as Quetzalcóatl is. These antipodes of spirit and matter must be reconciled. They are oppositions "which the poet, or the writer, has to reinfuse with life and mythology for the sake of mankind, for the sake of people" ("Myth" 81-82).[12] Jason, earlier in the novel, had objected to calling the rock *evil*: "It's not evil, it's only those who use it that are evil" (16). In *Heart* then, the rock becomes a door, and Clemente and Crispín begin their journey to the heart of Aztlán (129).[13]

At the end of the novel, Clemente's son Benji--who has become increasingly involved with drugs through Sapo, the drug pusher--falls from the water tower in the railroad yard. This water tower and the logo of the Santa Fe Railroad, which is a white cross on the water tank, are among the most ironic symbols in *Heart*, and a high point of its low-mimetic imagery. It is a human-industrial demonic tree of un-life nurturing machines, holding in unnatural suspension the life-death symbol of water contained in the irony of a circular tank displaying at once the symbol of the steel serpent and of the institutional church portrayed in the novel as holding the people in neo-colonial bondage. The cross points to a center. Raging with frustration at Benji's accident, Clemente tries to bring down the tower by pounding on it with a sledge hammer.

Some time after Clemente has recovered from the trauma of despair, he stops a threatened riot and declares a new Promethean fire in the highly stylized ending of the novel: "There is a heat more intense than the fire of the torch! Clemente cried cheerfully" (207). It is the fire of love. However, if the heart of Aztlán calls for the creation of a new paradise which essentially transcends moral evil, which is an option of on-going human choice, then Aztlán now can be only process. Hence the people cry out "Adelante!" and march forward led by Crispín strumming on his blue guitar (208-09).

I reflect that if Aztlán is accomplished in a state of perfect love, and God is love, then God is ultimate myth. Or, more precisely, myth is cosmic potency in God--Alpha and Omega. And the whole of cosmic evolution is the unfolding of this process, including people, in the sense in which Pierre Teilhard de Chardin expresses it through his opera (Chardin, *Heart* 199). In a more philosophical vein, we might conjecture on the relevance of the Werner Jaeger thesis commented on by León-Portilla (1, 9). Jaeger suggests that myth adumbrates philosophy, and that philosophy gradually makes explicit what is implicit in the religious imagery of myth. León-Portilla quotes Jaeger: "Authentic mythogony is still found at the core of the philosophy of Plato and in the Aristotelian concept of motion as the love of the world for the Unmoved Mover (xxi).

A final question imposes itself by way of corollary. Are the voices of myth, philosophy, theology, and science which speak to us about the reality of our experience, dispersed voices, or are they rather overlapping spheres in holistic confluence describing one epic quest between the two extremes of human knowledge identified by Parmenides and Heraclitus--stasis and dynamos seeking reconciliation? Or are these matters proper to mysticism and shamanic illumination? However, these philosophical and theological speculations are grist for another mill--without apologies to Javier Pacheco who remarked in his review of *Heart*: "[I]t will be interesting to hear the discussions popping up on the metaphysics of La Raza" (11).

In summary, I suggest that we should look at *Heart of Aztlán* from another point of view. Despite the criticisms leveled against the novel, it makes a contribution to our understanding of Chicano myth. This paper has focused on the function, structure, and movement of myth in *Heart*. The novel has served to distinguish between the uses of traditional myths and the need for the creation of myth in order to establish a basis for universalism in Chicano literature through the integration of our selfhood within our social realities. With Lévi-Strauss, the novel finds structure in the apparent chaos of experience. With the psychological school of Carl G. Jung, the novel calls for a return to the source and heart of myth in the collective unconscious in order to create a transcendent synthesis as we move through critical junctures of experience requiring a re-definition of our individual and collective selves. Finally, with Northrop Frye, the novel moves through a quest myth that escapes from romantic irony into the revolutionary dimension of myth. Rather than seek an irretrievable paradise lost, it challenges us to aspire to the creation of another ideal through the *terra incognita* of psycho-moral space and time. Throughout the novel, Anaya poses opposites and seeks the reconciliation of dichotomies. In other words, you can't make a one-sided tortilla, and anyway when all is said and done, it is still one tortilla. However, Anaya is ambiguous about reconciling the tensions between what Frye calls the secular scripture and the sacred scripture. It remains to be seen whether in the creation of myth, *la gente* will transcend the sacred scripture to some syncretic form of neo-Amerindian and/or secular humanism. Perhaps the *criollo* José Vasconcelos was right in that part of his theory of *La Raza Cósmica* that describes the mestizo as a person who cannot go back, but can only go forward, a person who points to the future. So I describe the Chicano as *una lucha viva. Y digo que nuestro destino es luchar para humanizar.*

NOTES

[1] In my opinion, the reviews by Bruce-Novoa and Karl Kopp are especially helpful in presenting different perceptions of *Heart of Aztlán*. Of all the works consulted, the most helpful in dealing with the novel were the interview with David Johnson and David Apodaca (Anaya, "Myth"); as well as the round table held at the University of California, Irvine, at which Alurista and Anaya were present along with María Herrera-Sobek, Alejandro Morales, and others (Anaya, "Mesa"). **Both of these works appear by way of appendix at the end of this volume**. The article by Antonio Márquez in *The Magic of Words* (Márquez, A.) should also be noted. Two especially useful bibliographic resources for identifying critical writings on the work of Anaya were those of Ernestina N. Eger (Eger) and the bibliography of María Teresa Huerta Márquez (Márquez, T.), **which has been adapted and also appears at the end of this volume**. María Teresa Huerta Márquez and I are preparing the following title for the Greenwood Press: RUDOLFO A. ANAYA A BioBibliography as a title in the Series Bio-Bibliographies in American Literature.

[2] Octavio Paz once made a passing remark about the demands sometimes made on writers that they be explicit and "involved" in their social commentary. He stated--in incidental remarks made to me and to some of my students after a presentation at San Diego State University, which we taped--that in his opinion a non-militant writer such as Juan Rulfo is more political than many of those people who go about shouting: "Viva México, hijos de la tiznada!"

[3] See the work in this volume María Herrera-Sobek: "Women as Metaphor in the Patriarchal Structure of *Heart of Aztlán*."

[4] See Tomás Rivera, " . . . y no se lo tragó la tierra." Also see my study, "Archetypes of Integration in Chicano Literature: Tomás Rivera's *Tierra*." Paper presented at the March 12-14, 1986, Symposium: *Cultural*

Expressions of Hispanics in the United States. Centre Interdisciplinaire de Recherches Nord-Americaines (CIRNA). Institute d'Anglais Charles V; Universite Paris III, Sorbonne Nouvelle; Paris, France. The paper is in the Tomás Rivera Archive at the University of California at Riverside. It is scheduled to appear in the Autumn 1989 issue of *Confluencia.*

[5] See Ron Arias, *Road to Tamazunchale.*

[6] This brings to mind Leal's statement quoted at the beginning of this paper that Chicanos must create a new synthesis ("Problem" 4). This is not meant to imply that Leal is endorsing a Jungian theory of myth.

[7] The waters of baptism in Christian rituals symbolize death to the old person and the rebirth of the new person. And in the Old Testament we have the pneumatic symbol of the spirit of God breathing on the waters of primeval chaos to bring forth life. Water is the instrument of death in the story of the flood, but the medium of life sustaining the ark of Noah. It is the way to life for the Israelites crossing the Red Sea, but brings death to the army of Pharoah. "The sea," Frye tells us, "is particularly the image of an unconscious which seems paradoxically to forget everything and yet potentially to remember everything" (*Secular* 148).

[8] And in *Tortuga* it is the ex-drug addict Benjie, as identified by Roberto Cantú, who is the chosen one to bear the blue guitar.

[9] See the study, in this collection, by Heiner Bus: "Individual Versus Collective Identity and the Idea of Leadership in Sherwood Anderson's *Marching Men* (1917) and Rudolfo A. Anaya's *Heart of Aztlán* (1976)." Bus sees Jason's gesture of throwing the raw meat to the dogs as an act of displacement at his irritation with his own weakness after his confrontation with El Super on New Year's Eve.

[10] Frye makes corroborative comment in this regard: "But, just as the literary critic finds Freud most suggestive for the theory of comedy, and Jung

for the theory of romance, so for the theory of tragedy one naturally looks to the psychology of the will to power, as expounded in Adler and Nietzsche" (Frye, *Anatomy* 214). Also see Heiner Bus's work in this collection: "Anaya makes [Clemente] face the logical consequences of his individual defeat and liberates him from 'the chains of isolation and loneliness' (*Heart* 68) and from mainstream concepts through identification with the collective experience, both ethnic and regional. To put it differently, while Anderson largely confines himself to Freudian categories, Anaya also applies the complementary findings of C. G. Jung."

[11] In his review of *Heart*, Bruce-Novoa states that "the narration needs more text, or a return to the dense, super-signifying power of *Ultima*. The same lack of space severely limits our appreciation of Clemente's mysterious pilgrimage and the brief references to the myth of the Sun-deer" (62). I asked Anaya to elaborate on this myth in an interview March 31, 1985, subsequently published in Imagine 2.2 (Winter 1985), which appears as an appendix to this book. Anaya's speaks of his views of the writer as shaman as well as of the roles of nagual and dream.

This response also has some relevance to my interest in Anaya's and Alurista's views concerning the matter of the creation of myth. Alurista has at least twice insisted to me that no single person sits down and writes a myth: Once, in San Diego, on Sunday, October 27, 1985, as a member of a panel discussion forum, "The Concept of Aztlán"--part of the *Made in Aztlán*, Fifteenth Anniversay Celebration of the Centro Cultural de la Raza. (The other panelists were Juan Felipe Herrera, Tomás Ybarra-Frausto, and Túpac Enrique). Alurista made a similar comment in the public discussion that followed his presentation on March 14, 1986, at the conference, *The Cultural Expression of Hispanics in the United States*, in Paris, France.

[12] Lévi-Strauss notes the central role of the mediation of opposites in myth: "We need only assume that two opposite terms with no intermediary always tend to be replaced by two equivalent terms which admit of a third one as mediator; then one of the polar terms and the mediator become replaced by a new triad, and so on" (224). See also Enrique Lamadrid: "Myth as the

Cognitive Process of Popular Culture in Rudolfo Anaya's *Bless Me, Ultima*: The Dialectics of Knowledge." *Hispañia* 68.3 (Sept. 1985): 496-501.

[13] The beating of the heart can be interpreted in a Jungian sense of the role of will--responsible choice--in the development of selfhood. It may also be seen in the Nahuatl sense of the role of will in developing a face or personality. "The face," writes León-Portilla, "reflected the internal physiognomy of man, and the beating of the heart symbolized the source of dynamism in human will" (115).

WORKS CITED

Anaya, Rudolfo A. "Barrio Life in Albuquerque." *Albuquerque Journal*, 13 Feb. 1977.

___. *Bless Me, Ultima.* Berkeley: Quinto Sol, 1972.

___. *Heart of Aztlán.* Berkeley: Justa, 1976.

___. Interviewed by César A. González-T. San Diego, CA, 31 March 1985. Publication pending in *Imagine: International Chicano Poetry Journal.* 2.2 (Winter 1985). Eds. Tino Villanueva and Luis Alberto Urrea. [**Reprinted as an appendix in this volume.**]

___. "Myth and the Writer: A Conversation with Rudolfo Anaya." Interviewed by David Johnson and David Apodaca. *New America* 3.3 (Spring 1979), 76-85. [**Reprinted as an appendix in this volume.**]

___."The Writer's Landscape: Epiphany in Landscape." *Latin American Literary Review* 5.10 (Spring-Summer 1977), 98-102.

Brito, Aristeo, Jr. "Paraíso, Caída y Regeneración en Tres Novelas Chicanas." Diss. University of Arizona, 1978.

Bruce-Novoa, Juan. Review of *Heart of Aztlán. La Confluencia* 1.3-4 (July 1977), 61-62.

Cárdenas de Dwyer, C. "Myth and Folk Culture in Contemporary Chicano Literature." *La Luz* 3.9 (Dec. 1974), 28-29.

Carpenter, Lorene Hyde. "Maps for the Journey: Shamanic Patterns in Anaya, Asturias, and Castaneda." Diss. U. of Colorado at Boulder, 1981.

Carrasco, David. *Quetzalcóatl and the Irony of Empire: Myths and Prophecies in the Aztec Tradition.* Chicago: U of Chicago P, 1982.

Carrillo, Loretta. "The Search for Selfhood and Order in Contemporary Chicano Fiction." Diss. Michigan State University, 1979.

Chardin, Pierre Teilhard de. *The Heart of Matter.* Trans. Rene Hague. New York: Harcourt, 1978.

Eger, Ernestina. *A Bibliography of Criticism of Contemporary Chicano Literature.* Berkeley: Chicano Studies Library, U of California P, 1981.

Elizondo, Sergio. "Myth and Reality in Chicano Literature." *Latin American Literary Review* 5.10 (Spring-Summer 1977), 23-31.

Frye, Northrop. *Anatomy of Criticism: Four Essays.* Princeton: Princeton UP, 1957.

___. *The Secular Scripture: A Study of the Structure of Romance.* Cambridge: Harvard UP, 1976.

Gerdes, Dick. "Cultural Values in Three Novels of New Mexico." *The Bilingual Review* 7.3 (Sept.-Dec. 1980), 239-48.

Gish, Robert F. "Curanderismo and Witchery in the Fiction of Rudolfo A. Anaya: The Novel as Magic." *New Mexico Humanities Review* 2.2 (Summer 1979), 5-13. (Abstract in *Explorations in Ethnic Studies* 1.2 (July 1978), 67.)

Haddox, John. "Heart of Aztlán." *El Paso Times*, "Sundial," 15 May 1977, 20.

Henderson, Joseph L. "Ancient Myths and Modern Man." Carl G. Jung, et al, eds. *Man and His Symbols.* New York: Dell, 1964. 95-166.

Jaeger, Werner. *Paideia: The Ideals of Greek Culture.* 2nd ed. Trans. Gilbert Highet. 3 vols. New York: Oxford UP, 1945.

Janowski, Jack. "New Novel Vividly Shows Albuquerque Barrio Life." *Albuquerque Journal*, 27 Feb. 1977.

Jung, Carl G. *The Archetypes and the Collective Unconscious.* 2nd ed. Trans. R. F. C. Hull (Bollingen Series 20). Princeton: Princeton UP, 1969.

___. and C. Kerenyi. *Essays on a Science of Mythology: The Myth of the Divine Child and the Mysteries of Eleusius.* Trans. R. F. C. Hull (Bollingen Series 22). Princeton: Princeton UP, 1969.

Kopp, Karl. Review of *Heart of Aztlán. La Confluencia* 1.3-4 (July 1977), 62-63.

Lattin, Vernon E. "The Quest for Mythic Vision in Contemporary Native American and Chicano Fiction." *American Literature* 50.4 (Jan. 1979), 625-40.

Leal, Luis. "In Search of Aztlán." Trans. Gladys Leal. *Denver Quarterly* 16.3 (Fall 1981), 16-27.

___. "The Problem of Identifying Chicano Literature." *The Identification and Analysis of Chicano Literature.* Ed. Francisco Jiménez. New York: Bilingual, 1979. 2-6.

León-Portilla, Miguel. *Aztec Thought and Culture: A Study of the Ancient Nahuatl Mind.* Trans. Jack Emory Davis. Norman: U of Oklahoma P, 1963.

Lévi-Strauss, C. *Structural Anthropology.* New York: Basic Books, 1963.

Lomelí, Francisco A., and Donald W. Urioste. Review of *Heart of Aztlán.* *De Colores* 3.4 (1977), 81.

López Hoffman, María. "Myth and Reality in *Heart of Aztlán.*" *De Colores* 5.1-2 (1980), 111-14.

Márquez, Antonio. "The Achievement of Rudolfo A. Anaya." *The Magic of Words: Rudolfo A. Anaya and His Writings.* Ed. Paul Vassallo. Albuquerque: U of New Mexico P, 1982. 33-52.

Márquez [Huerta], [María] Teresa. "Works by and about Rudolfo A. Anaya." *The Magic of Words: Rudolfo A. Anaya and His Writings.* Ed. Paul Vassallo. Albuquerque: U of New Mexico P, 1982. 55-81.

"Mesa redonda con Alurista, R. Anaya, M. Herrera-Sobek, A. Morales H. Viramontes." *Maize* 4.3-4 (Spring-Summer 1981), 6-23. [**Reprinted as an appendix in this volume.**]

Nava, Gregory. "Bridging the Gap between Myth and Reality." Interviewed by Francisco X. Alarcón, Juan Felipe Herrera, and Victor L. Martínez. *Revista Literaria de El Tecolote* 5.1 (junio 1984), 3, 12.

Pacheco, Javier. Review of *Heart of Aztlán. Rayas* 1 (Jan.-Feb. 1978), 10-11.

Rodríguez, Juan. Comments on *Heart of Aztlán. Carta Abierta*, 7 (Feb. 1977), 3-4.

Rogers, Jane. Review of *Heart of Aztlán. Latin American Literary Review* 5.10 (Spring-Summer 1977), 143-45.

Schell, Jonathan. *The Fate of the Earth.* New York: Avon, 1982.

Wilson, Carter. "'Magical Strength in the Human Heart': --The Framing of Mortal Confusion in Rudolfo A. Anaya's *Bless Me, Ultima*--." *Ploughshares* 4.3 (1978), 190-97.

Women as Metaphor in the Patriarchal
Structure of *Heart of Aztlán*

María Herrera-Sobek
The University of California at Irvine

> The most fundamental values in a culture
> will be coherent with the metaphorical
> structure of the most fundamental concepts
> in the culture. (Lakoff and Johnson, 1980:6).

> Metaphor is a device for seeing something
> in terms of something else. . . . A metaphor
> tells us something about one character
> considered from the point of view of another
> character. And to consider A from the point
> of view of B is, of course, to use B as a
> *perspective* upon A." (Kenneth Burke, 1945:
> 503-04).

Rudolfo A. Anaya's novel *Heart of Aztlán* (1976) depicts the vicissitudes of a Chicano family who has been uprooted from its traditional way of life and environment by the forces of an ever-encroaching Anglo society and its capitalist mode of existence.[1]   The work falls within the purview of the social protest genre category but follows the Anaya tradition of simultaneously interlacing and weaving myth and harsh reality in his novelistic tapestry. However, in spite of the interweavings of myth in *Heart of Aztlán*, the novel does not achieve the sensibility, vigor, and majesty of his masterwork *Bless Me, Ultima* (1972).   I believe this is due in part to the structuring of the female characters as metaphoric entities signifying various aspects of a patriarchal system in disarray, rather then flesh and bone, full-bloodied personages. In this study, I analyze the representation of women in Anaya's *Heart of Aztlán* and posit that the construction of the female characters in the novel's universe is that of metaphoric entitites representing the loss of Chicano (male) power in the Anglo capitalist system depicted in the novel. That is to say, the women in *Heart of Aztlán* are not free agents *per se*, but serve the larger interests of the structure of the novel which is to present the plight of the dispossessed, disenfranchised, and marginalized Chicano population. I further affirm that although this specific metaphoric function assigned to the female existents works to perfection in conveying the *primary message*, it, nevertheless, weakens the novel's overall impact and impedes the realization of its full potential.

The novel exhibits a definite patriarchal structure whose framework can be schemetically represented in terms of the following diagram:

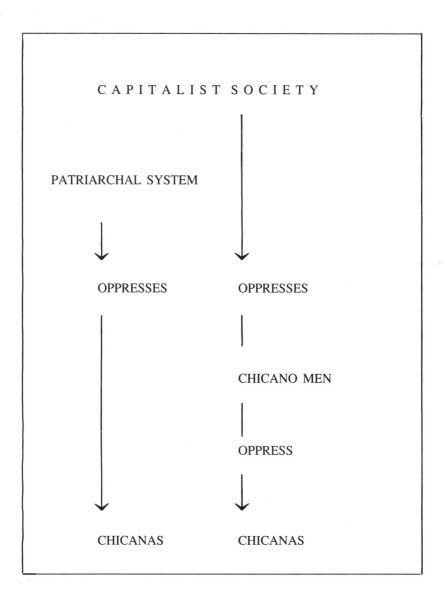

Here the overriding capitalist mode of production economically exploits and oppresses both Mexican American men and women. Simultaneously, and perhaps unconsciously, the New Mexican author depicts the oppression of women through the novel's delineation of the patriarchal system extant in Mexican American society as well as most other cultures in the world today.[2]

Anaya's exposé of the Anglo-capitalist system's corrosive effects on Mexican American traditions, lifestyles, and survival are clearly presented in the basic coordinates of the novel's plot: Clemente, the "patriarch" of the family, has been forced to sell his land and is moving his family to a barrio enclave in the city (Albuquerque). In the hostile environment of the city, Clemente is buffeted by the loss of his job and self-esteem, followed by immersion into alcoholic binges, with the consequent loss of paternal rule over his daughters, sons, and wife.[3] The disintegration of the Clemente Chávez family is nearly complete toward the end of the novel. Two events help unite the family again: Clemente's emergence as the leader of his people through his magical journey into the heart of the "piedra mala," and Benjie's unfortunate near fatal fall which leaves him crippled for life.[4]

The presentation in *Heart of Aztlán* of an exploitative, capitalist Anglo world is clearly conceptualized by the author. However, there is a certain ambiguity with respect to the representation of the female characters vis-a-vis their oppression and exploitation. On the one hand the negative *machismo* of most of the characters in the novel is so transparent that the reader might easily suppose that Anaya intends a double exposé.[5] This initial hypothesis is quickly canceled, however, by the pervasiveness of the oppression of women at all levels of society in Anaya's constructed literary universe and the patriarchal ideology implicitly expressed throughout the narrative. I contend that it is precisely this specific blind spot regarding the subordinate status of women in the fictionalized patriarchal society created by the author which backfires and makes the novel falter and prevents it from achieveing its obvious potential as an outstanding literary work.[6] There are a few flashes of insight in the novel regarding the inequality of women (i.e., the *Las*

Golondrinas or *putas* scene and Anaya's realization of the *pachucos'* double standard toward women), but on the whole the message conveyed seems to be that of a return to the traditional patriarchal structure with the male as head of the family and the women and children subordinated to him.

In Anaya's *Heart of Aztlán*, we can categorize the female characters as serving the function of structural metaphors. We define structural metaphors as those constructions in which "one concept is metaphorically structured in terms of another." (see Lakoff and Johnson, 1980:6). Thus a primary theme in *Heart of Aztlán* is the loss of manhood. The theme is structured in terms of a capitalist, uncaring society which strips away the possibilities for the male Chicano "head of the family" to be the mainstay of his family, as ideology and cultural expectations in all patriarchal societies dictate. The manhood theme becomes deformed and degenerates into the cynical and exploitative desires of adolescents to be "real men." Jason's teenage gang and their continual attempts to prove their manhood at the expense of women in general form a significant part of the subplot of the novel.

Women, therefore, serve as metaphors for the Chicanos' loss of economic and political power and will be transformed into signifiers which will encompass, within this metaphoric signifying function, the possibility of the men's recapturing their perceived loss of power, through the symbolic sexual act of "possessing" them. Ironically there is no discrimination when it comes to the sexual exploitation of women by these young Chicanos: they seek sexually to possess *gabachas,* old *putas*, Chicana virgins, and young Asian women. The pervasive desire of Jason's (Clemente's upright teenage son) gang to "have a piece" and to perceive women in general terms of sexual objects transforms the female characters in the novel into structural metaphors which effectively underscore the Chicano loss of power in the economic and political sectors of Anglo dominated society.

Sexual prowess, identified in a patriarchal system as a positive attribute, is the only "power" left to these adolescent Lotharios. The young male characters, therefore, will focus their full energies searching for sexual conquests.[7]   It is indeed significant that sexual conquest is referred to metaphorically as "scoring."   Benjie, Clemente's youngest son, for example, is described at the inception of the narrative as having "taken Consuelo beneath the bridge and scored his first piece" (l) at the tender age of fourteen. In the competitive game of "acquiring" women, in terms of sexually possessing them, males keep "score."   The male with the greatest number of sexual encounters with women then supposedly is victorious in this patriarchal game of sex.   Furthermore, there is evident pride in the "cuates" being "the lovers of the barrio" and keeping "the Country Club girls happy . . . " (44). Sex, the signifier of political and economic power is also perceived as signifying racial superiority in this sphere.   The above quotes connote sexual prowess at the level of racial competition for women between Anglos and Chicanos; it implicitly assumes that Anglo male youths cannot keep "their girls" sexually satisfied.   The Chicano, on the other hand, according to the teenage braggadocio extant in the narrative, is portrayed as a sexual powerhouse.[8]   The theme is important because it demonstrates how women are used as pawns in this deadly game of upsmanship between males.   Thus the loss of power in one sphere--i.e., economic and political--requires compensation in another, in this case through sexual activity, with the consequent use and abuse of women.

The theme of sexual power on the part of teenage Chicanos is reiterated several times. For example in chapter five we have a delirious Pato gurggling happily over being invited to Cindy's party--Cindy is a wealthy teenage Anglo girl in the novel--and ecstatically planning to "drink her old man's booze and screw all the gabachitas from the Country Club!" (55) Cindy, the blonde "gabacha" cheerleader, epitomizes the ultimate sexual "catch" for Chicanos: "Cindy's the blonde we saw at Tingley Beach Saturday, remember?   She's the one all the vatos were trying to score with" (55). Furthermore the narrative will portray this highly prized "number one cheerleader at la Washa" (55) as having "the hots" for Jason.

The youths are constantly "on the make" searching for sexual gratification and make a point of demeaning women throughout. This type of behavior, however, is not deemed suitable for the women they intend to marry.

The double standard applied to the sexual mores of women is clearly enunciated in the pronouncements articulated at different points in the novel: "My old man says, keep the women home and keep them busy with children, and they're happy" (47). This, after Dickie had parroted: "I expect the girl I marry to be a virgin!" And Pete agreed: "It's all right for the man to screw around, but not the woman. That's the way it's always been!" (46) The portrayal of this type of adolescent behavior in *Heart of Aztlán* is of course a parody and a caricature of traditional Mexican American family values and family life. However, the sexual mores projected by the youthful braggarts have been and, to a degree, still are those of the community toward women.

The depiction of the prostitute scene indicates Anaya's sensitivity to and awareness of these issues: specifically, how the loss of political and economic power on the part of Chicanos is linked to the sexual degradation of both Chicanos and their Mexican American sisters:

> "¡Yo soy hombre!" "We are men!" "Golondrinas! You are going to feel a man like you never have before!"
> They boasted and drank the wine that fanned the fire in their loins, and they shouted and slapped each other on the back to work up their resolution so that they would not feel the empty, gnawing fear in their stomachs.

The young men continue their debauchary at the expense of their Chicana sisters:

> They fell upon the whores, and realized that in the conquest of their ruined sisters they could find themselves. . . . "¡Yo soy hombre!" They boasted, and having proved their manhood they slid off sweating thighs.
> Las Golondrinas sung lullabies for their conquerors, but the new men turned away and felt a sickness gnaw within. The wine was gone. Only the emptiness remained. (54)

In spite of the narrator's realization of the emptiness of such sexual acts, the chapter ends with a reaffirmation that this is a *rite de passage* for boys. "In the silence of the night the bottles crashed against gnarled cottonwood trees which, like old grandfathers, shuddered at the painful growth of boys, the boys of summer who wound their way towards winter gray" (54). Implicitly delineated is the age-old patriarchal assumption that prostitutes fulfill the function of initiating young males into sexual adulthood.[9]

The diminishing power of Chicano males is also metaphorically expressed in terms of the loss of power of the *pater familias* vis-a-vis his wife and daughters. Again the women in *Heart of Aztlán* serve as structural metaphors for the decreasing power of the head of the family--Clemente. For example at the novel's inception Adelita, Clemente's wife, is portrayed as a paragon of loyalty, devotion, and obedience; she is the stereotypical, unidimensional Chicano wife so often portrayed in Mexican American literary works.[10] Clemente's daughters Juanita and Ana are likewise obedient and submissive to their father's authority. However, as the action progresses the daughters, in particular, begin to pull away from their father's rule. Ana, the younger daughter, drops out of school and becomes a pachuca "moving away from the familia," as the narrator puts it, "to a wider identification with the pachuco movement of the barrio" (63).

Clemente's *pater familias* status is definitely challenged in the drunken scene described on pages 73-75: "And where is my family?" he cried out. "Is the man of the house to eat alone! Like a dog! I want my family around me when I eat!" (73)

He becomes acutely aware of his loss of power and blames his wife for this turn of events:

> "You!" He cried angrily, "You cannot give them permission! Since when does the woman play the man's part!" . . . He saw her plotting with the other forces that were vent on destroying his position as head of the family. . . . She would ruin his family if he didn't put a stop to her meddling and reaffirm his rightful place, and so he

hounded his daughters out of their bedroom and into the kitchen. . . . "¡Ay! ¡Vívora [sic]!" He lashed out [at his wife], "You encourage your children not to obey their father! Since we came to this cursed city you have plotted to separate me from my family, and now you do it openly!" (74-75)

An explicit reason for the father's irrational behavior is that his drunkeness is caused by his loss of economic power in Anglo society. However the implied message is that under normal conditions the "ruler" of the household is the male and when his authority is usurped complete disintegration of the household occurs. It is evident in the narrative that there is a yearning for the traditional way of life, which means a return to the belief that women should be under the leadership of the "strong" father.

Other characters in the novel reiterate approval of a patriarchal system. Manuel's analogy between a strong father and a strong pueblo's leader makes this point very clear: "[T]he familia without a strong father soon falls apart, and . . . a   pueblo without a good leader is not united in its efforts to serve the people, and a country without a good, strong man to guide it is soon overrun by its enemies" (83).

Even female mythic figures serve as metaphoric constructs in the delineation of a Mexican American patriarchal structure in disarray. The mythical figures of "La Llorona" and "La Bruja" are incarnations of evil and destruction in *Heart of Aztlán*. José Limón has done a penetrating analysis of the Llorona figure and perceives this mythical figure in the following historical and social light:

> [M]y analysis will propose La Llorona as the third, comparatively unacknowledged, major female symbol of Greater Mexico social-cultural life. If articulated with this history and not merely with local contexts, she may be understood at two levels: first, as a positive, contestative symbol for the women of Greater Mexico and second as a critical symbolic reproduction of a socially unfulfilled Utopian

longing within the Mexican folk masses who tell her story. She speaks to the social and psychological needs of both Greater Mexican sectors, needs left unmet by the hegemonic, hierarchical, masculinized, and increasingly captitalistic social order imposed on the Mexican folk masses since their beginning. (1986:59-60)

The basic kernel of the Llorona legend is that of a betrayed woman who kills her children in a fit of revenge and who wanders across the earth (principally near bodies of water) wailing and searching for her lost progeny as punishment for her deed.[11] Whereas Limón, the anthropologist, presents the Llorona legend as a subversive narrative articulating the needs of the betrayed Mexican and Mexican American masses, Anaya's depiction of this shadowy, phantasmagoric figure is constructed into a negative figure; she is outlined in the novel as an instrument appropriated by the Anglo capitalist system to oppress and murder Chicanos. The female figure of La Llorona in the literary space of *Heart of Aztlán* through its association with the police sirens menacing the barrio becomes a symbol of death, destruction, and oppression in the Mexican American neighborhood.

> "Los vatos locos, the real crazy vatos on the street say there's only one Llorona now," Dickie added, "and that's the siren of a cop's car. That mother friggin' ley comes blaring down the street, busting heads, throwing the vatos in the can, and they rot there, they die there--"
> "Maybe so," Willie said, "It's funny how things aren't like they used to be. It used to be la Llorona was a ghost, a shadow, a cry one heard in the brush of the river or near la 'cequia. Now its becoming more and more real, now it's the cop's siren, now we can see it, we actually see it eating up the men of the barrio--"
> "The men of the shops call the whistle la Llorona," Pete added. (49)

The institutions oppressing Mexican Americans are associated with the menacing figure of La Llorona, i.e., the police and the dehumanizing industrial factory. Both are perceived as "destroying" the Chicano population. The contrast between the Llorona of old, "a story, a shadow," and the modern day Llorona is underscored in this scene (49). The old mythic figure was harmless, but the Anglicized version is deadly both to the spirit (the factory) and to the body (the police). As in the case of La Malinche--the Indian woman who accompanied Hernán Cortez in the conquest of Mexico and who became the symbol of treachery and whoredom--a feminine mythic figure is once again cast as a villian in literature.

The patriarchal structure of *Heart of Aztlán* is delineated in the figure of the witch, "La Bruja," represented stereotypically as the dark, evil "hag" living at the outskirts of the barrio. She is the keeper of "La piedra mala," the magic rock which holds the secrets of economic and sexual salvation for a price--a man's soul.

The perceptive chapter on European witchburning in Mary Daly's searing feminist study *Gyn/Ecology: The Metaethics of Radical Feminism* (1978) asserts that the label of "witch" was targeted at those self-sufficient women who disdained patriarchal control and authority:

> For the targets of attack in the witch craze were not women defined by assimilation into the patriarchal family. Rather, the witch craze focused predominantly upon women who had rejected marriage (spinsters) and women who had survived it (widows). The witch-hunters sought to purify their society (The Mystical Body) of these "indigestible" elements--women whose physical, intellectual, economic, moral, and spiritual independence and activity profoundly threatened the male monopoly in every sphere (184).[12]

The witch in *Heart of Aztlán* is conceptualized in exaggerated stereo-typical terms. Clemente's first experience with her is described as follows:

> A bony hand touched his shoulder and he turned and saw the cloaked figure of the old woman who kept the magic rock. She hissed and the dogs backed away, then whimpering they disappeared into the

shadows. She turned and beckoned, and he followed her into her mud hut.

A sputtering candle made the shadows dance on the walls. An acrid, sulfurous smell filled the room. The shelves of the walls were filled with rotting carcasses of animals; roots and herbs hung in disarray around the room. A small fire glowed in the woodburning stove where a foul-smelling concoction simmered. The hunchbacked old woman stood in front of the candle and removed her heavy cloak. Clemente gasped as he looked into her face. It was old and shriveled, and seeing her thus sent a shiver through him. (87-88)

The witch in Anaya's novel can be construed as a metaphor for the patriarchally constructed negative feminine principle who guards the secrets of life and death. She is analogous to the patriarchal conceptualization of Mother Earth or the Aztec goddess Coatlicue who is perceived as the producer of life sustaining nourishment and at the same time as she who has all living things return to "her womb"--the grave.[13]

However, although "La Bruja" guards the secret of ultimate salvation which Clemente seeks, she is conceptualized in terms of evil, desirous of leading a man to his physical as well as to his spiritual death. We see, moreover, how the witch reinforces the patriarchal structure of *Heart of Aztlán* in the juxtaposition of the figure of La Bruja with that of Crispín. Both characters possess "magic." But whereas the female existent is associated with evil ("La piedra mala"), Crispín, the bard and oral historian of the pueblo, is the repository of the "blue guitar" whose melody and magic brings life and hope to men. Both the "piedra mala" and "blue guitar" trace their ancient origins to a mythical space and time. The magical blue guitar, however, retains its positive aura and is a beneficial force weilded by Crispín to help his people, whereas the "piedra mala" loses its benevolent power and is depicted as having passed from the "positive" male (priests') domain to the implicitly negative female (the witch's) sphere:

The god's tail was made of fire, but when he walked on earth the fire cooled and turned into rocks with strange magical powers. The rocks contain the melody of the universe within them, and they could speak and cure people . . . but when the plumed god was cast out the rocks lost their power of good, and they became las piedras malas del mundo, stones with evil properties which men extract to do their bidding--" (125)

Ironically it is the "evil" witch which serves as midwife and mediator for Clemente's rebirth into a new man possessing leadership and knowledge. Unconsciously stated perhaps is the belief that it is only through the integration of the masculine and the feminine principle (i.e., the raging waters of the river of knowledge) that man can achieve his full potential. If Anaya meant to convey this message, his continual depiction of the witch in pejorative, denigrating terms weakens the full impact of the message which becomes lost in stereotypical representations.

In an otherwise favorable review of *Heart of Aztlán* written by Jane Rogers (1977), the critic points out a lack of "some of the charm of *Bless Me, Ultima.* Jason and Clemente do not evoke the reader's affection as readily as do Antonio and Ultima, who are developed from Antonio's youthful and naive perspective" (145). I propose that the initial strategy of incorporating women in the novel as structural metaphors to convey the oppression of Chicanos served well at that level. However, at a deeper level it weakened the novel by depriving it of full-blooded female existents.

If Chicano literature is to continue developing and evolving into a world-class body of literature, authors must pay careful attention to the structuring of all its woman characters. In the past, some Chicano works have neglected this important aspect and, consequently, suffered. The quest for equality in "real life" means an equally important quest for equality in those wonderfully created "fictional" worlds.

NOTES

[1] Rudolfo A. Anaya, *Heart of Aztlán* (Berkeley: Editorial Justa Publications, 1976). All quotes cited will be taken from this edition. Other major novels by Anaya include his most successful work, *Bless Me, Ultima* (Berkeley: Quito Sol Publications, 1972), and *Tortuga* (Berkeley: Editorial Justa Publications, 1979). For a bibliography on works on and about Anaya see María Teresa Huerta Márquez's updated bibliography included in this volume. Also see the forthcoming publication by the Greenwood Press: *Rudolfo A. Anaya A Bio-Bibliography* as a title in the Series Bio-Bibliographies in American Literture. María Teresa Huerta Márquez, and César A. González-T., editors.

[2] Two classic studies dealing with the status of women in a patriarchal society are Frederick Engels, *The Origin of the Family, Private Property, and the State* (New York: Pathfinder Press, 1976), first published in 1884; and Simone de Beauvoir, *The Second Sex* (New York: Random House, 1974) first published in 1949. More recent studies which treat the relationship of women and patriarchal systems include: Rosalind Coward, *Patriarchal Precedents: Sexuality and Social Relations* (London: Routledge & Kegan Paul, 1983; Peggy Reeves Sanday, *Female Power and Male Dominance: On the Origins of Sexual Inequality* (Cambridge: Cambridge University Press, 1981); Annete Kuhn and Ann Marie Wolpe, editors, *Feminism and Materialism: Women and Modes of Production* (London: Routledge and Kegan Paul, 1978); Zillah R. Eisenstein, ed., *Capitalist Patriarchy and the Case for Socialist Feminism* (New York: Monthly Review Press, 1979); Gerda Lerner, *The Creation of Patriarchy* (New York: Oxford University Press, 1986); and Nancy Chodorow, *The Reproduction of Mothering: Psychoanalysis and the Sociology of Gender* (Berkeley: University of California Press, 1978).

[3] The theme of Chicano family disintegration has been frequently incorporated in early Chicano novels. See for example José Antonio Villarreal,

Pocho (New York: 1959); Richard Vásquez, *Chicano* (New York: 1970); and Alejandro Morales, *Caras viejas y vino nuevo* (México: Joaquín Mortiz, 1975).

[4] Clemente's journey into self-knowledge adheres perfectly to Joseph Campbell's adventure of the hero monomyth as delineated in his seminal study *The Hero with a Thousand Faces* (Princeton: Princeton University Press, 1973). Campbell writes: "The standard path of the mythical adventure of the hero is a magnification of the formula represented in the rites of passage: *separation-initiation-return*: which might be named the nuclear unit of the monomyth." Campbell summerizes the kernel of the monomyth: "*A hero ventures forth from the world of common day into a region of supernatural wonder: fabulous forces are there encountered and a decisive victory is won: the hero comes back from this mysterious adventure with the power to bestow boons on his fellow man.* (p. 30). The meeting with the witch in *Heart of Aztlán*, corresponds with "The Meeting with the Goddess" in the trajectory of the hero monomyth (see Campbell, pp. 109-20).

[5] The term *machismo* should be employed with extreme caution given its indiscriminate use by contemporary news media. I view negative *machismo* as that complex of male characteristics associated with the term in the last two decades, i.e., exaggerated male virility, intransigence with women, etc. Chicano revisionist historians and sociologists are questioning previous assumptions regarding the term. See Ronald E. Cromwell and René A. Ruiz, "The Myth of Macho Dominance in Decision Making within Mexican and Chicano Families," *Hispanic Journal of Behavioral Sciences*, 1(December, 1979), 344-73; Alfredo Mirandé, *The Chicano Experience: An Alternative Perspective* (Notre Dame: University of Notre Dame Press, 1985); Miguel Montiel, "The Social Science Myth of the Mexican American Family," *El Grito* 3(1970), 56-63; and the excellent studies undertaken by Maxine Baca Zinn, in particular see "Chicano Men and Masculinity," *Journal of Ethnic Studies*, 10, No. 2(1982), 29-44 and "Mexican-American Women in the Social Sciences. Review Essay," *Sign: Journal of Women in Culture and Society*, 8(Winter, 1982), 259-72.

For an excellent discussion of the term itself see Américo Paredes, "Estados Unidos, México y el Machismo," *Journal of Inter-American Studies* 9(1967), 65-84.

See also some views on *machismo* expressed from a Mexican perspective Rodríguez Baños, *Virginidad y machismo en México* (México: Editorial Posada, 1973), Rogelio Díaz-Guerrero, *Psychology of the Mexican* (Austin: University of Texas Press, 1967), and Octavio Paz, *The Labyrinth of Solitude: Life and Thought in Mexico* (New York: Grove Press, 1961). See also Vicente Urbistrondo "El machismo en la narrativa hispanoamericana," *Texto Crítico* 4(1978), 165-83.

[6] On the other hand, Anaya's undisputed masterpiece *Bless Me, Ultima* portrays the figure of a strong female character. That is not to say that the portrayal of a strong female character guarantees literary success. However, the portrayal of stereotypical personages does mean ultimate mediocrity.

[7] For a study on the relationship between sexual ideology and patriarchy see Gerda Lerner, *The Creation of Patriarchy*, pp. 101-60.

[8] An interesting comparison can be made between the sexual prowess attributed to Blacks and Latins by Anglo society. For a discussion of the Latin Lover image see Allen L. Woll, *The Latin Image in American Film* (Los Angeles: UCLA Latin American Publications, 1977). Anaya's male youths seem to accept this Latin Lover stereotype of themselves.

[9] See Gerda Lerner, *The Creation of Patriarchy*, Chapter 7.

[10] See Judy Salinas, 1979:191-240; Yolanda Julia Broyles, 1986:162-87; Elizabeth Ordoñez, 1983:316-39).

[11] The more well-known studies on La Llorona include: Bacil F. Kirtley, "La Llorona and Related Themes." *Western Folklore*, 19(1960), 155-68; Robert A. Barakat, "Aztec Motifs in La Llorona," *Southern Folklore Quarterly*, 29(1965), 288-96; Bess Lomax-Hawes, "La Llorona in Juvenile

Hall," *Western Folklore,* 27(1968), 153-70; Betty Leddy, "La Llorona in Southern Arizona," *Western Folklore*, 7(1948), 272-77; Michael Kearney, "La Llorona as a Social Symbol," *Western Folklore, 27(1968)*, 199-206; Mark Glazer, "Continuity and Change in Legendry: Two Mexican-American Examples," in *Perspectives on Contemporary Legend: Proceedings of the Conference on Contemporary Legend* (Sheffield, England: The Centre for English Cultural Tradition and Language, 1984), 108-27; Jane Rogers,"The Function of La Llorona Motif in Rudolfo Anaya's *Bless Me, Ultima, Latin American Literary Review*, V, No. 10(Spring-Summer, 1977), 64-69. See also my study "La Llorona: The Weeping Woman Legend in Orange County," presented at the "International Conference on Legendry," Omaha, Nebraska, 1977.

[12] See also Julio Caro Baroja, *The World of the Witches* (Chicago: The University of Chicago Press, 1964; and Charles Alva Hoyt, *Witchcraft* (Carbondale: Southern Illinois University Press, 1981).

[13] See Erich Neumann, *The Great Mother: An Analysis of the Archetype* (Princeton, New Jersey: Princeton University Press, 1974).

WORKS CITED

Burke, Kenneth. *A Grammar of Motives.* New York: Prentice-Hall, Inc., 1945. 503-04.

Broyles, Yolanda Julia. "Women in El Teatro Campesino: 'Apoco Estaba Molacha la Virgen de Guadalupe?'" *Chicana Voices: Interactions of Class, Race, and Gender.* Ed. National Association for Chicano Studies Editorial Committee. Austin: Center for Mexican American Studies, 1986. 162-87.

Daly, Mary. *Gyn/Ecology: The Metaethics of Radical Feminism.* Boston: Beacon Press, 1978.

Lakoff, George and Mark Johnson. *Metaphors We live By.* Chicago: The University of Chicago Press, 1980. 6.

Limón José. "La Llorona, The Third Legend of Greater Mexico: Cultural Symbols, Women and the Political Unconscious." *Renato Rosaldo Lecture Series Monograph Vol. 2 Series 1984-85.* Ed. Ignacio M. García. Tucson: Mexican American Studies and Research Center, 1986. 59-93.

Ordóñez, Elizabeth. "Sexual Politics and the Theme of Sexuality in Chicana Poetry." *Women in Hispanic Literature: Icons and Fallen Idols.* Ed. Beth Miller. Berkeley: University of California Press, 1983. 316-39.

Rogers, Jane. "Review of *Heart of Aztlán. Latin American Literary Review* 10(1977):143-45.

Salinas, Judy. "The Role of Women in Chicano Literature." *The Identification and Analysis of Chicano Literature.* Ed. Francisco Jiménez. New York: Bilingual Press/Editorial Bilingüe, 1979. 190-240.

The Author as Communal Hero:
Musil, Mann, and Anaya

Bruce-Novoa
University of California at Irvine

> In the beginning was the
> Word. . . . And the Word
> was made flesh and dwelt
> among us. . . . Do this
> in memory of me.

For many readers, the power and appeal of Rudy Anaya's fiction lies in its mixture of fantastic or magical elements and a moral message. Another way to state it could be that Anaya's prose, although set in apparently realistic environments in New Mexico, consistently places the action in the realm of myth in which life follows familiar patterns of initiation rites or quest rituals, from which the characters emerge with a new consciousness and a sense of purpose. Realistic contextualization is little more than the stage on which the author plays out a confrontation between evil and good, a barely veiled mythical allegory of archetypal forces in primal conflict. In addition, in his most successful novels, *Bless Me, Ultima* and *Tortuga*, there is the added dimension that the protagonist, who must fulfill the mythical quest, the hero who battles the forces of evil--in traditional terms--or simply ventures into the feared, unknown side of life, has been assigned the destiny of becoming a writer. And in both works, the narrator is the same protagonist who has undergone the mythical initiation, and so the text we read is the proof of the successful completion of the assigned task. *Tortuga* is the focus of my analysis here.

No one would try to claim that the general idea or the basic plot line of *Tortuga* is original. Centuries of religious practices and mythical formulae call for the retreat of a chosen one into a secluded place--the desert, the forest, the mountain, a distant temple, a monastery, etc.--where, through penance, mortification, meditation, and perhaps dialogues with peers and masters, or an apprenticeship to learn a specific skill, the person is transformed into a new, enlightened man--and I say "man" because traditional myth reserves this role for men, and Anaya, although he grants women the key function of facilitators, has not allowed them the status of heroic protagonist. That the purging of the demands of the flesh and the nurturing of the knowledge of the spirit produce a new man explains the similarities between, on the one hand, the retreat motif and initiation rites, and on the other, between the former and the redemption and transformation ritual of sacrificial death--descent into hell--and resurrection.

Before a religious leader can utter the sacred word, or a wiseman speak true knowledge, they must pass a series of difficult tests, not only to learn information--any student can mouth the words--but to dispossess themselves of egotism and accept that they speak, not their own words, but those of the totality of forces that govern life and constitute the ultimate source of all knowledge, whatever name one chooses to give it. This is such a commonplace that perhaps we forget just how deeply ingrained it is in our culture. Christians yearly hear the gospel story of Christ in the wilderness. Martin Luther King's "I have been to the mountain" sermon just before his death is only one well-known example of the traditional rhetorical motif by which a preacher proclaims to have received divine guidance and the power to lead people. Readers of medieval literature, members of fraternities and sororities, or followers of guru cults are familiar with some form of the ritual. Yet this in no way invalidates the tradition or its structure. Far from signifying an untruth, as the word is so often misused in popular speech, myth is a symbolic representation of what is held to be a universal truth, so its repetition over centuries, and on multiple levels of social interaction, only reinforces its essential qualities. New works can still be created following the old patterns, and Anaya is in good company with *Tortuga*.

In the contemporary context, the literary paradigm for *Tortuga* remains *The Magic Mountain* (1924), Thomas Mann's masterly novel about the young Hans Castorp who spends seven years at a sanatorium retreat in the Swiss mountains, from which he emerges, just before World War I, a radically changed man. However, before discussing this obvious intertextual allusion, I would call attention to the echoes of another classic from the early period of the century which should linger in the sensitive reader's mind: *Young Törless* (1906), by Mann's friend, the Austrian writer Robert Musil.

Young Törless and *Tortuga*

While *Törless* is also a Bildungsroman, it differs from *Tortuga* in that instead of a sanatorium, the action is set in a boarding school. This difference should not distract us, however, because schools, especially boarding schools, are to adolescents what sanatoriums are to the sick adult: an isolated space in which one encounters, and is expected to master, the necessary skills to return to society. Törless, like the protagonist of *The Magic Mountain* and *Tortuga*, will become involved in the dialectical struggle of good and evil in the form of conflict among his young peers and between socially defined concepts and personal experience. Like Tortuga, Anaya's protagonist, at the end Törless has matured, leaving his retreat in the forest a changed man, one having garnered from a difficult moral and spiritual encounter with the dark side of violence and sex, a positive moral attitude in which the source of values in life must come strictly from the human presence in the world. If the spirit exists, and Törless feels that it does, it can only be apprehended through the body. Thus, the traditional God is absent or indifferent, and experience can have various and variable meanings, often contradictory, when considered from the perspective of rational systems of thought.

Törless summarizes the lesson of his education at the end of his boarding school experience when he is called to testify in front of the school masters who will, after they hear him out, expel him.

"I'm not afraid of anything any more. I know that things are just things and will probably always be so. And I shall probably go on forever seeing them sometimes this way and sometimes that, sometimes with the eyes of reason, and sometimes with those other eyes. . . . And I shan't ever try again to compare one with the other." (170)

Törless' discovery of peace of mind through the acceptance of the simple existence of the world as world, with no real comparative order, and the arbitrariness of perspective and judgment, finds an apparent reprise in *Tortuga*, when Mike, Tortuga's friend and guide in the outer wards of the hospital, relates his own version of learning the lesson of equanimity.

"What I finally learned to do is to quit looking for a reason or an answer as to why it happened. When I realized that things just happen, that there's no reason, that there's no big daddy up in the sky watching, whether you burn or not . . . much less caring, then it helped. Things just happen. They just are." (47)[1]

Later, as Tortuga progresses through his indoctrination into the philosophy of the hospital wise man, appropriately named Salomón, he will hear the lesson authoritatively restated in more explicit terms and with an extremely important corollary:

No, Tortuga, Salomón had said, the garden of cripples is not a place of punishment. Don't you see that punishment would give meaning to our existence. If we could say we're being punished then it would follow that God is punishing us, and we would be worse off than we were before . . . we would go on fabricating lie upon lie . . . It's very difficult to accept the fact that our existence has no meaning to the absent god. The only meaning it has is the meaning we give it . . . we can't blame the gods. (159)

This absence of the traditional sense of purpose and meaning in the world has the effect of deconstructing the moral hierarchy of society, revealed as a sham and a rhetorical justification for enslavement. Released from the dictates of absolutist morality, both Törless and Tortuga must readjust their behavior to an existential system of morality which imposes on them the right, as well as the responsibility, to define and choose. The effect of this revolution in their personal philosophy is forcefully brought home to the reader through sexual imagery. In Törless' case, although at first he is perturbed that his mother and the local prostitute remind him of one another (39), by the end of the novel he seems to able to abandon himself to the smell of his mother's body after having just moments before been reminded of the prostitute. That is to say, in a world devoid of god or absolutes, there remains little distance between what society places at opposite ends of the moral spectrum. The framing of the novel with this repetition of an action allows Musil to demonstrate how far Törless has come in his evolution. In Tortuga's case, he discovers that within the realm of desire and love, there is no reason to distinguish between his beautiful girl friend Ismelda and the ugly hunchback Cynthia. Both offer him love, and love in itself is positive. In addition, while having sex with Cynthia, Tortuga can project into a reality outside of himself his love for Ismelda. Anaya also frames the novel between these incidents, with Tortuga violently rejecting Cynthia at the beginning. He, too, evolves into a maturity similar to that of Törless.

The absence of God is a metaphor for the collapse of the traditional system of values upon which society and culture have been based. In both novels there is also the implication that society's systems of differentiating must be totally revised, for if individual identity is blurred to the point of being at times indistinguishable and substitutable, then the old system has lost its foundation. All humans are to be freed from a priori categories and judged on their value in particular situations and from the perspective of the observer. Törless' discovery has definite class implications, juxtaposing as it does women from such different economic levels, while Tortuga's seems more strictly focused on aesthetics and morality. Yet in the latter case, physical deformity and illness are obviously metaphors for all other social stigma, including those attached to class, and by implication synecdoches for all value systems based on binary oppositions, i.e., good versus bad. The apparent chaos which the cutting away of traditional moral absolutes can produce, in both cases, is given the perturbing significance of a re-evaluation of all social values, which affect the characters in their most intimate relationships. Nothing should remain the same after the novel's lessons are learned.

However, this apparent similarity should not hide the fact that *Tortuga* differs from *Törless* in one essential matter. Musil is relentless in his application of the freedom from values. If there is no system of essential, transcendent significance within the existential arbitrariness of life, then he must reject the possibility of claiming transcendent significance for experience itself, even that of his protagonist. Thus we learn that Törless will not better himself with his experience, but simply grow larger, like a tree adding another ring (162). In the end, Törless still cannot distinguish in absolute terms between evil and good, nor is he willing to attribute exclusive values to objects. He refuses to compromise to the social demands of his peers and teachers, because he intuits the need to state his experience as he feels it, not as it should be. This is Musil's way of rejecting the traditional claims for the redemptive power of the very rituals his protagonist undergoes. Yet they are still present in the culture, serving as models and patterns. Hence the justification of parody. His novel calls attention to the pits of nothingness over which culture suspends itself, inventing rhetorical distractions in an effort to forget its perilous venture. Like Törless himself, the novel refuses to ignore the pits, but neither does it attempt to close them. As his own character says, traditional society proceeds by leaping over the void as if there were a safe bridge over it, because there really are no absolutes with which to fill it (90). *Young Törless* is a parody of those old forms through which they are denounced as void of real signifying power, while admitting that they are the only cultural structure we have.

Anaya, however, insists on a more traditional position. While he wants to deny the validity of all previous value systems, he holds out the hope and promise of a new redemption, one which, while based on the future and the rejection of the past, simultaneously insists that the future will only be possible through the learning of lessons from the past. Anaya's break with the past is to be selective: he would have the protagonist purge himself of the concept of a divine purpose in suffering and its corollary of guilt, yet he insists that life does function according to an essential plan, a design intricately woven into the fabric of existence. The void of nothingness is not real, as in Musil, but only an illusion due to the human inability to perceive that, as Salomón says, "one great force binds us all" (102).[2] How else are we to interpret the fact that Tortuga's actions seem foreordained; that Salomón seems to know everything before it happens, as well as knowing everyone, even characters outside the novel; and that actions and even people repeat themselves, albeit it in different avatars. While Anaya seems to agree that visible order depends on the artist's vision and ability to recreate it in art, he simultaneously affirms the presence of order in the world itself, something that Musil, coming as he did from a school of empiricism, denied.[3] How can these apparent contradictions be resolved?

Mike is not the protagonist of *Tortuga* exactly because he does not understand that his position, "things just happen," is, like the hospital itself, only one station on the way to full comprehension of life. This flaw in his character keeps him from being Salomón's full heir. He remains suspended in an intermediate phase of the apprenticeship process outlined for Tortuga by Salomón:

> *First we question why? Then we curse the gods that send the punishment . . . then the despair enters, and there is only the chaos of nothingness left . . . a void in which we sink eternally, a plane of life so still and lonely that we think all of the creation has abandoned us . . . and still, it's but a station in life, a form we cannot see.* (41)

"Station" implies movement and direction, while "invisible form" alludes to hidden design, to purpose and to order, not chaos. Mike cannot make the last step to seeing the form behind the surface, the spirit within the material world, because he rejects the possibility of a signifying system.

Anaya may not know of Musil and his classic *Törless*, but *Tortuga* dialogues directly with it in the intertextual space of literature. Through the character of Mike, Anaya's novel utilizes the deconstructive value of arriving at a position in which one cuts oneself free from the crutch of God, but, like crutches themselves in the novel's context, this must not be the end of one's rehabilitation, but simply a station on the way to full ambulatory power. Remaining at midpoint can lead to the acceptance of a floating existence without progress, which in turn, in a moment of crisis, can cast one back into the traditional explanations for life. In other words, *Tortuga*, while bespeaking through Mike a nihilism similar to that of the character of Törless, does so only to transcend and ultimately reject it. It is important to understand how and why this happens.

Mike follows the steps of the ritual as defined by Salomón, as we hear when he tells Tortuga the story of his first year in the hospital. His asking-why phase took the form of blaming everyone, including himself, for the accident that burned his legs. Finally he blamed God, thus entering to the cursing-God phase. He passed through the nothingness phase, with its sinking into the void, symbolized by a year of lying in his own blood and feeling the skin patches falling from his body. Then Mike seemed to recover, assuming the position that "things just happen" and that there is no God. Yet he progresses no further. Although he represents a positive pole of thought, and despite his apparent closeness to Salomón, Mike limits his goals to the mere material level. His one rule, "get out," focuses strictly on the rehabilitation of the body, to the exclusion of any exploration of questions which might distract one from that end. He has cut himself off from learning or drawing any benefit from his suffering by remaining in what should be a temporary phase. This attitude allows him even to become comfortable in the hospital, a situation he himself recognizes as dangerous.

> "I'm tired of anything that's easy! For crying out loud! We're not supposed to be enjoying ourselves here! We're supposed to want to get the hell outta here! This is a prison, don't forget that . . . That's what they want us to forget, so they make it nice and easy for us. . . . they even let us get away with a little drinking and a little screwing on the side! Just enough to make us forget that our real purpose it to get out! . . . I'm getting used to this place . . . hell,

I'm only a step away from the vegetables! The only difference is I can move around." (138)

Mike is perceptive enough to realize that what he is doing is wrong and self-defeating. He even warns Tortuga about finding pleasant recreation in the hospital, because taking any form of comfort has historically made the patients dependent on the support they receive from the staff and the protective isolation of the sanatorium, leading to their inability to leave, even when they improve to a point where they could. The context of his warning to Tortuga, however, should also alert us to the flaw in Mike's position: it comes as a supporting argument for his admonition against loving Ismelda, whom Salomón has characterized as a guide to Tortuga's destiny. Mike is consistently almost right, almost well, almost the true disciple of Salomón. Yet, he is equally consistent in just falling short of the goal. His position is intrinsically weak, leaving him vulnerable. Thus, in a moment of crisis, when Tortuga imposes on the group the necessity to ponder the question of life and death, without reference to any guiding principle but their own conscience, Mike, instead of transcending his stasis by leaping forward into the freedom represented by the acceptance of full responsibility, rejects the opportunity. As a result, he slips back into a previous phase of rehabilitation: "'Blame it on God!' Mike cursed" (137).

Mike's failure to fulfill the necessary steps on the path to enlightenment by following Salomón's teachings fully, despite his rather complete familiarity with what Salomón says about almost everything, not only makes him unsuitable as the heir to wisdom, but leaves the patients without a heroic savior. Salomón is incapacitated, bedridden, one step away from pure spirit, unable to venture back into the world carrying the banner on which the stories of the forgotten cripples are written. This prepares the situation for the coming of another possible hero. The failure of Salomón's most promising disciple, Mike, makes it necessary for Tortuga to arrive and renew the influence of Salomón among the hospital inmates.

The state of despair and existence in a void that had prevailed in the hospital before Tortuga's arrival is summed up by Ronco. Danny accuses Tortuga of causing discontent among the healthier patients of the outer wards by bringing back into their conscious minds and conversation the subject of the inner wards, where the worst patients--the vegetables--are kept, which by turns forces an open reconsideration of the question of life and death, and whose responsibility it is to choose between the two. Danny claims that Tortuga's attribution of significance to the living vegetables is senseless, provoking the following defense and explanation:

> "It makes some sense," Ronco said, "because at least Tortuga went to see them. We had pretended they weren't there, then Tortuga came along and reminded us of all those poor vegetables. Now that's what's bothering us. We're blaming Tortuga for bringing all of this out in the open again. . . . most of us weren't even listening to Salomón any more, then when Tortuga came we had to start listening to him again. A lot of times we didn't like what we heard, but we had to listen. And Tortuga trusted Salomón, maybe he realized how smart that little bastard is . . . anyway, Tortuga at least was listening." (134-35)

Note how Ronco's words are a veiled denunciation of Mike, because if no one was listening to Salomón anymore, then Mike had lost faith, had never really trusted Salomón's teaching. Two pages later Mike slips back into cursing and blaming God, openly revealing his lack of firm commitment to Salomón's position, and even to his own.

Tortuga, on the other hand, does much more than listen; he provokes the retelling of stories, the restating of history, the reorientation of the community towards the essential questions of existence. If a system of blame were still viable, Danny would be right, because Tortuga does force the vegetables back into the conversation. Actually, he serves to recentralize Salomón's teachings, and in so doing fulfills his apprenticeship. At this point he is acting like Törless in refusing to adjust his vision to that of his peers, which would allow them to dismiss the disturbing presence of one of those voids gaping open beneath them. In this stubborn fidelity to a more profound, questioning spirit, Törless and Tortuga exercise the heroic function of communal consciousness raising.

For Musil, as for many existentialist writers, the communal hero need not pass any further in his activities. His main function is to provoke consciousness by questioning the status quo. He does not provide answers, because he cannot base any answer on essential, permanent, and, therefore, transcendent truth, for there are none in existentialism. Far from discrediting Törless as a communal hero, his attitude makes him the archetypal existential communal hero, refusing to lie or to compromise, and one who, by his actions, accepts the responsibility for choice which others reject. Anaya's belief in essentialistic truth and transcendent order demands a different type of hero, one who, while passing through the questioning phase when necessary for the communal good, eventually transcends it in order to lead the community into a higher realm of existence, one in which the essential, transcendent order of being can be recognized and followed in daily life. Tortuga became, first, Salomón's student, then his disciple, and finally a type of reincarnated Salomón. He suffers through the despair of losing the orientation and security that having a God gave his mother, but he is rewarded with a faith in the ordering and signifying power of a new creative principle based in the regenerative power of the word. It is that new faith that brings him much closer to Thomas Mann's Hans Castrop than Robert Musil's young Törless.

The Magic Mountain and *Tortuga*

From the beginning of the novel, the end is perhaps too obvious, but we must always remember when reading Anaya that his is not a world of realism, but one of mythical cycles which tend to the predictable. Tortuga is to learn a lesson in the hospital, and he will learn it from Salomón. That Salomón has the power to transform Tortuga, even kill him--in myth the two actions are often synonymous--is revealed in Salomón's first didactic monologue, which coincides with Tortuga's first dream. This in itself is significant in that, even before the two men meet, their individual texts meld into one at the level of the unconscious. Solomón relates a mythical tale of his initiation into an Indian tribe, during which he beheaded a giant turtle, English for *tortuga*. When the headless beast escaped back into the river, Salomón's destiny was sealed. He became a story teller, waiting at the brink of death ("that stygian bank") for the turtle's return from the water or waters (a traditional symbol of the life-death process) so he can either "finish the kill, or return its life" (25). Salomón will actually do both: kill the old Tortuga through a symbolic ritual of suffering and sacrifice so that he can return to life a transformed man.[4]

Tortuga's descent into symbolic death takes the form of a voyage into the inner wards of the hospital, to which he is sent by Salomón. There he encounters the burning question of the absurdity of life sustained by machines, in children who can no longer breathe on their own. This discovery triggers the desire to escape his situation and the recognition that he is powerless to achieve that goal. That is to say, he falls into despair, from which he would do anything to be free, even if it requires abandoning himself to death. This is exactly what Salomón needs in order to carry out the transformation of Tortuga, because from despair--the rejection of present life as meaningless and useless--there can come a new, reoriented life. Significantly, Tortuga reaches the nadir of despair when he allows himself to be taken to the swimming pool and cast into the water to drown. At this point, Tortuga is delirious, out of his head, but he refuses to die; that is, he is symbolically beheaded, just like the turtle in Salomón's mythical tale of origin, but also as in Salomón's tale, the attempt to kill the Tortuga fails. The water actually begins to stir in him the will to live. Thus, when Tortuga is rescued from the water, he returns a new person, one who draws even closer to Salomón. This parody of Salomón's myth is at once a death ritual, reenacted as part of Tortuga's spiritual apprenticeship. Appropriately, the soaking in water also causes Tortuga's body cast, into which he had been placed on arrival at the hospital and which had led to his being given the name Tortuga (Turtle), to become waterlogged, and thus necessitating its removal. The death ritual truly transforms the character, sending him one more step towards his destiny: at this point he quite literally comes out of his shell. But first, like a mythical pilgrim on a dangerous quest, he has had to pass through the portals of death and resurrection. Or like a new born child, he had to be baptized in the waters of life.

Tortuga must prove himself worthy of the role he is to play, but only after a series of tests and trials does he eventually learn the import of his destiny from Salomón. To readers familiar with mythical structures, however, it is clear from the start. Yet Tortuga, like the reader, must follow the traditional course of the apprenticeship quest through the novel to earn the right to that destiny, and this involves becoming the focal point of discussions and conflict between spokesmen for radically opposed principles. Like Mann's protagonist, Hans Castrop, who becomes both the battleground and the disputed prize in the debate between Settembrini, the representative of reason and humanistic values, and Naphta, the Jesuit defender of irrationality and the primitive forces, Anaya's Tortuga is the object sought by Mike and Danny, as well as the space itself--both physically and mentally--of a battle for communal survival between life and death. Mike appears to be a disciple of Salomón, while the latter proclaims faith in God. One should not expect Anaya's characters to reach the brilliant heights of Mann's--a feat matched by few, if any, writers--but that is not the point of the comparison. One would not ask young men with no pretensions to higher education to speak like European intellectuals, but then Anaya is not debating the entire history of Western civilization. He is content to encapsulate the archetypal dualities of good and evil, the rational and the irrational, the body and the spirit, in elemental portraits. Thus Danny, whose body is literally wasting away, represents a fanatical faith in the spirit, as well as the traditional belief that suffering must have significance because there is a God, which then leads him to assume that either he is being punished for some evil, or that God is unjust. Either conclusion destroys him. Mike, as we have seen, preaches the absence of meaning, the arbitrariness of life, and the pragmatic rule to get out of the hospital. His position is that of a modern rationalist or pragmatist, focusing on material reality. He also urges Tortuga to follow Salomón's lessons. I call attention to the similarity, even in their great difference, between *The Magic Mountain* and *Tortuga* to emphasize two points. First, in their intertextual relationship, *Tortuga* is a parody of its antecedent, whether Anaya meant it to be or not. Second, that there is another key lesson, the ultimate one of both books, that we must arrive at.

The first point is important because it lies at the heart of Salomón's teaching. Parody is the repetition of previous texts in different texts, in which the first serve as models, even when those that follow take liberties with the predecessors in the process of creating themselves. New texts continue the old, yet renovate them as a step towards the future. This reveals a culture in healthy regeneration. Texts die only when they cease to function as the source of parodies, or at least as a voice in intertextual dialogues. Mann was one of the arch practitioners of parody. *The Magic Mountain* itself parodied the tradition of the German Bildungsroman, whose paradigm is found in *Wilhelm Meister*. The Mexican critic Juan García Ponce has explained that Mann found parody necessary because society no longer could supply the solid foundation for fiction (191). Mann turned to literary forms for a firm base and a reliable tradition. Perhaps Anaya knows nothing about Mann's great project, but his character Salomón certainly has much in common with the German novelist. Salomón also recognizes that the contemporary situation of society lacks the strength and unity to provide a solid foundation for healthy life. Speaking in the terms of the novel's mythical imagery of the initiation of a cultural hero, Salomón explains to Tortuga that all the old heroes--and thus the heroic systems, another term for societies--are obsolete because they, like Danny, blame their suffering on a God. He criticizes Prometheus, Sisyphus, and even Christ.

> *No, Tortuga, we are beyond the last Greek hero . . . we are beyond all the heroes of the past . . . We have come to a new plane in the time of eternity . . . we have gone far beyond the punishment of the gods. We are beyond everything that we have ever known, and the past is useless to us.* (160)

As we have seen, the lack of a centralizing God casts values adrift. The question then arises, from whence does the artist draw inspiration and learn forms.

While Mann reached back into the literary history of written forms, Anaya's draws on the communal oral tradition. This is also obvious from the start. Salomón's fate is to be a story teller, just as Tortuga's is to be a singer: two forms of voicing stories, with an identical function with respect to the community they serve. The songs Tortuga is to sing are the stories he learns from his fellow patients, including Salomón. Moreover, they are not original stories, but repetitions of previous versions, or the retelling of stories which were already being retold when Tortuga first hears them. Actually, everyone in the hospital seems to have heard the stories before, and those who haven't are constantly asking what was said, and being told. Salomón's stories are repeated by several voices, and in reality it is often Tortuga who must learn them, because everyone else seems to know them already. His task is to accumulate the stories so he can repeat them. He will be, as someone says, "a walking story" (77). Later, when his cast, on which the patients had scrawled their stories, is taken off, someone complains that he has lost the stories, but Mike counters that Tortuga "hasn't forgotten what he's seen and felt" (129). Both Anaya and Mann resort to a form of parody for their support in a world which seems void of substance, but they seem to differ as well. While Mann utilizes the written tradition, Anaya seems to deny it as a source. He prefers the oral. Yet they share the need to write novels at the same time as they express their doubts about the written tradition. They question their literary tradition as they revitalize it.

Both Anaya and Salomón emphasize parody because it is basic to their beliefs and art. The oral tradition is essentially parodic: a story is heard and repeated; the unwritten condition allows for variations, and the applicability of the story to new situations--a proof of its value and truth--demands the flexibility provided for by substitutions and emendations to everything but the essential structure. Thus characters and places can change, as they do in the novel, but the story goes on. Salomón needs someone to come and learn the stories so they can be carried on once he is dead. He could write them down, but then they would not be lived nor living words. So he needs someone to voice them, and that introduces the possibility of parodic repetition. Yet, as

I have explained, it is in that very quality of adjustments around the basic structure that makes the oral tradition valid within it own terms. Anaya's art has always been the reformulation of the communal stories into his own mythical interpretations. Some see this as a universalization of the communal stories, but actually it is the application of the oral tradition to the art of the novel. Thus, his novels are parodies by definition. In the context of mainstream literature, Anaya, like Thomas Mann, seems to see the rule of individual originality as foreign, perhaps even as absurd--a position that places him in harmony with the postmodernist movement--and produces parodies of Bildungsroman, which are actually the dialogical intervention of the oral tradition into the written canon. Thus Anaya, like his character Salomón, requires parodic creation to fulfill his goals.

At the heart of Mann's novel, as García Ponce has also explained, lies the significance of Hans Castrop's strange dream that comes to him when he is trapped in a snow storm and literally at the brink of death (the "Snow" chapter of *The Magic Mountain*, 469-98). When Hans is awakened by a change in the dream from images of a paradise to those of horror, Hans remains in a drowsy state and rethinks the dream. He interprets it to be a representation of the struggle between the Apollonian and Dyonisian forces that have been battling over him all along, but the true importance of the dream is that he can give it meaning by transmuting it to the realm of order. By being able to conceptualize the dream, "he becomes capable of controlling it and gains a new equilibrium" (García Ponce 196).

The significance of Tortuga's dreams lies, similarly, at the heart of *Tortuga*. As we have seen, from the start, the protagonist begins to mind-meld with the spiritual master of his destiny in his first dream. In the ensuing series of dreams he will continue to question his experience, until the last dream, after Salomón's death, in which all the patients, including those who have died, are gathered together into "Salomón's army" (186) in a celebration which culminates in a communal escape from the condemned world via the liberated and high-flying mountain called Tortuga. This dream is the culmination of Tortuga's apprenticeship, but we must take all the dreams together, and add to them Salomón monologues--their initial coincidence allows us this reading--to match the dream in *The Magic Mountain*. Actually, Tortuga's entire experience at the hospital is like the short event in the snow in *The Magic Mountain*, a period of isolation in which the character is suspended between life and death, shifting from lucidity to the deep unconsciousness of the dream, yet somehow blurring the border between the two. Anaya's creation of the magical and mythical environment make the novel function like the world of Hans Castrop's dream, so it is only in the restatement of the total experience that Tortuga matches the conceptualizing act of his parodic German ancestor.

Likewise, it is in the capacity to conceptualize these dream-like experiences into a controlled form of narrative that Tortuga shows that he has become the artist of his destiny. Mann and Anaya teach the same lesson: when society, split as it is into dialectical warring camps and cut off from its supposedly harmonious origins, no longer is capable of orienting life, then it falls to art and the artist to counter both chaos and false order through the structuring of experience into a meaningful form. It is most probable that Hans Castrop becomes the interior narrator of *The Magic Mountain*, repeating the conceptualization process discovered during his adventure in the snow, although from Mann's famous ironic distance that makes him sound like a totally different character. Tortuga's destiny as the recreator of stories can be affirmed with much more assurance. We see him receiving direct instructions. Salomón indoctrinates Tortuga, infusing him with purpose, or what is called in the novel his destiny. He tells Tortuga that the rest of the characters will only achieve freedom if they

> *lie like my poor vegetables . . . until we think ourselves out of existence . . . [becoming] characters who are not yet born! . . . For if we are not, then we can become, and we will become what you sing of us, Tortuga! . . . Isn't that great! To become what you will make of us in your song!* (54-55)

Tortuga's destiny is as a storyteller/singer empowers him with the capacity to transmute his dreams into an signifying order, which is a task the absent gods will not perform, and the disoriented society can no longer achieve.

The hero, therefore, is not simply the questioner of the past or the status quo, nor even the provocateur of communal unrest, but rather the artist of the future text. As Salomón explains, the past is useless, except perhaps as a form to be renewed, but there is a goal that must be realized. Once again, Salomón prescribes the manner of fulfillment.

> *We must create out of our ashes. Our hero must be born out of this wasteland, like the phoenix bird of the desert he must rise again from the ashes of our withered bodies . . . and he must not turn to the shadows of the past. He must walk in the path of the sun . . . and he shall sing the songs of the sun. It may be that we will find someone who crossed the desert in Filomón's cart, someone who suffered like us as he felt the fire in his body go dry and the juices die in his bones . . . someone who has felt the paralysis of life, and walked in the garden with his brothers and sisters, and who will sing his adventures . . . (160)*

Tortuga is guided by all concerned in the hospital to prepare himself to fit Salomón's description. Without detailing here how he passes through, point by point, Salomón's enumeration above,[5] we can affirm with certainty that Tortuga comes to deserve his destiny. It is equally certain that, in a fashion befitting the belief in parodic forms discussed above, Tortuga is shaped by others into his destiny, almost as if he had no choice:

> . . . I felt [I was being drawn] into a complex web. Somehow Ismelda and Salomón and Filomón and all the others I had met were bound together, and the force created was sucking me into it. . . . When I asked her questions she would smile and tell me that my concern should be with getting well. But I had the vague, uneasy feeling that other things were in store for me. (101-02)

The feeling becomes a certainty when Tortuga inherits the magical blue guitar from Anaya's second novel, *Heart of Aztlán*, and is forced to accept that he will be the singer of songs about his fellow patients. This inheritance also makes him the reincarnation of another guru figure, Crispín, the magical guide who had escorted Tortuga's father, the protagonist of *Heart of Aztlán*, on his voyage of personal discovery in the magical mountain--a voyage parodied by Tortuga in his first dream, where he meets Ismelda, who leads him "deeper and deeper into the mountain's heart" (22). Tortuga has been marked for his destiny from all sides, apparently even from before the beginning of the novel by his father's mystical friend. He has no choice in the end, for in spite of his reluctance, he has become the hero and savior of the people: "Don't you see, my friend," Salomón tells Tortuga the last time they speak to each other before the young master's death, "you're the one hope that the darkness will never cover us completely!" (172) The conceptualization of those dreams is the novel itself, narrated by Tortuga from somewhere and sometime after the end of the experience.

That the artist is the servant of the community, and not the originator nor owner of his material is clear in that the source of the text, the dream, is specifically defined as communal. Although the following quote comes from Hans Castrop's musings, it could just as easily have come from Salomón, or from the transformed and resurrected Tortuga.

> Now I know that it is not out of our single souls we dream. We dream anonymously and communally, if each after his fashion. The great soul of which we are a part may dream through us, in our manner of dreaming, its own secret dreams, of its youth, its hope, its joy and peace--and its blood-sacrifice." (495)

In the beginning Tortuga's dream is Salomón's oral text of the myth of his own origins, but by the end, Tortuga's final dream is communal. Mike, Buck, and Ronco seem to have had the same dream as Tortuga, a coincidence which Ismelda states in a matter-of-fact fashion befitting her status as accomplice in the plot to transform Tortuga: "It was a beautiful dream to share," Ismelda affirms, with no need of being told what Tortuga had dreamed--she knows they are identical with an absolute certainty that Törless would have deemed impossible even in the case of common objects.

Dreams per se, however, are only one facet of the communal experience that Tortuga must be brought to understand and participate in. For example, from Salomón he will learn to see light and colors as a sign of the path towards a better future: Salomón's particular material manifestation of his harmony with the world is the butterfly, but he recalls that in his first encounter with one it glowed "*with the iridescent colors of the rainbow*" (41). Yet Tortuga had already been oriented towards such admiration and harmony through that image:

> I remember the rainbows of my childhood, beautifully sculptured arches reaching from north to south, shafts of light so pure their harmony seemed to wed the sky and earth. My mother had taught me to look at rainbows, the mantle of the Blessed Virgin Mary she called them." (2)

When, on the very next page, our protagonist encounters the mountain which bears the same name by which he will be known in the hospital, he sees it as a presence rising into the sky so magically "that it seemed to hold heavens and earth together" (3). Obviously--perhaps too obviously again--the metonymic lines of the web into which Tortuga later feels he is drawn are clearly stated from the start. Salomón also compares his butterfly to a hummingbird, which is then revealed as one of Ismelda's images when she and Tortuga finally unite in the act of love (195).

All the characters seem to fit into a common dream dreamed by the spiritual or magical force of harmony, although, as Mann stated, each being only a part of the dream, expressed in a particular manner, but ultimately being one and the same dream. Furthermore, Tortuga's destiny is to be the singer of songs made up of the dreams and stories he will hear in the hospital. Although this is revealed to us and to Tortuga as a special destiny reserved for the hero, ironically everyone in the hospital sings constantly. The references to singing are repeated so often as too border on the irritating. Tortuga would have to be totally insensitive not to notice his operetta-like environment. It could be attributed, perhaps, to the reformulation of experience by Tortuga-the-future-narrator-of-the-text, who, in his role of transmitter of tales, also has the obligation to liven them up, to infuse them with joy. *"[P]ity the sleeping plant,"* Salomón instructs Tortuga, " . . . *for the pain it feels--but celebrate its dance* . . . . [sic.]" (64). By the time Tortuga receives the blue guitar, he has been bombarded by so many different types of songs, and been told so often that he is to be a singer, that he has no choice. Salomón tells Tortuga that he will create his fellow patients through his songs, but in reality it is they who impose their will on him. *"Yes, you too will have your butterflies, because you will be a singer,"* the all-knowing Salomón blatantly informs Tortuga just before sentencing him to a lifelong participation in suffering: *"but your song will be full of the sadness of life . . . Your destiny has become ours, Tortuga . . . "* (117). One feels at times that this collective project of shaping Tortuga to his destiny is a thinly veiled, Gothic tale of possession (see note 4). Whether one would call it demonic or angelic depends on the interpretation, although certainly Anaya intends for us to take it as positive, just as Robert Musil and Thomas Mann meant us to take their novel.

Conclusion

   Young Törless, *The Magic Mountain*, and *Tortuga* all end with the departure of the protagonist from the site of their education. The last we see of Törless and Tortuga, they are being driven back home. Törless is still pondering the breakdown of identities and the perturbing blend of apparent opposites in the form of the mother/prostitute. His has been a voyage inward, and despite the departure from the school, somehow he continues to move inward, guided by some dark, perverse intuition of sexual love's capacity for undermining identity and opening one to experience beyond the limits of rational thought. Tortuga, on the other hand, is definitely moving in the opposite direction. He has become the singer everyone demanded he be, and his song spills out from him, filling the surrounding space. His inward voyage has turned outward. He moves back into the world as the representative of the community of the oppressed and forgotten.

We know nothing of Tortuga's future, but perhaps we can carry out the comparison with *The Magic Mountain* just a bit further to chance a prediction. Hans Castrop descends from the mountain into World War I. He moves into what Mann termed "this universal feast of death" (716). Tortuga also moves towards a situation of strife and violence. Readers of *Heart of Aztlán* will remember the conflict in which Tortuga's community was engulfed. Part of that violence led to the gunshot wound and the fall from the train yard water tower that shattered Tortuga's (then still known as Benjie) hand and vertebra, resulting in his hospitalization (198-99). *Tortuga* contains small references to the continued struggle, so we can expect Tortuga to be involved in it. After all, he has become the voice of redemption and harmony, and we would expect him to preach his gospel to his community at home. His will not be a feast of death on the scale of W.W.I, but there will be conflict, and perhaps even more deaths.

Much more important, however, is the promise of hope expressed by both authors that their character will apply the key lesson of his experience. As Tortuga rides homeward, his eyes closed, and perhaps at the edge of a dream, Solomón's voice comes to whisper his final instructions: "*Make a song of rejoicing from all that you have seen and felt! Sing a song of love, Tortuga! Oh yes, sing of love!* (196) The narrator of *The Magic Mountain* closes the novel in a similar vein:

> Moments there were, when out of death, and the rebellion of the flesh, there came to thee, as thou tookest stock of thyself, a dream of love. Out of this universal feast of death, out of this extremity of fever, kindling the rain-washed evening sky to a fiery glow, may it be that Love one day shall mount? (716)

Mann closes with the characteristic note of distance and ambiguity, signalled by the question mark. Anaya is much more optimistic, ending the novel with the spreading out of Tortuga's song of love which seems to have the power to awaken the desert, like a loving rain. Yet, in each case, the novel itself is the real proof that, out of the experience of suffering and death, love emerges triumphant: the characters, even the hideous monsters, are all lovingly brought back to life as a community. The protagonist has become their savior and hero; the hero, an artist of love.

NOTES

[1] It is interesting that the same sentence, "*Ich weiss: die Dinge sind die Dinge und werden es wohl immer bleiben*," translated as "I know that things are just things and will probably always be so" in the text of the novel, was freely rendered differently by John Simon in his "afterword" to the same edition. His version reads, "Things just happen: that's the sum total of wisdom" (189). Simon's rather free rendering, while it takes, perhaps, unjustified liberties with the original, ironically is supported by Anaya's character Mike, who combines the two statements as if to repeat the same essential idea, but in two different manners: "Things just happen. They just are." Accuracy demands that we quote the translation most faithful to the original. However, the Simon's version seems more faithful to the spirit of Törless' insight into the arbitrariness of the human condition. And as an epigrammatically expressed thought, it sounds better. The Mexican writer García Ponce--himself a translator of Musil and other Austro German writers--in the original Spanish version of the essay cited below, agrees as well, rendering the phrase in a literal translation of Simon's version: "*Las cosas simplemente pasan; ésa es la suma total de la sabiduría*"

[2] In this, Solomón echoes Ultima when she explains to the protagonist that his problem with the apparent opposition of forces is that he has "been seeing only parts . . . and not looking beyond into the great cycle that binds us all" (113). Considering the eventual revelation in *Tortuga* that everything is part of a complex and vast net of interaction, there is the possibility that someone other than Solomón speaks these words, perhaps even Ultima. Tortuga says: "I thought I heard Salomón say," which contrasts markedly to the unambiguous attribution of a statement to Salomón in other cases.

[3] For an explanation of empiricism and the novel see, Bruce-Novoa, "Juan García Ponce y la ficción empírica," *Iberoromania*, 20 (1984), 109-16.

[4] A mythical reading of Salomón's initial story could be the following. He represents the presence of an alien in the community: he is a non-Indian entering the tribe. This easily could be seen as the Mexican presence in New Mexico, but also as any new idea entering a traditional community. His act of initiation is incomplete, but also it is an act of destruction that splits reality in half. Symbolically it can stand for the rational philosophy of the European that opposes the rational and the physical realms. Salomón beheads the Great Turtle, who returns to the river as a body only. In punishment, Salomón becomes a head without a body. He even turns the pages of his books with a pencil held in his mouth. He symbolizes a primal split in existence which can only be resolved if the head and body are rejoined. Yet this demands a body willing to lose its head, as well as the eventual death of Salomón's body. Salomón's ideas--his figurative head--will move into Tortuga's head, thus reuniting what was split in primal violence. As such, as I suggest at the end of the essay, the novel can be read as a tale of possession, in the Gothic Novel tradition. A conspiracy of believers, including Crispín from *Heart of Aztlán* and all the characters in *Tortuga*, manipulates events to send Tortuga, alias Benji, to the sanatorium where he will be turned into a body for Salomón, the reincarnated Great Turtle reunited with its killer. Salomón can be seen as a type of vampire figure, but in a positive sense; or even as a Christ figure in need of human bodies in order to move around in the world of material bodies. Possession need be neither negative nor evil. The sacred pilgrimage, or the holy quest, or the kingly voyage of regeneration can all be seen as a cleansing of the body through which the spirit of the divine enters into the body of the pilgrim/knight/king and turns them into new men, marked by their experience and empowered to move back into the world to redeem it. The ritual achieved, in classic mythical fashion the world will be renewed, the people delivered from darkness and fear, and communal life set back into the harmony of the universe.

[5] The basic steps can be found on pages 25-26, 40, chapter 14, page 118, and chapter 16, although the process and the narration are, in a real sense, synonymous.

WORKS CITED

Anaya, Rudolfo. *Bless Me, Ultima*. Berkeley: Quinto Sol, 1972.

___. *Heart of Aztlán*. Berkeley: Justa, 1976.

___. *Tortuga*. Berkeley: Justa, 1979.

García Ponce, Juan. "El sueño en la nieve," in *Entrada en materia*. México: Universidad Nacional Autónoma de México, 1968, 225-263. The page references in the text are to the English translation, found in *Entry Into Matter, Modern Literature and Reality*. Normal: Applied Literature, 1976. 172-199.

Mann, Thomas. *The Magic Mountain*. New York: Knopf, 1953.

Musil, Robert. *Young Törless*. New York: Signet, 1964.

Journey into the Heart of *Tortuga*

María Elena López
University of Northern Colorado

It is a terrible thing when the
foundations of faith fall apart. A
great vacuum opens up, one wanders
lost in that void. There is little
meaning to life.

Rudolfo A. Anaya

In *Tortuga*, Rudolfo Anaya plunges us into the chthonic depths of
the unconscious through hierophantic dreams, and then releases us with a
symbolic ascent of transcendence to walk the path of the sun. The author
intersperses Tortuga's mythic journey to salvation, his quest in search of
cosmic unity, and the "Philosopher's Stone" with shamanic dreams, archetypal
figures, and healing moments of communion with the sacred mysteries of the
mountain landscape. The oppressive institutional sterility of the hospital is the
wasteland from which Tortuga, paralyzed in a full body cast and surrounded
by barren, destructive forces, must escape. Magical thought and mythic
shaman save Tortuga from an attempted suicide and the hell of his existence.

Tortuga completes the trilogy of Anaya's novels which incorporate
experiences from three periods of Anaya's life: childhood in rural New Mexico
in *Bless Me, Ultima*; adolescence in the urban setting in *Heart of Aztlán*; and
an unfortunate hospital stay in *Tortuga*.[1] The third novel has its
autobiographic base in a personal accident suffered by Anaya as a young man.
He and his friends went swimming in an irrigation canal. Anaya dove in, hit

bottom, fractured two vertebrae in his neck, and floated to the top face down, drowning, unable to avoid swallowing the water because the injury to his neck had instantly paralyzed him. Eventually his friends pulled him out and saved him. The paralyzed protagonist of *Tortuga* shares the suffering of Anaya:

> The novel is loosely based on my experience in a hospital, but it quickly became more than that. The theme of healing still occupied my thoughts. How do people get well? I looked around and saw that we had created a society that was crushing and mutilating us. People were sick, physically and spiritually. How could those people be helped? The hospital I created became an existential hell, symbolizing our own contemporary hell. (Anaya, *Contemporary Authors* 26)

In *Tortuga*, as in the other novels of the trilogy, Anaya's message is that the destructive forces of our time must be faced with a spirituality based on myth, tradition, and unity with the land.

Tortuga is a novel of initiation.[2] A young boy, paralyzed as a result of an unexplained accident, is forced to make the transition from one stage of life to the next in a remote hospital for crippled children where he struggles to understand the reasons for his paralysis and to overcome the limitations of his condition. Unlike the other cripples of the hospital, he faces his physical and psychological injuries and emerges as a new person. His is a symbolic death and rebirth. The *renovatio* is due to the magical powers of nature, the guidance of a tutelary figure, and the mediation and encouragement of a young girl. The end of the novel coincides with the end of the journey; he leaves the hospital victorious and triumphant.

Tortuga, the paralyzed young boy, is chauffeured to an isolated desert hospital by an "ancient" old man who is forced to drive through total darkness during a severe winter storm. Moments before the arrival, the sun breaks through the rain and darkness; the old man stops the ambulance and points out a nearby mountain which is illuminated by the afternoon sunlight. He informs the boy that it is a magic mountain with huge internal caverns through which run powerful rivers of holy waters. The old man delivers the boy to the hospital, tells him that he'll be better in the spring, and disappears. The symbolic motifs of the novel have been established: journey, desert, wise old man, cyclical rebirth, magic mountain, sacred rivers, internal caverns, and illuminating sunlight.

The journey to the hospital is more than a passage through space; the spiritual and symbolic equivalents are revelation, illumination, transformation, and the search for new and profound experiences. The desert isolation alludes to the desert as a place of purification. The ordeals that the boy will endure in the hospital will become rites of purification leading to health and salvation. The ambulance in which they travel is in reality a converted old hearse. The connection is established: the chauffeur is Charon, the mythological figure who rows the souls across the river of death. The delivery by Charon and the abandonment in which the boy is left symbolize death. The actions of the old man establish him as both Charon who delivers unto death and the archetype of the wise old man whose wisdom in this case presages spring's rebirth. The storm which they have endured has a sacred quality about it. Rain in most mythologies is regarded as a symbol of life and spiritual influences.

In universal tradition a mountain is a sacred symbol. A mountain becomes the Sacred Mountain when it is a symbol of the inaccessible and of spiritual elevation. The Sacred Mountain is always considered to be the *Centre* of the universe. As a cosmic center, it is the meeting point of the three cosmic regions: heaven, earth, and hell. In almost all traditions, the mountain has this profound significance because the vertical axis from the peak to the base is associated with the *axis mundi*, the stationary central point about which the earth may be imagined to revolve. Mircea Eliade explains:

> The center, then is pre-eminently the zone of the sacred, the zone of absolute reality. Similarly, all the other symbols of absolute reality (trees of life and immortality, Fountain of Youth, etc.) are also situated at center. The road leading to center . . . is arduous, fraught

> with perils, because it is, in fact, a rite of passage from the profane
> to the sacred, from the ephemeral and illusory to reality and eternity,
> from death to life, from man to divinity. (*The Myth* 17-18)

One is consecrated when one arrives at the center. A great many ritual acts have the sole purpose of finding this immutable center where God, perfection, and absolutes are said to reside. Tortuga's descent into the mountain will be a most sacred journey. It is the spiritual and physical relationship between the mountain and the boy that establishes the thematic and structural development of the novel. The symbolic objective of the boy's solitary journey is to enter the mountain, to discover the secret at its core, to be healed by its powers and illumined by its knowledge.

The underlying significance of the cavern is that of concealment. "For Jung, it stands for the security and impregnability of the unconscious" (Cirlot 38). To the alchemist the hollow cavernous mountain was a symbol of the philosopher's oven in which would be incubated the "Philosopher's Stone," the substantive equivalent of *Centre*. The legendary stone contained the quintessence of things, could turn base metals into gold, and. even more significantly, could cure the human body of all its weaknesses and give it health.

Spirituality, linked to light, illumination, and to the sun as the supreme source of light, becomes concretely evident in the development of the novel. The amount and type of light in every scene of the novel is regulated to reflect and complement the stages of the journey. We oscillate between darkness and glorious sunshine. The light of the sun becomes "strands of golden light," "glorious light," "eerie pearl light," and "weak saffron rays of light." By association with the sun, and to the gold of the alchemist's quest, the word "golden" becomes the adjective of Anaya's predilection. The constant dialectic of light and darkness converts Anaya's settings into a chiaroscurist canvas.

The boy embarks on the arduous journey from a dark abandoned room. The first stage of the journey is symbolized by the color black, which represents the stage of death and putrefaction, the stage at which one recognizes one's worthlessness and disintegrates into the level of *materia prima*. The boy has been symbolically entombed in a full-body cast which literally makes him smell and rot inside for several months. The cast gives him the appearance of a turtle whereby he acquires the name "Tortuga." His original identity disintegrates; we never know him by any name other than Tortuga. By virtue of the cast, he literally becomes one with the land, the microcosm of the magic mountain whose internal caverns he must explore.

Tortuga evolves into a multifarious protagonist. He is now a mountain-turtle-man. As a "turtle" he is the animal of the primordial waters, of the subterranean depths, a symbol of material existence. In alchemic tradition the turtle represented the *massa confusa*, the complete negation of any aspect of transcendence. By its subterranean nature, it is the antithesis of the bird which universally signifies elevation of the spirit. The quest for spiritual purification and transcendence must begin in the chthonic depths, at the level of the turtle.

Viewed psychologically, the symbolism of the novel refers to the process of individuation, the process by which consciousness and unconsciousness regulate and accommodate each other to produce a mature, integrated personality. The mountain is the impenetrable totality of the self. The visible mountain peak represents the ego. The internal caverns are the unconscious. The secret core becomes the Self. To enter the cavernous mountain is to enter the realm of the unconscious. In Jungian psychology, dreams are considered the mechanisms by which the unconscious communicates with consciousness. Dreams delivers messages of both a personal and collective nature. Dream messages, if understood, will produce positive psychic growth--the process of individuation.

The opening sentence of the novel states: "I awoke from a restless sleep." The tragedy of paralysis has punctured the unconscious and stimulated the intense dream activity which produces the restless sleep. Throughout the novel, Tortuga is repeatedly awakening from a restless sleep. The unconscious is providing a constant flow of significant dreams, and the psyche is regulating the flow of significant childhood memories. Archetypal figures surface from his unconscious. The archetypes of the anima, the shadow, and the self are personified by the people he meets at the hospital. The anima, a positive mediating force, is a young girl named Ismelda. Danny becomes his shadow. Salomón is the tutelary figure who personifies the self.

Immediately following the delivery to the desert hospital, Tortuga is met by Ismelda who, as a personification of the anima, is omnipresent--at his side during the day and in his dreams at night. Tortuga recognizes this when he says: "Ismelda had become a strong link between my dreams and the mountain and what happened to me. Somehow she was always near me" (55). By touching his forehead and brushing back his hair, she sends tingles running down his back and arms. These are the first sensations he has felt since the paralysis. And Ismelda's healing touch becomes a recurring theme throughout the novel. This concrete manifestation of the inner spirituality of human beings is a universal mythic belief which attributes great power to the hand. In many cultures the touch, or the laying on of the hands, generates healing forces.

Ismelda brings him water from the mountain, food from home; she bathes and feeds him regularly. Mystery and magic surround her. She knows the mountain, and perhaps she is the mountain, for often in her eyes is seen the outline of the mountain. When she sits beside Tortuga, there is another presence hovering over them. She represents the eternal feminine force: "[I]n some strange unfathomable way she was all the women who had touched my past and forced me to become a man" (109).

The magic of Ismelda's healing touch is counterbalanced by the nefariousness of the shadow, the negative, destructive, and regressive forces of the ego. The touch of the shadow forebodes a curse. Shortly after his arrival at the hospital, Tortuga finds himself abandoned in a dark and empty ward, a propitious moment for the arrival of the shadow, personified by Danny who enters stealthily and advances toward Tortuga. He thrusts a rancid, scaly, dirty hand over Tortuga's mouth and threatens to silence him forever.

Danny epitomizes Christian fanaticism. His mission as gatekeeper to the ego is to forbid the escape of messages from the unconscious. His aim is to destroy Tortuga's incipient belief in the magic of the mountain, repeatedly proclaiming all such beliefs as "bullshit." In his role as inquisitor, he must prevent the influx of pagan thoughts and mysticism, especially since Tortuga has abandoned his faith in the saints and the sacraments and is in need of a new spiritual focus to fill the void. When Danny is faced with what he considers heresy, he becomes hysterical and has to be restrained physically. Afterwards, he spends countless hours in the art room painting bloody mangled Christs. And in an attempt to heal his crippled arm, he orders a pint of miraculous dirt from the Santuario de Chimayo. But this only serves to irritate the disease further and to accelerate its spread.

Danny, furthermore, is a victim of rationalism. When the preacher shouts that everyone should open up his heart for all to enter, Danny gets a surgical saw and removes the casts of several children in order to permit God to enter their hearts. His logic leads him to the conclusion that if everything is made of atoms, and atoms are comprised of empty space, then he should be able to walk through walls. He succeeds only in injuring himself.

Danny meets Tortuga shortly after Tortuga arrives at the hospital, and accompanies him thereafter. The shadow, as a personification of the negative aspects of the ego, is by necessity omnipresent. Tortuga says of his shadow:

> He had been a constant companion. Whenever I opened my eyes, he was lurking nearby, like a vulture waiting for death to peck the answer from the riddle of life. He stood waiting, yellow eyes burning with insanity which drove him to mumble God's phrases over and

over, his dry arm hanging uselessly by his side, bent over by the
hump that was beginning to develop on his back. (122)

When Tortuga reaches the nadir of existence, Danny employs a very logical
story to convince Tortuga that death is better than suffering. Tortuga agrees
to die, and Danny takes him to the pool and attempts to drown him. When
the process of individuation is completed, Tortuga leaves the hospital; Danny
remains in intensive care in a state of physical and psychological
disintegration.

With the guidance of Ismelda to shield Tortuga from the rationalism
and fanaticism of Danny, he embarks on a journey of initiation. Tortuga"s
destiny is to surrender to the power of Salomón, a small paralyzed child with
angelic features, who is the personification of the universal which Aristotle
called the "unmoved mover, which the alchemist called the *lapis
philosophorum*, and the psychologist calls the "Self." Salomón, the
personification of the Self, is presented as the archetype of the Child.
According to Jung, this archetype symbolizes the formative forces of the
unconscious, of a beneficent and protective kind. And while in Christian
iconography children are portrayed as angels, embodiments of the soul, other
traditions present the child as a mystic child who solves riddles and teaches
wisdom. Salomón is the mystic child; his "angelic lips" utter the secrets of
the universe.

Salomón is literally the "unmoved mover." This frail creature is
completely paralyzed and helpless, alive only because his eyes move,
something which permits him to read incessantly. He lives with the terminally
ill in a ward known as the "vegetable patch." Dark hallways, rows of beds
and iron lungs lead to the center of the labyrinth which is Salomón's private
room. The nurse points out that "it's the only room in the ward . . . he needs
privacy, and besides, he's been here the longest" (39). His small cubicle is
lined with bookshelves containing books, potted plants and vines. The room
is a *temenos*, a protected area, set apart and dedicated to a god. He is the
immobile center of the hospital and those who dare must come to him.

Salomón has developed a solar cult and a solar theology. By walking "the path of the sun," man makes himself a sun that will shine on new worlds. The tenets of Salomón's philosophy include the following: the Sun is the divinity that binds all things; all that lives or exists in the world is a part of the sun; the Sun is the energy of the cosmos and the hidden essence in all of nature; man can gain salvation through illumination; life is a cycle of rebirth and regeneration, and the path of the sun is the path of love.

The tenet of divine immanence is a fundamental one. Man must walk the path of the sun for the purpose of discovering the god within himself. Based on this principle, man cannot fear the gods, nor blame them. Hence, Salomón turns iconoclast and attacks the Greek hero Prometheus, Christ the Saviour, and even the modern Sisyphus. They must no longer be considered viable heroes because they have proven that they cannot endure the pain of suffering without cursing the gods. Man must not follow the examples of heroes who bemoan moments of great anguish:

> *No, Tortuga, we are beyond the last Greek hero . . . we are beyond all the heroes of the past . . . We have come to a new plane in the time of eternity . . . We have gone far beyond the punishment of the gods. We are beyond everything that we have ever known, and the past is useless to us. We must create out of our own ashes. Our hero must be born out of this wasteland, like the phoenix bird of the desert he must rise again from the ashes of our withered bodies . . . and he must not turn to the shadows of the past. He must walk in the path of the sun . . . and he shall sing the songs of the sun.*
> (160)

Society must create new heroes. These heroes must control their own destinies; they must not allow themselves to be used as pawns by whimsical gods. If the faith in our Gods is shattered, if the foundations of our faith fall apart, if there is no meaning to life, we must plumb our own depths for our own salvation. We must revive our myths to work our way out of despair and depression.

Salomón is the sun. His moment of illumination is provided by a giant butterfly that cames through the open window and showers him with golden dust. Following the tenet of divine immanence, the butterfly contains the cosmic numen, and the cosmic numen contains the butterfly who is the ubiquitous *Centre*. The secret core of the mountain flies to him and gives him the "touch" of love. We hear echoes of Pascal, and of the many who have used the famous phrase: "God is an infinite sphere of which the center is everywhere, the circumference nowhere."[3] This is a moment of grandeur and beauty. A simple butterfly illumines a broken, withered body buried in a sterile hospital ward. It is the point of epiphany which Anaya speaks of in his "Writer's Landscape."[4]

The story of Salomón is a journey within a journey. A crippled child despairs, blames the gods, attempts to kill himself, but is saved by the "touch" of a butterfly. From his ashes will rise a hero, a crippled boy who has despaired, cursed the gods, and attempted to kill himself. The cyclic nature of life assures eternal regeneration. The name Salomón has a multiple significance. It is a Hebrew name which means "peaceful"; hence it associates the boy with the historical King Solomon who is known for his infinite wisdom and for his song of love. But the name Salomón also provides the boy with the nickname "Sol," which the nurses in the ward use to refer to him. It is a revealing nickname, because the word, in Spanish, means "sun."

Ismelda, Danny, and Salomón, Tortuga's constant companions, must be dealt with as comrades in the process of individuation. They personify the vital inner forces of Tortuga. However, dreams are the messages of the unconscious; they regulate the process of individuation. In *Tortuga*, there are nine principal dreams which structure the development of the novel. I will analyze three. They develop progressively into a symbolic ascent of the mountain. The first dream, symbolizing the plunge into the unconscious, is subterranean taking Tortuga to the center of Tortuga Mountain. The dream about the first communion girls presents, at length, one of the recurring memories of Tortuga's transition from childhood to adolescence. The last dream is a celestial coronation. Its setting, which finalizes the process of individuation, ends on top of the mountain.

The first night in the hospital, Tortuga falls into a restless sleep. His first dream is a revelation. Salomón, whom he has never met and about whom he knows nothing, appears to him and explains why man is in a state fallen from grace. Tortuga is escorted into the dream-world by Ismelda. She takes his hand and leads him into the mountain. Together they tumble into a spring of bubbling waters. She holds him to help him overcome his fear of drowning. She leads him deeper and deeper into the mountain until they reach the source of the internal rivers. Ismelda tells him that the source is the "place of power." There on the bank sits a small thin boy who knows the mountain because he is the mountain. The boys tells a story.

Clearly, the first dream is a descent to the mystic *Centre* of the mountain. Tortuga is escorted by his anima whose role it is to protect and guide. Together they tumble into the bubbling waters of the underground rivers and swim to the source. It is a ritualistic preparation and purification for a sacred event. Ismelda introduces Tortuga to Salomón who is the personification of the Self: "[This] Self usually appears in dreams at crucial times in the dreamer's life--turning points when his basic attitude and whole way of life are changing. The change itself is often symbolized by the action of crossing water" (Jung, et al, *Man and His Symbols* 198). In Jungian psychology, voices heard in dreams are considered to contain sacred messages. The Salomón of the dream speaks to Tortuga about primordial times.

In the beginning, Salomón says, man fell away from the path of the sun. Man must restore himself to his vanished eternity. Salomón's version of original sin is a variant of the universal myth of the accursed hunter. In many mythologies and legends, the figure of the hunter represents man's attraction to worldly things. The hunter, by his pursuit of temporal pleasures, brings ruin upon himself. Salomón tells how he was the adventurous hunter of primordial times. As a young man he abandoned his father's way of life to pursue the excitement of the hunt. The father was a farmer and he walked the path of the sun. Having fled his father's way of life, the young man attempted to join a tribe of hunters. He was defeated by the dark underworld forces when he failed to kill an ocean turtle during an initiation rite. The headless turtle overpowered the hunter and returned to the ocean waters from whence it was able to haunt him for the rest of his life.

Salomón reveals, with the myth of the accursed hunter, why man is in a state fallen from grace. But the first dream augurs deliverance and regeneration. Tortuga has touched the sacred *Center*. The Salomón he meets in this dream later materializes as the paralyzed cripple of the vegetable patch, and as such, becomes the shaman whose revelations will lead him out of the shadows and into the light.

The second dream deals with the First Communion, a dream of prior initiation: Tortuga's initiation into adolescence, his introduction to sexuality. It also marks the moment when Tortuga unveils the pagan gods hidden beneath the robes of the Christian sacraments. At that moment he loses faith in his mother's gods; he transcends the strictures of Catholicism. On the Easter Sunday of his First Communion, Tortuga bravely questioned the ritual. The children had gone through the ordeal of the dark confessional and the purification of penance. Why were innocent children confessing sins when there were no sins to be confessed? Did Communion signify a rebirth into a union with Christ? What was the meaning of Communion?[5] The answer to his question is revealed immediately after Communion as they are leaving the church. At that moment "the Lord blessed my girls again, teased them with his power, stripped the veil of innocence and revealed the soft, pink flesh of their eager tongues . . . Great, white petals of snow floated down from the clear sky (140-41).

In imitation of Zeus, the pagan god Dionysus transforms himself into spermy, glistening snowflakes and lasciviously rains down upon the First Communion girls. The intricate, crystalline hosts land in the mouths of the innocent girls.

Dionysus claims privileges to his rites of fertility. Tortuga screams in fear and runs to hide by the river.

He had discovered the "Mysteries" hidden in the Sacrament of Communion. The host and the wine of the Christian ceremony are modern sublimations of the Dionysian ritual of wine and erotic union. The Dionysian ritual celebrated man's animal nature and the fertility of the Earth Mother. Christianity dispelled these mysteries, but they were deeply ingrained in the memories of early Christian followers. They eventually modified the pagan rituals and incorporated them into the Christian Mass. Tortuga feels betrayed. His faith in God is lost.

Intrigued by the pagan origin of the Sacrament, Tortuga incorporates the sexual aspect of the ancient ritual into his own celebration of the First Communion. Down by the river, with several of the First Communion girls, he experiences his sexuality. The dream of the First Communion is the memory of puberty rites. This initiation symbolizes a break from maternal protection; it places him out in the world on his own.

The initiation into sexuality produces a radical change on the conscious and unconscious levels. The "mother archetype" within the child loses the vague identity of the personal mother with whom the child no longer participates extensively. As the child grows up the mother archetype "recedes from consciousness and the clearer the latter becomes, the more distinctly does the archetype assume mythological features" (Jung, *Four Archetypes* 36). The archetype now acquires fabulous and mysterious qualities. It may transform itself into the Great Mother who could develop as a benevolent goddess or a malevolent and dangerous woman. Tortuga, right after his first experience with sexuality, encounters the mythical "Llorona" down by the river. La Llorona, Tortuga's personification of the Great Mother, perhaps the Terrible Mother, thereafter appears to him in his dreams.

Tortuga's final dream occurs to him on the day of Salomón's death. Danny, the shadow of Tortuga, has pulled the switch and cut off all power to the ward of the vegetables where Salomón lives. It is a symbolic sacrifice; and, following the archetype of rebirth, Salomón will transform into another mode of being. As the phoenix bird of the desert, Salomón will rise from his ashes to be reborn into the hero Tortuga, whose identity has disintegrated upon arrival at the hospital, and needs to be re-established before his departure. However, the concept of rebirth is not always used in the same sense. Salomón's rebirth, most likely, takes the form of a reincarnation.

The final dream is an apocalyptic vision, a revelation that culminates his journey with a glorious ascent into the solar system. Tortuga is accompanied by Ismelda and all of his friends from the ward; together they sing and dance to the music of the blue guitar. A triumphant procession introduces the dream. Tortuga and his friends abandon crutches, braces, and wheelchairs. Dressed in flowing white robes, they dance and sing to the plants and the flowers. Slowly they ascend the mountain. They perform a May dance at the *axis mundi*, a juniper tree centrally located in a meadow at the very peak of the mountain. Golden strands of light and love bind them together. Then the mountain breaks loose and begins to float into the solar system. They were "rising like a glowing sun into the indigo of night, rising to take our place in the spermy string of lights which crowned the sky" (187).

In the dream, the group becomes a "glowing sun," and they become one of the suns in the solar system. The revelation is presented to him as a *solificatio*, a solar coronation. In alchemical terms, they have attained the final stage, symbolized by the color gold which is chosen to correspond to the sun and to that ultimate substance of the alchemist's quest. There is an analogy between dream symbolism and the symbolism of alchemy. Mircea Eliade tells us that Jung, in his studies of the unconscious, discovered the parallels:

> [H]is discovery amounted in substance to this: in the very depths of the unconscious, processes occur which bear an astonishing resemblance to the stages in a spiritual operation--gnosis, mysticism, alchemy--*which does not occur in the world of profane experience,*

and which on the contrary, makes a clean break with the profane world. (*The Forge* 223)

The unconscious, therefore, operates within a sacred realm, and the dreams which it regulates may contain revelations. Furthermore, Jung's studies reveal that "alchemy, with all its symbolism and operations, is a projection onto matter, of archetypes and processes of the collective unconscious. The *opus alchymicum* is in reality the process of individuation by which one becomes the Self (Eliade, *The Forge* 224). For centuries, the Self has been revealing its symbols and processes; in some traditions, that knowledge was systematized and called alchemy. As expressed by the alchemical symbols of his dream, Tortuga has experienced a sacred revelation; he has become his Self, which Salomón had personalized until his death.

For Tortuga, the dream of the solar coronation signifies the end of his journey of initiation. For as Eliade tell us, "In philosophical terms, initiation is equivalent to an ontological mutation of the existential condition" (*The Quest* 112). He distinguishes three types of initiation: puberty rites or collective ritual for transition from childhood to adolescence, rites for entering a secret society, and the personal experience connected with a mystical vocation of a shamanic nature (*The Quest* 112). The dream of the First Communion is the memory of a collective ritual which provides Tortuga the transition into adolescence. The dream of the solar ascent is unquestionably a shamanic initiation. Eliade tells us that these "consist in ecstatic experiences (e.g., dreams, visions, trances) and in an instruction imparted by the spirits of the old master shamans (e.g., shamanic techniques, names and functions of the spirits, mythology and genealogy of the clan, secret language)" (*The Quest* 115). Tortuga's dream of initiation provides him with a rebirth that would be classified as a *renovatio*, a radical change occurring to a person within the span of his own lifetime (Jung, *Four Archetypes* 48). Salomón has functioned in the novel as an old master shaman, whose voice is heard continually as he communicates the mythology and the tenets of his cult. The voice of Salomón alternates with the dreams of Tortuga and the events in the hospital.

The dream, moreover, is an apocalyptic vision. The magic mountain, on which Tortuga stands, breaks loose from its desert captivity and ascends into the sky. Those who have believed are saved; they are the redeemed who will regenerate the world. And as the mountain tears loose, oceans of lava and water sweep down upon the unbelievers. The holocaust destroys those who never walked in the path of the sun.

The day after the dream, Tortuga leaves the hospital to return home. He proudly carries with him his only possession--the blue guitar, bequeathed to him by the deceased poet Crispín, which will endow Tortuga with Crispín's poetic numen. This musical instrument becomes Anaya's version of the "Philosopher's Stone"--the "stone which is not a stone, a precious thing which has no value, a thing of many shapes which has no shapes, this unknown which is known to all" (Eliade, *The Forge* 164). The poetic numen of the blind poet Crispín, who is Homer himself, and the instrument are bestowed on Tortuga a few days before Salomón's death. Salomón had prophesied that Tortuga was destined to become a singer. The concurrence of these two events appears fortuitous because Salomón and Crispín did not know each other. However, Salomón's prophesy and the arrival of the guitar form a strange but meaninful coincidence known in Jungian terms as "synchronicity": an unconscious force causing events to coincide meaningfully despite the absence of all causality. The power of cosmic harmony is seen as the cause of such events.

Crispín and the blue guitar also appear in Anaya's second novel, *Heart of Aztlán*, where we discover that

> *the blue guitar was carved from the heart of a juniper tree. Its color was the blue of the mexican sky, its strings are the rays of the golden sun. Wise men tuned it to tell the legends of the people, and in it were stored the myths of the past. . . . It was there when the people arrived to carve the calendar-sun and it was there when the cross of Christ was driven into the flesh of the earth . . . (Heart of Aztlán 27-28)*

The attributes with which the blue guitar is described (heart, gold, knowledge, timelessness) reveal it as the ubiquitous "Philosopher's Stone." Crispín, another personification of the archetype of the "old man," and the blue guitar, moreover, form a symbol of unity. The guitar is feminine by virtue of its shape and its receptacle-like interior. In it reside music and poetry which are the expressions of the inner truths which link all things. Crispín and the guitar form a symbol of "Oneness," the alchemical *coincidentia oppositorum*. Tortuga, having achieved individuation, will go out into the world with his blue guitar to live as his tutelary shaman had instructed: "Sing a song of love, Tortuga! Oh yes, sing of love" (196).

There is an all-encompassing, sincere and worthwhile message in *Tortuga*: man must turn to his unconscious to satisfy his spiritual need since the mechanized, technological rationalism of our age cannot.[6] Man must create new myths--myths that will turn the tide of the rational attitude which recognizes only intellectual enlightenment as the highest form of understanding and insight. Rationalism endows man with an evolutionary vision: science and progress move mankind forward an upward in a never-ending linear progression. Yet, the mythic memory of man manifests a transformative vision: man, as an integral part of nature, functions in an Eternal Return in harmony with the cycles of the universe. Whereas consciousness and reason guide us in a linear progression, the unconscious mythical mind gives us a cyclical view of time and returns us to the archetypes.

José A. Argüelles, in his book *The Transformative Vision*, argues that society needs modern visionaries to offset the dangerous imbalance created by the supremacy of rationalism and the evolutionary vision. We must, Argüelles says, work for a "major reversal of the specialization typified by the scientist and the artist, until the two roles are merged into one" (289). The merger of the scientist, symbolizing intelligence, and the artist, symbolizing intuitive knowledge, will provide society with the visionaries who "will combat the great rush of progress, so contrary to the cyclical order of the universe. . . ." (288). Society and man must be regenerated and transformed in order to offset the debilitating horrors of progress. Our age has been creating a system of intellectual and practical organization that favors mechanical automatism and abolishing human autonomy. Too much of our progress turns out to be life-eliminating.

We must turn to the myths of our collective heritage to find new strength and comfort. With Anaya, our archetypal figures become Ultima in *Bless Me, Ultima*, Crispín in *Heart of Aztlán*, and Salomón in *Tortuga*. Ultima, as an archetypal figure, is grounded in our Southwest folk motifs and oral tradition. She speaks to and about our cultural experience. Salomón, the Sun God, reborn later as Tortuga, is skillfully grounded in Jungian psychology, but much further removed from Southwest mythology and cultural tradition. In *Tortuga*, therefore, Anaya presents us with a beautiful vision for the redemption of society. This novel, like the others of the trilogy, attempts to tap the spiritual and mythical roots of our Southwest Hispanic culture in the hopes that people will identify and redefine themselves in accordance with forgotten cultural values.

NOTES

[1] *"Tortuga* was my hospital stay, and thus a very difficult novel for me to write. Yet I believe it to be one of my best works" (*Contemporary Authors* 26).

[2] All subsequent page references refer to the 1979 Editorial Justa edition of *Tortuga*.

[3] The circle (circumference and center) is the most immutable of the archetypal symbols. George Poulet, beginning with the medieval concept of God as an infinite circle whose center is everywhere and whose circumference is nowhere, traces its origins and studies the symbolic meanings of the circle in literature.

[4] He defines epiphany as the "natural response to that landscape, a coming together of these two forces. And because I feel a close kinship with my environment, I feel constantly in touch with that epiphany which opens me up to receive the power in my landscape" ("Writer's Landscape" 98-99).

[5] Anaya's young protagonist in *Bless Me, Ultima* also questions the meaning of his First Communion (210-11).

[6] In this article I have limited myself to studying the myth of Tortuga, the process of individuation through which Tortuga advances, and three of the principal dreams within his process of individuation. Anaya's mythopoesis searches the unconscious for what he calls the "truth in the heart," the constructive foundations on which to rebuild our faith. However, we cannot overlook the fact that the unconscious contains forces that are not constructive, negative forces that can return us to a primitivism that offers even less than the rationalism and pragmatism of our age. And these negative forces are present throughout the novel. They are there in the language and sexism of the other young hospital patients. They culminate in the movie theater scene. Here, unfortunately, Anaya effectively taps cultural roots many of us abhor. While he signals the need to return to spiritual values, he does so by

interspersing the spiritual journey with incessant conversations about "aching peckers," "swollen tools," and "desires for a good piece of ass."

WORKS CITED

Anaya, Rudolfo A. *Bless Me, Ultima.* Berkeley: Quinto Sol, 1972.

___. *Heart of Aztlán.* Berkeley: Justa, 1976.

___. *Tortuga.* Berkeley: Justa, 1979.

___. "Rudolfo A. Anaya." *Contemporary Authors Autobiography Series*, (vol. 4). Ed. Adele Sarkissan. Detroit: Gale Research, 1986. 15-28.

___. "The Writer's Landscape: Epiphany in Landscape." *Latin American Literary Review* 5.10 (1977): 98-102.

Argüelles, José A. *The Transformative Vision: Reflections on the Nature and History of Human Experssions.* Berkeley: Shambhala, 1975.

Cirlot, J. E. *Dictionary of Symbols.* New York: Philosophical Library, 1962.

Eliade, Mircea. *The Forge and the Crucible: The Origins and Structures of Alchemy.* Trans. Stephen Corrin. New York: Harper, 1962.

___. *The Myth of the Eternal Return: Cosmos and History.* Trans. Willard R. Trask. Princeton: Princeton UP, 1974.

___. *The Quest: History and Meaning in Religion.* Chicago: U of Chicago P, 1975.

Jung, Carl G. *Four Archetypes.* Trans. R. F. C. Hull. Princeton: Princeton UP, 1973.

___, et al. *Man and His Symbols.* New York: Doubleday, 1964.

Márquez, Antonio. "The Achievement of Rudolfo A. Anaya." In *The Magic of Words: Rudolfo A. Anaya and His Writings.* Ed. Paul Vassallo. Albuquerque: U of New Mexico P, 1982, 33-52.

Poulet, George. *The Metamorphoses of the Circle.* Baltimore: Johns Hopkins UP, 1966.

Tortuga: The Black Sun of Salomón's Wards

Ernesto Padilla
California State University, Bakersfield

Within Rudolfo A. Anaya's oeuvre, *Tortuga* has received limited recognition, but time will prove its power to endure. The novel presents an inspired vision that ennobles the reader, that provokes the range of human emotions: rage, pity, guilt, anxiety, laughter, euphoria, peace, and, above all, love. The novel also presents a controlled, mature aesthetic and merits careful attention. Edward Elias is right in his somewhat hyperbolic praise of the novel's "pictorial images, beautiful metaphors, peace, and . . . final joy" (87). However, it is my contention that the novel achieves its remarkable quality by understating the non-essential trappings of what is traditionally considered aesthetic, and by building responsibly on a single theme: the human instinct for love. *Tortuga* is a passionate attempt to replace John Calvin's and the seventeenth century Puritan's doctrine of "election," a passionate attempt to replace the conception of man as "depraved" and "evil" with the idea that man is innately loving and nurturing. Calvinists believed that some men (only a select few) were "elected" by God (predestined) and others were innately depraved, innately evil. Since the time of the Puritans, Americans have transferred this extremely negative religious teaching to the secular realm, and this secular legacy is what *Tortuga* negates.[1]

And yet, in spite of its power, *Tortuga* has the aesthetic defect of lack of character development; and the ideological defect of advocating dreams, magic, and cosmic mysticism as solutions for human problems. Both defects detract from its poetic power. Yet, the novel has a stubborn moral insistence and an intense focus and movement which mark it, in some ways, as more powerful than Anaya's first novel, *Bless Me, Ultima*, considered by many to be his best. In *Tortuga* we discover a poem with emotion that teaches compassion with more craft than is at first apparent.

Unlike *Bless Me, Ultima, Tortuga* is a deceptively simple poem, not ornately plotted, nor peopled with larger-than-life characters; it is the tale of a journey from innocence to experience, which travels through hate and despair, ending in love. *Tortuga* is a love poem that pins down a society too often impatient to pause and draw moral lessons from literature, especially if that literature is drawn from the experiences of the deformed. Within such a context, *Tortuga* focuses on love and compassion: what should be our response to the suffering of the world?

The protagonist of the novel, Tortuga, is destined to achieve the only thing that is not expendable for humanity: a simple love that asks for no reward other than to love. His principal shaman--the quadriplegic vegetable, Salomón--guides Tortuga to that spiritual insight, speaking to him primarily through dreams, waking and sleeping. Salomón's mesmerizing voice comes out of nowhere to teach Tortuga:

> *[Y]ou walked through the halls of the orphans and the cripples of this life . . . and you held us in your arms and offered us love . . . Oh, we sang with joy when you offered us your love! Our pain and suffering had meaning in your heart! We're not concerned with why we're here anymore. . . . Now is the time for singing and rejoicing! Now is the time to dip into the electric acid of life and burn our souls with its joy! Don't you see, my friend, you're the one hope that the darkness will never cover us completely! Even battered, crippled men will follow the path of the sun . . . bathe in its light . . . sing its songs.* (172)

This dream tells the whole tale. It is Tortuga's destiny to love his people and to speak on their behalf. He will minister to them spiritually by singing of their experiences. When he has accepted this destiny, the tale will end. Maureen Dolan has best articulated the circle that the novel charts: "It is as though [Tortuga's] destiny triumphed over his will until the latter was humanized, and became one with the former" (57). And yet, to appreciate *Tortuga* fully, we must take into account its weaknesses as well as its strengths.

An ideological weakness is the novel's emphasis on magic and cosmic mysticism revealed in dreams. The problem lies in the implication that dream, magic and cosmic mysticism are a viable solution for mankind, available to all who will believe and submit to the priesthood of cosmic forces.[2] But setting aside the difficulty of cosmic mysticism for a moment, let us take up the matter of how Anaya utilizes dream as a vehicle for the process of teaching the protagonist.

In his use of dream as a primary plot vehicle, we wish Anaya were not so much influenced by Carl G. Jung, as by Sigmund Freud. To say this is not to deny the presence of dream as an important reality in the life of mankind, nor to deny the power of faith in humanity as a central force in human motivation. But we want a story that is accessible to us, human mortals. The problem with the dreams is that they are, in fact, well organized, apocalyptic visions. They are the voices of the forces of nature speaking to Tortuga both while asleep and while awake. Elias suggests that Salomón, the shaman guide, "speaks as an oracular voice disembodied from a credible character. His counsel is akin to that of the wise Solomon of biblical texts." Salomón's wards, Elias continues, "appear constantly in the narrative as if they were reflections of Tortuga's conscience, his reveries or intuitions; in fact, the sage's teachings are disconnected from actual meetings or dialogues between the two characters" (83). It is true that the dreams are admirable for their poetic power, for their power of metaphor, but it is this very clarity, this left brain organization that destroys the novelistic illusion.

The dreams in *Tortuga* are not the highly symbolic, chaotic dreams that we find in *Bless Me, Ultima*--dreams common to humanity, dreams which can be analyzed according to Freudian dream interpretation. The dreams in *Tortuga* are not the kind of dreams which might be narrated, for instance, by the detached narrator that Henry James perfected. James's narrators make the reader work; they do not provide omniscient perspective analysis. Instead, the James reader must actively participate in the journey of knowledge, understanding, and moral growth, just as Freud had to work to make left brain sense of his patient's chaotic dreams.

It is lamentable that the reader of *Tortuga* need not work to achieve understanding and emotional maturity by means of the novel. The dreams are too obviously the poetic vision of the narrator imposing itself upon the drama. We want some right-brain dreams, more disconnected, more like Antonio's dreams in *Bless Me, Ultima*, more like those Freud reports in his *The Interpretation of Dreams*. In recognition of the apparent chaos of logic in dreams and in an attempt to make sense of the disconnectedness of the dream content, Freud proposed a "psychological technique which makes it possible to interpret dreams" so that "every dream reveals itself as a psychical structure which has meaning and which can be inserted at an assignable point in the mental activities of waking life." Freud tried to "elucidate the processes to which the strangeness and obscurity of dreams are due and to deduce from those processes the nature of the psychical forces by whose concurrent or mutually opposing action dreams are generated" (35). It is my contention that this quality of "strangeness and obscurity" is largely absent from the dreams in *Tortuga* while it is wonderfully present in *Bless Me, Ultima*.

Still, the dreams constitute a primary vehicle. Through them the narrator tells Tortuga that he has a destiny to fulfill, but they are not otherwise integrated into the story. A typical dream, as propounded by Freud, would present a chaos of logic and emotion. This chaos might then be interpreted by another, wiser character. The following statement by Freud elucidates the deficiency in the dreams of *Tortuga*:

> The dream-content . . . is expressed as it were in a pictographic script, the characters of which have to be transposed individually into the language of the dream thoughts. If we attempted to read these characters according to their pictorial value instead of according to their symbolic relation, we should clearly be led into error. (312)

The dream-content in Tortuga's dreams forms a one-to-one correspondence with the theme of the novel, with the final illumination. There is one language: that of the narrator announcing the plot, as we have already seen in the dream quoted above. The narrator's voice overwhelms the story line, destroys the illusion of reality, intrudes with poetic and inspired passages that are presented as dreams and waking euphoric experiences. And yet, although the dreams are counterproductive in that they destroy the illusion of reality, in that they lack verisimilitude, they are, one has to admit, inspired, inlaid with Anaya's best poetic craft. Some of them are poems in and of themselves.

But it is not just in dreams that the narrative heavy-handedly plots to organize all elements so that they magically reinforce and guide Tortuga to his pre-ordained destiny. This too-obvious conspiracy of magic and cosmic mysticism begins even on the first page. Clepo, a minor character who knows the Arizona desert, speaks of a desert storm as if he had no experience of it: "It's never been this dark before." Clepo must be instructed by Filomón that he has to "know the desert to know rain don't last. It can be raining one minute and blowing dust devils the next" (3). But Clepo does know this southern desert because he has made the ambulance trip south with Filomón many times: "Ah, Filo . . . you've stopped here every time we bring a new kid. Don't you ever get tired of showing them that damned mountain?" (3) It is too obvious that the dialogue is meant to instruct the reader and not the experienced Clepo.

The reference to the ominous sky foreshadows Tortuga's journey to the "inferno" (Dante's journey) in which he will experience the "heart of darkness," Conrad's vision of man's utter depravity and degraded condition. Unfortunately, however, Anaya trivializes the experience by asking the reader to accept Tortuga's phantasmagoric spiritual journey of conversion to the heart of the mountain by means of a magic-mushroom-inward journey, à la Carlos Casteneda. Tortuga mountain is a spiritual mountain to which people flock "to bathe in the mineral waters from the springs" (3). Again, on the next page:

"These old villages cling to the river like the beads of a rosary . . . the springs of Tortuga, the place of the healing water--" Thus, Tortuga's spiritual ascent and cleansing is foreshadowed, as is the triumph: "Just wait till spring, and you'll be better" (5). In a brief span of pages, we have a call to shamanic magic and Catholic faith.

It is dark, it is winter, and Tortuga, who is yet to be christened after the mountain, is completely paralyzed. The only hope for the universe of the novel is faith in the mystic healing powers of the mountain. Filomón is only the first in a series of shamanic guides that will lead Tortuga to the priesthood of communion with the mystical magic of the mountain which in the final analysis will turn out to be the power of faith, love and compassion. The novel presents a timeless horizon of magic, witches, shamans and myth. But evil is not an abstract, pre-existing force; instead it is the temptation of the stronger to subdue the weaker. This selfish act is a transgression against the common good. In presenting evil as if it emanates from mystico-religious powers greater than man, Anaya dehistoricizes the human condition, attributes the common motivation of greed to powers or forces beyond man, thus implying absolution and tolerance. Enough said about the inaccessibility of this magic. *Tortuga* does, in spite of the unfortunate fairy tale element, make a sincere and inspiring statement on behalf of simple human compassion, and for the inspiration that empathy and example engender.

A second deficiency in the novel is the lack of character development, an important aesthetic deficiency. We see that Tortuga grows in maturity and selflessness, but this development is not fleshed out. His destiny is to inherit Crispín's mythical blue guitar, to play the role of wise man and spiritual guide to his people. Crispín will be for Tortuga what Ultima was for Antonio: an inspirational teacher who practices white magic. Tortuga, as has been foretold, finally accepts his role as poet-singer for his people but only after he makes sense of the universe:

> [M]y thoughts were making connections with everything, and without
> knowing I was humming a song. It was a song about the mountain
> and about . . . everyone who had come into my life . . . I sang and

filled myself with hope, a hope against the dark fear which returned
to haunt us and force us into dark shells, a hope which rejoiced in
what Salomón had said. (185)

We can chart, step by step, Tortuga's inspirational progress toward
unselfish love, his despair at the prospect of never again walking; his revulsion
at the helpless life forms interminably laying in their own spit, vomit, urine,
and human waste; his rejection of those more deformed than he, his lust for
the healthy physical-therapist, his attraction to the healthy and sensuous
Ismelda, his refusal to believe in either the symbolic, magical mountain or the
mystic call of Salomón, and, finally, his gradual love, eventual loyalty and
committed determination to help his fellow disabled and all of suffering
humanity. Yes, this gradual journey of self moving from ego-centrism to
selflessness is there, and it is an inspirational statement of compassion.

But, *Tortuga* contains few illuminations about the nature of the world
of the protagonist; that is, there are few spontaneous, apparently random
illuminations, the kind that give one the impression that character rather than
plot or theme is more important. We want to know how the protagonist
perceives the world on a more concrete level, on a more intimate level, and
we want these perceptions to be, at least upon first impression, unrelated to the
plot and theme. Instead, Tortuga's illuminations are thematic, staged,
organized to lead us to the heart of the mountain after which he is named.
But we, as readers, want to know *who* Tortuga is, without the insistence of
the plot and theme compelling us in an economy that is overly obvious. We
want the random luxury of nature, of apparently unrelated incidents. We want
a density and flux of experience and incident out of which we discover that
love and compassion give meaning to life, and that they are the only
transcending qualities that distinguish mankind. We want to see this potential
embedded in the character of Tortuga.

Strip the novel of its magical elements, its unrealistically structured
dreams, its opportunistic symbol, and we have a simple story, a much more
accessible story of a boy that matures. Then add more incident and

illumination--the kind of self-discovery and exploration that is so successful in *Bless Me, Ultima*--and we have a much more compelling tale.

Another, less important, defect of the novel is its exaggerated concern with the sexual (here, again I acknowledge this defect to be ideological instead of aesthetic). I refer to the sensationalization of sex, and even more unfortunately the sexism, the glorification of male sexual dominance and female subordination. This stereotyping would not, perhaps, be so disturbing if it were not so redundant and graphic. Not that we are squeamish readers, but we want Tortuga's compassion to speak both to women as well as to men--to inspire an attitude of equal regard. These negative aspects of Anaya's portrayal of sex are counterposed by an important dimension in a positive direction which Maureen Dolan articulates well:

> Sexuality . . . is conveyed in many ways, and physical desire and sexual activity are presented as manifestations of love, and not merely what by 'conventional' standards would be termed lust. Physical love is a curative for spiritual suffering. (60)

Dolan observes that the "coupling between deformed adolescents at first produces disgust." Here she is referring to the love-making orgy at the local movie-house. Dolan continues:

> Against the backdrop of the rejection of Frankenstein because of his ugliness, the reader is forced to accept that in devoting so much attention to physical appearance, Western culture, instead of portraying love, really only portrays physical lust. Anaya, by presenting a scene in which the sexual partners are not physically attractive, stresses the spiritual side of love-making. (60)

Hence, the novel contains contradictory elements: a tendency to view women as sexual objects and the portrayal of sexual love-making as spiritually liberating and curative.

Although I have extended my remarks about the tale's deficiencies, there is much more to say about its power. The novel inspires evocatively on almost every page. See, for example, Salomón's transference of priesthood from Crispín to Tortuga:

> *Ah, Tortuga, I'm so glad to see you. I see you've come walking like a man. . . . And what is that slung around your shoulder? Could it be the blue guitar? . . . has it come at last? That means Crispín is dead . . . passed into another form of this vast drama we are weaving . . . But he left you the guitar. He sang his time on earth and now it's your turn. Oh, how can we be sad when a man passes away but leaves us so much of his life . . . leaves another to take up his place. Now it's your turn to sing, Tortuga. My heart is full of joy that this has come to pass!* (171)

Crispín also appears with his blue guitar in Anaya's second novel, *Heart of Aztlán,* where he is a symbol of hope and inspiration to all who will listen with an open heart. Passages such as this are rendered with craft. They have a poetic dream quality. Note the three consecutive questions, each leading to immediate revelation, followed by a smooth flowing interpretation: Crispín is dead, has "passed into another form of this vast drama we are weaving." This kind of clarity, insistent logic, inspirational wisdom, and easy flow of words is characteristic of Anaya's mature style.

Perhaps the most notable element of the novel is the Dantesque journey to evil, a journey which intrigues and astounds. Here is a journey into Conrad's *Heart of Darkness*, and into Hawthorne's evil forest in "Young Goodman Brown"--the conventional literary journey toward experience. This inward journey takes Tortuga to an understanding of the attraction of evil, and to an illumination that strength in goodness is the only means for overcoming evil, for returning to the world of human need equipped to help others. This journey is the centerpiece of the novel. If the message of the novel is love, then this journey is the vehicle leading to that love, the journey into the self. Unfortunately, the journey is proposed as a spiritual/magical/shamanistic experience. Most of humanity does not have shamanistically inspired journeys. Instead, we may go to the palm reader or the *curandero* only to find them no more wise, inspiring or potent than our own parents or grandparents. Fortunately, Tortuga's journey can simultaneously be perceived as a psychological/philo-sophical journey into the self.

This journey is announced early in the novel when Tortuga realizes that the "twisted, dying bodies," were a part of him, and that he "would never be free of them." He adds:

> But they would only live in the farthest niche I had found in my shell, the shell which would protect me from the searing acid of the damned path of the sun and the pain of the bitter songs, which were really not songs, but the whimpering of the babes of limbo, the living dead . . . I was empty . . . that's all I felt, emptiness. (119)

Here, succinctly stated, are the parameters of Tortuga's journey into adulthood, his *rites du passage*: he will have to face a hyperbole of human suffering and the problem of evil as personified by the polio-deformed children in the inner ward, and he will have to face their suffering directly, in the light of the sun, the "black sun of Salomón's wards" (133). Instead of suppressing the knowledge of their suffering as he does here at this early stage, he will have to seek it out, confront it, answer the question of why they suffer. Obviously, Tortuga already possesses the compassion to love these twisted bodies, otherwise, he wouldn't anguish over them. His journey is towards experience: self-knowledge and knowledge of the world about him. This knowledge will bring with it answers, or at least fashion responses. But first he must confront the evil, the darkness, directly. He must, using Anaya's metaphor, walk the "path of the sun."

This early passage begins Tortuga's journey of anguish that eventually leads to an understanding that he will never be free of the "babes of limbo" until he understands that it is his mission not only to endure the "pain of the bitter songs" but also to sing the songs to humanity. He feels empty at this point because he suffers empathetically, passively without having solutions.

When he learns that telling the story of the suffering handicapped provides catharsis, raises the consciousness of humanity, then he will agree to sing. But not at this point; first he must mature. Salomón, however, knows better. From the beginning, he has told Tortuga that he must grow out of his egocentric shell, that his mission in life is to help humanity selflessly. The metaphor for the egocentric life is the "mad dash for the sea." As the turtle who lays her eggs on the sand and then abandons them, people are involved in a mad dash toward gratification; however, people, unlike the beasts of the wild, have a greater capacity to sacrifice themselves for the betterment of the species. As Tortuga discovers the love that Ismelda and Salomón have for him, and as his own body functions begin to return, he comes to realize that he is on the road to selfless love and compassion for humanity:

> . . . I wanted to shout that I was no longer afraid of the strange cries I heard at night. I wanted to tell him that my life was more than a mad dash for the sea. The emotions gripped my throat and I was about to spill everything when he spoke again . . .

> *Of course you want to shout, he whispered, that is why you have come here. You have found your destiny, but you have not yet found your song . . . That is why you must go farther, deeper, to the very last ward of the hospital. . . . My friend, my friend, this is only the beginning of the nightmare we have made of life. . . . You have only begun your journey. . . . you must go to the very roots of sadness before you let out this shout of life that bursts in your lungs. . . . Your destiny has become ours, Tortuga . . .* (116-17)

Salomón, mysterious shaman and quadriplegic, sends Tortuga to experience the degradation and hopelessness of humankind. Those that exist at the "very roots of sadness" are totally helpless, terminally ill abandoned souls. Humanity in its heartless depravity denies their existence. The abandonment of these human sufferers constitutes the dark side of people. It is easy to love that which is beautiful and elegant, difficult to love that which is repulsive. Some among us would kill the repulsively and hopelessly ill: we call it euthanasia.

Danny, the bitter, hopeless handicapped boy whose arm is rotting before our eyes, opts for this solution when he turns off the electricity, killing all the helpless polio victims who are in iron lungs. Humanity is not quite ready to do as Danny does, but, in abandoning these disabled children, humanity has nevertheless turned its back on them, and this is the euthanasia of neglect. Tortuga's destiny is to experience despair, suffering and tragedy and fathom the depths of humanity's depravity. His destiny is to experience the "heart of darkness" and, unlike the embittered, negative Young Goodman Brown in Hawthorne's tale, to become cleansed, to dedicate his life to helping his fellow sufferers.

The first time that Tortuga attempts to enter the inner wards that contain the most repulsive of the suffering vegetables, he suffers a violent spasm of rejection: "'No!' I pleaded, 'Salomón! No! Please no more! I've seen enough! I've suffered enough! Let them die!'" At this point, Tortuga withdraws into himself: "The weight of the mountain was falling on me, darkness was settling over me as I burrowed into my shell." He strikes out violently at a fellow disabled companion and faints from the exertion into a "frightful darkness which opened like a monstrous mouth to receive" him (118).

A few days later he awakens from the dark sleep and again enters the inner ward of "comatose orphans." He tells us: The "images of the twisted, dying bodies which had filled my nightmares were burned into my brain." He knows that they are forever a part of him, that he would "never be free of them," but he still thinks that he can deny his responsibility: "they would only live in the farthest niche I had found in my shell, the shell which would protect me from the searing acid of the damned path of the sun and the pain of the bitter songs, which were really not songs, but the whimpering of the babes of limbo, the living dead . . . I was empty." He claims not to care. He retreats inwardly into a spiritual catatonia: "I was retreating, moving deeper and further into my shell, covering my hurt and pain with layer after layer of . . . meaningless silence" (119).

At this point, Tortuga personifies the emotional frigidity of humanity.

He has experienced those whom humanity rejects, and he also reacts irresponsibly. He denies his accountability: "I am free. I am nothing. I won't be responsible for anything. I denounce my destiny. There is no destiny . . . there is no fate" (120). The journey toward the heart of darkness is both outward and inward. Just as the narrator of Conrad's tale travels physically toward an uncharted part of Africa while psychically experiencing the total rejection of the moral values of Western society, so Tortuga moves outwardly through the wards which manifest human neglect and an egocentric pursuit of physical beauty, while inwardly journeying toward a progressive realization of evil. His initial rejection symbolizes humanity's rejection. And Danny, in killing the helpless vegetables carries out what humanity would do, yet lacks the courage to carry out. Danny's act of euthanasia, reprehensible as it is, brings Tortuga to an understanding of how depraved his own denial is. Danny does the deed, but Tortuga, who knows better, is a party to the deed by denying responsibility.

This then is the nadir for Tortuga, the experience of the "heart of darkness." His mighty effort at denial is followed by a growing awareness of what is right and by a counter-resurgence of his instinct for compassion. Appropriately, this movement toward the path of the sun is presented through powerful passages, inspirational because they advocate love and compassion.

Before Tortuga finally accepts his destiny, Salomón's guidance comes in dreams that have a songlike, poetic quality. Salomón's dream-voice is represented in italics throughout the novel.[3] However, once Tortuga accepts his destiny, we have another voice equally songlike, equally as poetic as Salomón's. It is Tortuga's own voice, his inner voice. It is also presented as a dream, but this time it is Tortuga's own dream, and, therefore, it is not in italics, as follows:

Perhaps I can never love again   never hold Ismelda in my arms
again without holding the girl who lies wasting in the iron lung
Perhaps the shadows which pursue me will drag me down   into the pit
of shrunken bodies and withered souls   Never see a child run and play

again without seeing the endless rows of crippled orphans   the orphans
of a world without love   the innocent tortured by the hatred which
lurks in all souls   and pursues me in my nightmares
　　　Perhaps not even Ismelda's magic can erase the memory of the dark
wards   the stench of the living dead   the helpless creatures dying
breath by breath
　　　Perhaps I will never dance again   Never laugh again
　　　Perhaps I will never run and play again
　　　Never love again
　　　Never be free again
　　　Perhaps the sun will never shine again   never see the path again
Only the black sun of Salomóns wards will guide me through the air
stale with death   cries of death
　Perhaps I will never turn again, to see the shimmer of light on green
leaves, to feel the cool breeze of summer touch my forehead, to learn to
love again
　　　My love is the love I brought with me from the dark wards a love
unknown to you   a love which you fear to draw into your heart
　I will sleep eternally with the cripples of the desert share their
bed   eat their bread   drink their water   I will lie by their sides
all my life   as I touch you and caress your glowing skin
　　　Perhaps that is my love   a growing love   a love you must reach
to share
　　　Perhaps you cannot love and touch our cripped bodies
　Perhaps it is you who cannot walk in our dark wards and reach out to
touch . . . (133)

　　　The rhythmic flow of this passage is insistent. It flows, it crescendos,
without stops, colons, semicolons, nor periods to interfere with the stream.
The lines do not begin and end at the left and right margins.   Spaces
throughout the passage give it a translucent, a diaphanous look, a feeling of
hesitancy and of being overwhelmed which corresponds to the emotionally
inspired content. The emotion leaps as does the eye in reading the depth of
words. It looks and reads as a poem. Perhaps, it is the most potentially

epiphanic dream that man can dream, and yet, ironically, it talks of the hatred that "lurks in all souls" and which "pursues" Tortuga in his "nightmares." This hatred in mankind has its own kind of light, its own kind of vision, its own sun: the "black sun of Salomón's wards" which lights the way to the

> "stench of the living dead   the helpless creatures
> dying breath by breath"

This poetic passage foreshadows the resolution. Tortuga's conscious mind does not, at this point, accept what his unconscious mind has already accepted. Note that this brief dream is articulated in the conditional mood, except for the four lines beginning with "my love is the love." It begins with six repetitions of the conditional, "perhaps," followed by the declarative and assertive, and returning to the conditional. The emphasis on the conditional implies an uncertainty, a weakness, but upon closer inspection one finds that the same conditional tone towards the end is positive and assertive. The first conditional phase is a personal lament, an inward directed lament of the loss of love. It internalizes an outward reality. The reader identifies with a first-person narrator mourning his personal loss of hope. But the declarative phase signals a shift in address. Suddenly, the lost soul who has learned love but cannot find hope turns the tables on the reader. The narrator no longer addresses himself, his soliloquy is now replaced by an accusative direct address. The narrator has learned to love with a love which the reader fears to draw into his heart. The narrator will "sleep eternally with the cripples of the desert." Following the accusation, Tortuga returns to the conditional, but now the understanding of who is to blame for the emotional deprivation of the disabled is clear to him, as is the remedy. However, characteristically, Tortuga tones down his accusation and ends with the conditional "perhaps you cannot love" as if to suggest, perhaps you *can* love.

The pattern of confusion moving to clarity, this *I-you* tension in the poem is akin to the logical pattern in the Italian sonnet in that the first two-thirds of the poem creates one unified experience and emotion, and the last third contradicts in such a way as to lead to illumination. This tension of "self" address and "self" flagellation leading to "other" address and "other" accusation parallels the movement from the "black sun of Salomón's wards" to the "path of the sun." The movement is from inside to outside, and it is sustained. The reader is inside the *I* long enough to experience the despair and arrive at the illumination that the responsibility lies within all of us and that the solution is acceptance by all of humanity.

The key to the achievement of the poem is encoded in the word *touch*. The shift in mood and address parallels the act of reaching out to the reader. The anguish of the first part of the poem leads to the illumination of who is to blame. The pivotal sentence introducing the shift in mood and address also introduces the merging of the *I* and the *you* in common concern: "my love is the love I brought with me from the dark wards   a love unknown to you   a love which you fear to draw into your heart." In this sentence the first person *my*, *I*, and *me* appear together, separated from the second half. The *you* appears in the tag-on part of the sentence separated from the first part of the sentence by something other than the traditional comma; there are four spaces separating the first person from the person addressed. This is a declarative sentence announcing how things are.

The following sentence is assertive. The narrator has achieved understanding and realizes that the remedy is union with humanity, so now we have the *I* and the *you* in the same syntactic unit, *I touch you*, joined by the significant verb, *to touch*. This is both a spiritual and a syntactic act of union. This joining of the *I* with the *you* by means of the very human and warm verb, *to touch,* is what this novel is about: A unity of *I* touching *you*,[4] the process of *you* becoming *I*: ego-centrism collapsing before empathy and compassion. Appropriately, this dream passage ends with the conditional question "can you love?" as well as with the bridging word, *touch*.

The dream posits a "black sun" which bodes evil, but this metaphor contradictorily turns on itself and, in the end, turns out to be the same "path of the sun" which Tortuga's shamanic guides want him to follow. The reason for the confusion between the "black sun of Salomón's wards" and the "path of the sun" is that one leads to the other. (I take the "path of the sun" to refer to the bright, healing light of the sun outside, in contradistinction to the knowledge and psychological illumination of the reality of the darkened inner wards.) To achieve a heightened, purified state of spirit, one must first comprehend the most profound depths of evil of which people are capable. Yet, through Tortuga as vehicle, the "black sun" is subsumed, integrated and eventually illuminates the "path of the sun." Heraclitus in his philosophical meditations deals with the tension between apparent contradictions such as Anaya's "black sun" and his bright "path of the sun": "men do not know how what is at variance agrees with itself. It is an attunement of opposite tensions. . . . It is the opposite which is good for us," and again he asserts "the one is made up of all things, and all things issue from the one" (72-3). For Heraclitus identity is not distinct; it is, rather, a continuum, a spectrum of one leading to the other. In this sense the sun which is also black is the central metaphor of a novel that achieves it epiphanic illumination in contrapuntal movement. The "black sun" leads to the "path of the sun" in a movement of opposition, creating a contrapuntal tension that convinces.[5]

This dream (occurring three-quarters of the way through the novel) is the pivotal point of the novel because it achieves vision, leading, in turn, to acceptance, opening the door for the only possible solution. At this point the passage ends in the conditional. It only *suggests* going beyond the conditional, but there is yet time for more clear assertion. By the end of the novel, the song of love of humanity and self-sacrifice for humanity will be strong and clear. This epiphanic dream occurs during Tortuga's most depressed hours, and symbolically, it also occurs in winter. By the end of the novel, on his return to his family in Albuquerque, Tortuga is well, and it is spring. His sunlight images are no longer "black":

> The bus glowed with the bright light of the sun. . . . Butterflies played in the sun. . . . It was a good time to be going home. I reached for the blue guitar and cradled it in my arms. My fingers felt the strings and strummed a melody, and I heard the words of my song fill the bus and flow out the open window and across the awakening desert. (197)

Spring brings renewed life and hope. The desert is awakening just as Tortuga's dead hope for himself and humanity has reawakened. All about him is life, color and song. With his magical blue guitar he will sing his song to all humanity. Tortuga has cast off his shell and will reach out to life. Leaving behind the magic mountain, he makes a song of rejoicing out of all that he has seen. This song will be a "song of love, Tortuga! Oh yes, sing of love!" (196).

Anaya is an important Chicano novelist and *Tortuga* is an inspiring work. If the lack of character development in the work is problematic, the ideological deficiency is more serious. The concept of the euphoric, shaman-guided journey through experience that leads to a clear vision of one's mission in life is a thing of beauty to contemplate, but it does not propose viable answers. Creation of myth works against practical solutions. Disease, deformity and the abandonment of the helpless is a social reality, a social problem that collectivities can solve. Magic water flowing from a mystical mountain will not induce humanity to insist on continued efforts to prevent birth defects, nor will magic and mysticism induce humanity to accept the deformed as loved and respected equals who participate fully in providing for the common good, according to their physical capacities. Although it is true that, as Vernon Lattin points out, "the critic who accuses Anaya of failing to see the evil that exists in the world has not read this novel [*Tortuga*] with care. One can hear its pain, page after page" (*Focus* 356) After reading *Tortuga*, few will accuse Anaya of not portraying evil concretely and accurately. It is Anaya's solution that falls short. María López speaks for many when she asks of *Heart of Aztlán*: "has contact with the myths provided a real tool to correct social injustice?" (qtd. in González-T., *Focus* 134)

The ancient Greeks created myths and proposed that only super-men could resolve man's socio-political-philosophical impasses. Only gods, kings and princes could be the protagonists of their dramas. But twentieth-century people have moved beyond classicism, neo-classicism and romanticism. The heroes of realism, naturalism and the post-Kafkian novels can be ordinary men and women who stand up against societal injustices in both large and small ways. The answers to suffering are derived logically and practically, not through inspiration, especially not when inspired by the gods or beings greater than ordinary men and women. On the other hand, Anaya's work is realistically inspired and admirable to the degree that it emphasizes love and compassion. It registers very real feelings of confusion, hatefulness, hopelessness, anomie and disorientation. There is a degree of emotional verisimilitude that leads the reader to ask, "Did Anaya, personally experience these events?"[6] If the hands that lead us into the fields of myth are not wise and protective, the hands that lead us to till the fields of human compassion and love are.

In *Tortuga*, Anaya has succeeded superbly in creating what he intended, an "existential hell, symbolizing our own contemporary hell . . . and existential wasteland" (*Focus* 385). The eternal, relentless suffering of the crippled is extremely depressing, and the novel almost doesn't succeed in bringing the reader out of the horror, the "existential" horror. Nevertheless, the love and hope in the heart of the protagonist at least points the reader in the direction of regeneration.

Take away the magic mountain, the blue guitar, and the shaman, and we find an effective bildungsroman, eloquently portrayed, a tender human story about a boy that awakens to the brutality of experience and to the cruelty of a society organized so as to dispirit and dehumanize those who do not measure up to its ideas of beauty. This novel helps to shatter the myth that equates human physical perfection with human value. Even though the handicapped are not fleshed out, the reader comes to accept their need, their human cry for regard and love. *Tortuga* challenges the reader, and, most important, it does it with love, a love for humanity that reaches out to the reader from every page. There is a song of innocence and experience in the "black sun of Salomón's wards" and it sings in the purest of tones. This song has called to us through all three of Anaya's novels, calling with greater focus in *Tortuga*.

NOTES

[1] For a definitive study of American Puritanism and the doctrines of predestination and election, see Perry Miller, *The New England Mind: The Seventeenth Century*, as well as his *Jonathan Edwards*.

[2] This is also a weakness in Anaya's two earlier novels. Although in *Bless Me, Ultima*, magic and cosmic mysticism are more integrated within the novel; and the dreams especially are more believable as belonging to a young boy obsessed with magic and, therefore, riding a current of auto-suggestion.

[3] In discussing *Heart of Aztlán*, before he had published *Tortuga* (see "Myth and the Writer: A Conversation with Rudolfo Anaya" first published in 1979 and **reprinted in this volume**), Anaya explains that he reserves italics as a device to signal "reality," "truth." The italics signify, in Anaya's words, "extra-reality." He goes on to explain that the voice presented in italics is a mysterious narrator: "you don't know who the narrator is that's dropping this" (see *Focus*, page 434-35). However, in *Tortuga* the mysterious speaker is not unknown. The speaker is supposed to be Solomón, but the effect remains the same in both *Heart of Aztlán* and *Tortuga*: Here, obviously, is the inner voice of "truth," a truth that floats in out of nowhere similar to the choruses of early Greek tragedy.

[4] The subject of the sentence, *I*, is joined with the "other" by means of the act of touching. The *toucher* is touching, and they are one, but seemingly the direct object, *you* (although now, syntactically, much closer to the you than in the previous sentence where *is* was relegated to a tag-on) is not *one* with the toucher. The *you* is in the direct object position. There is a seeming grammatical disjunction because of the accustomed perception of disjunction between subject/predicate and the direct object; however, Chomsky in his "rewrite rules" for predicates asserts that the direct object assigns its meaning to the verb. He suggests that the verb absorbs the direct object

semantically. According to Chomsky, there are three linguistic levels of perception involved in the perception of written communication: the orthographic (analysis of characters), the grammatical (analysis of pieces), and the semantic (analysis of meaning). Chomsky asserts that the third level is more useful. Emotionally the reader intuits what Chomsky claims.

This phenomenon of the direct object collapsing to the subject/verb occurs in other languages. In Spanish, for example, *dámelo* joins all three syntactic units: subject, verb and direct object.

It is interesting to note that there are even correspondances in the physical universe: if a particle comes within the range of a larger body, the larger body will pull the particle into its gravitational field. It will either absorb it or hold it within its gravitational field. If we perceive the verb as the larger body--the greater force--and if we perceive the direct object as a particle, then we can understand how they are experienced as one.

This poem/passage is dense with signification and has more to yield. I suggest the need for further semiotic analysis.

[5] Here again Dolan synthesizes the idea of pain and suffering (the black sun) leading to selflessness and love (the path of the sun): "he comes to see that pain is partly what saves the world from selfishness: pain binds people together. By purposefully descending into the realm of suffering, Tortuga can find happiness in the knowledge that he is sharing part of the very essence of life with others (57)."

[6] In Anaya's autobiography [**Reprinted in this volume**], he admits for the first time that at about the same age as the protagonist, he was paralyzed as a result of an accident and spent some time in a hospital.

WORKS CITED

Anaya, Rudolfo A. *Tortuga*. Berkeley: Justa, 1979.

___. *Bless Me, Ultima*. Berkeley: Tonatiuh, 1972.

___. "Rudolfo A. Anaya: An Autobiography." *Contemporary Authors Autobiography Series*, (vol. 4). Ed. Adele Sarkisan. Detroit: Gale Research, 1986. 15-28. **Reprinted in this volume.**

Conrad, Joseph. *The Heart of Darkness*. New York: Norton, 1971.

Dolan, Maureen. "Aspects of Chicano Reality With Reference To The Novels of Rudolfo A. Anaya." Masters Thesis. Glasgow, Scotland, 1984.

Elias, Edward. "*Tortuga*: A Novel of Archetypal Structure." *The Bilingual Review* 9.1 (January-April, 1982): 82-7.

Freud, Sigmund. *The Interpretation of Dreams,* Ed. and Trans. James Strachey. New York: Avon, 1965.

Hawthorne, Nathaniel. "Young Goodman Brown." *An Introduction to Literature,* 8th ed. Eds. S. Barnet, et. al. Boston: Little Brown, 1985, 84-95.

Heraclitus. "The Word." *The Portable Greek Reader*. Ed. W. H. Auden. New York: Viking, 1964, 69-77.

Lattin, Vernon E. "Chaos and Evil in Anaya's Trilogy." *Rudolfo A. Anaya: Focus on Criticism*. Ed. César A. González-T. La Jolla: Lalo, 1990, 349-58.

López, María. "Myth and Reality: Heart of Aztlán." *De Colores* 5.1-2 (1980): 111-14.

Miller, Perry. *The New England Mind: The Seventeenth Century.* Boston: Beacon, 1968.

___. *Jonathan Edwards.* Amherst: U of Massachusetts P, 1981

The Search for a Center: The Shamanic Journey of Mediators in Anaya's Trilogy, Bless Me, Ultima; Heart of Aztlán, and Tortuga[1]

Jean Cazemajou
The University of Bordeaux
Bordeaux, France

Anaya's trilogy forms a closely interwoven network of stories set not only in a real landscape of northern New Mexico: the small hamlet of Las Pasturas, the quiet little town of Guadalupe, and the big city of Albuquerque; but set also in a mythical universe organized around primordial archetypes: the river, the plain, the goat-path, the bridge, the mountain, the sun, the moon, the sea, the eagle, the nopal--to name only the most frequently recurrent which function as so many landmarks in shamanic journeys.

His characters are, to a large extent, products of these specific settings, especially in *Bless Me, Ultima*, a novel in which, Antonio, the young narrator, establishes a clear-cut distinction between two cultural heritages: that of the Lunas, a race of farmers and peace-loving people, and that of the Márez, a race of conquistadors brought by the sea--whose respective bloods mingled giving birth to him. Antonio, who himself describes his initiatory journey, is an apprentice shaman.

But whether the action takes place in the midst of nature, or in the city, a link of some sort with the natural world survives, symbolized in *Heart of Aztlán* by the Chávez's coffee can filled with earth from their garden in Guadalupe, to be scattered over the "hard city soil" of their new home in Albuquerque (18). The religion with which these narratives are imbued obviously encountered Catholic tradition and ritual on its way, but it has partly outgrown this heritage and persistently looks for the source of a more ancient faith which implies a mystic relationship with the earth. It includes old Indian legends such as that of the Llorona--the "Weeping Woman"--whose appearance is a bad omen; that of the golden carp--Anaya's own invention; magic practices with herbs and talismans; and, of course, a deep veneration for the "brown" Virgin, the *Virgen de Guadalupe* who is the patron saint of the little town and close relative of Tonantzín, an Aztec goddess of fertility. All of this projects a syncretic vision in which time never appears as an abstraction, but as a concrete cyclical force linked with the elements and the seasons.

A "sense of place," a total harmony with the "raw, majestic and awe-inspiring landscape of the Southwest" (Anaya, "Writer Discusses" 40), remains the prime mover of the creative process. The vantage point from which Anaya observes life is the "land of the eagle and the nopal"; and, beyond the llano, the blue mountains (*Heart* 8). His most enlightened protagonists can absorb the power of this landscape and use it at times for magical purposes. Thus the relationship between man and the physical universe does not function along naturalistic lines.

Anaya's major characters are not one-dimensional, although their psychological underpinnings are often allegorical. Among them are typical local color types--the cowboy or *vaquero*; the farmer, occasionally uprooted and trying to adapt to an urban setting; the moderately successful Chicano businessman, the priest, the young man in search of God and of his own identity, the authoritarian father, the loving mother, the village or barrio outcast, the vato loco, the pachuco, the adolescent girl liberated by an urban environment and access to outside work, the exploited worker, and the more or less radicalized community leader.

Towering over them looms the figure of the mediator: Ultima in *Bless Me, Ultima*, Crispín in *Heart of Aztlán*, and Ismelda in *Tortuga*. They preserve an indispensable contact with the world of nature and the supernatural forces inhabiting this universe which, as the Indians say, have always been with us. "The rivers still flow, the grass still grows." The mediator plays a role similar to that of the *santero* in contemporary forms of Caribbean religious practice, but occupies a somewhat marginal position in the community. He or she is not a natural leader, but merely there to inspire and guide potential leaders or future mediators.

There are not many strong leaders in Anaya's fiction; however, community life is strengthened by the presence of the various mediators--the major ones already mentioned and their apprentices and assistants who relay the magic power dormant in nature and transmute it into beneficent action. Their difficult task is made somewhat easier because, in spite of socioeconomic differences, the group in which they operate is fairly homogeneous. It is essentially a society of *Mestizos* and Indians in which the Spanish element is hardly ever found in pure unadulterated form; and the Anglos, even if they are close by, tend to live by themselves.

The central problem of mediation for a writer has to do with the very instrumentality and scope of literary communication. Anaya's first target audience is a community of *compadres* who need little explanation, but there is also a larger audience waiting somewhere to hear his voice. As a Chicano novelist, he is fully conscious that he is addressing both at the same time. In an interview in 1979, he said: "In taking . . . responsibility for my own actions and my own creation, I therefore take responsibility for everyone in all of the universe" ("Myth" 80). Hence, the writer's program is very ambitious and not at all restricted to an isolated New Mexico microcosm.

However, since the starting point of his creative process is "a sense of place," something is needed to prevent the distant reader from feeling out of place in Anaya's universe with its rich Aztec and Pueblo heritage. The first instrument that he uses is the power of *myths*, so well dramatized in many legends and *cuentos* of New Mexico, but which were already present in those primordial images that Jung called the "Great Mother" and the "archetypal light" (9). Clemente, in *Heart of Aztlán*, partakes not only of the plumed serpent's duality--heaven and earth combined--a fusion of contraries recurrent in the Nahuatl religion, but also of the duality in Christian mythology: "Christ the man being also Christ the God. . . . having all the powers of the godhead and yet being composed of the clay of the earth" (Anaya, "Myth" 81).

The second level at which mediation operates is that of the *texture* of the writer's creation: the concatenation of stylistic effects linked with all the emotions triggered by a diglossic situation in which Spanish remains the language of the heart and English that of formal communication. Anaya's craft thrives on this linguistic dichotomy, embracing both the robust spontaneity of an oral language and some of the literary devices which are the stock-in-trade of contemporary mainstream writers. An implicit and continuous battle of words with the occasional head-on collisions of two different sensibilities generates many humorous effects.

The most interesting level of mediation is also the one which gives Anaya's fiction its poetic and semi-religious quality. It concerns the very heart of the mediation process since it brings into play the *mediators* themselves within the framework of individual stories. They are, all of them, ordinary people with a touch of the divine in them. And their apparent fragility is no obstacle to the accomplishment of their mission. They fulfill their preordained tasks dutifully, reawakening or maintaining communal bonds in human groups threatened by inner conflicts.

Anaya's highly poetic and finely crafted prose uses myths, symbols, and archetypes frequently linked to a pre-Columbian cosmogony. Besides the divine powers associated with the sun and the moon in this world vision, it seems to me that he constantly returns to the Nahuatl veneration for the quincunx with its symbolic representation of an ideal center. He dramatizes this search by contrasting the labyrinth of the city with the reassuring landmarks of nature, and the mountains in *Heart of Aztlán* are not merely those of New Mexico, but also replicas of the symbolic pyramid in the center of the Nahuatl quincunx.

In 1981 at a symposium of Chicano writers when Anaya said, "I define myth as the truth in the heart ("Mesa" 11), he was trying to expand and universalize the concept of myth, but he emphasized at the same time the contribution made by Chicano authors to a rediscovery of myth that mainstream literature had failed to provide. On this occasion, he jousted with Alurista and Alejandro Morales on the definition and use of myth in literature and contemporary life. According to Alurista, some of the myths that Chicanos had tried to use--for instance Christian mythology--had not proved very useful, but Aztlán, of course, met with his approval as a "unifying tool" (8) in the present Chicano struggle. He warned, however, that it should not "become an opiate" (15). On the contrary, Anaya, supported by Morales, noted that such an abundance of archetypes in the Chicano imagination was an asset, especially if we compare it with the mythological poverty of contemporary mainstream literature. Anaya presented myth as the survival kit of the modern world--a world plagued by fragmentation and fascinated by the prospect of total annihilation. In this context, myth keeps alive in us values present both in archaic and modern man, but eroded by the frictions of modern life. Thus, as he puts it, "the mythic element is the unifying element" between past and present and between different cultures (19).

Anaya's fiction, seen in this perspective, cannot be described with the reductive phrase "minority literature." The author's great familiarity with various Mesoamerican mythologies and his early immersion in mainstream American literature place his work at the meeting point of numerous cultures. Indian and Spanish, Pueblo and Aztec strands of thought merge with symbols anchored in a mainstream Anglo tradition. Anaya's syncretism should make his trilogy attractive to a universal audience since, like Ralph Ellison's narrator in *Invisible Man*, he seems to address his distant reader as follows: "Who knows but that, on the lower frequencies, I speak for you?" (469).

Mythic statement is always a priority in Anaya's fiction, and he has elaborated in the trilogy a complex emblematic web, sometimes derived from ancient legends, but always adapted to modern circumstances. Writing as he does in a period of ethnic revival, he was bound to use the myth of Aztlán--the central myth in Chicano culture, launched by Alurista in 1968 and acquiring an official status and a symbolic significance with the Denver Conference of 1969.[2] This myth, associated with the bitter reality of dispossession and oppression by a hostile Anglo culture, operates as a magic springboard for the author's imagination. The merging of the eagle and the serpent in Aztec mythology was revived by Anaya in *Heart of Aztlán* where these two mythic animals exchange roles with the steel snakes of the exploitative railroad and the eagle-eyed leader of the strike who will become similar to the "hombre volador" of legend (84, 86). And the search for Aztlán seen as a sort of lost paradise becomes in the novel a pilgrimage to the magic mountain--a ritual journey present in the three volumes--which teaches Clemente that the real Aztlán is not a geographic place, but a feeling of spiritual union with his people, buried deep in his heart.

However, the two thrusts of the narrative compete for prominence. And we may wonder whether *Heart of Aztlán* is a *Bildungsroman* with Jason Chávez as its central character, or a social novel, with his father, Clemente--an uprooted farmer turned into an alienated city worker slowly acquiring the stature of a leader--as its main protagonist.

Anaya himself has never claimed that he was a social novelist, and he has sometimes been attacked for underplaying the political dimension of the Chicano struggle in his fiction. *Heart of Aztlán* has been the main target of such criticism. Some reviewers have objected to the character of Clemente whom they find unconvincing, or they have objected to the use of myth as an inadequate political tool. Anaya has replied on many occasions to such an approach to this work. He wrote in 1977: "My interest in writing is to explore the magic in realism" ("Writer Discusses" 40). One year later, interviewed by Prof. Juan Bruce-Novoa, he declared:

> The role of a writer is vis-à-vis the universe itself, chaos versus patterns. I fit easily and completely into the Chicano communi-ty--that's where I was born and raised, that's where my family resides--and the Movement, because I was active in it and have seen its different areas of development. I think that in part I fit into the mainstream society, what you call U.S. society. I know it's fashionable for many Chicano writers to say that they do not belong to this society that has oppressed minorities. Nonetheless, the fact exists that we are a part of that society. (190)

With such an approach to the act of writing, Anaya reactivates the myth-making faculty which seems to have become dormant with most Anglo writers, often lost in narcissistic navel-watching. The author of *Heart of Aztlán* responds to an opposite urge which launches his characters on shamanic journeys, prepares the best of them for mediators' tasks, and prioritizes in modern man--as well as in archaic man--the consciousness-raising powers of myth. As prerequisites to the mediation process, we find the reconciliation of opposites, transcending the boundaries of time and space; and, generally speaking, the search for a center, for harmony in a world that is more and more threatened by fragmentation and atomization. The mediator is the indispensable force, since he or she works in order to preserve or rediscover harmony. Except in the case of Ultima--the *curandera* in *Bless Me, Ultima*--the mediator (as do many characters in Flannery O'Connor's fiction) is at the outset often reluctant to walk the path of grace which Anaya is more likely to call "the path of the sun." Clemente is a case in point in *Heart of Aztlán*. He needs the assistance of Crispín to accept the challenge of facing his new task as a leader of men, and, consequently, as a potential mediator.

This novel, with its barrio setting, is a bold attempt at writing a kind of musical composition in prose, and it is no accident if the haunting figure of Crispín, "the man with the blue guitar," is the one which remains branded in our memories when the book is closed. He blends together a great many feelings and emotions into a flow of sounds, and he exerts a powerful appeal not only on the barrio as a whole, but also on the reader. Crispín is no ordinary character. His blue guitar operates as the depository of legends and mysteries which Anaya wishes to introduce into the narrative. And, on the structural level, this treasured legacy of a remote and composite Indian past finds its best expression in the passages printed in italics which form a mythic counterpoint to the story-telling process.

Heart of Aztlán is a kind of cultural symphony which also incorporates elements from many sources outside the central fund of Aztec and Pueblo mythologies. One may be surprised to find that it owes a literary debt to Wallace Stevens, who appears to some critics as the very embodiment of aesthetic hedonism, but who is highly respected by Anaya as "one of the major poets of the imagination" (Interview, González-T. 4). In a more subdued manner, another voice occasionally makes itself heard in the novel, that of Stephen Crane. One should not interpret that phenomenon as a direct influence of a mainstream writer on a Chicano novelist, but rather as the unexpected communion of these two authors in their passionate love for the open spaces of the West--both of them tending to perceive landscape in archetypal terms.

Anaya's interest in Wallace Stevens, as reflected in *Heart of Aztlán*, is essentially linked to two poems: "The Man with the Blue Guitar" (1937) and "The Comedian as the Letter C" (1923)--the latter having a central character, who is a voyager called Crispín. Wallace Stevens' voyager does not resemble Anaya's Crispín physically nor psychologically, but both characters are confronted with a common problem which is that of man's relation with reality. The opening lines of Stevens' poem

> Nota: man is the intelligence of his soil,
> The sovereign ghost . . . (30)

in typical Wallace Stevens fashion, lead to a counter-statement approximating what Anaya calls his "sense of place" and "the harmony which is inherent between man and his place" ("Writer Discusses" 40-41).

> Nota: his soil is man's intelligence.
> That's better. That's worth crossing seas to find.
> (Stevens, "Comedian" 38)

Both Stevens and Anaya then tend in different ways to emphasize the physical aspect of an authentic knowledge of the world; but, as Helen Vendler pointed out, "the physical world will become, for Stevens, a minor *point d'appui* on which the immense structures of his imagination are erected" (51). Anaya's creative process follows a similar pattern, but there is a sincere need in him for what he calls "epiphany in landscape," that is to say, for an experience which releases man from the constraints of civilization and brings into play the secret sources of his being ("Landscape").

In order to find these, ordinary people need the assistance of a mediator. In *Heart of Aztlán*, it is Crispín--a Wallace Stevens character originally--who performs this task. Crispín's "blue guitar . . . carved from the heart of a juniper tree," has come to replace "the [broken] flutes of the priests," and this musical instrument in which "were stored the myths of the past" becomes a cultural symbol of the Chicano people as a whole. So, when the enlightened mediator, Crispín, tells Jason the story of the blue guitar and says: "*It was a new instrument, a subterfuge, passing from poet to poet it wove the future OUT OF THINGS AS THEY ARE . . .* " (27) (EMPHASIS ADDED), we can hear then a distant echo of Stevens' poem "The Man with the Blue Guitar" in which the anonymous speaker makes the following pronouncement:

> Poetry
> exceeding music must take the place
> Of empty heaven and its hymns,
>
> Ourselves in poetry must take their place
> Even in the chattering of your guitar. (54)

And we remember that the phrase "things as they are" runs like a burden throughout Stevens' poem, dialectically contrasted with the poet's and the artist's creative imagination.

Crispín, in Anaya's novel, is not merely an anonymous barrio musician, but also an archetypal blind man provided with clairvoyance and supernatural healing powers, i.e., both mediator and shaman. Whereas Father Cayo, Barelas's priest, proves to be unable to assist his flock and is even hypocritical, Crispín officiates at all the major ceremonies in the life of the community. Exposure to the sun blinded him when he crossed the desert to move from Mexico to "the land the ancients called Aztlán" (28), in a ritual journey from the present to the past and the place of origin; but, ironically, he sees and knows everything.

He is the one around whom the community gathers to celebrate the arrival of the Chávez family in the barrio. His guitar has the same power as that of his counterpart in Wallace Stevens' poem who says: "And things are as I think they are / And say they are on the blue guitar"(70). This statement is clearly echoed by Crispín's remark in chapter one of *Heart of Aztlán*: "Things as they are never appear the same on the blue guitar . . ." (14).

The blue guitar is thus the identity marker of the mediator. It is handed down from one barrio bard to another, and each of them in turn, after serving a long apprenticeship, is finally allowed to take up this magic instrument. In *Tortuga*, the unnamed young protagonist--who is in fact Benjie, Jason's younger brother--learns through a letter from his mother that Crispín is dead, but left him his blue guitar. Salomón, Tortuga's best friend and mentor in the hospital, also acts as mediator and interpreter since he tells Benjie, shortly before he is released from the hospital, to assume fully the task thrust upon him by fate: "*Crispín is dead . . . passed into another form of this vast drama we are weaving . . . But he left you his guitar. He sang his time on earth and now it's your turn*" (171).

This passage, printed in italics, functions as the last will and testament of Salomón--a terminally-ill patient--whose voice has kept reaching for Tortuga from the "vegetable patch" where he is slowly dying with the other "vegetables." Salomón had chosen Tortuga for this future mission, and his training is almost completed. Salomón's earthly task is also accomplished; and his death, just like that of Crispín, is compensated for by Tortuga's return to life and the beginning of his long journey as singer of songs.

But the stature of Crispín dominates that of all other mediators in the trilogy. His ties to the past are not ambiguous as are those of Ultima; and compared to nascent mediators such as Antonio Márez or Benjamín Chávez, he is a full-fledged shaman. So, in *Heart of Aztlán*, Crispín can do a number of things with his music: sing a dirge after Sánchez' accidental death in the railroad yard (24), or play on his guitar the "music of life" when Benjie falls from the water tank, in order to save this young life from the grasp of death

(202). He can also "strum a tune of liberation on the blue guitar" (208) when the strikers cheer the charismatic figure of their new leader, Clemente, who himself needs the assistance of Crispín's blue guitar producing "the sound of a drum" (206) to arouse the "fire of love" and a revolutionary spirit in the strikers (207).

Whatever we may think of this combination of politics and love, the final image of the book, showing the strikers marching to the tune of Crispín's guitar, cannot leave the reader indifferent. And the river metaphor, often used in revolutionary rhetoric, acquires a new momentum because of Anaya's finely crafted prose: "That infusion of spirit into flesh which generations of wise men have described throughout the ages was the simple bond of love that gave the river its strength to surge and roar and cut its new channel into the future" (208).

Music, then, is the most constant and efficient community-building element in the story: Crispín's blue guitar functions as a rallying point and a source of inspiration. It strengthens the cohesion of the community; and, with its mysterious power, changes a pathetic barrio drunk into a leader and drives passive workers to political action.

The interplay between some of Stephen Crane's works and Anaya's *Heart of Aztlán* is more tenuous but worth exploring just the same. In his long introduction to Thomas Beer's *Stephen Crane* (1923), Joseph Conrad reminisced about his young friend of the late 1890s, who looked to him as mysterious and laconic as an Indian and who was fond of using the term "Indian" to designate some of his closest friends. It may have been something of a pose and also a means for Crane to shelter himself from the endless questions of London writers and critics about his works. But we must also take into account the tremendous impact that Crane's trip to the West and Mexico, at the beginning of 1895, had upon his creative imagination. It is true that he shared some of the prejudices of the Easterner and the Anglo-Saxon, but the humor of his western tales is not only directed at western customs and traditions, but also at the self-complacency of Easterners. And, in Mexico, his anti-Mexican bias is compensated for by a more sympathetic way of looking at Indians:

The Indian remains the one great artistic figure. . . . In his serape, with his cotton trousers, his dusty sandals upon which his bare toes are displayed, and his old sombrero pulled down over his eyes, [he] is a fascinating man. . . . He is a mystic and silent figure of the darkness. (Katz 65-66)

Now, to hint at any kind of a relationship between Crane and Anaya may seem rather odd; but, after all, Anaya himself pointed out that "in the beginning [he] had the U. S. American novels to work with, not the Mexican models" (Bruce-Novoa 191). It is a safe guess to infer that he encountered Crane's work at a very early age. Like Crane, who grew up in a very different part of the country, Anaya is extremely sensitive to his physical environment, and both writers are inclined to use "the forces in [their] landscape" for aesthetic and symbolic purposes ("Writer Discusses" 41).

To Crane, the impressionist, landscape had a lot to do with the effects of sunlight on the greens, browns, and greys of nature at all times of day. But to Crane, the Jungian writer, the sun was an archetype associated with fire and blood--something Anaya had probably internalized through the combined influence of Aztec and Pueblo mythologies. The famous line concluding chapter nine of *The Red Badge of Courage*, after Jim Conklin's horrible "danse macabre": "The red sun was pasted in the sky like a wafer" (which, in the first draft, read "like a fierce wafer"), and Crane's reference to war as "the red animal, the blood-swollen god" (Crane 51-52) call to mind the human sacrifices required in the Nahuatl religion to placate the fierce battle god and sun deity, Huitzilopochtli, whose life and brilliance could be preserved only though such sacrifices.

So, when Anaya writes, in chapter one of *Heart of Aztlán*: "The sun hung like a gold medallion in the blue sky" (6), the laconic power of this arresting image--appearing as it does after a reference to the violent death of Guillermo, Clemente's brother--strikes us as having a distinct Cranean ring to it.

In another passage of the same novel, at the close of chapter nine, the ritual rumble between the pachucos and the young cowboys has taken place; and there is, in the tone of the narrative, the same gentle irony that Crane leveled at his would-be hero, Henry Fleming, another youth tormented by the problem of manly conduct under stress. Anaya captures just the right note of equivocal pride in the young pachucos when they return home after the fight: "They laughed and entered their barrio proudly, carrying their wounds like badges of courage" (98).

Granted, their wounds are real ones won on the parking lot which was the site of the fight between the two gangs, but are they authentic "badges of courage" or simply battle scars which do not prove anything? Henry Fleming got his wound from the rifle butt of a retreating comrade from whom he was trying to learn the whereabouts of his own regiment that he had left in a great panic in the midst of action. Using this spurious badge of courage, he pretended, when he met his friends again, that he had been shot by an enemy bullet. So he is truly an impostor. His counterparts in *Heart of Aztlán* are much less introverted and only play as best they can the archetypal war games of young boys all over the world.

In spite of its allegorical title, Anaya's book often functions as a realistic tale in which only Crispín, Clemente, and Jason are fully integrated in a symbolic representation of reality. However, Anaya's long fiction, on the whole, displays a vast range of symbols, myths, legends, and folktales in which animals play significant mediating roles. For example, in *Bless Me, Ultima*, an owl--a bird associated with the god of the netherworld in Aztec mythology, and in the novel with Ultima, the curandera--operates in the story as an interesting fusion of opposites: both tutelary spirit and messenger of death. In *Tortuga*, an identical union of contraries is found in the turtle-- earth-ridden and almost pinned to the ground, but also a heavenly symbol associated with the magic mountain bearing the same name. Furthermore, the golden deer racing across the sky in *Heart of Aztlán* combines in a striking image the positive qualities of the most useful animal in Pueblo culture and the centrality of the sun in Aztec mythology. Above all, it stands for the fifth sun--the sun of movement and cosmic unity, thus bringing together two antithetical ideas.

This Indian heritage clashes with the Spanish Catholicism which, in different ways, pervades the three novels. Anaya best dramatizes the conflict between these two cultural forces in *Bless Me, Ultima*. In this novel, Jason's Indian, Cico's legend of the golden carp, and Ultima's long and patient initiation into the secrets of nature finally win the young protagonist's heart and prepare him for his future role as mediator in this constant exchange between earth, heaven, and man which, from now on, will be his new religion.

The three novels are closely interrelated. Although Benjie's name is not mentioned in *Tortuga*, the young hero turns out to be Jason Chávez's younger brother, paralyzed by his fall from the water tower. Sent to a hospital for crippled children, he is placed in a heavy plaster cast--hence his nickname, Tortuga. There he is completing his shamanic training while modern medicine looks after his body. Ismelda, a pretty, young nurse, fully attuned to the natural world and the messages sent by the magic mountain, provides the major contribution to his initiation. A heavy-breasted black nurse, who gives him therapy sessions, also provides some sexual titillation and reawakens the hero's "need to love" (149). This need is fulfilled in his sexual encounter with Cynthia during the horror movie episode, after which, Tortuga tells us, "The last brittle remnants of my shell fell crashing to the floor" (151). This clear evocation of the rebirth myth has taken the hero from "limbo" (89) to his journey through the desert--which at Solomon's request has forced him to see with his own eyes the worst wards of the hospital where "in each lung lay a twisted pretzel" (117); to the sexual encounter with Cynthia which literally breaks his shell and turns him from a turtle into "a lizard" (159); and thence to the final liberation when Ismelda symbolically invites him to "throw away [his] crutches" (185).

The protagonist of this last novel of the trilogy has thus come a long way. After being a drug-addict and a cripple in the last chapters of *Heart of Aztlán*, he entered the hospital at the beginning of *Tortuga* as if it was the antechamber of death. But, thanks to the combined assistance of all the mediators--Ismelda, the nurse, the therapy session assistant (KC), the other inmates of the hospital, but more especially Salomón, Danny, Mike, and Cynthia--he is now a new man, ready to sing "a song of love" that takes him back home (196-97). And this song, which "fills the bus and [flows] out the open window and across the awakening desert," (197) binds past, present, and future together and keeps the line of shamans unbroken, for Tortuga is now cradling Crispín's blue guitar in his hands.

According to Lorene H. Carpenter, shamanism in literature makes use of the following six elements: "equilibrium, integration, dreaming, initiation, healing and animal/human transformation." And writers and shamans have something in common: "Both know the power of the word to create worlds and both use narratives of shamanic journeys . . . to transform the awareness of their audiences" (17).

This set of assertions can easily be verified in Anaya's trilogy, but what strikes us most in Anaya's handling of shamanism is what Mircea Eliade calls the principle of "separation": shamans "are separated from the rest of the community by the intensity of their own religious experience" (*Chamanisme* 24). It is true of Ultima, because of her ambiguous status as curandera; of Crispín, because of his blindness; of Salomón, because he is a terminally-ill patient and knows it; and of Tortuga himself, because he feels that a tremendous responsibility has been thrust upon him by Salomón--that of taking over from Crispín after the old barrio bard has "entrusted the blue guitar to [him]" (170). This is precisely the most excruciating episode in his shamanic initiation--a fight with this mysterious call which will prevent him from "leading a normal life" (170). For to become a shaman means the acceptance of being different, ecstatically inclined, and prone to solitary meditation. Moreover, according to Anaya, it also means the ability to strengthen community bonds by the mysterious power of the human voice or that of music.

The various forms taken by shamanic journeys in different religious systems have always included images of ascent and heavenward flight, and, in each case, there is an attempt to reach a sort of equilibrium between heaven and earth through what Mircea Eliade calls a "Center" or the "Axis Mundi"

(*Mythes* 143). Anaya's own system, although it is a transformational one using Pueblo, Aztec, and Catholic cosmogonies as its raw material, is no exception to the rule. The juniper tree growing on the slope of a hill or mountain often provides this "Axis Mundi" which facilitates mediatory tasks in Anaya's trilogy. Flexibility is the rule in his mythic constructs. They are characterized by a broad syncretic vision which embraces an endlessly unrolling tapestry of cyclic time with the whole universe as its backdrop.

Anaya is not blind to the presence of evil forces in the natural world or in the world of men. In fact his potential shamans only acquire the ability to guide and heal after crossing a desert of experienced or vicarious suffering. Furthermore, mediation, which operates in his stories most of the time as a positive factor, can occasionally take on negative connotations. Several characters act as mediators in the positive sense of the term, as we have already seen, and facilitate the difficult journeys of the central characters--Antonio Márez, Clemente Chávez, and Benjie, in the three respective volumes of the trilogy. Since Antonio is the youngest of the three and seems to be essentially an apprentice and a beneficiary of the mediation process, we might think that *Bless Me, Ultima* is the story only of his initiation. But Antonio, like Clemente and Benjie, is actually at the intersection of the two vectors, receiving and *giving* at the same time. By the side of Ultima, he participates in positive magic practices: first, in the exorcistic healing of his Uncle Lucas, then in the lifting of the curse on the Téllez family. But he can also go it alone. He gives a dying man the last rites and hears his confession in chapter fourteen.

Negative mediation, however, also operates in the devil's territory. For example, in *Bless Me, Ultima*, Tenorio and his daughters act as agents of an undetermined evil power and leave behind them curses and innocent dead wherever they go. This clearly shows that Anaya is not an inveterate optimist. As a writer, he has sensed, like Isaac Bashevis Singer and Flannery O'Connor, a revival of Satan in a world which once thought it could explain everything in rational terms.

Through the use of transformational myth and a clever handling of the diglossic situation of Mexican Americans in New Mexico, Anaya has managed to weave a tightly knit network of relations between narrator, reader, and characters. Some readers may find that he has painted too rosy a picture of what he himself calls, "the indigenous people" ("Mesa" 23), and that his fiction is not a direct call to political action. But this is precisely what he did not want it to be. Literature, he feels, should not be reduced to political manifesto. Besides, Anaya never wrote about the barrios of very big cities, and his fictional world cannot be compared to those of John Rechy or Alejandro Morales. He also strikes a compromise between the way these two novelists handle language--refusing, in the trilogy, the all-English or all-Spanish form of narrative. He uses Spanish in reference to family or community structures, to express prayers, blessings or curses, and to deal with anything having to do with the depths of the natural world--love, nurturing, and mourning. English dominates in his prose, but there is no artistic clash between the two since they serve two different purposes. Their conjunction dramatizes very well the dilemma of young protagonists who have to use a vehicular language with the out-group and another one with the in-group and with their peers.

Whereas Chicano poetry has remained the best instrument of direct political challenge for the Chicano militant, so much so that Rafael Jesús González has called it "our Huitzilopochtli" (136), a certain number of Chicano novelists--and Anaya is one of them--have tried to come to terms with their mixed cultural heritage and with the paradoxical situation that Anglo society has created for Chicanos in the Southwest since 1848. We might be tempted to call up the image of Quetzalcóatl to designate this attempt at a synthesis, but the range and variety of Chicano fiction forbids such an oversimplification. Anaya's trilogy, with its various levels of mediation and its persistent reference to mutual love and comradeship as the best instruments of mediation, occupies a privileged niche in a literature that is warm, robust, and extremely dynamic.

NOTES

[1] This essay is the final development of the author's reflection on the theme of mediation in Anaya's trilogy, which began as a presentation made at the Paris Conference of March 12-14, 1986, on "Hispanic Cultures and Identities in the United States." It has been published, in an abbreviated version, as part of a collection, under the following title: "Mediators and Mediation in Rudolfo Anaya's Trilogy: *Bless Me, Ultima, Heart of Aztlán* and *Tortuga.*" *European Perspectives on Hispanic Literature of the United States.* Ed. Genvieve Fabre. Houston: Arte Publico, 1988. 55-65.

[2] For an interesting summary of the role of Aztlán as symbol and myth see Luis Leal. "In Search of Aztlán." *Denver Quarterly* 16 (Fall 1981): 16-22.

WORKS CITED

Anaya, Rudolfo. *Bless Me, Ultima*. Berkeley: Quinto Sol, 1972.

___. *Heart of Aztlán*. Berkeley: Justa, 1976.

___. Interviewed by César A. González-T. San Diego, CA, Sunday, 31 March, 1985. See *Imagine: International Chicano Poetry Journal* 2.2 (Winter 1985). Eds. Tino Villanueva and Luis Alberto Urrea. **Reprinted in this Volume.**

___. "Myth and the Writer: A Conversation with Rudolfo Anaya." Interviewed by David Johnson and David Apodaca. *New America* 3.3 (Spring 1979): 76-85. **Reprinted in this Volume.**

___. *Tortuga*. Berkeley: Justa, 1979.

___. "A Writer Discusses His Craft." *CEA Critic* (November 1977): 40-43.

___. "The Writer's Landscape: Epiphany in Landscape." *Latin American Literary Review* 5 (Spring-Summer 1977): 98-102.

Bruce-Novoa, Juan. *Chicano Authors: Inquiry by Interview*. Austin: U. of Texas P, 1981.

Carpenter, Lorena Hyde. "Maps for the Journey: Shamanic Patterns in Anaya, Asturias and Castaneda." Diss. Univ. of Colorado, Boulder, 1981.

Crane, Stephen. *The Work of Stephen Crane*. Ed. Wilson Follett. New York: Knopf, 1925-27. Reissued, New York: Russell, 1963.

Eliade, Mircea. *Le Chamanisme et les techniques archaïques de l'extase*. Paris: Payot, 1983.

___. *Mythes, rêves et mystères*. Paris: Gallimard, 1957.

Ellison, Ralph. *Invisible Man*. London: Penguin Books, 1965.

González, Rafael Jesús. "Chicano Poetry/Smoking Mirror." *New Directions in Chicano Scholarship* 1 (1984): 127-138. [University of California at Santa Barbara: Center for Chicano Studies. Ricardo Romo and Reymund Paredes, eds.]

Jung, Carl. *Four Archetypes*. Princeton: Princeton UP, 1970.

Katz, Joséph, ed. *Stephen Crane in the West and Mexico*. Kent State UP, 1970.

Leal, Luis. "In Search of Aztlán." *Denver Quarterly* 16 (Fall 1981): 16-22.

"Mesa redonda con Alurista, R. Anaya, M. Herrera-Sobek, A. Morales y H. Viramontes." *Maize* 4.3-4 (Spring-Summer 1981): 6-23. **Reprinted in this volume.**

Stevens, Wallace. "The Comedian As the Letter C." In *Opus Posthumous*. Ed. S. F. Morse. New York: Knopf, 1957.

___. "The Man with the Blue Guitar." In *Wallace Stevens: Selected Poems*. London: Faber, 1953.

Vendler, Helen. *On Extended Wings*. Cambridge: Harvard UP, 1969.

The Surname, the Corpus, and the Body in Rudolfo A. Anaya's Narrative Trilogy

Roberto Cantú
California State University, Los Angeles

> *He who has eyes to see, and ears to hear, becomes convinced that mortals can keep no secret. If their lips are silent, they gossip with their fingertips; betrayal forces its way through every pore.*
>
> --Sigmund Freud[1]

I. The unconscious speaks more than one dialect

In his essays and interviews, Anaya often deploys significant terms such as "collective subconscious" and "archetypes," producing an over-encoded reader within the margins of his narrative. At such revealing moments, Anaya is tacitly legitimizing with his authorial blessing a specific reader theoretically composed of recognizable psychological and cognitive features. A similar operation occurs frequently in his narrative, particularly after 1972, where one finds intertextual allusions and connections to a myth, a film, or a novel, thus providing a "background" which clarifies or expands the textual meaning. It would seem that in order to understand Anaya's writings one must read simultaneously at several levels (the story, mythological allusions, symbolic patterns, etc.), very much like medieval monks reading Scripture. On the other hand, there appears to be in Anaya's selected discourse a compelling wish for a given "message" to be firmly grasped by his authorial audience and, concomitantly, a compulsive desire to beguile the gullible. The result has been an implied attempt for absolute authorial control over textual meaning; it follows, then, that the "clues" being transmitted, or the "truths" being disclosed, remain concealed like Ultima's revelations, which are a riddle, almost a hieroglyph, therefore, unknown to those who, like Antonio Márez Luna, do not have eyes to see. In a strange parallel, Antonio's fate in *Bless Me, Ultima* (BMU) is that of the trusting authorial audience: to "misread" the signs and to be blind to the textual truth which, by the rules of the narrative game, is none other than the site of the transcendental signified. The critical question, therefore, leads us directly into problems of reading, textual lordship and, like border coyotes, to a transgression of limits and undocumented entries.

The question of challenging Anaya in his role as a critic of his own writings suggests a similar action towards Anaya criticism, for within its ranks there is a growing satisfied consensus as to what is emblematic in Anaya, producing, as a result, a stereotype now associated with magical realism, a geographical mystique, dream narratives, and the repression of history. In our desire to return (with the intent of remembering) to the Anaya who remains buried and concealed underneath a growing mountain of critical documentation, I propose a *coyote* reading. What would it be like? As a plot against the Anaya stereotype, it would be a reading that is undocumented, undomesticated, therefore alien(ated). Since that is my intent in this critical study, the ground to be covered shall be limited to the range of a narrative trilogy constituted, according to Anaya, by BMU, *Heart of Aztlán* (HOA), and *Tortuga* (T). The resolution is to accept Anaya's implicit challenge to read his trilogy as his "autobiography," and, along the way, to propose other theoretical (coyote) entries into Anaya's narrative--e.g., the problem of the (Chicano) subject, the analysis of the unconscious in narrative texts, Anaya's idea(s) regarding the act of writing; his concepts of the *body* (mystical, social, physical, literary) and of the *surname* ("Anaya" as the name-of-the-father); and, finally, the theoretical conditions for a reading of Chicano autobiography.[2]

Based thematically on cultural transgressions, Anaya's narrative seems to call for coyote readings to the extent that such a nocturnal scavenger is an active signifier in the history of racial relations in New Mexico. The signifier "coyote," according to Theresa Meléndez,

> has a range of meanings that have little, if anything, in common. However, the tenor of most of the approximately fifteen connotations, is attempting to bridge opposing forces or cross boundaries, as in the coyote of mixed ancestry, or in case of the smuggler who literally crosses borders.[3]

Born in New Mexico, how could Anaya escape from the pressing realities of local unwritten laws and social codes? In his narrative, one readily locates reconciling figures who represent the bridging of differences and the crossing of boundaries (e.g., Ultima, Crispín, Salomón), along with coyotes of mixed ancestry (e.g., Cindy's "unborn" child conceived by Benjie in HOA). Meléndez discusses various coyote signifieds which include the stigma of offspring born from interracial unions (Mexican and Anglo-American), generally considered to be "outcasts" and "perpetual outsiders"; youngest members of a family (in this sense, Antonio and Benjie are coyotes); the underdog or dupe; the coyote as "other" or trickster; and the coyote's power of identity transfiguration or metamorphosis, along with his ability to travel "from one level of meaning to another."[4] The free play allowed by the coyote signifier reveals other dimensions of Anaya's narrative, keeping the textual "meaning," like the Márez blood, in continuous dispersal and disjunction. Within this nomadism of the signifier, the coyote reading scans Anaya's ideological dislocations which occur after the publication of BMU. As a result, the Anaya stereotype splits, shatters in Anaya fragments, producing a plural Anaya who, nonetheless, retains compulsive repetitive traces of the same. This Anaya, who is the same, though always different, is captured in the metaphor: that rhetorical operation which carries signifieds "from one place to another," where comparison is always an implicit possibility. How else is one to think or interpret Anaya's obsessive play with a few signifiers, such as the tree, the bridge, the mountain, the river, and the (resurrected) body?

Anaya criticism tends to accept the self-referential commentaries of Anaya towards his narrative as the ultimate source of textual authority (the question seems to be, who knows more about Anaya's narrative than Anaya?), thereby admitting the author as the Fa(mo)ther of his literary creation. Critics, therefore, tend to indulge in unproblematical assumptions regarding the identity between author, narrator, and protagonist, assumptions which, I admit, Anaya continues to encourage. In this respect, Anaya's narrative *fiction* has become virtually his *autobiography*, and Antonio's prophetic powers have been transferred to the "real" Anaya. Test your critical skills in the following passage written by Anaya in *A Chicano in China* (ACC) as his boat glides through the Yangtze River, and as his mind drifts across distant memories of his life in New Mexico:

> [M]y task as a writer is to enter those streams of time. I remember the early fear and fascination I felt as a young man when I first discovered this. . . . is the work of a *brujo*, the task of the shaman, to fly into the other realms of time or heaven or hell and to rescue the souls of our characters. This is the work of the writer, to learn to fly. (ACC 123)

Why does this passage, along with similar statements by Anaya, appear to be a parody of Carlos Castaneda, forcing a smile, perhaps laughter, followed by the impression that Anaya is "misleading" his critics on purpose, leading them to further "research" undisputed influences, sources, and authorial secret powers? This passage is an example of Anaya's writing of disclosure and concealment, for in the inscribed cosmological topography (heaven, earth, and hell), Anaya is revealing much of the "cosmological" structure of his narrative trilogy, with BMU, HOA, and T, respectively, as the texts corresponding to each plane or level. Anaya critics, however, would read this passage as "proof" that Antonio is a *brujo* and a *curandero*, for isn't he Anaya's double? What is certain--at least in my view--is that Anaya's autobiography cannot be understood through anecdotal resemblances with Antonio, Benjie, and Tortuga. Furthermore, if the reader's generic definition of autobiography is "a retrospective prose narrative produced by a real person concerning his own existence, focusing on his individual life, in particular on the development of his personality," then the reader may ask, how can Anaya's autobiography be read in a narrative form known for its elaborate rhetoricity?[5] Either Anaya was a child prodigy (and has become its adult version), or else he is rubbing the shepherd's wool over our eyes.

For the purposes of this study, autobiography cannot be understood in its positivistic sense, that is, as a "retrospective prose narrative" recounting the life of an "individual"; instead, it will be understood as that narrative register with recurrent thematic patterns, compulsive repetitions, and the so-called obsessive metaphors which manifest the illusionary hold on "realism" as well as the regressive tendencies of desire. The perception of Anaya's "I," as it remains concealed behind his narrative and self-disclosures, cannot, as a result, be seen as a unified, integrated self who resembles the "real" Anaya. The "I" with the Anaya surname and imbricated in an autobiographical narrative, is a linguistic construct or, in Jameson's view (via Lacan), "one further text in its turn, a text on the level with the other literary texts of the writer in question and susceptible of forming a larger corpus of study with them."[6]

In sum, since Anaya considers his narrative trilogy to be autobiographical, the task will be to examine the traces of self-inscription in the actual moments of writing (as recollected by Anaya), followed by an analysis of Anaya's descriptions or formulations regarding his surname, ideas of brotherhood, the (Chicano) collective body, and notions related to a *resurrection paradigm* wherein what was collectively dead (the *dismembered* bodies) either "resurrects" through science, resulting in an aberration (e.g., Frankenstein), or conversely follows a path of ascension leading towards "higher" forms of life (e.g., the *re-membered* body of Christ). Anaya's account of his almost fatal accident, paralysis, and "resurrection" when recovering the use of his limbs, finds its narrativization in the trilogy and gathers a richer meaning within this resurrection paradigm. The narrativization of Anaya's "life," therefore, is not analyzed in a positivistic mode, but read as rebuses and hieroglyphs which recantan Anaya's "psychography." It is in this semiotic region of the unconscious that Freud's proposition--"the unconscious speaks more than one dialect"--borders and crosses into Anaya's Pentecostal discourse.[7]

II. An Eye, An "I," and Anaya

In Anaya's writing of disclosure and concealment, the eye is the main organ of an exceptional sensorium.   There seems to be always a punctual narrative return to an exemplary encounter between a *spectator* (e.g., Antonio, Anaya, etc.) and the *scopic master* (e.g., Ultima or one of her counterparts). A variant of this encounter occurs in relation to the *scopic adept* (the spectator who suddenly knows "how to see"), and the New Mexican landscape whose beauty is revealed through the teachings of a wise benefactor (again, Ultima, old *ancianos*, Cruz, etc.).   To illustrate this point, open your eyes to one of the first instances in which Anaya, in an operation that transforms narrative fiction into autobiography, skillfully rewrites the original plot function of Antonio's encounter with Ultima:

> I feel constantly in touch with that epiphany which *opens me up* to receive the power in my landscape. . . .   [M]y vision was limited until I was taught to see the stark beauty which surrounded me.   I was fortunate to meet a few, old ancianos who taught me to respond to my landscape and to acquire the harmony which is inherent between man and his place. . . . Antonio's eyes have to be *opened* by Ultima so that he can see for the first time the beauty of the llano and the valley (emphasis added).[8]

Anaya's account clearly divides his life into two phases: one of scotomized vision ("my vision was limited"), and another of scotopic perception, acquired through the teachings of "a few old ancianos."   In addition, the differences between "fiction" (i.e., BMU) and "real life" are swiftly cancelled with the explicit reference to Antonio's epiphanic experience as having been Anaya's, but rewritten in fictional form.   In other words, as of 1977, Anaya claims an autobiographical affiliation with Antonio; interviews and his autobiographical essay expand this kinship to Benjie and Tortuga. Anaya concludes this essay with the admission that, in spite of his disclosures, they really explain "only a small part of the creative process that occurs in writing" (102). The impression of having been in Anaya's intimate circle (what Anaya has candidly given you) lingers, and the reader may be left assuming there must be more in Anaya, but, due to limitations of space, or authorial discretion, it is better left unsaid (therefore, Anaya takes away). In a concluding comment, Anaya describes the act of writing as follows:

> The private writing place becomes a madhouse, and the writer a mere guide as to the course of the character's lives. . . . [T]hat which is honest to me and, therefore, to my writing comes from my deepest felt experiences . . . the exploration into my world is a process through which I come to know myself and my earth better. For the moment, I am content to continue this exploration, and to convey to my reader the center of my universe. (102)

If one observes Anaya's metaphors of *body ingress* ("that epiphany which *opens me up*," "Antonio's eyes had to be *opened* by Ultima"), and correlates them to variants of *body fragmentation* (the Frankenstein model in HOA, but particularly in T), an anticipation will be posited regarding the "splitting" of an ego which, in the quoted passage, occurs in a field where reason or conscious mind are subverted by the rebellion of lunatic characters who--now masters of the house--delegate to Anaya the task proper to a "mere guide," to the doorman of the asylum, confounded by the logomania and collective madness of the "unconscious" residents emerging from Anaya's "deepest felt experiences." The act of writing, as a result, is metaphorized as a subversive drama taking place in the writer's psyche. On the other hand, Anaya shifts from the madhouse image to an archaeological metaphor where *honesty* (now synonymous with the act of writing) has *subterranean origins* ("deepest felt experiences"). To write, therefore, is equivalent to an exploration of unknown regions of one's unconscious ("my world") with the intention of achieving self-knowledge ("to know myself and my earth"). Proposed implicitly as a lifelong process ("for the moment"), Anaya willfully accepts his dual role as explorer of his psyche and as reporter of his findings ("to my reader . . . of my universe"). The shift, consequently, occurs not only from a madhouse to an archeologist's site, but also moves from a subterranean level (the unconscious) to a macrocosmic dimension ("my universe"). The act of writing, hence, is described as an operation which takes the writer--and later the reader--through coyote channels, that is, "from one place to another." In a passage which appeared almost ten years after this article, Anaya remembers his encounter with Ultima as follows:

> She laid her hand on my shoulder and I felt the power of the whirlwind. I *closed my eyes* and saw the heart of the lake, the deep pool of my subconscious, the collective memory and history of my people. . . . In the process of writing, the serious writer enters planes of vision and reality that cannot be induced with alcohol or drugs. . . . [W]hen the juices flow and the story begins to write itself, the soul of the writer seems to enter the story. The trance can only be explained as a kind of spiritual high. . . . I feel that connection right now as I write these ideas down. The flow is natural. Life itself. . . . Ultima *opened my eyes* and let me see the roots of my soul (emphasis added).[9]

From the explorer/reporter roles, Anaya now turns to diving tropes to describe how, by submerging himself into the pool of his subconscious, he enters into the collective memory and history of his people. The move is from ontogeny to phylogeny, from a personal search for plenitude to a remembrance of an always already absent collective history; from a condition where the "exploration" is done under his will, to one in which someone else (Ultima) serves as a directing, Plutonian force. The locus of polarization occurs at the transition to Chicano *writing*; the metaphysics of presence, however, remain in constant form. The extraordinary experience is, again, of at least two kinds: a personal encounter and the act of writing, conventionally encoded as the artist's inspiration (a muse) and the actual process of literary creation. In this passage, however, Anaya insists on the factuality of the apparition ("Those who don't know me . . . ") and on the veracity of his trance ("a kind of spiritual high"). The ancient convention of the artist's muse, therefore, is inappropriate for a full understanding of this passage. But in the attempt to reinstall reason in Anaya's discourse, can one read this passage literally (and seriously)? I will return to this question shortly; for now, it is clear that the visual metaphors remain active ("*closed* my eyes," "Ultima *opened* my eyes"), although dramatically changed from a personal quest for self-knowledge to one of the key metaphysical features of *Chicanismo*, namely: the appropriation of a collective history and culture. The scopic perception, as a result, is the vision of a *remembered* collective history (previously in a state of *dismemberment*). Anaya, after Ultima's advent, becomes a virtual microcosm of a people, producing in his self-portrayal a profile of Antonio Márez Luna who now clearly turns into his allegorical "double," thus legitimizing the readings proposed by Anaya criticism in the 1970's. This marks, as well, an instant of textual undoing in Anaya's narrative for it enters into contradiction with itself in its attempt to resurrect what Anaya all along considers "dead" beyond redemption. Hence, Anaya's conflicting messages: on the one hand, an apocalyptic image of the world (the decay of an old cultural era along with the rise of a "higher form," basically the message in BMU and T); on the other, the past viewed as worthy of being brought back to life, for it represents the collective history and culture of the people (the structural metaphor in HOA, Anaya's most "Chicano" novel).

Besides metaphors of visual perception (from scotomized to scotopic precision; from a life of darkness to one of light and an extraordinary sensorium, etc.), one also finds seminal metaphors which suggest procreation; writing, then, becomes the analogue, or sublimated act, of sexual, bodily ingress, leading to conception and birth of the literary child ("the juices flow . . . the soul of the writer seems to enter the story . . . The flow is natural. Life itself"). The artistic experience associated with the act of writing is thus returned to one of its conventional topos: a regression to a "life" origin where literary creation is linked conceptually to childbirth, with the sublimated difference resting on Anaya's reversion to acts of penetration and conception as if to emphasize the moment during which the writer, in an instant of divine frenzy (hence unconsciously, involuntarily), inscribes himself in his story or narrative ("the writer seems to enter the story"). BMU's *conception* (metaphorized through an *annunciating* Ultima; Anaya's *spirit* entering into the story; the *work* itself, etc.), suggests, then, a parodic role-inversion of the archangel Gabriel (the supreme messenger between heaven and earth, hence a "cosmic" coyote), now rewritten as the herald of literary conception (Ultima), and God (as Demiurge) and the Virgin Mary proposed simultaneously through the androgynous figure of the artist as creator and carrier of the seeds of literary life (Anaya). Anaya's idea of the act of writing, along with much of his narrative, may be understood, consequently, as artistic procreation or self-creation ("I wrote . . . I created my own spirit," Autobiography 24) fulfilled through a *crossing of frontiers*: heaven/earth, self/text, the old/the new. For Anaya, each scriptural *conception* becomes the equivalent of a child, the carrier of his surname and a member of the Anaya narrative corpus. Anaya's *body*, in other words, increases with each kinship unit, thus becoming a *literary body* which unites the offspring in a spiritual brotherhood or in a narrative community. Yet the writer's task corresponds to the work of fallen Adam; the artist is cursed, procreating "children" who are flawed from birth: "Perhaps the writer or artist is a person who is damned . . . we must flee into writing to assuage the pain" (Autobiography 23).

An overview of Anaya's descriptions of the act of writing allows us, at this point, to illustrate a problem found in every attempt to bring premature closure to "meaning" in Anaya, for how can one do so (even in the eventuality of "consistency") when confronting such "nomadism," concealment, and compulsive "erasures" from the part of the writer? If one were to look for a rhetorical pattern governing the various descriptions of the act of writing (to satisfy one's "rage for unity"), one could indicate that such act occurs either (1) on cosmological planes (heaven or hell, through the *brujo*); (2) in a metaphorical madhouse (i.e., the novelist's unconscious; an underground archeological site); (3) at the writer's desk, turned metaphorically into a marital bedchamber; or (4) in a place of atonement and remembrance of former pains. It follows, then, that for the sake of unity, one must shuttle back and forth-- like the coyote signifier which traverses various levels of meaning--between *cosmological planes*, a *madhouse*, a *bedroom*, and an *expiatory site*. Writing, as a result, more than the rescuing of souls, the surveillance/super-vision of lunatic characters, the digging or diving into oneself, the act of (self)procreation, or the act of atonement, is marked by a crossing of frontiers, which is a "crossing over" and a "crossing out," or the name of that gesture "effacing the presence of a thing and yet keeping it legible."[10]   Before inquiring further into the nature of such gesture which is Anaya's writing, let's recall that such an act is accompanied by a condition which is always one of perfect vision, at times made synonymous with orgasm, or with the living present in which (as with Antonio in BMU) time stands still while one sees and feels all that has been and all that is to come. In his 1977 essay, Anaya touches on these matters while elaborating on the concept of "epiphany":

> At that moment time is infused with power. As man and woman at the peak of their love break the shell of solitude that holds them apart and in tension, man and place achieve a similar climax in the realization of this essential metaphor.[11]

Anaya's repeated associations of the act of writing with *vision, sex,* and *knowledge,* suggest the presence of an intricate triad in which, as Freud proposes, an eye becomes a trope for a phallus; castration, consequently, is that condition in which man is blind, hence, unable to read or solve riddles.[12] The rewriting of Freud's idea of castration as the radical separation from the (m)Other adds a Lacanian dimension that makes castration applicable to both males and females, thus transforming the phallus into something more than just a male organ. Anaya's triad of vision, sex, and knowledge subsumes under its domain notions of females as purveyors of truth ("Woman, appear! . . . I seek to go to the truth, the door which opens to the mystery of the universe," commands Anaya in ACC, 100); of scopic adepts whose bodies "tremble" in ecstasy during an epiphanic communion (particularly when Anaya's characters have the uncanny feeling of "having been there before"), and so on. In this incessant crossing (over and out) of frontiers and acts of body ingress--all such acts proposed as personal moments of truth--an important occasion is Anaya's marriage: he married "a woman from Kansas."[13] Anaya, consequently, crossed a state frontier, marrying into a different "clan," very much like Gabriel and María in BMU, with the difference that this "woman from Kansas" has her proper name crossed out, becoming Anaya's (m)Other or, at times, his "double"; the latter, both in the sense of a relation to knowledge, or in scopic abilities when viewing landscapes:

She is glued to the new and mysterious sights the river presents us; she whispers she *has been here before*, in another time. . . . The people are friendly, all smile, they act like *they have never seen a Chicano walking with a Gringa* down the streets of Chengdu. . . . We wave. We are especially attracted to the babies. (ACC 121, 99; emphasis added)

How do these people from Chengdu "act" when they see a Chicano walking in China with a "Gringa"? Do they "see" the differences between a Chicano and a Gringa (i.e., do they know the meaning of "being" a *Chicano* or *Gringa)*, but conceal their prejudice ("are friendly, all smile") in regards to interracial couples? Are they really aware of such differences, or is it Anaya's projected vision that "sees" in Chengdu the presence of a New Mexican street (he also "has been here before"), a street in which Mexican-Anglo couples are seen with "precision"? The knowledge of having transgressed an unwritten law, a regional (racist) taboo, does it create a consciousness of being constantly watched (by God, fate, society), therefore, the indefatigable attempts to conceal, erase, cross-out or camouflage self-revelatory texts, writing in riddles, personal codes and, at times, in a discourse of madness? It is in these various modes of writing that Anaya's circumlocutions are subject to the betrayal of his fingertips, "forcing its way through every pore," as indicated in my epigraph.

There is a visible modulation in the thematic development of interracial unions from BMU to HOA. In BMU, the image of the *city* (Guadalupe) is associated with a *multiracial population*; in HOA, the theme of Anglo-Mexican unions surfaces from a negative, and presumably not personal, point of view.[14] In the first instance, the theme of forbidden marriages is presented under a positive light; in HOA, as an utter failure. Yet in this crossing of frontiers, Anaya should be beyond ethnocentrism by reason of family history and personal conviction, duplicating his mother's frontier marriage: "My mother left the river valley to marry a man from the *llano*, a *vaquero*, a man who preferred to ride horseback and work with cattle, not a farmer" (Autobiography 16). From this autobiographical disclosure one is suddenly back within the pages of BMU, with Antonio "torn" and undecided between the Márez (people of the llano) and the Luna (people of the river valley), and ultimately deciding that he will be *both* (the syncretic tendency of the coyote). Anaya states in his autobiography that his mother was first married to a man from the llano, his name being Salomon Bonney. This same name will be split and inverted in Anaya's trilogy, as if symbolic of a *double parentage*, or perhaps as a homage to a mother's memory of a former husband. In BMU, one reads that Gabriel's friends,

> *old amigos like Bonney* or Campos or the Gonzales brothers would come by to visit. Then my father's *eyes lit up* as they drank and talked of the old days and told the old stories. (3; emphasis added)

In the closing of the narrative trilogy, Salomón is Tortuga's *spiritual guide* and almost a voice from the underworld or from the beyond. Whereas Anaya criticism may have been directed to assume a symbolical correspondence between Salomón and its biblical antecedent, the name may have a different, more personal meaning. An instructive feature of Salomón's story is his own crossing of frontiers, forsaking his home and "doomed" to storytelling:

> My father was a farmer who planted corn on the hills along the river. . . . *[A] wild urge in my blood drove me from him. I went to join the tribe along the river.* . . . I forgot the fields of my father. . . .
> I, Salomón, tell you this so that you may know the meaning of life and death. . . . I tell you this because since that day *I have been a storyteller*, forced by the order of my destiny to reveal my story. (T, 22; emphasis added)

Salomón displays himself as a symbolic model of Anaya's storyteller (e.g., Antonio in BMU), being an instrument of fate ("a wild urge . . . drove me"), committing a transgression, and becoming a (compulsive) storyteller ("forced by the order of my destiny"). What emerges with some measure of legibility from Anaya's narrative is the kinship notion of exogamy as the foundation of a *communal body* (Mexican and Anglo), erased and rewritten in the conventional Spanish/Indian opposition, *resolved* in Mexico, culturally as well as racially, therefore undisturbing, admissible, thinkable. In his writing, Anaya crosses a state line to marry a "woman from Kansas"; his mother, likewise, travels across toponymic differences and marries a "man from the *llano*"; Salomón, in turn, joins a "tribe along the river," forgetting (dismembering) the fields of his father and obeying a wild urge of his blood (hence, he is not to blame). Anaya's personal mythology, consequently, seems to be governed by these border "transgressions," revealing its contents through adversary relationships resolved by means of forbidden marriages; expatriations, either self-imposed or in compliance with fate; syncretism in culture (instead of endogamy and ethnic "purity"); and, in regards to Anaya's idea of a "personal credo," to eclecticism, a veritable epistemological variant of Frankenstein insofar as it is a body integrated with members from different sources.

In his autobiographical essay, Anaya informs the reader that the marriage between his father (who had a daughter by a previous marriage) and his mother (who had a son and a daughter by Salomon Bonney) produced a family of ten children (therefore, in three "groups"), with Anaya as the youngest male (therefore, the Benjamín and the coyote of the family). Anaya's birth, under the light shed by Providence, could be seen as the will of fate, for someone died (Salomon Bonney) so that another (Anaya) could live; someone almost drowned (Anaya), yet was saved by Eliseo (therefore, Anaya was born *a second time*). Overall, the idea of the "nurturing" female is best exemplified in fiction (e.g., Ultima) as well as autobiographically (Anaya's mother and wife); such a maternal icon represents women of *vision*, possessors of knowledge, and transgressors themselves of *frontiers*. Anaya, the *youngest male* in the family, finds his truth in "three inevitable relations," and acquires, in his father's eyes, the symbolism of Death: "A silence fell between me and my father. Why? Did the familiar story tell him that to his way of life his youngest son was lost?"[15]

Besides these frontier crossings, there are in Anaya other rhetorical variants, such as that of scriptural creation, knowledge empowerment, or the revelation of truth, which appear encoded in metaphors of *body ingress*. An illustration of such metaphor is found in ACC where Anaya describes the symbolical conjunction between one of China's supreme cultural codes (the dragon) and Anaya's body:

> I sleep, and in my fitful sleep, a dragon enters my body. . . . Only when I no longer resist does China rest in my heart. The dragon settles itself in me, *its eyes breathing fire through my eyes* . . . The tail of the dragon spreads to my feet. The dragon sex now goes into my balls and penis. Finally, *it has entered me completely*. I am still. I have made peace with China. When I awaken, I feel refreshed, a new man. (45-46, 194; emphaisis added)

The comprehension--both as understanding and containment--of a *foreign body*, like the smuggling of an alien code, is subject to appropriation insofar as the "seeker of truth" makes room for a metaphorical *interracial union* between that which is Mexican and the other which is Chinese; the trespassing of a border (in a dream, or while awake), like the entry into the body of the "other," has the lure and the conditions for learning a "truth," that is, for personal (bodily) growth while one travels in foreign lands. In the illustration of the dragon, the union is both *reprehensible* for its implied bestiality (dragon + human), as well as for being a *forbidden marriage*: China (through its metonymical male dragon) and a Chicano (who becomes a metaphorical bride ["Finally, it has entered me completely"] in the tradition of the great mystics). In retrospect, every moment of revelation and of extraordinary cognition in Anaya's narrative is rhetorized in imagery of *visual trances*, in a discourse of rapture and communion where one hears and visualizes a trembling body, an elevation to a plane of eternity (Anaya's metaphysics of presence), and the brief disclosure of harmony coming into perfection. In the revealing moment of the dragon visiting Anaya's dreams, the communion recalls a former paralysis ("It has entered me completely. I am still.") translated into a moment of *transgression* in the form of a *symbolical rape* which concludes in the reconciliation of opposites and renewal ("I feel refreshed, a new man").

The study of Anaya's autobiography, as rhetorized in his narrative trilogy, must then be based on these passages of "effacement" and "legibility" and not on a psychobiographical signified that is found outside and away from Anaya's writing.[16] Reading Anaya is, in a manner of speaking, like dream analysis: one can easily be sidetracked by the manifest contents, when one should be tracking what is latent, condensed in the writing. Analysis, as a result, must be based on these moments of "self-inscription," of textual ingress by the "soul" of the writer (one of Anaya's favorite images) or, conversely, on the penetration of the writer's metaphorical, or oneiric, body by the *presence* of the alien "other" (e.g., China's dragon) which rushes in, undocumented, alien, undomesticated and nocturnal, crossing borders and permeating all with its faculty of comprehension and containment, making Anaya feel refreshed and new.

III. The Surname, the Corpus, and the Body

Anaya's autobiographical essay, with its unnumbered twelve sections and his claim to have been born with the umbilical cord around his neck like a *hanged man* (#12), displays Anaya at his best in terms of the writing that is simultaneously one of disclosure and concealment. The narcissism of Anaya-the-wonder-child is balanced with the telling of bitter memories, such as the accidental shooting of Santiago Chávez's eye ("a bad memory of that haunts me still," 18); Anaya's crippling accident and the ensuing loneliness; the sudden racism which divided Anglos and Mexicans in Anaya's immediate world ("We who had always been *brothers* now separated into Anglos and Mexicans. I did not understand the process" 19; emphasis added); then, a shaken faith, a lost love, the unfulfilled parenthood, and the bothersome hounding of the literary critics. What draws these memories into one condensed field is the feeling of fragmentation and the ensuing exclusion which continuously threatens Anaya's sense of integrity, harmony, and communion. Of all, the crippling accident seems to have marked Anaya for life ("the scars I still carry" 20), therefore, analysis must move from a reported biographical incident to its inscription in Anaya's narrative:

> I have not spoken or written about this accident before . . . I
> learned that indulging in confession did not really help me. . . . *We*
> *learn very well to hide* our disabilities. . . . [W]e are reminded how
> little our friends know us . . . We *learn to hide* our pain, to live
> within, to build a new faith inside the shell of bones and muscle.
> (20; emphasis added)

The pronominal shift from "I" to "we" is an almost imperceptible
transition from Anaya's youth to the narrative characters ("we") who recontain
his biographical past. Anaya adds: "It is easier to ascribe those times and
their bittersweet emotions to my characters." (22)[17] Anaya's brush with death
is narrated almost as poignantly as is his professed religious disenchantment
("a faith shaken"), which surfaces in BMU through dialogues between Antonio
and Florence. The friend who saves Anaya from drowning (Eliseo) is
rewritten as *Mike*; he saves Tortuga from drowning ("strong hands lifted me
out of the water. . . . I smiled," T, 125). In BMU, however, Antonio does
not drown; the one character who has no one to lift him out of the water is
Florence; he is, then, the only "double" who integrates the trinity formed by
Anaya-Antonio-Tortuga (or Benjie), either through the theme of "a shaken
faith" or a (barely escaped) drowning. Yet, Florence is also the one character
who represents a radical difference, for he is blonde:

> He was tall and thin, with curly blonde hair that fell to his shoulders.
> I had never seen anyone like him, *so white and speaking Spanish*.
> He reminded me of one of the golden angel heads with wings. (BMU
> 33; emphasis added)

Does one perceive at this narrative instance a possible idealization of
"Anglo" features presented as Spanish (with a subterranean homology with the
"Spanish" Márez)? Or is Florence--in the underworld of Anaya's cosmology--
a code character for Salomón and, biographically, for Salomon Bonney, whose
death allowed Anaya to live? For the moment, the duality that emerges is
that of death/life in the context of *fate*, with the same conceptual pair

suggestive of a cosmological hierarchy or variation (above/below, day/night), so that Florence could be the Sun King (with his long, blonde hair) who, after his daily "fall," allows night (i.e., Tortuga) to rise and govern the "heavens" (what is above). The symbolical *darkness* appears in Tortuga's hair: "My hair had grown almost to my shoulders." "My hair hung nearly to my shoulders" (T 129, 163). This Christ-like cluster, with latent connections to Samson, stimulates discussion at various symbolical planes, all variations of the Sun King (long hair, the journey to the underworld, and the rise to a celestial origin). If Anaya's birth can be interpreted as being an *act of fate*, his early contact with death at *the river* (while being "upsidedown"), and his last-minute rescue, must have given Anaya a sense not only of a *double birth*, but that God was watching and saving him for better things:

> . . . I dove first. Then *the world disappeared*. . . . I floated to the top of the water, opened my eyes, saw the light of the sun shining in the water. . . . I struggled violently to move . . . to *turn upside down* so I could at least breathe and keep from drowning. . . . Then I saw Eliseo tentatively approach my floating body. . . . He turned me over. . . . *I had been saved for a new role in life*. (Autobiography 20. Emphasis added)

This structural theme appears displaced throughout the trilogy either in the form of the golden carp (BMU, 227), Florence (BMU, 229), Henry (HOA, 107, 110), or Tortuga (T, 124-125). Whereas the first is a *river god* (therefore a chthonic ruler), and the other characters *descend* to the underworld (i.e., they die) either *literally* (Florence and Henry) or *metaphorically* (Tortuga, who "ascends" with a new role in life), the overall process would seem to indicate a necessary "death" prior to rebirth.

In a family of several brothers and sisters--some by a different parent--how does one establish a sense of *brotherhood* in spite of acknowledged "differences" (e.g., racial)? How does one ignore the surrounding racism that introduces the wedge of disharmony in social or family relations? Anaya was troubled by the division ("We who had always been brothers now separated into Anglos and Mexicans" Autobiography 19). Since the children of Anglo and Mexican intermarriages are called *coyotes*, these "outcasts" are by definition *without* a brotherhood, without a "pack"; unlike the wolf, the coyote runs alone. Seen from this angle, idealized brotherhoods (a constant thematic pattern in Anaya's narrative) could be understood as symbolical resolutions to a coyote condition, the result of the racism which dehumanizes the children of interracial couples.

Anaya, in one of his trips to Spain, learned that "Anaya" means *brotherhood* or *brothers of a clan* in Basque. Any discussion of brotherhoods in Anaya's narrative must begin, therefore, with the surname. According to Anaya, this discovery suggested *anarchy* and *rebelliousness* (instead of what the name suggests: a fraternal contract, the obedience and submission to the Name-of-the-Father; in other words, the brothers' acceptance of the Law). The surname, in Anaya's interpretation, also clarifies a feature of temperamental lineage:

> There is a story of an Anaya who had a strong argument with the parish priest. . . . Knowing the anarchistic and independent nature of the Basque people has provided me as much of a clue to my father's nature as all the years I knew him. Perhaps I remember all this only because it sheds light on my nature. There is something of the rebel and the anarchist in me. (Autobiography 17)

The symbolic function of names and surnames in Anaya's narrative has been examined amply by Anaya criticism to a point that the above disclosure can hardly surprise us; nonetheless, is this passage to be taken as the gesture of a Chicano who has decided to acknowledge either his Basque ancestry or to rationalize his own alleged temperamental inclination? If we return to the meaning of the surname "Anaya" (both as *brotherhood* and *anarchy*), it becomes a fusion of both surnames (Anaya + Mares, i.e., Anaya's maternal surname), combining *father* and *mother* as the (dual) conceptual foundation of his narrative: a search for community as a *social body* and *brotherhood* ("Anaya"), coupled by an inherent tendency towards *anarchy* and *rebelliousness* (Márez in BMU, Mares in "real" life), i.e., the defiance of the

Law, the crossing of frontiers, and the overturning of one's "prescribed" fate. From yet another perspective, "Anaya" (interpreted in its isolated *Ana*-rchy) is the synecdoche of a *linguistic coyote*, for Basque is the "outcast" language of Europe (where does it belong?), the language of a lost brotherhood, the presumed native language of Iberia which survives in spite of several waves of conquests, cultural impositions, and Basque "submersion." The Basque, like the Native American and Mexican memories of Guadalupe, are a *repressed memory*.

How did Iberia's (m)Other tongue survive? In the surname "Anaya" the dyadic value of *brotherhood* and *anarchy* becomes the contra-diction (language in an adversarial mode) and the compulsion to repeat a repressed Mother Tongue. The contradiction results in a muffled, obstructed discourse (it "comes out" in the language of conquest), while the repetition, the tautological redundancy, is the stammering of a desire expressed through the (m)Other's repressed tongue:

> Language is a code; it is a way of getting close to each other. . . . I retreat to the comfort of my own native language, Spanish. The woman in the dream comes to speak Spanish to me and to comfort me; I need to hear the sounds of my native language to keep my reality together. I need the words I know and understand and can roll on my tongue to give focus to my being. (ACC 138-39)

The notion of brotherhood formulated from such grounds as the surname and its Basque meaning becomes, consequently, a connecting thread that gives integrity to Anaya's narrative corpus and unity to Anaya's idea of a community body. It is in this sense that Anaya's paradigmatic hero--a young man in search of his "destiny," in the manner of self-knowledge or knowledge of the world--is the man on a personal search for plenitude, on a journey or quest for an always already absent ideal society where the hero truly belongs. Based on propositions advanced in this article, one could assume that Anaya's "politics"--antiracist and pacifist--is an advocacy for a society that would be Pentecostal in its language diversity, and plural in its cultural diversification. It is for this reason that Anaya's interest in *Aztlán* as a "reintegration" of a native population (Mexicans, as direct descendants of Aztecs, now returning to their land of origin) is an ideological eccentricity in his narrative corpus, but is clearly expressive of the ethos moving much of the Chicanismo of the early 1970s. The free association of the surname, the body, and the corpus as conceptual terms in Anaya's trilogy allows, therefore, for the imaginary recall of a fourth term--brotherhood--and for the analysis of the ideological permutations of brotherhoods (as family clans, regional affiliations [e.g., people of the *llano*], as *ideal corps* or groups of initiates [e.g., the brotherhood of the golden carp], as a people returning to its land of origin, etc.).

Anaya criticism has had a tendency to bring ideological closure to its readings of BMU through propositions of clan resolutions or *synthesis* (Márez + Luna) as they occur in Antonio, thus neglecting the analysis of the membership, and apparent cultic goals, of BMU's ideal brotherhood, composed of youths (Samuel, Cico, and Antonio) and adults (Ultima, Jasón's* Indian, and Narciso). The cult is concerned with origins and with an advent, that is, with the prophecy of a god's return to rule the land (Guadalupe), a site of multiethnic convergence, therefore, an analogue of the universal city or empire. The world at large, sundered by military violence, becomes the macrocosmic homologue of a regional enmity of protracted duration (Mexicans invading Native American territory; Anglo-Americans then invading Mexicans, etc.).

* [Editor's Note: *Jasón* is accented throughout *Bless Me, Ultima*. In *Heart of Aztlán, Jason* is Anglicized; hence unaccented, except for a single instance on page 7. We use both formats when referring to the name as it appears in the novels, respectively.]

Since Guadalupe is the original site of the "covenant" between the *people* and their gods--who sent them on a long pilgrimage to found their city--this urban site becomes the diachronic construct of four settlements, all having the utopian goal of establishing a *brotherhood* in the form of a community body: the (original) *people*, Native Americans, Mexicans, and Anglo-Americans. Given that Guadalupe (in Arabic, "wolves by the river") is surrounded by water--therefore a metaphorical island--the end of the world is expected to be in the form of a deluge, with the carp's advent to occur by the waters of the river (in the manner of Anaya's floating body before being pulled out--and saved--by Eliseo). Lupito's (i.e., Guadalupe's) slaying symbolizes, consequently, the anthropomorphic representation of an urban fate: global violence, madness, and death at the hands of one's own neighbors (brothers, given the regional affiliations).

With the exception of Antonio (who is not disposed to violence), the brotherhood of the golden carp seems to be "besieging" the town of Guadalupe, as if to induce the *second advent* of the golden carp. Antonio's role in this drama is complex and somewhat similar to Samuel's and Cico's in terms of character symbolism, for Antonio's middle name (a name of power) is "Juan." Therefore, as Juan--and because of Antonio's residential correspondences (his hill and Tepeyac), as well as physical resemblances to Juan Diego--Antonio is an important structural element in a "micronarrative" which extends to two historical antecedents: to Juan Diego (Mexico, the Spanish Empire, XVI century), and to John of Patmos (Christians, Roman Empire, first century A.D.). The micronarrative, as a result, involves a man known by the same name, in an analogous geographical setting ("island"), with comparable visionary experiences. If one extends this character "telescoping" to Samuel and Cico, then they themselves--along with Antonio--will be seen in their full complexity as diachronic constructs made with biblical antecedents or with elements taken from Mexican history (e.g., Juan Diego, the Virgin of Guadalupe and her apparition, etc.). From this perspective, Samuel and Cico (= Ezequiel) are both symbolical counterparts of their biblical namesakes. Samuel, as a priest, is the primogenital child born of a mother of six children whose husband has *two wives* (i.e., the theme of double parentage); in addition, as a priest, Samuel's role is to serve, first, Saul ("a man from the land of Benjamin," I Samuel, 9:16), and second, to serve the *youngest* of Jesse's sons: David (therefore, the "Benjie" or coyote of the family). Ezequiel, on the other hand, is the prophet who has a vision close to a river (much like Cico, associated with prophecy and the river); and is "among the exiles by the river," (Ezequiel 1:1-2). In addition, Ezequiel is often seized by the spirit of God, "trances" described through images of *body ingress* ("As he spoke, his spirit came into me," 2:1-2, 3:23), and associated with modes of revelatory truth. Both Samuel and Ezequiel treat the subject of a *foundation*, either of a *genealogy* (Jesse's "mystical tree" which leads from David to Jesus), or a *Universal City*, to be ruled by Christ (according to the New Testament). Furthermore, the Book of Ezequiel, divided into *eight* sections (which is David's number--himself being the eighth child), follows three phases: the prophecy of Jerusalem's fall, the city's destruction, and the advent of a ruler (David) whose "restored theocracy" is to be eternal (Ezequiel 48:35). Jerusalem is destroyed because of its sinfulness and violence. Its reconstruction will result in a period of peace (34:25-27) and in a "multiethnic" community where aliens and "coyotes" are not ostracized, deported, or killed (47:21-23), for Jerusalem itself is "interracial," of an Amorite Father and a Hittite Mother, 16:3-4. One must note as well that both books have an obvious *political unity* through David: Samuel relates David's *terrestrial* rise to power; Ezequiel, conversely, celebrates David's return as a *spiritual* power (37:24-26). Both prophets are marked by times of strife and urban deterioration, much like the world depicted in BMU. One of Ezequiel's first commands will return our attention to BMU: "Jerusalem [read Guadalupe] . . . it will be the besieged and you [read the brotherhood of the golden carp] the besieger" (4:1-3; see also 16:1-4). When contrasted to other youths, this ideal brotherhood reveals the following differences:

BROTHERHOODS

Golden Carp
Samuel, Cico, Antonio
("We shared a secret that would always bind us," 108)

Sheepherders/the llano
Jasón, Samuel, Vitamin Kid, and Antonio
(live "across the river," 32)

Farmers/Delia boys
George, Willie (and Antonio)
("We banded together. . . ." 55)

Los Jaros
Horse, Bones, Abel, Florence (and Antonio)
(live "across the tracks," 33)

Antonio's virtual membership in all four brotherhoods exhibits various factors that can either explain "spiritual" polarities (the Los Jaros boys as a demonic parody of the cultic brotherhood composed of visionaries and privileged chosen) or economic differences among the local youth (ranching and farming). As a demonic parody, the Los Jaros gang--specifically Horse and Bones, who are described as "swinging like monkeys in the bell ropes," (190), and Bones as being brought up "on raw meat" (148)--are portrayed as wild youths having an *infrahuman* nature (hence, proper to the underworld, chthonic, demonic), and living "across the tracks" (therefore, associated with the railroad, i.e., with the culture destroyed by the *iron horse*). This contrasts with the *spirituality* of the brotherhood of the golden carp who live "across the river" (hence associated with "rebirth"), await a second advent and the coming of a New City, and besiege Guadalupe, precipitating its doom with actions and sacrifices (e.g., Ultima) which serve as indexes of a (desired) forthcoming reintegration of the social body. The fact that Antonio is found in all four brotherhoods insinuates a "splitting" of his identity (from shepherd to farmer, from initiate to gang member, that is, from Antonio to Benjie), as well as his idealized "other," this being expressed through the composite form of Samuel/Cico or Florence, who becomes, then, by virtue of his brotherhood membership, an *underworld double* of Antonio and the one to die by the river, as a sacrifice to the golden carp (now turned into its "double") offered by the cult. It follows, then, that the "falling" into or from the water (tank) by Florence and Benjie, correspond, in a subterranean manner, to Tortuga's own fall and metaphorical death (paralysis), along with his eventual Spring "resurrection."[18]

The possibility of this reading, when added to BMU's overall plot structure (and, in an underground form, extending it to the narrative trilogy), redirects our attention along two parallel levels or plot-tracks mutually aligned on a course which concludes with a sacrificial death of a scapegoat (Ultima, Florence) symbolically resolving community contradictions at the youth and adult levels. In BMU the brotherhood membership contains *racial differences, including* Jasón's Indian, Mexicans, and the "Anglo" looking Florence, who becomes a metaphorical cult member at the moment of his death. These differences will be resolved with the second advent of the golden carp. In HOA, the emphasis is on Mexicans who are returning to their *Indian* origins (i.e., to Aztlán) with the intentions of "remembering" or recollecting, so to say, the communal or *tribal body*, dismembered throughout Mexico over centuries of southern migrations. IN BMU the brotherhood besieges Guadalupe (in a simulacrum of a regional Armageddon) in order to hasten its fall (anticipated by the children, and the conceptual core of the prophecy), and to foreclose a period of ecumenic and local violence. In HOA, on the contrary, there is a celebration of a return to origins, the crossing of *political* frontiers (but not of "racial" borders), and the return to the *mythical body* (Albuquerque) which, in HOA, is the original site of Aztlán (HOA 9, 11). The Aztlán motif will be part of a larger Chicano construct which incorporates the figure of the pachuco, now implicitly made into a historical antecedent of the Chicano movement:

Ana identified closely with the *pachuco brotherhood*, the *carnalismo of the barrio*. She adopted the pachuca's style, the language, and she had gone as far as tattooing a blue India ink dot on her forehead. With that she had sealed her independence and had begun to move from the circle of the familia to a wider identification with *the pachuco movement* in the barrio. (HOA 70; emphasis added)

Ana's grotesque profile is drawn in such a manner as to create a parody of a female's emancipation from family bonds, suggesting, therefore, a parallel to Benjie, who also believes he has "sealed" his independence by joining a gang and by his use of drugs. In his involvement with his characters, however, the omniscient narrator at times adopts a pachuco "discourse," thus undermining the propriety of the distance guaranteed by the third person mode of narration:

The children . . . fell asleep in the arms of a mother, a sister, una tía or an abuelita, anyone. They were all one family. . . . Outside the dance hall los vatos locos mounted those hours on the thin wings of marijuana smoke . . . [Benjie] was high on mota. . . . (40-41)

The contrast is clearly established between a domestic somnolence of children, who may rest secure in the safety of the family's arms ("anyone"), and the profane space in which the youth ("los vatos locos") waste themselves in the somnolence induced by drugs. The implied thematics of the mystical body as a community, a brotherhood, or a spiritual kingdom is rewritten in HOA as the Barelas barrio (to whom the novel is dedicated), the pachuco movement, and Aztlán, respectively. Anaya's manner of depiction, however, has been in the form of parody; therefore, our reading remains crossed between what purports to be exemplary and yet, simultaneously, appears to be a caricature of a true community or brotherhood.

Anaya's characterization suffers after BMU due to the ideological "overload" that burdens his characters. One must be redirecting one's attention somewhere else to a dimension where Anaya's heroes acquire a different narrative purpose. For example, Clemente Chávez, as a signifier, is a condensation of three signifieds easily identified by an informed authorial audience, particularly regarding contemporary Chicano history. These signifieds are found condensed in a leadership paradigm composed of César Chávez, Reies López Tijerina, and Rodolfo "Corky" Gonzales. Clemente is the signifier for all three Chicano leaders by virtue of the activities he assumes as *labor organizer* (168-69); to issues related to *land grants* (103); and as a *community organizer* of a "Crusade for Justice" (141). Read in this manner, HOA appears to be Anaya's homage to three Chicano leaders (with Anaya's embedded view against violence), as well as a tribute to the people of Barelas; the result (formulaic, predictable, ideologically obvious) is a faithful mirroring of the early phase of Chicanismo.

Wishing to write a narrative thematically related to the Chicano movement, Anaya proposed two heroes (Clemente and Jason) who would represent *organizational* efforts at two different community levels, namely: adults (working class), and youth ("the gang Jasón had found," 44). The two heroes are portrayed simultaneously in only four chapters (1, 2, 3, 19), with Clemente active in seven (7, 8, 10, 13, 14, 15, 21), and Jasón in nine chapters (4, 5, 6, 9, 11, 16, 17, 18, 20). The reader is lead to certain logical assumptions regarding both Clemente and Jason Chávez as probable "heroes." But in retrospect, particularly from the vantage point provided by T, such assumptions are not fulfilled, for Crispín dies. Clemente has not resolved anything (T 168), and, more important as a plot element, neither Clemente nor Jason inherit the guitar: Tortuga (i.e., Benjie) does. Yet both have been groomed as potential inheritors of Crispín's guitar (hence, the reader is mislead). At the end of the narrative, each hero adopts the role which corresponds to the quest assigned by Anaya: Clemente reintegrates two *collective bodies* (his family and his community) thanks to the "fire of love" (207); Jason, consumed within by the fire of love he feels towards Cristina, wins the heart of his beloved. What of Benjie? While Clemente has become impregnated with the desire to lead his people and reunite his family, and Jason, unable to consummate his love with Cristina, organizes a local gang while attempting for several chapters to prove his innocence in regards to Cindy's pregnancy ("Everyone knows you are the father of the coyotito that mocosa gabachita went away to breed!" 175), Benjie, on the contrary, has become Jason's *demonic double*: he crosses a *frontier*, violates a local unwritten law, and succeeds in impregnating Cindy (the "gabachita," 181). Benjie, as a coyote himself (the youngest son), acts true to form: he is the scavenger who "consumes" what others (Jason) disdain or leave behind (Cindy). As could be expected, the violation of the law results in a *ritualized exile* for both: the gabachita goes away "to breed," and Benjie, after his accident, also leaves town (within the logic of the trilogy, he would then go to the hospital, as Tortuga).

HOA's narrative, consequently, follows a course of action starting from a point of disintegration of the collective body (family, community), to its reintegration either in the form of brotherhoods (gangs), a workers'union, family or community:

> Old friends from the different barrios of the city met and the nexus was kept intact as the different barrios formed one larger community. . . . "--La familia has been torn apart and scattered before, but it will come together again--" (HOA 62, 205)

HOA's conclusion furnishes a contrast: after Clemente's momentary catatonia, there follows the *mobilization* of the community (a reintegration and movement of a "body") and the *paralysis* of Benjie (whose subsequent "reintegration" and movement is narrated in T). Benjie's injury, then, is none other than a retribution for his cultural transgressions (a strong term in BMU), such as his youthful impudence, his distaste for pastoral life, his easy abandonment to urban ways (his emancipation from the "old ways"), culminating in an interracial liaison with Cindy. Clemente's family, on the other hand, finds its last minute hold, its unity, in spite of the lacerations caused by urban deculturation.

In this semantic field of paralysis/movement, death/resurrection, the disintegration of the Mexican rural family, as a *problem*, will be resolved with the emergence of a strong leader:

What Manuel had said was true. They needed a leader . . . Manuel continued. "You know that the familia without a strong father soon falls apart, and that a pueblo without a good leader is not united in its effort to serve the people, and a country without a good, strong man to guide it is soon overrun by its enemies. Our own revolutions have taught us the value of a wise leader, now we must find that man among ourselves--" . . . one of the men called to Crispín to sing them a song that would help bring them together again. (82, 83)

The telescoping of three "bodies"--familia, pueblo, country--is achieved by connecting the figure of the "strong father," the authoritarian ruler who, by virtue of charisma and personal omnipotence, keeps his people within the fold. This ideological dimension of HOA reveals how "political" Anaya's narrative can be and how misguided most criticism is when denouncing Anaya for not being "political." Seen from this perspective, the political dislocation which occurs from BMU to HOA actually becomes a translation of a metaphysics of government (siege of a city to hasten the end of the world, heralding the Second Advent of a Christ-figure), to an authoritarian government, with the strong leader as the Father of all. But, fortunately for us, Clemente (even though meaning well) is an overburdened signifier, hindered as a character by the weight of Anaya's messages, encumbered by the gravity of pre-Columbian, Christian, and Mexican intertextual determinants. He becomes, therefore, almost a parody of the strong leader, particularly in the final scene, at the front of a *river* of people, burning with the madness of acquired mobility and the fire of love. Approximately a year later, "the battle here has continued. It is like a war. Nothing is settled" (T 168). So the "fire of love" resulted in violence, after all.

The besieged city, either Guadalupe in BMU or Albuquerque in HOA, remains distant from becoming an ideal society or collective body, as envisioned by local brotherhoods. Yet there are no tears shed for the cultural past. The trilogy's conclusion does not propose a plan for a social reintegration according to *traditional* forms, for now Tortuga functions--in his capacity as a *guitarrero*--as the "messenger" of collective cultural change. The message is to be encoded in the form of *underworld* songs whose content proclaims the *death* of the cultural past. Someone dies so that somebody may live. Death is the foundation of life; therefore a cultural past must pass away to allow for the creation of a new cultural world. Anaya's apocalyptic message is consistent throughout the trilogy, proposed through liminal characters who represent the end of an era and the (hoped for) transition to a new cultural stage; what remains concealed, however, is the nature of such a cultural world as envisioned by Anaya.

Anaya's "doubles" (Antonio, Benjie, Tortuga) are structured according to a process of inversion and transformation, confirming Benjie and Tortuga as demonic parodies of Antonio who, *during his dreams*, ascends to a level of visionaries, hence to an ideal community, while Benjie and Tortuga descend to the "depths" of hell, both in its urban and metaphorical variants. In terms of character inversion, Antonio is innocent, kind, and credulous; Benjie and Tortuga, on the other hand, are "tough," cynical, and transgression-prone. Antonio has *symbolic* contacts with women, particularly with Ultima; his demonic parodies have *literal* contacts which, on two occasions, are also marked as social transgressions (Cindy, the "gabachita," in HOA and T), or merely endogamous (Ismelda in T). More important, however, is the transformation from a non-heroic role (Antonio) to a "heroic" one, culminating in Tortuga. Through these three characters, Anaya appears to be forming a heterogeneous triad which can, upon analysis, be reduced to a dioscuric couple whose inversions and transformations suggest the imaginary development of a cosmological topography (heaven, earth, hell), and the embryo of Anaya's body of beliefs:

> I was molded into a good Catholic, insofar as any Anaya can be molded into one. I kept asking . . . questions which had to do with the nature of the *Trinity* and the *geography* of heaven. . . . Years later when I read Dante's *Divine Comedy*, I discovered that his inferno was like my hell. . . . If the sisters of Santa Rosa had read Dante, they would have been able to answer my questions about the *geography of hell*. (Autobiography 17-18; emphasis added)

304 ♠ *Roberto Cantú*

Taking this passage at face value, one readily sees Anaya's trilogy as the account of a *cosmological topography* consisting of three levels, with BMU = heaven, HOA = earth, and T = hell, and with two characters standing as direct opposites, namely: Antonio and Tortuga. These intertextual connections have their corresponding articulation in other character doubles, such as Tortuga/Danny. Danny's function in the logic of events as Tortuga's double is revealed in his decision to pull the switch which controls the electricity sustaining Salomón's ward. In other words, Danny carries out consciously what Antonio in BMU executes unconsciously as an instrument of fate, namely: he is the master's downfall. Danny's action against Salomón and his ward could be the result of his mounting paranoia which leads him to a decipherment of another "puzzle" ("I see it now! I see the plan now!" T 161). Tortuga's moment of recognition, on the contrary, is a puzzle whose decipherment results in the discovery of his destiny--precisely in the manner in which Antonio's *anagnorisis* has been read, wrongly, by Anaya criticism:

> He knew! He had known all along that Crispín would send me the guitar! That's why he kept saying I would learn to sing. But how did Crispín know? Did all of these people know something about my destiny which was revealed to me only in flashes of insight, like now, when *everything suddenly seemed to fall into place and make sense.* (T 169; emphasis added)

Besides being Tortuga's double, Danny and his two companions-- Mudo and Tuerto--constitute a parody of the brotherhood of the golden carp, more specifically of Ultima. First of all, alarmed and fearful of the malignant growth spreading throughout his arm and body, Danny turns to readings of the Bible ("He knew in detail the stories of every cripple in the Bible" 91); awaits the end of the world and Christ's second advent ("Danny . . . and the gruesome twosome . . . started sending everyone who would go to the recreation room because by that time they really believed that's where *the second coming* would take place" 95; emphasis added); and, along with his two "gruesome" friends, Danny is associated with violence as a means of hastening the end (they pull the switch on two occasions 93, 181). Second, Danny, Tuerto, and Mudo are a parody of Ultima inasmuch as their names are indicative of a specific lameness: Mudo = mute; Tuerto = "one-eyed"; and because Danny is "one-handed," he would be known as "Manco," just like Tortuga, who is a one-handed bard. This parodic triad, as a result, expresses physical disabilities (close to Anaya's memories of youth) related to *speaking*, *seeing*, and *touching*, which form the basis of Ultima's mode of *supercommunication*, as exemplified in BMU's initial passage and first encounter with Antonio. It follows, then, that Danny, who is associated with a "contact" disability, will be the symbolical "amputation" of Ultima's powers and the inversion of Ultima's juniper tree (of resurrection), given his condition as a metaphorical *tree of death* ("[H]is arm is drying up . . . It's turning dry and brown like an old tree branch. . . . [T]he damn curse has spread up his entire arm" 93). Anaya's obsession with rhetorical twists surfaces again in the tree signifier, for Tortuga, destined to *resurrect* from the hospital-cemetery, will return home with the blue guitar ("carved from the heart of a juniper tree" HOA 27); hence, Tortuga is associated metonymically to the juniper tree (by contiguity), while Danny, who is destined to remain *underground* (i.e., with no hope of "resurrection"), has an arm which resembles a withering tree branch. He is, in a synecdochical manner of speaking, a *dying tree*.

An in-depth analysis of the logic of T's plot actions, which I can only outline in passing, would produce the following salient features: Tortuga visits Salomón's ward on *three occasions*: chapters 5, 15, and 22 (with two intervening magical numbers--"10" [chapters 5-15], and "7" [chapters 15-22]-- expressed in the sequence of chapters 5, 15, and 22, which form the signposts of Tortuga's *recovery* and *return* home). In the first occasion, Tortuga is taken to Salomón's ward by mistake and is *unable to move* (38); the second, in a wheelchair (i.e., *indirect mobility*) and by his own free will ("I felt Salomón was going to tell me something that had to do with that nagging question and my reason for being here" T 115); in the third and last occasion, Tortuga *walks* to Salomón's ward and accepts his "destiny" as a *guitarrero*, i.e., as a people's bard ("Destiny had suddenly converged on me and illumined my path" 172). Along with the theme of recovery, symbolically read as resurrection, one finds the subtheme of having a "change of heart" from non-acceptance of "freaks" or monstrosity, to a condition of sympathetic response and identification. The first phase ("I don't belong here!! . . . Freaks . . . please God . . . take me from this hell . . ." 40), however, foreshadows Tortuga's reaction during his second visit ("Damn all of you! . . . This is a hell you've created! Pull the plug and let them die!" 118), and *Danny's action* in chapter 24, for he (Tortuga's double) is the one to pull the plug (181, 182).

Tortuga's recovery fulfills Filomón's prophecy that he would get better in spring (T 5). Shortly after Tortuga's arrival at the hospital, Ismelda appears and "squeezes" his hand, producing another miraculous effect: "Ismelda held my hand. Now my body seemed to want to come alive" (11). One could dismiss these passages as just more examples of the "magical realism" that is so important, according to Anaya criticism, in Anaya's narrative. Yet rereadings of this novel always seem to conclude with the following dilemma: either Tortuga's account (in first-person narrative mode) is the story of a narcissistic madman who finds meaning in every gesture, action, or batting of an eyelash (interpreted as a wink of complicity), or else Tortuga is surrounded by inhabitants of the underworld, i.e., by the dead. (How else can one explain the fact that "everybody" seems to be expecting Tortuga's arrival, that all are supportive of Tortuga's return to the world "out there" by spring, that narrative characters have the same dream, and, through something resembling telepathy, read each other's thoughts?) Tortuga's arrival at the hospital acquires, consequently, features associated with a journey to the Plutonian underworld, with Filomón as the ferryman and counterpart of the mythical Charon, and Tortuga as the Chicano Aeneas who has descended to Hades to consult with his "father" (Salomon Bonney?) regarding his destiny. Incidentally, this underworld which welcomes Tortuga could be viewed as a *multiethnic cemetery* (a parody of the ideal city in BMU), having Native Americans (Jerry), Blacks (the nurse known as "KC"), Anglo-Americans (Buck), and Mexicans.

Along with this death/resurrection construct, and its winter and spring seasonal phases, Anaya diligently overloads his narrative with images of zoomorphic transformations (e.g., from a worm to a butterfly, from turtle to lizard; from Tortuga in a cast [metaphorically in a coffin] to Tortuga on his way home. Hence we find transformations from earth to air, from water to earth, or again from earth to air, respectively, resulting in a continuous *crossing of frontiers*), and references to films, explicitly to *Frankenstein*, and implicitly to *One Flew Over the Cuckoo's Nest*, with its "mute" Native American, its riotous boat trip in the harbor (an appropriate parallel to the medieval Narrenschiff), and its institutional condemnation. Tortuga, as a result, not only recovers *mobility* (a metaphorical return from the grave), he also discovers that he is to be a people's bard, a "one-handed guitar man" (190). The return of life to Tortuga's stiff limbs is portrayed as involving tenacity, anger, much support from "local" friends, and pain, which is posited as a conjecture in regards to the resurrection of the dead, considered to be excruciating. In the narrative, this motif emerges precisely at the juncture where KC is introduced (60); during the viewing of the *Frankenstein* film (148); and in the correspondences between film and the plot actions (183). At the narrative's conclusion, the thematic construct integrated by a death/resurrection trinity (Lazarus, Jesus, Frankenstein) manifests its pervasive influence and ultimate function:

Level:	**Empirical**	**Symbolic**	**Imaginary**
Strong Term:	Tortuga	Resurrection	Jesus
Weak Term:	Danny	Putrefaction	Frankenstein

The basic conceptual framework produced from the above construct allows us to integrate the opposition life/death into its epistemological variant: God's wisdom/man's knowledge (derived from a "tree"). Frankenstein's function in Anaya's narrative, then. more than being a meaningful "body" for his autobiographical writing, serves as the prototypical example of man's vain attempt to be like God (through his science and technology) by either extending the limits of life (therefore Anaya's position in favor of euthanasia) or resurrecting the dead (e.g., in Shelley's novel). As a demonic symbol of resurrection, Frankenstein is a corpse integrated with members of the collective, social body (i.e., from the local cemetery); hence, he remains science's *Adamic scandal*. Yet Frankenstein also brings to mind the attempts, particularly in

Anaya's eclectic writing, to integrate a body or dogma of beliefs made from the fragments of destroyed cultural eras and the mythological debris of the historical past. In Anaya's narrative corpus, only from such region of death and devastation can a new cultural world emerge.

IV. Recollecting Anaya's Corpus: The Archaeology of Grave Digging.

Anaya's testimony would make us believe that T represents the acquisition of form, the reintegration of his personal credo, and that his narrative trilogy is his autobiography. One of the purposes of this study has been to examine such assumptions and to analyze the ideological contrasts between BMU and the subsequent two members of the trilogy, marking the dislocation of Anaya after he was "swept" by the Chicano movement. After BMU, the domain of the story becomes secondary and subordinated to the ideological investment of the narrative. In other words, what Anaya proposes in terms of artistic *evolution*, both at the level of craftsmanship and ideology ("body of beliefs"), does not find its empirical support. There is, however, an underground symbolical continuity between BMU and T, composed of a discourse of death and resurrection in which culture in general in the United States is portrayed as in its own apocalyptic moment--in the throes of decay and rebirth ("the past is useless to us. We must create out of our ashes" T 160). Such discourse--generally associated with notions of cultural "deficiency" or conflict--may have more profound sources, such as a personal history with a birth commanded by fate (Salomon Bonney's death) and an early brush with death. As a result, the view of life as a process emerging from someone's death can be identified as one of the primal scenes in Anaya's narrative. The unconscious in Anaya's narrative, consequently--as seen from Lacan's rereading of Freud--expresses itself through a discourse encoded with the (m)Other's desire. At this point, Anaya's narrative trilogy can be abstracted into this schematic outline:

	BMU	HOA	T
Utopian Aim:	Carp's Second Advent	Return to site of origin (Aztlán)	Cultural renewal
Brotherhood's Politics:	End of the World	Reintegration of scattered members of the community's body.	To *mobilize* the physical body and culture of Tortuga and his people.
Time:	Future	Past	Future
Youngest *Son*:	Antonio	Benjamín	Tortuga
Conflict:	Genealogy	Urbanization	"Immobility"
Surrogate Victim:	Ultima/Florence	Frankie	Salomón

The relations established in the last category can be cleared by recalling that when Tenorio is about to shoot Antonio, Ultima's owl intervenes, is shot, and Ultima dies (to save Antonio); in HOA, Sapo intends to kill Benjie, but "Frankie" is shot instead (HOA 195); in T, Danny attempts to drown Tortuga (simulating euthanasia), but Tortuga is saved at the last minute; later, Danny turns off the switch to Salomón's ward, who dies so that Tortuga may live.[19] Salomón's teachings, based on the mystery of life arising from the *inanimate* (e.g., the earth), are transcoded in anthropological terms related to *cultural change*, which corresponds to border crossings, cultural transgressions, forbidden marriages, etc. Similarly, other structural features, such as riddles, lame heroes (blind, like Crispín; one-armed, like Tortuga), and the resurrection of bodies, are intrinsic to the Oedipus myth, a constant theme in Anaya's narrative, presented through notions of destiny, fate, sphinxes who "seduce" boys (e.g., Ultima), and the heroes' blindness.[20]

In summary, the belief that everything in life is infused with meaning, that life itself is a miracle, and that one is constantly surrounded by hieroglyphs, rebuses, and riddles (and that the artist must be a rebus himself), would by itself reserve for Anaya's narrative a singular place in Chicano literature. But in Anaya, one finds, moreover, a utopian discourse composed of catastrophic and apocalyptic features that reinscribe Chicano history within the process of Western civilization, calling forth the reappearance of notions regarding the body and the collective destiny of humanity, and simultaneously burdened with an inherent inability to conceptualize the "end of the world" other than in conventional biblical imagery.[21] Anaya's compulsive return to the theme of a world-historical destiny, in spite of the traditionality of its writing, raises Chicano literary discourse to a truly universal level, conceived on what has been a Mexican cultural legacy on both sides of the international border. In Anaya, the cunning of reason manifests itself through multiple forms, while his quest for brotherhood--rewritten in the surname--is, like desire itself, constant and unfulfilled.

NOTES

[1] Sigmund Freud, "Fragment of an Analysis of a Case of Hysteria," quoted by Peter Gay, *Freud: A Life for Our Time* (New York: W.W. Norton, 1988), xix.

[2] The texts to be discussed and quoted more frequently are the following: Rudolfo A. Anaya, *Bless Me, Ultima* (Berkeley: Quinto Sol Publications, 1972); *Heart of Aztlán* (Berkeley: Justa Publications, 1976); *Tortuga* (Berkeley: Justa Publications, 1979); *A Chicano in China* (Albuquerque: The University of New Mexico Press, 1986); and Anaya's autobiographical essay published in *Contemporary Authors Autobiography Series*, Vol. 4, ed. A. Sarkissian (Detroit: Gale Research Col, 1986), 15-28; all references will derive from these editions and will be indicated by acronymic designation (with the exception of the Autobiography) and page number.

[3] Theresa Meléndez, "Coyote: Towards a Definition of a Concept," *Aztlán*, Vol. 13 (1982), 299-300. For other coyote signifieds, such as coyote as *seducer*, see Claude Lévi-Strauss, *From Honey to Ashes* (New York: Harper and Row, 1973), 113; coyote as demiurge/lord of the underworld, see Lévi-Strauss, *El origen de las maneras de mesa* (México: Fondo de Cultura Económica, 1970), 253; coyote as carrion/raw meat eater, see Lévi-Strauss, *The Raw and the Cooked* (New York: Harper and Row, 1975), 336; for coyote as trickster/carrion eater, see Lévi-Strauss, "The Structural Study of Myth," *Structural Anthropology* (New York: Basic Books, 1963), 224-225.

[4] Theresa Meléndez, op. cit., 304.

[5] The definition has been taken from Philippe Lejeune, "The Autobiographical Contract," in *French Literary Theory Today*, ed. Tzvetan Todorov (London: Cambridge University Press, 1982), 193.

[6] Fredric Jameson, "Imaginary and Symbolic in Lacan: Marxism, Psychoanalytic Criticism, and the Problem of the Subject," *Yale French Studies*, No. 55/56 (1977), 340, note 4. The Lacanian discourse of the (m)Other--the locus of the primary unconscious and the generating force of unmitigated Desire--allows for deeper insights in the study of Anaya's narrative. Consult the excellent study by Ellie Ragland-Sullivan, *Jacques Lacan and the Philosophy of Psychoanalysis* (Chicago: University of Illinois Press, 1986), 240, 279-280, 292-293.

[7] Taken from *The Standard Edition of the Complete Psychological Works of Sigmund Freud*, trans. and ed. by J. Strachey (London: The Hogarth Press, 1955), Vol. XIII, 177.

[8] Rudolfo A. Anaya, "The Writer's Landscape: Epiphany in Landscape," *Latin American Literary Review*, Vol. 5 (1977), No. 10, 99, my italics.

[9] Anaya, "Autobiography," *Contemporary Authors Autobiography Series*, 23.

[10] Gayatri Chakravorty Spivak, "Translator's Preface," in Jacques Derrida, *Of Grammatology* (Maryland: The Johns Hopkins University Press, 1976), xli.

[11] Anaya, "The Writer's Landscape: Epiphany in Landscape," 100.

[12] According to Freud, "this fear of damaging or losing one's eyes is a terrible fear of childhood. . . . A study of dreams, phantasies and myths has taught us that a morbid anxiety connected with the eyes and with going blind is often enough a substitute for the dread of castration. In blinding himself, Oedipus, that *mythical law-breaker*, was simply carrying out a mitigated form of the punishment of castration," in Sigmund Freud, "The Uncanny," *On Creativity and the Unconscious*, ed. B. Nelson (New York: Colophon Books, 1958), 137; emphasis added. For a different translation, see

this same essay in *The Standard Edition of the Complete Psychological Works of Sigmund Freud*, trans and ed. J. Strachey (London: The Hogarth Press, 1955), Vol. XVII, 231.

[13] Anaya, Autobiography, 22.

[14] There are in HOA three accounts of Anglo-Mexican unions or marriages which end in failure or separation. First of all, Clemente's brother, Guillermo, was "murdered by that pinche tejano who couldn't keep his wife home" (4); second, El Super's daughter, who marries "a gringo from the rich Country Club district" (40), resulting in an unhappy marriage, for "the daughter was in the last months of her pregnancy. . . . [H]er husband beat her, and so she returned to her parents" (151); and lastly, Cindy's pregnancy by Benjie ("she went to Benjie to get even with Jason!" 182). Of the three cases, two have a direct effect on Clemente's family, namely, a dead brother and a "dead" son. In addition, border stereotypes about Mexican husbands are reversed: Anglo males become wifebeaters; Anglo females, logically, are lusty, adulterous, easy "flesh." Jasón, acting like a true border hero, genealogically affiliated to the Gregorio Cortez lineage, refuses a possible marriage with the Anglo female (Cindy, whose name starts with a syllable that sounds like a transgression), preferring the Mexican Cristina, whose name suggests the presence of Christ, i.e., of death and resurrection (and didn't Jasón fall in love with her during a wake?).

[15] Anaya, Autobiography 17. On the occasion of a commentary on *King Lear*, Freud writes the following observation: "One might say that the three inevitable relations man has with woman are here represented: that with the mother who bears him, with the companion of his bed and board, and with the destroyer . . . the mother herself, the beloved who is chosen after her pattern, and finally the Mother Earth," in "The Theme of the Three Caskets," *On Creativity and the Unconscious*, 75. Anaya's "epiphanies" when feeling close to his "earth" are the conditions resulting from the "inevitable relations" Anaya has to Ultima and mortality.

[16] For a suggestive reflection on *pochismo* as imitation and identification with the other, see Derrida, *Of Grammatology*, Part II, chapter 3, in which Derrida analyzes Rousseau's ideas regarding pedagogy, imitation, and the economy of pity, along with the notion of "metaphorical ecstasy" (206).

[17] Anaya's character elaboration tends to deploy "doubles" throughout his narrative (e.g., Antonio/Florence; Tortuga/Danny) which act as elements of plot development or as semantic units in the narrative's ideological field. These doubles are linked by the reader in suggestive instances found in a continuum of questioning dialogues (e.g., God's mercy), moments of despair, or as demonic parodies of the "counterpart" (e.g., Benjie, as parody of Jasón in HOA). The category of the double, then, operates at different semantic planes, either establishing *correspondences* (e.g., Trementina sisters + clay dolls; Comanche Indians + bundles for crematory ritual), or *parodies* (e.g., Tenorio and his daughters, of Ultima; the *diurnal* Antonio while awake, a parody of the *nocturnal* Antonio, who dreams, etc.). It should be noted at this point that Anaya's trilogy is not a "trilogy" in the Balzacian tradition, where narrative characters reappear and are recognizable in different narrative spaces. In Anaya, the characters change from one text to the next. For example, in BMU, Chávez's brother is killed by a war veteran (Lupito), an act which serves to stress the war's "madness"; in HOA, on the contrary, Chávez's brother is "murdered by that pinche tejano who couldn't keep his wife home" (4). Now the reason is *adultery* between a Mexican and an Anglo's wife (the "tejano"); Clemente Chávez, therefore, changes along with his brother's identity: in BMU, Clemente's pain at losing his brother moves him to mob rule and lynching; in HOA (now identified as "Clemente" Chávez), on the contrary, he is portrayed as the leader who wants to transform the world through the "fire of love."

[18] At this stage of my study I can only suggest the rethinking of Florence's function in the narrative, for he seems to emerge (and fall) in a pattern similar to Ultima's, both in their anticlerical position (one subdued, the other explicit) as well as in their role as scapegoats. From the point of view of his function in the plot structure, Florence appears to be the *offering* being

made to the golden carp by the cult's infant membership (known only by Samuel and Cico, and ignored by Florence's "double," Antonio), with Ultima as the *pharmakos* of the adult world. The traditional scapegoat, as a result, is proposed in terms of an *intermediary* which allows for communication with the supernatural realm (Florence as an offering to the underworld), or else in terms of a *dismembered* body (Ultima) that is a symbolical reduction of the social world, torn apart by violence. It follows, then, that Florence acquires supernatural, chthonic characteristics immediately after his drowning by the river (portrayed as a golden, gliding body); while Ultima's death, occurring indirectly through the "dismemberment" of another body (the owl's), reintegrates the social body while serving as an intermediary with the supernatural world (i.e., with the "upperworld"). On the other hand, Florence's drowning occurs at a narrative juncture too precise to be coincidental, almost simultaneous with the carp's second advent (as witnessed by Antonio), and with Antonio's suggestion (to Cico) that Florence be initiated into the cult. One could argue that Florence's death is anticipated as of chapter 3, when Antonio meets Florence for the first time and hears him say that the boys from Los Jaros are going to hell; then in chapter 11, Florence suggests that all go swimming at the Blue Lake; then in chapter 21 he indeed drowns at the Blue Lake, therefore fulfilling his own "prophecy." What remains obscure is the reason for Antonio's thinking of death on two occasions and while watching two hawks over the road to Tucumcari: first, when Florence suggests going to the Blue Lake; second, when he drowns and Antonio flees from the "crowd." All this is clear at the plot level, yet Florence's drowning creates ripples that will have an effect on our reading of the cult's plan of action (a micro-Armageddon), while it embodies autobiographical remembrances of an accident (Anaya's brush with death).

[19] Since Danny can be viewed as a metonymical reduction of Frankenstein (associated with graveyards and "dead" limbs), the "Frankie" victim is repeated. Given that Salomón (Bonney) functions as a "father" figure, Tortuga's journey to the underworld becomes an Oedipal quest of identity and parricide (through a double, Danny): Salomón dies (twice: first as a "real" person; second as a narrative character) so that Tortuga may live

(the motif of the double birth). Since Tortuga, as a signifier, refers also to zoomorphic and to geographical signifieds (reptile, mountain) and, in addition, it is associated with *movement*, "Tortuga" suggests then (1) the *crossing of elements* (water → earth → return to water); (2) *topographical differences* (high/low); and *earthquakes* (mountain + movement). Lastly, given that turtle's eggs hatch *underground*, their birth suggests an unexpected simulacrum of Judgment Day: they literally *rise from the earth*, as if resurrecting from their graves (T, 81-82, 160, 186-87).

[20] See Claude Lévi-Strauss, "The Structural Study of Myth," 221-23.

[21] The biblical language found in Anglo-American political discourse remains an unexcavated, although implicit, text in this study. Consider, as an illustration of such discourse, an example deployed in the context of analyzing the Mexico-United States war of 1846: "Again, the pride of race has swollen to still greater insolence the pride of country, always quite active enough for the due observance of the claims of universal brotherhood. The Anglo-Saxons have been apparently persuaded to think themselves the chosen people, anointed race of the Lord, commissioned to drive out the heathen, and plant their religion and institutions in every Canaan they could subjugate. . . . Our treatment both of the red man and the black man has habituated us to feel our power and forget right." See A. A. Livermore, *The War with Mexico Reviewed* (Boston: American Peace Society, 1850), 8, 11, 12, quoted in Rodolfo Acuña, *Occupied America*, 3rd. ed. (New York: Harper and Row, 1988), 15. The sarcasm is evident; Livermore describes the United States through biblical imagery associated with *demonic* characteristics (e.g., pride, insolence), and not with virtues proper to a "chosen people," or to an "anointed" nation. Livermore mocks the ideological premises of Manifest Destiny through an ironical reversal of biblical discourse. Anaya's apocalyptic writing, therefore, stands as a challenge to a favored political discourse in the United States. On the theme of utopian discourse and the collective dialectic see Fredric Jameson, *The Political Unconscious: Narrative as a Socially Symbolic Act* (New York: Cornell University Press, 1981), 281-99; regarding the politics of the body within the discourse of Western civilization, consult M. Horkheimer and T.

Adorno, *Dialectic of Enlightenment*, trans. J. Cumming (New York: Continuum, 1986), 231-36.

The Writer as Shaman: A Reading of the Works of Rudolfo A. Anaya Through the Works of Carlos Castaneda

Margarita Nieto
California State University, Northridge

The works of Carlos Castaneda and Rudolfo A. Anaya, anthropological on the one hand, fictional on the other, and their successive appearance in print suggest structural connections based upon the reading of one text into another, a continuity of textuality, and the imbedding of texts through the phenomenon of reading and a shared vision. Both bodies of work depart from a premise posited by Mircea Eliade, among others, which is defined as a crisis or call that translates into a change of direction and focus in one's life. In his seminal work, *Shamanism: The Archaic Techniques of Ecstasy*, Eliade affirms that while the shaman may be a magician, healer, or medicine man, as well as a priest, mystic or poet at any given moment, it is the shamanic experience that separates the "shaman" from these other roles for it consists of a "technique of ecstasy" involving visions, dreams or trances. Furthermore, it is an experience that determines a change of life, a "calling," created by a crisis, a "psychic rupture" (22). Since this extraordinary experience must be shared and described to a society, it is by necessity, both narrative and artistic, be it oral, pictoric, or in written form as Joseph Campbell has pointed out:

> The healing of the shaman is achieved through art: i.e., mythology and song. And the practice of the shaman also is by way of art: an imitation or presention in the field of time and space of the visionary world of his spiritual "seizure." (265)

It is the shaman who is the storyteller, dancer, poet, musician, painter, and creator of myths. It is the shaman who creates structures emanating from his visionary world, structures applicable to prevailing constructs in those contemporary literary works which challenge accepted precepts of Western thought. In "Maps for the Journey: Shamanic Patterns in Anaya, Asturias, and Castaneda," Lorene Hyde Carpenter examines the creative relationship between the shamanic role and vision and the narrative strategies of these three writers as well as their utilization of "patterns of shamanic activity to provide a "path" or pathway to lead the reader and the shamanic initiate to the vision of unity that expresses the shamanic universe" (6). Those patterns are, according to Carpenter, equilibrium, integration, initiation, dreaming, healing, and animal/human transformation, patterns that are evident in any cursory reading of the works of Carlos Castaneda and Rudolfo A. Anaya. These works acknowledge first of all, that the premises of non-Western mythic tradition and praxis warrant exploration; they also share common temporal and spatial realities: they occur in a present shared by the reader and in the border areas of the Southwest.

It is probable that readers of Anaya have read Castaneda. The first volume of Castaneda's work (*The Teachings of Don Juan: A Yaqui Way of Knowledge*) appeared in 1968, and its influence has continued steadily through the publication of six successive volumes. All the books have appeared on best seller lists throughout this country. They have also been translated into every major language and his publishers abroad include Gallimard (France), Fischer Verlag (West Germany) and the Fondo de Cultura Economica (Mexico). Castaneda and his works were also honored at the Frankfurt Book Fair in 1971, and he was the subject of a *Time* magazine cover story on May 5, 1973.

Published and distributed by a major New York publisher since 1971, Castaneda had published three books of the series by 1972, when Anaya's first novel, *Bless Me, Ultima,* appeared in the well-known publication by Berkeley's Tonatiuh International. This sequence of events and distribution comparison contradicts the points of view of both Richard De Mille and Juan Bruce-Novoa in which they assert the influence of Anaya on the works of Castaneda, although their studies refer directly to the character of La Gorda María Elena in *The Second Ring of Power* (1977) and possible analogies with Ultima.[1] A careful reading of this work and *Bless Me, Ultima*, however, leads to a different conclusion since La Gorda is diametrically opposed to the archetypal representation of the old, wise, aged, and maternal *Curandera* Ultima.   On the contrary, La Gorda is a dynamic young *bruja* who has regressed in age and time as a result of being touched by the *Nagual*.[2] The mythical and literary archetype for La Gorda comes from a different source, that of the evanescent "Eternal Feminine," a figure that appears in Juan Rulfo's *Pedro Paramo* (Susana San Juan), Carlos Fuentes' *Aura*, and in the folk tale, "La Mulata de Cordoba (Nieto, "*tres hechiceras*").   It is evident, therefore, that the wide dissemination and popularity of the Castaneda books prepared a group of readers for participation in a shamanic text; that they were initiated and familiar with shamanic literary structures; and that Anaya's familiarity with Castaneda was, either directly or indirectly, unavoidable.

Another significant question, however, would touch on the "fact versus fiction" controversy that has raged around Castaneda's works, more specifically, as a result of his moving from the position of observer to participant.   The existence of his field notes and his non-academic narrative mode have also been called into question.   It is a curious problem, because, first of all, this concern with barriers and distances between observer and participant applies specifically to academic social scientists; other noted ethnographers (notably, Edmund Leach) and oral historians have rarely been asked to produce field notes; and, as Frederika Randall has pointed out, Castaneda is not the only scholar turned storyteller.[3] But this question concerning the reader-response to Castaneda's work refers to an issue of significance for our purposes, for in posing the question of documentation versus fiction within his work, Castaneda succeeds in eradicating the differences between the two genres, and as Lorene Hyde Carpenter has pointed out, he also succeeds in challenging the reader and freeing him from "traditional expectations of genre."

> Unsure of what set of expectations, those of fiction or non-fiction, to bring to the works, the reader is kept in a state of discomfort, which has the function of keeping his mind skeptical and therefore

open to the new. Carlos as an author has the opportunity to effect the same kind of transformation on his readers as he himself has undergone: the ambiguity of the status of the texts allows the reader to become the Carlos, and Carlos to assume the shamanic role of Don Juan. (8)

This issue, the role of the reader in the work, is implied in the topic before us because if the writer is indeed a shaman in these works, then, the reader must assume that he, the reader, is a fellow traveler, an apprentice or initiate who is embarking on a journey of discovery and knowledge. The text then, becomes the mediator between the worlds of the reader, which corresponds to an "actual" reality, and the magical or sorceric world of the text. In this regard, Wolfgang Iser, in his essay "The Reading Process: a Phenomenological Approach," states:

> The phenomenological theory of art lays full stress on the idea that in considering a literary work, one must take into account not only the actual text but also . . . the actions involved in responding to the text. (50)

In his ensuing discussion of Roman Ingarden's theories, Iser goes on to say that the process of bringing to light the subject matter of the work, is in itself *konkretesiert* (realized). The work is then, neither identical to the text nor with the realization of it, but halfway in between (50). The relationship of this theory to the relationship between the two world views before us lies in the understanding that these worlds are composed of what Imgarden calls, *intentionales Satzkorrelate* (intentional sentence correlatives):

> Sentences link up in different ways to form more complex units of meaning that reveal a very varied structure giving rise to such entities as a short story, a novel, a dialogue, a drama, a scientific theory. . . . In the final analysis, there arises a particular world, with component parts determined in this way or that, and with all the variations that may occur within these parts--all this as a purely intentional correlative of a complex of sentences. If this complex finally forms

a literary work, I call the whole sum of sequent intentional sentence correlatives the "world presented" in the work. (Iser 52)

But it is the reader who makes the connections between those correlatives, according to Iser, marking those points "at which the reader is able to 'climb aboard' the text." These sentences are not, after all, statements since "one can only make statements about things that exist." They are aimed "at something beyond what is actually said." That is finally, what brings about the actual content of the text itself. Each sentence becomes a "kaleidoscope of perspectives, preintentions, recollections," which previews the next and forms a micro-vision of what is to come (54).

In narrating these works, both Castaneda and Anaya present texts that are readily interpreted through the reading process, that is, through the possibilities offered to us as readers and participants in the creation of the work. What now lies before us, is to study the relationship between the two world views found in these texts. Based on the psychic jolt that comes about through the shamanic experience, they challenge our collective Greco-Roman and Cartesian rational world and cause us to examine the converging of one world upon another, the continuum of an "infinite text," and the possibility of one text being read in conjunction with the other. These texts are in turn, experienced by readers who share a common cultural base, and who have been "initiated" into the process of reading a shamanically structured work, through an anthropological work documenting the experience of a sorcerer's apprentice, and who then read another work classified as fiction, that of Anaya.[4]

The creation of the "world presented" in Castaneda's seven works, which begin with *The Teachings of Don Juan*, implies first of all, a dislocation on behalf of the reader. This confusion, this ambiguity, already defined by Lorene Hyde Carpenter, is marked by the two epigraphs that introduce the text itself, one by Don Juan and the other by Georg Simmel:

Para mi solo recorrer los caminos que tienen corazon, cualquier camino que tenga corazon. Por ahí yo recorro, y la unica prueba que vale es atravesar todo su largo. Y por ahí yo recorro mirando,

mirando, sin aliento.

[As for me, I would travel only those roads which have heart, any road with heart. That is where I move about; and the only test that matters is the crossing of the whole length of it. And that is where I go about seeing, breathlessly seeing. Trans. ed.]

[N]othing more can be attempted than to establish the beginning and the direction of an infinitely long road. The pretension of any systematic and definitive completeness would be, at least, a self-illusion. Perfection can here be obtained by the individual student only in the subjective sense that he communicates everything he has been able to see. (*The Teachings*)

Followed by a narrated explication of Carlos Castaneda's initial meeting with Don Juan and then by a conversational analysis of the meaning of the word "diablero," these three elements serve to introduce the two realities operant in the works and germane to the shamanic experience. Don Juan and Simmel represent two opposing world views, the magical world of sorcery on the one hand, and the rational world on the other. These two worlds circumscribe the realities that Castaneda describes and that he, (if one is to utilize the formula of shamanic patterns prescribed by Carpenter), will attempt to unify, to create as a totality throughout the course of the works. Yet, these two visions are in themselves correlative. Both refer to roads that are metaphorically referring to the same concept of a "journey" which is endless, which is an end in itself, and which leads one toward "seeing," ("mirando, sin aliento" and "everything he [is] able to see.") Both these references suggest openings toward the sorceric world to the reader. The matter-of-fact account of the initial meeting with Don Juan that opens the work, continues this reference to roads, journey and mobility:

The events I describe here began during one of my trips. I was waiting in a border town for a Greyhound bus talking with a friend. . . . Suddenly he leaned toward me and whispered that the man, a white-haired old Indian, who was sitting in front of the window was very learned about plants, especially peyote. (Castaneda, *The Teachings* 1)

Border town, Greyhound bus, and peyote are all signifiers of real or induced "journeys." This initial meeting also creates the relationship pattern between Don Juan and Carlos which is sustained throughout the seven books; the persona of the seemingly arrogant, "blind," academic university student, through his obvious questions, opens up the dialogue with the "man of knowledge," Don Juan for the purpose of guiding his readers. There is also an incomplete comprehension expressed through the *absence* in the text of the real meaning of this meeting.

> I then told him that I was interested in obtaining information about medicinal plants. Although in truth I was almost totally ignorant about peyote, I found myself pretending that I knew a great deal, and even suggesting that it might be to his advantage to talk with me. As I rattled on, he nodded slowly and looked at me, but said nothing. I avoided his eyes and we finished by standing, the two of us, in dead silence. . . . He said goodbye and left the station.

> I was annoyed at having talked nonsense to him, and at being seen through by those remarkable eyes. When my friend returned, he tried to console me for my failure to learn anything from Don Juan. He explained that the old man was often silent or noncommittal, but the disturbing effect of this first encounter was not so easily dispelled. (*The Teachings* 1)

That same annoyance is shared by the reader whose anticipation and expectation of the marvelous journey has been stirred and awakened, and because the bumbling arrogance of the narrator seems to have ruined it. Yet, as we find out in the succeeding pages, this attitude creates the dialectic for knowledge. And the candor and lack of pretension of the narrative lead the reader to experience the different phases of initiation, the meeting with "mescalito," the step-by-step transformation into a crow, along with the vacillations and refusals to accept *rationally* the extraordinary events and transformations to which he is both witness and participant. The wealth of experience and recorded phenomena of the books would entail a study in itself. The first recorded journal entry is dated June 23, 1961; twenty-five years later, the initiate to the reading is still bewildered, confused, and often caught in the terrifyingly magical sorceric world described by Castaneda.

In the books that follow, the *unsaid* becomes *materia prima*. The lapses, gaps, and factual explanations are revealed as functions emanating from a *partial* (right brain) memory of experiences occurring from an altered state (the second attention). Thus, as I have said elsewhere, books one through four (*The Teachings of Don Juan, A Separate Reality, Journey to Ixtlan*, and *Tales of Power*) constitute one recounting of events. *The Second Ring of Power* begins with the process of recalling and reconstructing events that took place simultaneously and which had been suppressed. The books, *in toto*, comprise a balancing of the world, an establishment of equilibrium and order between the two realities. This account continues through *The Fire From Within* along with the surprising revelations of the shamanic mode of escaping death--the ultimate objective of the warrior's way.[5]

Castaneda's works provide the literary pathway for a readership to confront a magical reality, and seemingly to suffer the same psychic shock that the sorcerer's apprentice himself has undergone, and which challenges the "world as we know it" by opening up other possibilities of reality. The narrative style is in itself, the key to that transformation. For the factual accounting of the unbelievable heightens a sense of awe and disbelief while engaging the reader in a dialectical interrogation with the text itself, opening up toward a genuine comprehension of the "world presented" through a sense of imagination, which as Hans Georg Gadamer points out, marks the difference between "methodological sterility and genuine understanding, . . . the capacity to see what is questionable in the subject matter and to formulate questions that question the subject matter further" (xxii). The Castaneda books are manuals of sorcery that explain Don Juan's world and its functions, including the balancing of the world, the art of dreaming, the art of intent, and the art of stalking. They are descriptive exemplifications of the shamanic world. They do not pretend to tell a story; they simply *relate* experiences.

A reading of Anaya's trilogy, *Bless Me, Ultima* (1972), *Heart of Aztlán* (1976), and *Tortuga* (1979) is based on a different narrative construct. While these experiences *may* be autobiographical, their construct is openly fictional. There is no basis for confusion in genre. Of the three, the thematic structure of Anaya's first novel, *Bless Me, Ultima*, introduces the most evident shamanic literary structures, and they have been analyzed by Lorene Hyde Carpenter.[6] In her interpretation, the shaman, Ultima, and her apprentice, Antonio, succeed in presenting shamanic functions of equilibrium, of integration of conflicting worlds, of dreaming, of initiation, and of the utilization of animal/human motifs--the most obvious being Ultima and her owl.

The reader's acceptance of this world, however, is diametrically opposed to the initial discomfort with Castaneda's world view. First of all, readers drawn to Anaya's text are fewer in number than those reading Castaneda. Second, they already share a cultural framework and view, possibly fostered through an initiation of reading Castaneda but also encouraged by their own cultural mythic and oral tradition.

In literary terms, the relationship between Ultima and Antonio, based as it is on the polar opposites of old age and wisdom versus innocence and youth, reduces the dialectical posits inherent to Castaneda's work. Antonio accepts Ultima. He not only accepts her, but also reveres her unquestioningly. Moreover, in contrast to the Castaneda works, the adventure begins in the first paragraph; there are no false starts, there is no sense of impatience. This pattern is strengthened by Antonio's subsequent oneiric interpretations of his selection and mission. Thus, the reader's anticipation and retrospection of Anaya's text constructs itself on the *familiar*, on a sense of solace and comfort which dilutes the psychic jolt. Does the journey begin with Tony's birth, with Ultima's arrival, and if so, what are the precepts or conditions that suffer change as a result of the revelation? At what point does the apprentice fly? The construct of the novel limits its sorceric possibilities through its predictability. The only real question confronting the reader has to do with Ultima's being a *bruja*, or a *curandera*, a question that reveals the rational

Western viewpoint that prevails in the novel. The narrator represents the Western tradition, although he is moved to consider other possibilities. But the "world as we know it" overcomes him. Yet In shamanic terms, while the question about Ultima's function in terms of *good* or *evil* is at best arbitrary, it is the only issue that contradicts and "jolts" the harmonic balance of the novel. Still, it is a familiar question, given the reader's cultural background and mythic and oral literary tradition. It is also a reference to the text's manner of anticipation and retrospection which, according to Iser, is the key to its transformation into experience:

> The manner in which the reader experiences the text will reflect his own disposition, and in this respect the literary text acts as a kind of mirror, but at the same time, the reality which this process helps to create is one that will be *different* from his own (since normally, we tend to be bored by texts that present us with things we already know perfectly well ourselves). Thus we have the apparently paradoxical situation in which the reader is forced to reveal aspects of himself in order to experience a reality which is different from his own. The impact this reality makes on him will depend largely on the extent to which he himself actively provides the unwritten part of the text, and yet in supplying all the missing links, he must think in terms of experiences different from his own; indeed, it is only by leaving behind the familiar world of his own experience that the reader can truly participate in the adventure the literary text offers him. (57)

Anaya's work is successful because its receptivity, its reading occurs in a vacuum that exists in texts experienced by readers prior to the appearance of the Castaneda and Anaya works. The reader's own cultural experience is the link between the oral literary tradition that preceds both bodies of work. The void becomes meaningful and is stimulated by the Castaneda success which opens up the possibility of texts based on mythical values similar to those remembered in the collective unconscious and in the oral tradition.

The success of *Bless Me, Ultima*, moreover, creates another challenge to both author and reader: what variants can be created through new textual explorations introducing shamanic patterns which might also break new ground in terms of the reader's own experience? Both *Heart of Aztlán* and *Tortuga* are partial responses to those questions in their presentation of conditions and constructs that explore other shamanic pathways by opening up the text to the possible function of operant non-Western beliefs and precepts.

In moving from the temporal and spatial references of childhood memory and specific archetypes to an omniscient narrator and to an urban setting in *Heart of Aztlán*, Anaya, nonetheless, utilizes an anticipatory sub-text in an oneiric voice that maintains a continuity with the preceding work. While it is the main device utilized, it is not the only one. Characters introduced in *Bless Me, Ultima*, Jasón Chávez and his family, are already known entities for the reader. What is different, and comes even closer to the shamanic patterns outlined by Carpenter, is the concept of the journey (the change of residence from Guadalupe to Albuquerque) which develops into the symbolic shamanic journey in Clemente's ascent of the mountain through his encounter with the power object (the "piedra mala") in the old *bruja's* hut. This is the psychic shock that *Bless Me, Ultima* suggests, but does not fulfill, for it is this ascent that inexorably alters the course of events for Clemente Chávez by breaking down perceptual barriers for him and for the reader, and by making him a visionary who seeks *clemency* for the injustices suffered by his people. Crispín, the blind guitarist and a symbolic Homeric bard, is Clemente's guide on the road to knowledge, as well as the shaman who establishes unity between both realities: the barrio on the one hand, and the vision of Aztlán on the other. Clemente also exemplifies Don Juan's precepts for warriorship because he ascends to the highest point after descending to the lowest, most wretched point of his existence (a drunk in the gutter). He seeks knowledge from the magical source because he has nothing more to lose, and from the moment of his revelation, he fears nothing.

For Tortuga, the narrator and main character of the novel that bears the same name, the meaning of nothingness and fulfillment through the shamanic journey functions in a similar manner. Immobile, suffering a physical state of paralysis, he is taken to a hospital clinic that lies in the shadow of Tortuga, the magic mountain. His journey and experiences (which, to a degree, parallel Thomas Mann's *The Magic Mountain*) consist of an upward ascent in which omens, dreams, power objects, and magical encounters abound. Crispín's blue guitar is the power object that maintains contact with the world of *Heart of Aztlán*. But Salomón, the mute invalid is the shaman who leads Tortuga from the horrors of the bed wards of the terminally ill (his garden), to health, through dreams and prophesies. Salomón, like Crispín is a curious combination of Western and non-Western metaphor: his wisdom emanates from that of the biblical king, but he is also mute: his wisdom is thus beyond words, and he communicates through visions and dreams. He is also beyond reason.

Ismelda who fulfills the role of healer, angel, and sexual fantasy is a female figure more like La Gorda than Ultima. She is a portent of the promise that lies ahead, of health, vitality, and spring, the season of regeneration, bringing health and release to Tortuga, and of the journey homeward.

The linear continuity in these three novels is established through what Carpenter refers to as the shamanic structures of equilibrium, integration, dreaming, and healing. They are structures that are dynamically utilized to further and strengthen personal and collective goals. In *Bless Me, Ultima*, that goal involves the qualitative difference between good and evil. Both *Heart of Aztlán* and *Tortuga* share a commonality of healing. Clemente's shamanic journey seeks justice and mercy for his people, that is, the healing of wounds and collective suffering. Tortuga's journey is a personal affirmation of healing through dreams and prophecy.

Oneiric time in these novels functions prophetically: a forewarning of events to come; and, at times, it coincides with the actual shamanic travel of the initiate. Its function is dissimilar to the "Art of Dreaming" in the Castaneda works, a function that Carpenter fails to understand, for in them, Don Juan *explains* "dreaming," and it is only in the final three books that Castaneda begins to consciously *realize* what the dreaming state is and to be aware of it.

This example of difference in narrative mode--the difference between narrative description-explication and fictional narrative--draws the line of demarcation between the two bodies of work. Castaneda's seven books consist of an overlaying and overlapping reading of events that occur within the same time period, but which becomes richer as the narrator's perceptual barriers are gradually broken down. The stratification of recollection and memory is gradually peeled away. The *re-writing* of the text, and its consequent *re-reading* is concomitant with the psychic jolt itself and with the erasure of Western linear reason. The reader is compelled to understand that all remembered experience is only partial, and that we are condemned to selective recollections of what we think we are.

Anaya on the other hand, utilizes shamanic devices and the awareness of his reader to create characters and events that parallel the "world as we know it," as well as to embellish and enhance that world with the possibilities of other realities. His world, unlike Castaneda's, is caught in the dichotomy of a Western literary tradition that struggles against a non-Western structure, the world of ancient meso-American myth and prophecy. It is a linear, yet dynamic *Weltanschauung* that experiments with imaginative, creative and original possibilities in contemporary fiction. Through a shared readership, these works form a continuum, a construct in which one reading serves as a preparation for the other, as an aperture introducing structures through "a world presented" which in turn supports another "world." They thus initiate and stimulate the reader's desire, active participation, and integration within a former "alien" shamanic world of a dialectic between both texts and readings which allow us to " . . . formulate ourselves and so discover what previously seemed to elude our consciousness" (Iser 68).

NOTES

[1] This issue is discussed in Richard De Mille, *The Don Juan Papers* (Santa Barbara: Ross-Erikson Press, 1980) which includes Juan Bruce-Novoa's article, "Chicanos in the Web of Spider Trickster."

[2] Castaneda's usage of the term "nagual" differs from the usage established by George Foster in 1944, "Nagualism in Mexico and Guatemala," *Acta Americana*, 2 (85-103) which went virtually unchallenged until the publication of Castaneda's fieldwork. Castaneda's definition is as follows: ". . . the undescribable principle, the source of everything." (*The Second Ring Of Power* (New York: Simon and Schuster, 1977), 220. And elsewhere he tells us: "The reason we called him the Nagual . . . is because he was split in two. In other words, any time he needed to, . . . something would come out of him, something that was not a double, but a horrendous, menacing shape that looked like him, but was twice his size. We call that shape the nagual and everybody who has it, is of course, the Nagual." (Ibid. 193-94). The accepted usage defines the "nagual" as a "familiar," as an animal that functions as a double, like Ultima and her owl, which is Foster's definition.

[3] In this article, Randall refers directly to Castaneda's unorthodox storytelling mode" and to Claude Lévi-Strauss' *Tristes Tropiques*, which she calls "part anthropology, part travelogue, part philosophic voyage." She then cites the cases of Marcel Mauss, Michel Leiris, Marcel Griaule, and Alfred Metraux and even Margaret Mead as examples of anthropologists who have had close ties with literary circles or whose narrative mode made them suspect among their social science colleagues.

[4] The construct for this critical interpretation is taken from a reading of Jacques Derrida, *Of Grammatology,* trans. Gayarti Chakrovorty Spivak (Baltimore: Johns Hopkins, 1976).

[5] In an article published in *La Opinion, (La comunidad),* and entitled,

"Fronteras en la obra de Carlos Castaneda," (Oct. 12, 1986), I discuss this aspect of Castaneda's work in detail.

[6] Carpenter's classificatory analysis of the shamanic patterns in Anaya's and Asturias' work functions well because these are works of fiction, and these classifications clarify aspects within them. In the case of Castaneda, however, she fails to observe the differences in narrative style from the first book through the seventh. In reading them, it is clear that Castaneda initiates his work by trying to create a schema and a taxonomy for the teachings. Castaneda himself explains this fact as well as his realization that the work defied Western categorization, which led him to narrate the works as they now read and appear. In so doing, however, Carpenter is following the oversights and mis-readings of other Castaneda critics including Peter Furst, Barbara Meyerhoff, and Richard De Mille.

WORKS CITED

Anaya, Rudolfo A. *Bless Me, Ultima.* Berkeley: Quinto Sol,   1972.

___. *Heart of Aztlán.* Berkeley: Justa, 1976.

___. *Tortuga.* Berkeley: Justa, 1979.

Campbell, Joseph. *The Masks of Mythology: Primitive Mythology.* New York: Penguin, 1976.

Carpenter, Lorene Hyde. "Maps for the Journey: Shamanic Patterns in Anaya, Asturias and Castaneda." Diss. Univ. of Colorado, Boulder, 1981.

Castaneda, Carlos. *The Teachings of Don Juan: A Yaqui Way of Knowledge.* Berkeley: U of California P, 1968.

___. *A Separate Reality.* New York: Simon, 1971.

___. *Journey to Ixtlan.* New York: Simon, 1972.

___. *Tales of Power.* New York: Simon, 1974.

___. *The Second Ring of Power.* New York: Simon, 1977.

___. *The Eagle's Gift.* New York: Simon, 1981.

___. *The Fire From Within.* New York: Simon, 1984.

___. De Mille, Richard. *The Don Juan Papers.* Santa Barbara: Ross-Erikson, 1981.

Derrida, Jacques. *Of Grammatology.* Trans. Gayarti Chakrovorty Spivak.

Baltimore: Johns Hopkins UP, 1976.

Eliade, Mircea. *El shamanismo y las técnicas arcaicas del éxtasis.* México: Fondo de Cultura Económica, 1986.

Foster, George. "Nagualism in Mexico and Guatemala." *Acta Americana* 2 (n.d.): 85-103.

Gadamer, Hans Georg. *Philosophical Hermeneutics.* Trans. and ed. by David E. Linge. Berkeley: U of California P, 1976.

Iser, Wolfgang. "The Reading Process: A Phenomenological Approach." *Reader-Response Criticism.* Ed. Jane P. Tompkins. Baltimore: Johns Hopkins UP, 1980.

"Magic and Reality: Don Juan and the Sorcerer's Apprentice." *Time* March 5, 1973: Cover Story.

Nieto, Margarita. "Fronteras en la obra de Carlos Castaneda." *La Opinión* (La Comunidad), Oct.12, 1986, n.p.

___. "El problema de la juventud eterna en tres hechiceras en *The Second Ring of Power*, "La mulata de Cordoba," y *Aura.*" *La Palabra* 4-5 (Primavera, Otoño, 1982-83): 81-92.

Randall, Frederika. "Why Scholars Become Storytellers." *The New York Times Book Review* (Jan. 29, 1984): n.p.

Voices in the Wind:
Anaya's Short Fiction

LUIS LEAL
Professor Emeritus
University of Illinois

The deserved recognition that Rudolfo Anaya has received as a novelist has detracted from the study of his short fiction. Although his novels have been thoroughly analyzed, his short stories have received little notice. This is unfortunate, for his short stories are excellent illustrations of his mastery of the art of fiction, as well as added examples of his magical interpretation of his native land and the people who have inhabited it for generations. At the same time, they reflect the writer's sense of life, which is representative of that of the people with whom he grew up and whom he knows so well. He has said that he feels fortunate to have been born on the llano. "The wild, nomadic vaquero was my father, sheepherders were my old *abuelos*, and a woman from the river valley was my mother" ("An Author's Reflections" 14). This *apego a la tierra* explains Anaya's ability to write about universal themes as they are interpreted through the perspective of a Chicano who sees reality as it has been seen by the people whose culture he has inherited. His is an interpretation which is not different from that found in the novels and short stories of some of the most famous Latin American writers, such as Miguel Angel Asturias (Nobel Prize, 1967), Alejo Carpentier, Juan Rulfo, and Gabriel García Márquez (Nobel Prize, 1982). Anaya, like them, has been able to create new visions out of old realities.

And yet, Anaya, like his Latin American contemporaries, speaks with a voice that has reached out beyond his immediate environment. The attraction that his works have had for European readers and critics attests to that fact. Alan Cheuse has observed that although Rudolfo Anaya may be the "Dean" of Chicano fiction writers, his collection of short stories, *The Silence of the Llano*, makes clear "he speaks in a firmly accented voice to questions that lie far beyond the boundaries of the American Southwest" (F-5).

In a brief essay, "The Writer's Inscape," written for the special number that the *South Dakota Review* dedicated to the subject of the writer's sense of place, Anaya defended the regional perspective but recognized that those who utilize this literary mode have to be skillful, otherwise they fail, especially if they let the materials "become more important than the human element behind them" (67). And that is precisely what Anaya never allows to happen in his own stories, for he is careful not to let them remain simple anecdotes. In this aspect, he resembles the New Mexico traditional *cuenteros* (storytellers), with whose art as oral raconteurs he is very well acquainted. Like them he recreates in story form the lore of his own people, for, as he says, their stories, representing the voice of the past, are "bright, piercing commentaries on life. The language of the people is alive in them. And each one speaks across the centuries as to the conditions of our contemporary life" ("Cuentos de los antepasados" 12).

In a way, in his short stories Anaya has assumed the role of the storyteller, or *cuentero*. As he tells us, these popular stories, although very old, are alive today. "We hear them," he says,

> in the wind which sweeps across our mountains and deserts. We sense them in the work of the people, [for] the stories are in the people as they work and dance. They are in the vision of beauty and art which has been kept alive in the craft of the *santeros*, the colors of the painters, in the songs the native poets sing, and in the *colchas* and rugs that women weave!" (*Cuentos: Tales* 8-9)

There is strong evidence showing that Anaya has been greatly influenced by the legendary *cuentos* of the people of Mexico and Spain which have survived in the Southwest, especially in New Mexico. The importance that he attaches to them is present in all his fiction. In *Heart of Aztlán*, he tells us, "I created Crispín, the old poet of the *barrio*, and around him the younger men gathered to listen to his *cuentos*" ("Cuentos de los antepasados" 11). His own childhood was much more "magical and mysterious and imaginative because of people like Ultima," and it was certainly enriched by his grandfather, who "told marvelous *cuentos* and side-splitting *chistes*" ("Cuentos de los antepasados" 11).

The words quoted apply also to the *cuentos* collected by Professor Juan B. Rael in southern Colorado and northern New Mexico, some of which were adapted by José Griego y Maestas and published in 1980, with Anaya's English versions, under the title *Cuentos: Tales from the Hispanic Southwest.* While translating these folktales in 1979, Anaya was struck, as he was as a child, "by their deep sense of the human condition" ("Cuentos de los antepasados" 12). In one of his own stories, "B. Traven Is Alive and Well in Cuernavaca," of the same year, he introduces a character, Justino, who has the characteristics of the *cuentero*. The narrator, who has gone to Mexico in search of short story materials and a place to write them, hears from Justino a *cuento*, "El pozo de Mendoza," about a very popular subject, the buried treasure. While telling the story Justino also makes reference to a popular legend, that of "La Llorona," which Anaya later turned into a novelette, *The Legend of La Llorona* (1984). Traven, according to Anaya's imagined story, had also heard from Justino the story about the buried treasure, and remarks that "people like Justino are the writer's source" (*The Silence* 144). In Justino, Anaya has created a character overflowing with humanity, doubtless inspired by some of the *cuenteros* he knows personally.

Besides the human content which Anaya so much admires, the *cuentos* have another important quality, the traditional form, which has become, since it has been repeated throughout the centuries, a classic structure. "The short story, when presented in the oral tradition," Anaya says, "can be a simple but compelling form" ("An Author's Reflections" 14).

Contrary to what may be thought, the use of these traditional forms does not limit the scope of the story or its universal appeal. Anaya knows this well, as revealed by what he had to say about this type of story, that is, that it "can also be made to move beyond its regional arena to engage language and form in the expression of a vision which reflects the writer's sense of life" ("An Author's Reflections" 14). And that is precisely what the reader finds in Anaya's own stories: his own sense of life, a sense of life that is manifested, as it is in his novels, by his sense of place and by the recreation of ancient native myths.

In one of Anaya's stories, "The Place of the Swallows," written, he says, "under the strong influence of *Bless Me, Ultima*, but not published until 1976 in the anthology *Voices from the Río Grande*, and included in *The Silence of the Llano*, a group of boys go hunting in the valley. At the end of the day they sit around the fire, and one of them, the storyteller, must recount the group's exploits. This simple anecdote has a universal theme, for, according to the author, it is "really about the art of storytelling and the role and function of the storyteller within the tribe, his social group. The tribe of boys reflects mankind" ("An Author's Reflections" 15).

By recounting the activities of the group, the *cuentero*, to paraphrase Tomás Rivera's words, is giving *forma a la vida*. Anaya himself has said that whatever suddenly rings with the tone and pitch which he has come to sense as a story is "the germ of the story." Once that small seed or germ is deposited, he has to write the story. "Life provides us with the seed; the writer as artisan must give it form" ("An Author's Reflections" 16). The narrator, in "The Place of the Swallows," says, "All day I have known that someone will have to tell the story of today's exploration; someone will be chosen to give form to our exploits. It is always like this" (*The Silence* 48). The internal story, of course, goes beyond the simple description of the events of the day and becomes a work of art by means of the rhetorical use of language:

> [T]here is a special time which the telling of the story creates, a time and place which become more important than the adventure lived. Why? I ask myself. What do the words create? In the story the small marsh becomes a swamp, slipping into mud becomes a

near-fatal fall into the quagmire, and the stoning of a harmless garter snake becomes the killing of a poisonous viper. In the shadows of the river I make them see great monsters, unknown enemies which I know are only reflections of the words I use. I choose details carefully and weave them all into the image; they see themselves as heroes and nod their approval. (*The Silence* 51)

This self-reflecting storyteller has not yet, at this point, reached the "germ of the story," which has to do with the senseless killing of innocent swallows. In this case, the function of the narrator of the internal story goes beyond that of being a mere storyteller, for his real purpose is to make the boys who are listening to him feel their guilt. And the same can be said of the function of Anaya as a fiction writer, since many of his stories make the reader reflect about his own actions. In the story the boys do not like to hear about their senseless action, and when it is over they walk away, one by one. The storyteller, however, must speak the truth, even if he has to walk alone. "Perhaps modern society has placed the storyteller in conflict with his social group. Now, to tell a lie is to live; to tell the truth is to die. For the storyteller it means a perversion of his original role" ("An Author's Reflections" 15). Thus, the storyteller's function is, in Anaya's fiction, universalized: he becomes humanity's consciousness. In the context of Chicano culture, the writer has become the conscience of the people. The storyteller, according to Anaya, "tells stories for the community as well as for himself. The story goes to the people to heal and re-establish balance and harmony, but the process of the story is also working the same magic on the storyteller. He must be free and honest, and a critic of things as they are, and so he must remain independent of the whims of groups" ("An Author's Reflections" 49).

In "The Place of the Swallows," as in most of Anaya's stories, the characters are always in close contact with nature. The voice of nature, indeed, seems to inspire Anaya more than any other factor. This is one of the characteristics to be found in his fiction that join it to the poetry of pre-Hispanic Mexico, as well as to the contemporary Native American writers, who, like their ancestors, consider themselves to be not the creators but the interpreters of the poetry to be found in nature.

In the story, "The Silence of the Llano," it is not only the author who hears stories in the wind, but all the people of the llano. And more important, the stories are an antidote to the oppressive silence: "When a man heard voices in the wind of the llano, he knew it was time to ride to the village just to listen to the voices of other men" (*The Silence* 10).

What gives form to this powerful short story is precisely the depicting of the loneliness of the people, which is the result of the silence of the llano, that is, the absence of the poet or storyteller. The life of the protagonist, the rancher Rafael, is presented as a case exemplifying the consequences of living in total isolation, both external and internal. In Rafael's solitary life there is but a short respite from loneliness, when he marries Rita. After a brief period of happiness--Rita soon dies giving birth to a daughter--Rafael returns to silence, a silence not to be broken for sixteen years. This is accomplished when he identifies his daughter with Rita, his dead wife. The simple anecdote serves Anaya to portray the relationship between human beings and their environment. Just like the silent llano, the two characters, Rafael and his daughter, are silent persons. This lack of communication, this absence of a storyteller, leads to tragedy.

The story, Anaya tells us, was inspired by the image of a silent girl in a ranch house:

> The llano is a lonely place. One comes upon lonely, isolated ranch houses. . . . I had seen the face of the young girl in the story peer at me, so many times. . . . One day the face of the young girl appeared again, and I sat down and wrote the story. . . . The story is about silence, what it can do to people . . . and it is also about the vast gulfs which can separate people when the word is not present between them." ("An Author's Reflections" 17)

The underpinnings of the story--and the same can be said of the other stories in this collection--are to be found in the magic description of the landscape and in the close relationship between *la tierra* and the characters.

The author has said that "The Silence of the Llano" is a story "which creates its own aura and ambiance." Its composition was not, apparently, done while Anaya was in the llano, for he adds, "When I wrote that story I felt myself returning to the llano, I saw and felt it again as I knew when I was young and growing up. The aura became very real for me. It became palpable" ("An Author's Reflections" 17). This is understandable, for Anaya has also stated that he composes from memory. In his essay, "The Writer's Landscape: Epiphany in Landscape," he says, "The relationship I feel with the earth fuses with time and memory and imagination and creates the scenes, characters, images, symbols and themes that are woven into the story. Sitting quietly behind the typewriter I evoke the epiphanies sleeping in memory and the flood begins" (101).

This evocation of the llano is, of course, highly colored by the writer's imagination, and the result is a landscape which can be considered to be the product of an artist observing nature through the perspective known in Latin American literary criticism as "magical realism." This can be demonstrated by comparing the descriptions of the llano in New Mexico done by Anaya with those of the Mexican novelist and short story writer Juan Rulfo, who has described another llano in central Mexico, in the State of Jalisco. The landscapes found in the stories of both writers are similar. Anaya writes:

> The people of this country knew the loneliness of the llano; they realized that sometimes the silence of the endless plain grew so heavy and oppressive it became unbearable. . . . They knew that after many days of riding alone under the burning sun and listening only to the moaning wind, a man could begin to talk to himself. When a man heard the sound of his voice in the silence, he sensed the danger in his lonely existence. Then he would ride to his ranch, saddle a fresh horse, explain to his wife that he needed something in the village, a

plug of tobacco, perhaps a new knife, or a jar of salve for deworming the cattle. It was a pretense, in his heart each man knew he went to break the hold of the silence. (*The Silence* 10)

In Juan Rulfo's masterful story "Luvina," from the collection *The Burning Plain and Other Stories*, the protagonist, who has just left the village of Luvina, located in the llano, describes the desolated community with these words:

"San Juan Luvina. That name sounded to me like a name in the heavens. But it's purgatory. A dying place where even the dogs have died off, so there's not a creature to bark at the silence; for as soon as you get used to the strong wind that blows there all you hear is the silence that reigns in these lonely parts. And that gets you down. Just look at me. What it did to me." (120)

Solitude is the theme of another of Anaya's stories, "Iliana of the Pleasure Dreams" (1985), in which the protagonist, a beautiful girl, lives in psychological isolation due to the character of her husband Onofre, who neglects her because he "believed in his heart that a man should take pleasure in providing a home, in watching his fields grow, in the blessing of the summer rains which made the crops grow, in the increase of his flocks. Sex was the simple act of nature which he knew as a farmer" (1986: 17). Unlike Anaya's stories about solitude, "Iliana of the Pleasure Dreams" ends on a happy note, with the husband and wife reaching an understanding and confessing their love for each other. But it takes a miracle to bring about the change.

Anaya's deep sense of place is matched only by his strong reliance on legend and myth, which he has used to advantage in his short fiction. To exemplify this trend we shall examine his short story "The Road to Platero." In this story the setting is the same as in "The Silence of the Llano," but the theme is that of the popular Spanish *romance* (ballad) "Delgadina," which often appears in Mexico and the Southwest in the form of a *corrido*. "Some years ago," Anaya has said, "while reading through old Mexican *corridos*, the ballads of the people, I came across the *Ballad of Delgadina*." As is well known, the *romance/corrido* "Delgadina" deals with the theme of incest, a theme that is, Anaya observes, "as old as mankind . . . the subject of many literary works, but the subject is still taboo, and it is a theme which is difficult to treat" ("An Author's Reflections" 16).

"Delgadina" is one of the best known *romances* in the Spanish-speaking world and in the Southwest among Hispanics. The Mexican folklorist Vicente T. Mendoza, in his classic study *El romance español y el corrido mexicano*, collected no fewer than twenty-one versions, from both Spain and Mexico (342-54). Professor Aurelio Espinosa added nine texts, and Arthur Campa three more. These two Mexican American scholars included versions found in both California and New Mexico.

Anaya's short story, "The Road to Platero," is entirely original. Of the *romance* "Delgadina" he only utilizes the theme of incest between father and daughter. He enriches the anecdote so much that it becomes a truly contemporary story unrelated to the old *romance/corrido*. If it were not because the author himself has told us that he was inspired by the theme of "Delgadina," no critic would have seen the relation between the *romance* and the short story. The theme, however, has been developed by Anaya in a play, *Rosa Linda*.

> I have been writing and revising that drama for a number of years, and so it is natural for the theme of the father/daughter relationship I am exploring in that drama to find its way into some of the stories I was writing at the same time. The theme begins to appear in *The Road to Platero*. In a sense, the story is almost a warming-up exercise for the bigger and more challenging story in the play." ("An Author's Reflections" 16)

In the *romance*, of early origin, the father is a king, while in Anaya's short story he is a *caballero* of the llano. Delgadina is, of course, a princess in the *romance*, while in New Mexico she is a *llanera*, a girl of the plains.

In the Spanish poem the incest is not consummated, as Delgadina is a virtuous girl who would not submit to her father's advances. As a consequence, she is placed in a cell, where she dies.

> When they came back from Mass, he embraced her
> in her hall;
> "Delgadina, daughter of mine, I want you to be
> my mistress."
> "Don't let it happen, my mother, nor you, all-
> powerful Virgin,
> for it is a sin against God and the perdition
> of my soul."
> "Come together, my eleven servants, and put
> Delgadina in prison;
> see that she is well locked up," said the king
> in great anger. (Paredes 15)

In the *romance* the king is not punished. In Anaya's story, on the other hand, the father is killed by his son-in-law. His daughter Carmelita--one of Anaya's most humane characters--unlike Delgadina, admires and loves her father, and the incest is consummated. Her son, who is the narrator, remembers the tragedy vividly: the death of his grandfather at the hands of his half-insane father; the daily outbursts of anger on the part of his father, who wants to avenge his disgrace; and finally the death of both parents, who kill each other in his presence. Carmelita wants to forget the past, but is unable to do so because her husband will not let her forget:

> "[Y]our father made sure that we could never forget the past. . . ."
> "Forgive? Oh no, your sin is too dark to be forgiven. . . . Your sin
> is the sin of hell, and you will do penance by serving me forever."
> (*The Silence* 40)

The husband, however, is afraid of the grandfather's ghost, who haunts the road to Platero and terrifies him. He, of course, blames Carmelita for the ghost's appearance: "It is you whose sin brings the ghost of hell to our doorstep. You will be happy with that devil!" (*The Silence* 41) In life Carmelita and her husband were separated by the presence of the ghost, symbolic of the transgression, but in death they are finally able to be together. In front of their bodies, which lie still, their son thinks, in a final internal monologue:

> It is done, the torment is done . . . I feel death enter the room. Strangely, a peace seems to settle over them as they lie in each other's arms. Outside, the wind dies and the streets of the village are quiet. The women of Platero sleep, a restless sleep. In the corral the mares shift uneasily and cry in the dark. The horseman who haunted the road is gone, and only the gentle moonlight shimmers on the road to Platero. *(The Silence* 42)

Throughout the story, the imagery that predominates is that which elicits in the reader the concept of machismo. As in Juan Rulfo's novel, *Pedro Páramo*, in "The Road to Platero" the presence of symbols associated with the *macho* predominate, especially those of the horse and the spurs. In the last scene, when Carmelita is killed, the instrument used by the husband is the spur:

> "Witch!" he groans and lifts his sharp spurs and slashes at her. My mother cries out in pain as the spurs cut a deep gash along her throat." (42)

The spurs also announced the arrival of the husband and their jingle had put fear in the boy's heart: "On the portal I hear his sharp spurs jingle, then the door opens and he fills the house like a howling wind, his harsh laughter echoes in the room" (39).

The other symbol that reappears throughout the story is that of the horse. The *macho* dominates his women as he does his horses. "My father rides with the vaqueros. For him the road is haunted, and every day I hear him curse God and torment his horse with whip and spur" (36). Carmelita believes that women are the slaves of men, and that even her own son will grow up to be a *macho*. Anaya very skillfully combines the two images to give expression to the theme of the story. Carmelita tells her son,

> "Will you too, raise your spurs and rake your mother's flanks when you are grown?" . . . "Yes, we are the slaves of our fathers, our husbands, our sons . . . and you, my little one, my life, you will grow to be a man. . . . " (36-37)

The stories selected here for analysis are representative of Rudolfo Anaya's short fiction. An extended treatment would reveal that his art as a short story writer is based on the principles pointed out in this brief study. Other interpretations are possible, as that is a characteristic of literary criticism. Anaya may even change his technique in the future, for he is a dedicated short story writer, and will undoubtedly write and publish many more *cuentos*. As he tells us, he is constantly in search for inspiration for his stories.

> But a writer just doesn't sit and wait for the story to begin. One learns to think continuously about stories. In fact, one's thought process becomes that of reinterpreting life as story. I call this process "story-thinking." . . . "Story-thinking" is part of the creative process, the dialogue with the world. It is an exhilarating process. ("An Author's Reflections" 16)

Life as a story. Indeed, Anaya has provided the reading public with an original interpretation of reality, especially of his environment and his people in New Mexico, as seen by a gifted short story writer. He and his works are as much a part of New Mexico as are the *cuenteros*, the *santeros*, and the many popular artists who have contributed with their distinctive and unique works to enrich our vision of that region, and, by extension, of the world.

WORKS CITED

Anaya, Rudolfo A. "An Author's Reflections--*The Silence of the Llano*--. *Nuestro* 7.3 (1983): 14-17, 49.

___. "Bless Me, Ultima." *El Grito* 5.3 (1972): 4-17.

___. "Cuentos de los antepasados. Spanning the Generations." *Agenda* 9.1 (1979): 11-13.

___. *Cuentos: Tales from the Hispanic Southwest*. Selected by and Adapted in Spanish by José Griego y Maestas. Retold in English by Rudolfo A. Anaya. Based on Stories Originally Collected by Juan B. Rael. Santa Fe: The Museum of New Mexico Press, 1980.

___. "Iliana of the Pleasure Dreams. "*ZYZZYVA* 1:4 (1985): 50-61. Rpt. in *Viaztlán* February/March 1986: 17-21.

___. "The Place of the Swallows." In *Voices from the Río Grande*. Albuquerque, New Mexico: Río Grande Workers Association Press, 1976, 98-106.

___. *The Silence of the Llano. Short Stories*. Berkeley: Tonatiuh-Quinto Sol International, 1982.

___. "The Writer's Inscape." *South Dakota Review* 13 (1975): 66-67.

___. "The Writer's Landscape: Epiphany in Landscape." *Latin American Literary Review* 5 (1977): 98-102.

Campa, Arthur L. *Spanish Folk-Poetry in New Mexico*. Albuquerque: U of New Mexico P, 1946.

___. *The Spanish Folksong in the Southwest.* Albuquerque: U of New Mexico P, 1933.

Cheuse, Alan. "Anaya's Hunting Landscape. A New Mexico Writer's 'Anglo' Debut." Rev. of *The Silence of the Llano. Los Angeles Herald Examiner* 24 Oct. 1982: F-5, 6.

Espinosa, Aurelio M. *Romancero de Nuevo Méjico.* Madrid: Revista de Filología Española, 1953. Anejo LVIII.

___. "Romancero nuevomejicano." *Revue Hispanic* 33 (1915): 446-560; 40 (1917): 215-27; 41 (1917): 678-80.

___. "Los romances tradicionales de California." In *Homenaje ofrecido a Menéndez Pidal.* Madrid: Casa Editorial Hernando, 1925, I: 299-313.

Mendoza, Vicente T. *El romance español y el corrido mexicano.* México: UNAM, 1939.

Paredes, Américo. *The Texas-Mexican "Cancionero": Folksongs of the Lower Border.* Urbana: U of Illinois P, 1976.

Rivera, Tomás. "La literatura chicana: vida en busca de forma." Paper read at the Annual Meeting of the AATSP, Chicago, 1971.

Rulfo, Juan. *The Burning Plain and Other Stories.* Trans. George D. Shade. Pan American Paperback Ed. Third Printing. Austin: U of Texas P, 1978.

Chaos and Evil in Anaya's Trilogy

Vernon E. Lattin
Arizona State University-West

Although a number of critics have recognized and praised Anaya for imaginative use of myth-making, few have discussed more than the sacred and holy in his myths. They have stressed the sense of religious unity, love, and harmony achieved in the novels. For example, Antonio Márquez correctly identifies mythopoesis as the "crux of Anaya's philosophical and artistic vision." He continues, "Anaya's conviction that harmony and the reconciliation of elemental forces are needed for spiritual fulfillment leads to the holistic philosophy that forms the thematic core of his three novels. . . . The oneness of things is repeatedly stated in multiple images and thematic motifs" (47-48). David Carrasco, arguing for a non-Christian understanding of the religious in Anaya, limits his approach to the sacred landscape and *sacred* human beings (2).

Other critics have agreed with Márquez about the centrality of a unifying vision in Anaya's works but have seen this myth-making as less positive, as a refusal to deal with the reality of social and political evil as it exists for Chicanos. Alurista has argued with Anaya for a more rational and realistic confrontation with the enemy of the human spirit ("Mesa" 6-23). María López Hoffman is even more direct in her attack on *Heart of Aztlán*. She rhetorically asks: "Can insight into the existence of a spiritual bond destroy oppression and end exploitation? Can the feeling of a shared communal soul destroy the chains of steel that bind the people? Is there not some other ingredient necessary in addition to a spiritual feeling of love? Has contact with the myths provided a real tool to correct social injustice?" (114)

Most critics, including myself, have failed to give full attention to the darker side of the mythopoetic process. We have failed to account for the chaos and evil that exists in Anaya's trilogy, an evil as dark and permanent as the parallel good also found in the novels. This evil assumes different manifestations; it may be seen as the dark night of Antonio's soul in *Bless Me, Ultima*, the malevolence of "la piedra mala" and the railroad's injustice in *Heart of Aztlán*, or the wasteland throughout *Tortuga*. Whatever their form, chaos and evil are central to the novels' themes and structure, for the novelist accepts the more primitive vision of evil and good, seeing them as two battling forces in a cosmic struggle.

This mythopoetic view of evil is hard for moderns to understand and accept. We tend to see evil as human and limited. Injustice is not part of the fabric of the world; it is a result of Jones or Hernández doing something concretely bad to his neighbor. Thus Hoffman cannot see a meaningful confrontation with evil in *Heart of Aztlán* because to her evil is a social/political reality, not a cosmic or mythic reality. Her questions imply a need for "tools" to correct social injustice rather than a need for a cosmic confrontation with evil in its satanic form.

Perhaps we can understand Anaya's view of evil by looking briefly at N. Scott Momaday's Native American novel *House Made of Dawn*. Abel, the main character of the novel, is forced to confront his fear, his enemy, in the form of a huge, grotesque Albino during the feast of Santiago. The feast is a fertility, rebirth ritual in which men compete by riding on horseback and trying to pull up by the neck a chicken which has been buried in the ground. Abel makes a dismal showing, but the Albino succeeds and then turns on Able and beats him brutally with the chicken until the blood and flesh are scattered everywhere in sacramental violence. The Albino is not just the white men and white world beating Abel; he is evil itself, a cosmic force with which Abel must reckon. Like all archaic people, Abel recognizes that evil is part of the total schema of things.

Later, when Abel battles the Albino and kills him, he is reenacting the spiritual confrontations between creative and destructive elements that have been going on forever. The white jury convicts Abel of murder, much as the critics convict Anaya of social blindness, because they do not understand the true nature of evil. But Abel knows better: "They must know that he would kill the white man again, if he had the chance, that there could be no hesitation whatsoever. For he would know what the white man was, and he would kill him if he could" (95). Similar to this is Abel's dream where he see his tribe running the race against eternal evil and chaos. He accepts what he sees: "Evil was. Evil was abroad in the night; they must venture out to the confrontation; they must reckon dues and divide the world" (96). Anaya's vision of evil and chaos in his trilogy is Abel's vision; it is what Eliade has described as archaic man's view of creation and destruction, the "return to the precosmogonic Chaos, to the amorphous and indescribable state that precedes any cosmogony" (89).

Reading *Bless Me, Ultima* with this understanding of evil in mind, one can quickly see how evil forces permeate the novel. As I point out in my article, "The 'Horror of Darkness': Meaning and Structure in Anaya's *Bless Me, Ultima*" (*Revista Chicano-Riqueña*, 1978), four major death scenes structure the novel and measure Antonio's spiritual progress and doubts. Moreover, Antonio's dreams are his dark night of the soul, revealing the "horror" out of which unity will evolve. Let me limit my further analysis of this novel to the confrontation between Ultima and Tenorio.

Bless Me, Ultima is a religious novel, but it celebrates the pagan rather than the Christian concept of good and evil. There are many forms of "la tristesa de la vida," but the most dominating embodiment of evil is certainly Tenorio Trementina. It is his struggle with Ultima that is the spiritual struggle between chaos and order, between cosmic justice and cosmic injustice, between good and evil. Tenorio and his three daughters are flesh and blood people, causing real problems in the community with their curses and schemes. But they are also part of the pagan web of reality that accepts evil as spiritual as well as physical. They are the destructive part of the "cosmic struggle of the two forces (that) would destroy everything" which Antonio dreams about (112).

Tenorio confronts Ultima three times in the novel and these three confrontations can help us understand the meaning of evil in Anaya's novel. The first confrontation is the result of a curse placed on Antonio's uncle Lucas by Tenorio's three daughters. Lucas is near death and Ultima has been asked to cure the curse. She accepts this task, warning that tampering with the fate of man may set in motion a chain of events over which no one will have ultimate control (80). Ultima is aware that the conflict between good and evil goes beyond social justice or correcting personal wrong.

Before Ultima enters into this cosmic struggle and sets the pattern of fate into motion, she attempts to get Tenorio to lift the curse. She enters a saloon to give him this last chance. Tenorio, whose description is a caricature of evil, has a face portrayed as "thin and drawn, with tufts of beard growing on it. [His] eyes were dark and narrow. An evil glint emanated from them" (87). In rejecting Ultima's offer, Tenorio continues the spiritual conflict between good and evil in human form.

Ultima successfully cures Lucas, and shortly after, one of Tenorio's daughter's dies. Tenorio, wishing to avenge his daughter's death but fearing a direct confrontation, accuses Ultima of being a witch and rouses the village to a witch-hunt. The men of the village, led by Tenorio, come to Antonio's home to kill Ultima. She is saved when Narciso takes holy needles and pins them on the door, "for a witch cannot walk through a door so marked by the sign of Christ" (126). Ultima passes this test at the moment that Ultima's owl attacks Tenorio, ripping out one eye. This second confrontation has ended again in the defeat of evil and the restoration of order. However, it has not ended the struggle, an increasing struggle which is more and more clearly becoming a spiritual battle with Tenorio, described as "the reincarnation of the devil."

The final confrontation is at the end of the novel. Tenorio has killed Narciso and his second daughter has died. He is becoming more desperate, wanting to believe that if he kills Ultima's owl, he will kill her spirit. On the last night of the novel, he does just that; in turn he is killed by Antonio's uncle Pedro. The two most significant manifestations of good and evil in human form are dead, but the struggle will continue. Evil has stalked the land. Anaya has presented the power of evil and the reality of chaos. Seven people, good and evil, have died in the course of human conflict. Moreover, in this vision of the world, it is clear that the end of evil is never absolute; the struggle will be repeated in other human forms.

Heart of Aztlán continues the mythic view of evil presented in *Bless Me, Ultima* but places the conflict in a urban setting. The Chávez family has moved from Guadalupe to Albuquerque. In the barrio Tenorio's evil has been replaced by the railroad and an economic system that exploits and kills the Chicanos. Our first view of the railroad makes it abundantly clear that the devil has devised a new hell to torment man:

> At the railroad shops the trains screamed as they came roaring into the yard to be serviced by the graveyard shift. A distant rumbling filled the dark and erupted in thunder and flashes of fire. Even at night the trains would not rest, they thrashed about like snakes in a pit and demanded service. Humble men, shadows of the night, moved to do their bidding. (18)

The railroad system is not evil because it provides a poor paying job, or because the work is hard, or even because the men are not allowed to organize a union. The trains are portrayed as giant steel serpents because they rob workers of their dignity and worth; they destroy in "dis devil's place" the human soul. (22) This is why the ultimate solution to evil must be a religious, mythic solution. This is why early in the novel, when a worker is killed, Anaya reminds us of the Aztec legend:

> *. . . there had been times of darkness, four times the earth and its life had been consumed in the void, and each time the blood of sacrifice had raised the light. Now the fifth sun, a blinding, white deer raced across the sky; a new legend would have to be told, a new myth created before the deer gave its power to the people. (25)*

The new legend, the new revolution, will be created by Clemente Chávez, but not until he has passed, like Antonio, through the dark night of the soul, not until pain and suffering sear his being. Like the mythic heroes of the past, Clemente must suffer and doubt; he will lose his job and his family will begin to disintegrate. His despair and suffering is parallel to the suffering of the barrio people. The reader must not make the mistake, however, of thinking that the mythic pattern negates the human suffering involved. Mythic heroes, like Oedipus and Odysseus, felt pain and confronted meaningful evil and personal chaos. Likewise, Clemente and the people of Barelas suffer from their enslavement.

> Accidents occurred daily. Stiff, frozen hands that did not move fast enough lost fingers, eyes went blind from sudden, careless explosions, sharp steel slashed at arms and legs, and everywhere bits of flesh clung to the searing-cold steel. The enslavement became final when each man withdrew into himself and was concerned only with his own individual survival. (120)

Clemente's despair reaches the point where he welcomes death, and in a drunken stupor he lies down in the snow to die. He is rescued by his spiritual guide, Crispín, much as Ultima helps Antonio survive and overcome his doubt. Through visions, Clemente learns that injustice is ancient; the struggle between good and evil has gone on forever. The images he sees allows him to touch the heart of the sacred earth and to renew his faith. He learns that revolutions are made by prophets more than by bullets.

At the end of the novel, Clemente leads the workers in revolution as they strike against the railroad. However, Clemente rejects the revolutionists who call for a simplistic solution of destruction and fire, and he replaces it with the fire of love. This ending, partly because of its rhetoric, has confused and angered readers demanding a fiery confrontation with the oppressors. They have complained that Anaya's "fire of love" and "river of humanity" are meaningless jargon and cop-outs, for they are not real weapons to battle human oppression. In their complaints, they fail to understand Anaya's mythic structure and to accept the idea that a spiritual transformation is essential to a meaningful confrontation with evil and chaos. Martin Luther King led his people into a *real* confrontation with injustice and was successful because he was able to move them spiritually. Likewise, Anaya is telling his readers that the eternal struggle between good and evil will continue and that for humanity to compete in this struggle, they must first recognize it and accept it for the eternal spiritual battle that it is. Ultimately, each reader will have to decide whether a purely temporary battle or an eternal battle is a more meaningful presentation of evil.

Also, we must not fail to recognize that Clemente is leading a strike against injustice at the end of the novel. Ultima did not avoid Tenorio and his evil daughters; she battled them actively until death. Likewise, Clemente is not just preaching a sermon. He is leading his people in revolution. They are marching to the railroad shops to confront the snarling watch dogs and the armed guards fingering "their rifles nervously." The sound of the sirens makes it clear that the police will be there to protect the shops, not the workers. The novel ends with the shout of "¡Adelante!" as the battle continues in earnest. Evil has again manned the barricades and the barrio people are marching to challenge it.

Anaya's third novel, *Tortuga*, is his most intensive look at the nature of evil in the world. The ancient cry of "Why?" echoes throughout the novel. Why are innocent children crippled and killed in a world supposedly governed by God and love? The novel presents an unflinching view of a wasteland of suffering, pain, and human chaos. There is a growing crescendo of torment as we see children doomed to a life of separation, isolation, physical and mental anguish.

The novel begins as a young boy wakes up, held in the grip of paralysis, on his way from home to his new hospital/home. His paralysis was the result of an accident, a sudden and unexplainable intrusion into his normal childhood that has left him paralysed and without hope. Moreover, he is a charity case, too poor for his parents even to afford to visit him. His own personal hell will be enclosed in a body cast which will further prevent his movement and activities at the hospital.

But "Tortuga" is not alone in this wasteland. Danny is there, whose hand and mind have long ago withered. Also there are the "brothers and sisters" of the hospital who are so twisted and deformed they leave their rooms to wander the halls only at night. There Tortuga sees the hard core cases, cripples, "freaks all of them. . . . bent and twisted with polio or MD or club feet, pigeon toed, curved spines, open spines, birth defects, broken backs, car wrecks, under-nourished kids who can't even stand up, even VD cases, kids that were smashed by their parents, looney cases" (35). There are the vegetables in Salomón's ward, those who live only in machines, who cannot even breathe for themselves. These are the ones that Tortuga thinks are dead when he first sees them: those of "the haunting eyes which burned in the hollow sockets," kept alive with "air and sugared water!" (39)

The critic who accuses Anaya of failing to see the evil that exists in the world has not read this novel with care. One can hear its pain, page after page. For example, Salomón describes for Tortuga the process all the children go through:

> [T]hen the despair enters and there is only the chaos of nothingness left . . . a void in which we sink eternally, a plane of life so still and lonely that we think all of the creation has abandoned us. . . . I tried choking on my own phlegm, and they cut a hole in my throat and made me breathe. I could not eat and they fed me through my veins. They fixed me for all time . . . in one place . . . a worthless piece of flesh rotting in the compost of self pity. (41)

In Anaya's novels we have a confirmation of Abel's statement: "Evil was. Evil was abroad in the night." That Anaya also presents a way out, a sense of love and hope should not blind us to his presentation of evil and chaos. His confrontation with death and suffering is as meaningful as the confrontation of the novelists who write social protest novels. It is a confrontation based on the pagan, archaic view of existence. It is, as Eliade and others have pointed out, a world view where modern man's anguish and tragedy are avoided because agony and death are always followed by the resurrection. Death is not a nothingness; trials and tortures, real and eternal, are preludes to a regenerated world. Anaya accepts this condition in his novels. He does not avoid evil; he subsumes it in this overriding myth. His view of evil, Indian and pagan, is not less substantial because he sees beyond chaos. It is only more difficult for modern Westerners to understand and accept.

WORKS CITED

Anaya, Rudolfo A. *Bless Me, Ultima.* Berkeley: Quinto Sol, 1972.

___. *Heart of Aztlán.* Berkeley: Justa, 1976.

___. *Tortuga.* Berkeley: Justa, 1979.

Carrasco, David. "A Perspective for a Study of Religious Dimensions in Chicano Experience: *Bless Me, Ultima* as a Religious Text." *Aztlán* 13.1-2 (Spring-Fall): 192-221.

Eliade, Mircea. *Rites and Symbols of Initiation.* New York, 1958.

López Hoffman, María. "Myth and Reality: *Heart of Aztlán.*" *De Colores* 5.1-2 (1980): 111-114.

Márquez, Antonio. "The Achievement of Rudolfo A. Anaya" in *The Magic of Words*, ed. Paul Vassello. Albuquerque: U of New Mexico P, 1982.

"Mesa redonda con Alurista, R. Anaya, M. Herrara Sobek, A. Morales y H. Viramontes." *Maize* 3.3-4 (Spring-Summer 1981): 6-23. **Reprinted in this volume.**

Momaday, N. Scott. *House Made of Dawn.* New York, 1966.

RUDOLFO A. ANAYA: AN AUTOBIOGRAPHY*

1937-

Womb of Time

What is it I remember about the first stirring of my imagination? I pause and listen, and I hear the wind blowing across the empty stretches of the plains of eastern New Mexico. This harsh but strangely beautiful land is my home; it is a land dotted by ranch houses, herds of cattle, flocks of sheep, the tough vegetation of the plain, gnarled juniper trees, cactus, mesquite bushes. By day, the wind plays a sad and mournful symphony across the land. By night, the wind is a lullaby, a fitting accompaniment to the surge of blood which flows around me, nurtures me, speaks to me, as I grow in my mother's womb. I hear her voice as she speaks to the children around her, siblings who have preceded me into the world of sun and wind.

Her name is Rafaelita. She is the daughter of Liborio Mares, a farmer from the Puerto de Luna Valley, a small village nestled along the Pecos River just south of Santa Rosa. They are farmers, a Spanish-speaking people who have been in the valley for over a hundred years. They came from the Rio Grande Valley, to farm, to raise their families, to adore their Catholic God

*Reprinted from *Contemporary Authors: Autobiography Series*, Vol. 4. 4, edited by Adele Sarkissan (copyright © 1986 by Gale Research Company; reprinted by permission of the publisher, all rights reserved), Gale Research, 1986, pp. 15-28. [Incidental editorial changes have been made, principally in accents and punctuation, with the permission and review of the author.]

and venerate His Blessed Mother, as their forefathers had done in Spain and Mexico before them. They speak Spanish to the few Anglo settlers who begin to come into the valley from the East. The Anglos learn the rudiments of the language of Spain. All settle into the life of the valley. They grow their crops; they raise pigs and sheep for meat, cows for milk. The horse is their beast of burden, their means of travel, the status symbol of the *vaquero*.

There are no pretensions on this land. The effort to survive cuts through all that, for this is not the land of milk and honey. My mother's family works from sunup till sundown. Life in the small village is difficult, but the joys of the *fiesta* sustain them. The feast day of the patron saint of the village, *Nuestra Señora del Refugio*, is celebrated. The men gather to clean the irrigation ditches that bring the water from the river into the fields. The harvest is abundant, the crops are gathered. They make *chile ristras*, the women boil jams and jellies, the men butcher their pigs to make the lard of winter, they store the meat in the *soterranos*, the cool earth pits. A good harvest sustains the isolated village through the winter.

My mother left the river valley to marry a man from the *Llano*, a *vaquero*, a man who preferred to ride horseback and work with cattle, not a farmer. My mother's first husband was Solomon Bonney. She bore him a son and a daughter. He died only a few years after their marriage. The land was not always kind to my people. A mistake can be final; a frightened horse that rears and throws its rider can kill even the best *vaquero*. A winter storm roaring across the empty *Llano* exempts no one, even the innocent shepherd caught unawares may freeze to death.

A widow with two small children has no time for a long romance. She married Martín Anaya, a man without pretensions, a man who knew how to work the cattle and the sheep of the big ranchers. The myth of the *caballero* courting the daughter of Spain was just that, a myth. For the workers of the *Llano* there was survival. A man needed a wife; a woman needed the warmth and safety of a home to raise her children. Out of that union in the small village of Pastura, my brothers and sisters came, and in 1937, I was born.

My father, too, was married before he married my mother. He had a daughter from that marriage. Later I will know her as a sister; I know nothing about the first woman in my father's life.

A family was born to Rafaelita Mares and Martín Anaya, my older brothers, Larry and Martin. I came sandwiched between the younger sisters. Edwina, Angelina, me, then Dolores and Loretta. My brothers were models for my manhood, but they were young men of sixteen and seventeen when World War II swept away the young men of the small towns of eastern New Mexico. I was in the primary grades while they fought the war. Awaiting their return, I grew up surrounded by sisters.

Why do I remember the dreams of life in my mothers's womb? Is it possible I felt the sting of the sun, heard the mournful cry of the wind, the lullaby of my mother's songs as she carried me in her womb? Why do I think I heard the cry of the *coyotes* at night, the bleating of goats and sheep? In the small village of my birth, Pastura, why do I remember the dim light the kerosene lamps cast on the adobe walls, the aroma of smoke from the wood stove where my mother cooked? Why do I remember the voices of the old women of the village as they visited my mother in her kitchen, drank coffee, smoked cigarettes, talked about the impending birth? The date was October 30, 1937, almost the eve of All Saints Day.

"You were born with your umbilical cord tied round your neck," my mother was to say many years later. "*La Grande* was there to help in your delivery . . . "

La Grande. That name will haunt my childhood. She was a woman of power, a power born of understanding. An intelligent woman who knew the harmony in nature. Some say she was a *curandera*, a woman who knew how to use her power and herbs to cure sickness. All my life I will meet such people, people who understand the power of the human soul, its potential. If I am to be a writer, it is the ancestral voices of these people who will form

a part of my quest, my search. They taught me that life is fragile, that there
are signs given to us, signs that we must learn to interpret.

That is why, if I am to write these short chapters of my life, I must
go to the beginning. For me, it began there, with the blood of a farmer's
daughter and a *vaquero*, commingling in the womb, to create a child who will
come strangling in his own umbilical cord, pulled into the world by the strong
hands of an old woman who understood life.

My father and his *compadres* got drunk that night and shot their
pistols into the frigid night air of the empty plain. My mother groaned and
made the sign of the cross. One more son was born alive. Strange signs
were in the air. The owls hooted in the hills and flew away at the sound of
gunfire. The *coyotes* lay quiet. Overhead the Milky Way was a river of
sperm, a river of life shining down on the lonely planet earth. I will always
wonder about the first stirrings of that journey to earth. Whence? Wherefore?

"When you were still a baby," my mother said many years later, "we
sat you on a sheepskin on the floor. We put different things around you.
Your father put a saddle. I don't remember who put a pencil and paper.
Perhaps it was me, because I had always yearned for an eduction. I had a
bright mind, but in those days the girls remained at home. Only my brothers
went to school. Anyway, you crawled to the pencil and paper . . . "

A silence fell between me and my father. Why? Did the familiar
story tell him that to his way of life his youngest son was lost?

The Child Rebels

In my childhood world the power of prayer was supreme. God
listened. The saints came down from heaven to comfort those who needed
comforting. The Virgin Mary would always intercede on behalf of those who
needed help. But the demonic powers of the devil were also a truth in the
world. The devil came to men, whether they had done evil or not, to tempt

them and claim their souls. Witches rode across the open plain disguised as balls of fire, disguised as owls or *coyotes*. They could appear at any time. Their power was equal to the power of the saints. Only the Cross of Christ could save one.

We moved from that little village of Pastura to Santa Rosa when I was a small child. Our new home was perched on the edge of a cliff, below flowed the Pecos River. The wind blew around the edges of the house, along the dreary and lonely cliff. Here I first heard the cry of *La Llorona*, the tortured spirit of a woman who had once murdered her children and gone insane. Now she was a witch who haunted the cliff of the river. With eyes burning with fire, clawlike fingernails, hair stringy, and her clothes torn and tattered, she came at dusk to haunt the river. Her cries were carried by the wind around the corners of our house. I felt a terror I had never felt before. *La Llorona* wanted me, she wanted my flesh and blood, she wanted my soul. She wanted to take me deep into her lair where she would consume me, as she had consumed her own children. I fled in fear into the arms of my mother.

Not yet a man, I found safety only in the arms of my mother. Later she, and the priest at the church, would move me one step further along the road to salvation. They would teach me that if I made the sign of the cross, *La Llorona* and all the witches and demons of hell could not harm me. Armed with the sign of the cross I could go out into the world and fear no evil. Ah, to be innocent again and to believe those foundations of faith which protect us from harm.

If I am going to look squarely at the forces which have formed my life, then I need to look at the church. My mother was a devout Catholic, but I was never sure about my father. Although he prayed and came along to Mass, I always suspected he was a rebel. He rebelled in his silence, he drank, the settled life seemed to torment him. He had lived life on the open *Llano*; those men of cattle and sheep were his only real friends. Now he was a *vaquero* without a horse. In many respects, a broken man.

I understood that streak of the skeptic in him years later when I read Angelico Chávez's book on New Mexico families. There is a story of an Anaya who had a strong argument with the parish priest. His crime was serious enough to cause him to be sent to Mexico City to be tried before the church fathers. He was made to recant, to apologize; then he was sent back home to New Mexico. Upon returning to his village, he dressed in a most outlandish costume, probably to imitate the cassock of the priest. And he rode his horse down the village street, sipping drinks from a bottle of *aguardiente*, boasting to the people, I am sure, that he had never apologized.

Many years later, while I was traveling in Spain, a guide who studied genealogy told me that Anaya was originally a Basque name. It means something like "brotherhood" or "brothers of a clan." Knowing the anarchistic and independent nature of the Basque people has provided me as much of a clue to my father's nature as all the years I knew him. Perhaps I remember all this only because it sheds light on my nature. There is something of the rebel and the anarchist in me.

My mother taught me catechism in Spanish. I grew up speaking Spanish at home. As far as I knew all of the world spoke Spanish. Even the sermons at *la iglesia de Santa Rosa de Lima* were given in Spanish. I was taught that the church was in charge of my salvation, that I needed the sacraments. I was molded into a good Catholic, insofar as any Anaya can be molded into one. I kept asking the sisters and the priest uncomfortable questions, questions which had to do with the nature of the Trinity and the geography of heaven. "You must have faith" was not an adequate answer for my inquisitive mind. I was breaking the chains of dependence, but I still feared the devil and his demons.

Years later when I read Dante's *Divine Comedy*, I discovered that his inferno was like my hell. I was thoroughly fascinated. If the sisters of Santa Rosa had read Dante, they would have been able to answer my questions about the geography of hell.

Life in Santa Rosa was good. I had friends, I played all day. We wandered into the open plain country, hunting. We spent entire days along the river, fishing and swimming. We made our own toys, boats and wagons and airplanes and wooden guns. I went to school and learned English. Moving from a world of Spanish into a world of English was shocking. I had very little help, except for the teachers at school. I don't know how I survived. A lot of my classmates didn't.

The Voices of Childhood

The seasons of the *Llano* are distinct. In the spring the wind blows, the dust clouds are thick, the tumbleweeds roll across the land. In the years of the late thirties and early forties, I remember sandstorms that blocked out the light of the sun. Imagine, a small boy coming from school, leaving the warm safety of the school and entering the terrible windstorm that obliterated every familiar landmark. Down the town streets and toward the river, across the bridge and up the rocky path I struggled to reach the safety of home.

Outside, the storm raged and tore at the tin roof, but inside was safety, warmth, hot *tortillas* with butter. Maybe I played paper dolls with my sisters, Edwina, Angie, Dolores, and Loretta, or I took out my marbles and trucks and played alone. Maybe I sat in the kitchen and asked my mother a lot of questions. Where does the wind come from? Where does it go? She always said I asked a lot of questions, that I was destined to go against the current of life.

The Chávez boys were my neighbors. We grew up like brothers, playing hide-and-seek, tag, football, fishing, swimming in the river, sitting around campfires at night where we told stories, sometimes fighting and swearing and tearing at each other like little animals. The town boys feared us. The battles we fought with them were fierce. Luckily no one was ever killed. I accidently shot Santiago Chávez in the eye with a bee-bee gun during one terrible battle. It is a bad memory that haunts me still. I saw one boy's eye smashed by a rock from a slingshot. A bloody mess.

How strange that I could grow up gentle and in a loving home, while outside the home I lived very much the life of a little savage. I grew tough and brown in the summer sun. No shoes, except for the movies in town on Saturday. My dog, Sporty, by my side, I feared no one. No one, that is, until the sounds and shadows of the ghosts in the bush reared their heads. I hated to travel alone along the river. In the deep brush lurked *La Llorona*. I heard her, I felt her, I saw her. As I cut wild alfalfa that grew by the river to feed my rabbits, it would suddenly grow dark, and I was alone, far from home, in a world full of strange powers.

Summer was the most joyous season. We could go into town and play baseball with the town boys, or go fishing in the lakes, streams, and rivers around the town. The town is unique in this part of the country, because it lay in a natural depression. Many springs and lakes are born out of the underground water--clear, precious jewels of water in an otherwise arid plain. Some of these lakes had beautiful golden carp in the waters; all were haunted by sirens, frightful fantastical sisters of *La Llorona*. To fish in the day along the rivers and lakes was fine, but no one was brave enough to be caught there at night. Nothing is as lonely or frightening as one of those lakes out in the middle of the desolate plain, at dusk, when the bats and nighthawks begin to fly. Even the friendly shapes of cows became shadows of ghosts, and to get home one had to cross the cemetery.

An aunt who had come to live with us died of cancer. I had grown very close to her. My father made her coffin from pine planks we bought at the lumberyard. We placed her in my mother's parlor, *la sala*, where the rosary was said at night and the family and friends gathered to pray. Coins were placed on my aunt's eyes because they would not close. When the rosary was done, a little girl and I were awarded the coins, and after that I had the gift of finding coins.

Death lurked in the bud and flower of summer. We accepted death as a fact of life. Like our destiny, it was there, waiting to manifest itself. It was a mystery, as the winds of spring were a mystery, but it was nonetheless a part of life.

There were only half-a-dozen *familias* on our little hill. I remember the Chávez family, my cousin Fio and his wife Amelia, the Giddings, the González Family. George González and I became good friends. His father, who had been the sheriff of the small town, was tragically killed. George became a man at a young age. He had a ranch to run, and I spent summers with him there, helping as best I could. The ranch was a terribly lonely and deserted place, but the experience helped me along my road to manhood. Only by looking back do we see how crucial are the steps that separate us from our mothers.

School was not difficult for me, but I was learning that I saw things in a different way. I would be running home and stop suddenly because I had heard a voice calling my name. I would stop and turn slowly around in a circle, looking for the source of the voice but seeing only the brilliant sunset, the red and gold and mauve which filled the large sky, the whirl of the nighthawks, the flutter of dusk. Who? I would ask. The sound would slowly fade, and I was alone, weak, wondering. The sun set, the clouds turned grey, the owl called on the hill. Was it the call of *La Llorona* along the river? Was it the call of my mother calling me to hurry home? Was it the mournful pleas of my dead ancestors asking me to remember them? Awakening from the brief trance, I would run home, still full of the mystery of that voice that called my name so clearly.

Winter on the plains is severe. The storms whip down from the northwest, there are no mountains to break their intensity. Sliding down the eastern slope of the Sangre de Cristo mountains they gather momentum, and by the time they reach Las Vegas and Clines Corners and Santa Rosa they are bellowing bulls of winter. The snows drift, the ice freezes everything solid, the trees along the river are transformed into ice palaces.

But the enchantment doesn't last long. The cold brought reality with it and the hardship of life. Our feet bundled in several pairs of socks and warm shoes wrapped in burlap (there was no money for the galoshes), we trudged to school. My mother was fanatic about school; not one day was to be lost. She knew the value of education.

A New Life

I attended School in Santa Rosa until the eighth grade. It was then that the gang of boys I had known began to fall apart. Some had moved away from the small town. Some began to fight with each other. Prejudices I had not known before appeared. We who had always been brothers now separated into Anglos and Mexicans. I did not understand the process. I had always known I was brown, that I was *mejicano* in the language of my community, that we were poor people. But those had been elements of pride, and now something had come to separate us.

We moved to Albuquerque in 1952. In a way, I was glad to escape the confines of Santa Rosa. But how could I escape it? Being fifteen was the same in most places, the process of finding a new identity as young men is the same anywhere. The pain in the blood and the flesh is a joy, a new awareness.

Albuquerque in the early fifties was a great place to be. The war was over, the boom was on. Cheap sand hills near the mountain became new and instant housing additions. The city was a young woman growing into womanhood, and I a young man ready to take her. We lived in the Barelas *barrio*, at 433 Pacific. There in the heart of the *barrio* I met new friends, and I quickly learned the rhythm of survival on the streets.

As before, life was easy, safe, sure, if I kept to the corners I knew, near people I trusted. My brother Larry lived in Barelas, and he knew the people and the street gangs. He was respected, so I had no trouble. Still, life for my discarded and poor people was tough. Country people were entering the city in search of work. On the streets, the gangs of *pachucos* were vicious, deadly. Small drug traffic. Baseball in summer in the park, football in fall. My friend Robert Martínez and I cleaned lawns in the Country Club for spending money. We stayed clear of the gangs, the *tecatos* on dope, but when we had to fight. We fought.

I attended Washington Junior High, later Albuquerque High School. Cars came into our lives, without a car you were nothing. Games, bebop dances in the gym, James Dean, the State Fair in the fall and wild rides with wild girls, after-school rumbles, Bill Haley and His Comets, Fats Domino, customized '48 Fords, learning to French kiss and always wondering about going all the way, *macho* men, fifties-cool dress, ducktails, tapered denims and black shoes with double soles . . . We were all pretending, growing up and pretending we were cool as Jimmy Dean. We pretended to know everything, and we didn't.

Not My Time to Die

There are events that change one's life forever. Each experience causes a perceptible change in the rhythms of the soul, and the ripples which flow outward measure the degree of the change. Slight or serious, the spirit adjusts and goes on.

It was a beautiful day, warm and carefree. The water of the irrigation ditch came through a culvert and created a deep pool. We had been there before, we knew the place. Laughing and teasing each other, we headed for the water, and I dove first. Then the world disappeared. The doctors would later explain that I had fractured two vertebrae in my neck, and I had gone into instant paralysis. I could not move a muscle.

I floated to the top of the water, opened my eyes, saw the light of the sun shining in the water. I tried to move. I couldn't. Face down, my shouts for help were only bubbles of water. I felt a panic I had never felt before. Death was coming for me, and I could not move in protest. I struggled violently to move, to kick, to swing my arms, to turn upside down so I could at least breathe and keep from drowning, but I could not move. The panic closed around me, I knew I was about to drown. But my instinct for survival had been sharpened too well for me to give up without a struggle. It was not my time to die!

I held my breath, but I knew I could not hold my breath forever. Panic turned to dread, then into a strange acceptance of my fate. I began to breathe water, felt it sting my lungs. A strange peace came over me, I prayed, surrendered my soul to God. My soul seemed to ascend into the air. Beneath me I could see my friends jumping and swimming in the water. Then I saw Eliseo tentatively approach my floating body. He thought I was playing, but I had been down a long time. He turned me over. I remember smiling and laughing at him, and with that I returned to earth. I had pulled away from the first step toward death.

I have not spoken or written about this accident before because I learned during the ensuing years that pity did not help rebuild my world. I learned that indulging in confession did not really help me. Perhaps it was that I withdrew too much into myself and refused to share that experience with others. Perhaps I learned too quickly that most people really do not possess the sensibility we call empathy. Most people are too much in their world, they find it difficult to understand the world of others, they do not have the sensibility to understand the feelings of others.

In later life I would meet friends and acquaintances who did not know my past and thus could not know or guess my pain. We learn very well to hide our disabilities. It is only when we are asked to do something we cannot do, like play baseball or volleyball or run, that we are painfully reminded of our limitations, and worse, because we have learned to live with those limitations, we are reminded how little our friends know us, how cruel the simplest invitation may sound. We learn to hide our pain, to live within, to build a new faith inside the shell of bones and muscle.

For the following weeks fever and fantastical monsters filled my tormented days and nights, leaving in the wake of pain the scars I still carry. But I lived, and I vowed to move again. I found slight movement in my fingers, worked from there to regain the use of my legs, then my arms. I spent the summer at Carrie Tingley Hospital, and when I returned home, I was walking with a cane, stiffly, but walking. Most of those with similar neck injuries never regain any movement. I had been saved for a new role in life.

One of the first things I did on my return was to go down to the YMCA, alone. I waited until the pool was deserted, then stepped to the edge of the pool. I did not know if I could swim. My muscles were stiff, very weak. But I dove into the water, floated to the top, smiled, dog-paddled out, got out as well as I could, sat panting on the side of the pool. I had conquered one fear within.

I walked stiffly through those following years, turning into myself, protecting the soft spot within. I learned the true meaning of loneliness, that is, how it feels to be alone. I had the support of my family. My mother nursed me through the worst part of the paralysis, daily massaging the stiff limbs back to life, and my friends never wavered. But I was alone, alone and wondering: Why me?

But I was so strong, or had been so strong, that I survived. I exercised, swam, re-entered the rough and tumble life. I accepted no pity, and really moved out determined to do more than my more abled friends had ever done. I fished, scaled the mountains of Taos, hunted with Cruz from the pueblo, finished high school, entered the university, married, and began to travel. I climbed mountains and crossed oceans and deserts in foreign places my old friends back home didn't know existed. So who is to judge whether an adversity comes to crush us or to reshape us?

Self-Discovery

I attended Albuquerque High School and graduated in 1956. I did nothing to distinguish myself at school. My grades were good, but there was little to challenge the imagination. Reading the *Reader's Digest* during free period in English class doesn't make for producing a writer. Anyway, a writer learns to live beyond his circumstance. He learns to be in touch with a stream of active imagination which is fed from deeper, internal sources.

The fifties, as we are being told by the historians of popular culture, were a great time. They were. We had the king, Elvis. John Wayne was still shooting them up at the Kimo theatre every Saturday afternoon. Stolen hubcaps adorned our cars. Rock-and-roll and bebop liberated us musically. The *Blackboard Jungle* and *Rebel Without a Cause* reflected part of our youth. We rocked around the clock, hung out at Lionel's, the local drive-in, and went to dances at the community center, always following the sweet fragrance of blossoming girls. But all times come to an end, and even heroes die.

Yes, the fifties were a good time, but one has to remember that historians do not see everything. There are huge pockets of people whose history, at any given time, is never told. The large Mexican-American population is a case in point. Moving through high school without purpose, never seeing Mexican teachers, never reading the history or the literature of the people, created in us a sense of the displaced. We knew our worth. It was reflected in our families, in our *barrios*, in the cities and ranches. We knew there was a long history of Hispanic presence in the Southwest United States, but the education we received did not reflect this. Society's melting-down process was at work, but the idea of the melting pot was a myth. Society did not accept, as equals, the black and brown people of the country. Prejudice did exist, racism was thriving.

Small wonder any of us entered professional fields. People ask me why I became a writer. My answer is that I became a writer in my childhood. That is why that time has been so important to me. The characters of my childhood, the family, friends, and neighbors that made up my world, they and their lives fed my imagination. All cultural groups develop an oral tradition, and the tradition of the Mexican-Americans is immensely rich. The stories of characters, fanciful and real, constantly filled my life. In the circle of my community, my imagination was nourished.

There is something in the Mexican character which, even under the most oppressive circumstances, struggles to keep art and its humanizing effect alive. I have seen this in the simplest details carved into door frames, the brightly painted walls, the decorative altars in the home, the gaiety of the music, the expressive language. The Mexican possesses a very artistic soul; I am heir to that sensibility.

My discovery of my past should not seem so profound, but it was, because nothing of that past had been intimated in the schools. We studied no Mexican history or art, no Indian religious thought or art. Even during my undergraduate days at the University of New Mexico, not a word or a suggestion that the cultures of these two groups existed. Of course I could have studied in the Spanish department, but in those days those scholars were *too* Spanish. Their concern was for the literature of another time and place, and rightly so, for every discipline needs its scholars. But in their assistance or encouragement, there was no sense that they either understood or cared about our needs.

I cannot say I found a more welcoming home in the English department, and yet, taking freshman English as it used to be taught, as the building block of a liberal education, I was suddenly turned on to literature. It was not easy. I had attended business school for two years, I was good at the work. More study, and a CPA could have been my vocation. Even that would have been more than many from my neighborhood aspired to in those days. But the study of business was unfulfilling, so I dropped out and enrolled in the university. I didn't have the money, but I worked every odd job imaginable. I kept books for a neighborhood bar; I worked for a state agency, anything to pay my way. Long hours of work by day, fitting classes into the schedule, and reading into the night became a way of life.

On the surface there was nothing new here in the life of a student, but there was a difference for us. We were Mexican students, unprepared by high school to compete as scholars. We were tolerated rather than accepted. The thought was still prevalent in the world of academia that we were better suited as janitors than scholars. English was still a foreign language to us; I had to work to dominate its rules and nuances. Even in university classes, I was still corrected for allowing my Spanish accent to show. We were different, and we were made to feel different. It was lonely time; many of us did not survive.

A Faith Shaken

The friendship of other Chicanos helped me survive in the university. Dennis, who later became my *compadre*, was there. Jimmy, who was studying Spanish and Latin American literature, was there. On weekends we got together, went out drinking, played pool, met girls. Dennis and I fished a lot up in the Jemez Mountains. The *barrios* of the city were always there to welcome us home. We knew we were moving out into a bigger world, but it was the old world we knew which provided our stability.

Reading created a new, turbulent world with ideas that challenged the foundations of my faith. I began to write poetry to fill the void. It is a terrible thing when the foundations of faith fall apart. A great vacuum opens up, one wanders lost in that void. There is little meaning to life. Suicide becomes a perverse companion. I felt betrayed. Life and the church had betrayed me. I lost my faith in God, and if there was no God there was no meaning, no secure road to salvation. All this may sound like the retelling of the crisis of faith which many young people experience, but it is important to verbalize these feelings. The depth of loss one feels is linked to one's salvation. That may be why I write. It is easier to ascribe those times and their bitter sweet emotions to my characters.

Love is most poignant when we are young. I fell in love with a young artist at the university, but in the tradition of that beatnik generation which was moving around the country, she moved away. I was shattered. My religious beliefs were being assaulted from every side. I think it is precisely those two elements which are the most difficult for young people to deal with: the loss of love and loss of faith.

What saves us? Something in the fiber of the soul will suffer the loss of meaning, be dragged to the depths of despair and depression, and still find threads which will not snap. Love is such a thread. Forgiveness is another. The will to *be* in the face of nothingness. The will to reconstitute the faith. Something in the stream of my blood and the blood of my community gave me the strength to begin my search anew. I can rebuild the foundations of my faith, I said. A realization slowly arrived at, one that came out of the difficult years.

I began to write novels of young people caught in the same despair which seemed to drown me. I wrote exclamatory poetry. "Man is born free! But everywhere he is in chains!" Reams of manuscripts. One novel, I remember, ran nearly a thousand pages. I burned all those old manuscripts. It was necessary phase for the budding writer, but no need to trouble the world with pure emotion regurgitated.

I received my degree and accepted a teaching position in a small town in New Mexico; later I taught in Albuquerque. So, I still had not left home except for brief journeys to New York, into the South, to St. Louis. Always in search of something, something I thought the eastern part of the American continent could give me but did not.

I married a woman from Kansas. Patricia. I think she was the one person who truly believed I could be a writer. Her encouragement was a new pillar in the foundation I was building. She became a good editor who could read my work and respond to its strengths and weaknesses.

Every writer needs a relationship with an editor, a sort of mentor. In our formative years especially, we need to see our work reflected in the eyes of another person. That person somehow represents our eventual readership. If he knows our desire to write, that person will quickly go to the strengths and the weaknesses, saving the writer time by focusing on areas that need revising.

For many writers, marriage is difficult. It seems to add to the storm of emotion which is the baggage of our work. I have needed a stable base from which to write, so for me marriage and home have been positive. Two miscarriages were the most difficult experiences of my married life. The flushing of one's own blood hurts more than anything I know. But time softens the memories and images and teaches us to forget and forgive. Still, the image of that loss remains sharp and clear in my mind, painful. Perhaps the writer or artist is a person who is damned not because he or she writes, but because those sharp and poignant images of joy and pain remain so clear in our blood and soul that we must flee into writing to assuage the pain.

In the sixties I had thrown out all my old work and I began work on my novel *Bless Me, Ultima.* I would teach by day, come home and write in the afternoon and into the night. It was a simple story, the story of a boy growing up in a small New Mexico town. I was still haunted by the voices of my childhood, and I had to capture the memory of those times and people. But I was still imitating a style and mode not indigenous to the people and setting I knew best. I was desperately seeking my natural voice, but the process by which I formed it was long and arduous.

Literary historians have not been kind to the literature of the Mexicans in this country. In many ways, history has cheated us. It has not reflected the true accomplishments of this cultural group. This slight we are just now setting right. But in the sixties I felt I was writing in a vacuum. I had no Chicano models to read and follow, no fellow writers to turn to for help. Even Faulkner, with his penchant for the fantastic world of the South, could not help me in Mexican/Indian New Mexico. I would have to find my way alone. I would have to build from that which I knew best.

Ultima Appears

I was working late one night, trying to breathe life into the novel that would one day be known as *Bless Me, Ultima.* The *curandera* Ultima had not yet entered the story. One light was on, a desk light near the typewriter. I heard a noise and turned to see the old woman dressed in black enter the room. This is how Ultima came to me, deep in that process of creativity, while I was struggling with the story. Old and bent, the fragrance of sweet herbs clinging to her dress, wrinkled, but with the fire of truth and wisdom burning in her eyes, she moved toward me.

¿Que haces, hijo? the old woman asked. I am writing a story, I said. Her presence in the room was strong, palpable. She laid her hand on my shoulder and I felt the power of the whirlwind. I closed my eyes and saw into the heart of the lake, the deep pool of my subconscious, the collective memory and history of my people.

One thing should be made clear about my meeting with Ultima. Those who don't know me may smile and suggest perhaps I had a little too much to drink, and in a state of weariness I was hallucinating. No doubt about it, I do enjoy good bourbon or scotch. Most writers I know are hooked on something or other, or it may be that writers just acquire a little bit more of public fame and think they have to keep up their notoriety. A bit of the *enfant terrible* syndrome. But I trained myself from the very beginning never to drink when I am writing.

In the process of writing, the serious writer enters planes of vision and reality that cannot be induced with alcohol or drugs. And in that stage of creativity, when the juices flow and the story begins to write itself, the soul of the writer seems to enter the story. The trance can only be explained as a kind of spiritual high. The writer's materials may be from the world of the profane, but in breathing life into those materials, the writer enters the world of the sacred. Even the most simple and mundane story might at any moment transport the writer into that flow of creativity which seems to connect him with the world of the story. At that moment everything is in balance, in harmony. The mind and the body keep pace with each other, the words flow, the story grows. I feel that connection right now as I write these ideas down. The flow is natural. Life itself.

I respect my work. I want nothing to get between me and the natural, creative high I discover there. So it was the night Ultima appeared. I told her about the story I was writing, the setting, the characters. I told her I wasn't satisfied with the story, that it lacked soul. I could imitate the writers I had read, but I couldn't write like me, Rudolfo Anaya, a *Nuevo Mexicano, hispano, indio, católico*, son of my mother and father, son of the earth which nurtured me, son of my community, son of my people. Ultima opened my eyes and let me see the roots of my soul.

I worked for seven years on *Bless Me, Ultima*. The process of discovery continued. Those realizations we later see so clearly actually came in small steps, and that's how it was for me. I began to discover the lyric talent I possessed, as the poet I once aspired to be, could be used in writing fiction. The oral tradition which so enriched my imagination as a child could lend its rhythms to my narrative. Plot techniques learned in Saturday afternoon movies and comic books could help as much as the grand design of the classics I had read. Everything was valuable, nothing was lost.

The First Novel Is Born

The sixties were turbulent years; the war in Vietnam created a national debate which tested the nation, tested communities and families. Most of the people I knew in education opposed the war. I circulated petitions to end the war, and I worked hard to organize the first teachers' union in the Albuquerque school system, an alternative voice to the lame classroom union that was in place. Around us the winds of the Chicano Movement, which were later to sweep me up, blew across the land. In California, César Chávez led the first organized *huelgas*; the farmworkers union was born. In New Mexico, Reyes López Tijerina led a group of private citizens to the courthouse in Tierra Amarilla, a small town in northern New Mexico. They went as private citizens to arrest the district attorney. A shooting incident erupted; the now famous Tierra Amarilla courthouse raid became a national incident around which Chicanos rallied, especially those who knew the meaning of having lost the ancestral lands of the old Mexican and Spanish land grants. Corky Gonzales organized the crusade for Justice in Denver, and La Raza Unida Political Party was born in Texas. Bobby Kennedy broke bread with César Chávez. The political activity of the Chicano Movement was spreading. The assassination of President Kennedy was deeply felt in the Chicano community. Black Friday was viewed as a symbolic striking back of the reactionary forces which guarded the power in the country, a power they did not want to share with the oppressed.

In the midst of these turbulent years, I struggled to learn the intricacies of writing a novel. I wrote incessantly, exhausted though I might be, I pushed myself to develop a strict schedule of writing. I knew the only difference between me and the other young writers of my university years was that they wrote sporadically, when the spirit moved them. I wrote every day. I created my own spirit.

I completed *Bless Me, ULtima* and began to circulate it. I started the only way I knew how, a slave to that American myth which deludes us into thinking that the only place for a young writer to begin is with the big publishers of the East. Little did I know that many of the old giants of the publishing world were dying, that American publishing was changing, that the small presses of the county were on their way to creating a publishing revolution. I went the old route, with dreams of New York, Boston if need be, sure that *Bless Me, Ultima* was a good novel, perhaps a great novel.

I approached dozens of publishers, the result was always the same. I collected enough form letter rejections to wallpaper the proverbial room, but I was undaunted. Sometime in 1971, I was reading a literary magazine published in Berkeley. It was *El Grito*, a Chicano magazine, one of the first and finest of the early Chicano Movement. It was founded by professors, students, and writers in the Bay Area, and it called for manuscripts. So I sent the editors a letter. Would they like to see my novel? Months later they responded. They wanted to publish the novel. Months later came the crowning achievement. My novel was to be awarded the prestigious Premio Quinto Sol Award for the best novel written by a Chicano in 1972. I went to Berkeley and met Octavio Romano, Herminio Rios, and Andrés Segura, the movers behind the fledgling Quinto Sol Publications. *Bless Me, Ultima* became an instant success.

It was a fabulous time to be alive. I was a novelist, a novelist whose work had been awarded a literary prize, an honor which carries great distinction in the Latino world. Everywhere I went I was lionized. It was a moveable feast! This sense of being destined to complete a purpose in life, the sense of being chosen, need not be as egotistical as it sounds. Every person who develops a healthy sense of self feels important, unique, chosen. Those who begin to do important work in life have the feeling of destiny heightened.

Bless Me, Ultima had touched a chord of recognition in the Mexican-American community. Teachers and professors were reading it, but most rewarding of all, the working people were reading it: "I gave it to my aunt, my uncle, my cousin." "I gave it to my neighbor." "The bus driver was reading it at the stop." "I saw it in a bookstore in Alaska . . . " My novel was moving out into the world. Most of the Chicanos who had lived the small town, rural experience easily identified with it. Everybody had stories of *curanderas* they had known in their communities. The novel was unique for its time; it had gone to the Mexican-American people as the source of literary nourishment. It became a mirror in which to reflect on the stable world of the past, a measure by which to view the future. I traveled all over the country, from California to Washington to Texas and Colorado, into the Midwest in Ohio and Michigan, and everywhere I found large communities of Chicanos. The Chicano Movement and the artistic work we were producing united us all and gave us a sense of worth and destiny.

I had made my connection to the Chicano Movement. The winds of changc which bcforc had only been felt as the stirring of the storm were now a gale of commitment to our people. The Mexican-American people, long suffering under their economic, political, and educational oppression were moving to change their destiny. In the universities, Chicano Studies classes and programs were created. Never again would we be denied a study of our history, literature, and culture!

The farmworkers organized across the Southwest. Years of frustration erupted in riots; some of our people died. But their efforts, the efforts of all, were to be rewarded. The movement changed the destiny of the Chicanos, changed in small part the way the society looks at this cultural group. The country was not completely changed, but a significant beginning was made. A feeling of renewed pride flowed in the people. Everywhere I went, the message was the same: It is good to be a Chicano!

The Search for Aztlán

During the sixties I was teaching junior high school, then later, high school in Albuquerque. My wife's parents had moved from Kansas to Taos where they built their retirement home. I had been to Taos, had stayed in the pueblo with Cruz and Tonita. I learned to hunt with Cruz in the Taos mountains. I was also doing a lot of fishing in northern New Mexico. Growing up in rural New Mexico, I had hunted rabbits, *coyotes*, small game, but with Cruz the hunt took on a deeper meaning. The deer was a source of nourishment for the pueblo, the deer is also a brother. The hunt is a ceremony involving the energies of life: man and animal. I had been privileged to understand the delicate balance of nature from Cruz, something which bordered on the sacred. More important, the time I spent with him began to reveal to me the vibrations of my Native American soul.

Patricia and I began to take trips into Mexico. At first we went as tourists, down the western coast to Mazatlán and Guaymas and later into Mexico City. As we became drawn to the country, the tourist baggage dropped away. I was on the trail of clues of roots which seemed to speak to my identity. We had no family in Mexico. The Anayas had been in New Mexico for centuries. My father's father had been one of the incorporators of a land grant in Albuquerque: *La Merced de Atrisco.* So our roots were New Mexico, but now I was making my connection to other, more distant roots in Mesoamerica.

The land grant which my father's family had helped incorporate consisted of a huge area of land stretching for miles along the Rio Grande in Albuquerque's south valley, and then for miles west into desert as far as the Rio Puerco. The land grant had always been a bone of contention between my parents. My father, as heir to the land grant, had received some lots in the forties and sold them very cheap. My mother, having that peasant *Nuevo Mexicano* instinct and love for the land, saw the land grant as a source of our values. Take care of the land and it takes care of us. She believed that someday we would all own a piece of that grant which had been handed down for generations. The real history of the Spanish and Mexican land grants of New Mexico would prove her wrong. Most of the big land grants were stolen away from the true inheritors.

It was part of those themes which I incorporated into my second novel, *Heart of Aztlán,* a novel about people living in the Barelas barrio in the early fifties. It was an exploration of the relationship the *Nuevo Mexicano* of New Mexico has to the land. How did the relationship change as the old communal villages lost their sons and daughters to the cities? How were we affected by the symbols and knowledge of Mesoamerica which the poets and artists of the Chicano Movement were finding in Indian Mexico? I knew I was discovering an association to Indian Mexico. At the height of the Chicano Movement the myths, legends, and symbols from Aztec pre-Columbian Mexico began to be a very important ingredient in Chicano poetry and thought.

The artistic arm of the movement also aligned itself with the farmworker who became the symbolic hero of the young activists and artists. The three headed figure of the *mestizo* appeared in posters everywhere. The eagle of the farmworkers became the flag of the movement. The Teatro Campesino used people and experiences from the farmworkers' community to reflect the reality of people's lives. Everywhere there was a feeling that the artist had to return his art to the people, to the pueblo.

From the cave man, whose art on the wall of the cave is partly inspired by the need for communal food, to the priests past and present who pray to the gods for the community's spiritual well-being, man has developed his spiritual and artistic self as a reflection of the group's needs. Writers have always reflected on their life in the group. By extolling the virtues of the heroes of the group or by challenging the pettiness of restrictive group rules, they have been the mediators between what is and what can be.

But all social and political and artistic movements have shortcomings. All movements have individuals within their ranks who want to dictate the role of each person in the context of the movement. Within the Chicano Movement there was a small band of Marxist-Leninist critics who insisted that Chicano writers had to follow their ideology. The struggle was of a working people against capitalistic oppression, they said, so the role of the arts was to present that theme and nothing else. That, to me, was a limited perception of what I felt to be the creative spirit. *Bless Me, Ultima* was attacked by the Marxist critics as having no social value relevant to the working class. Yes, I had many defenders of my work, but I also had to face the few detractors.

In *Heart of Aztlán* my inclination was to follow the symbols I was encountering. The concept of Aztlán began to dominate my thoughts, and the novel reflected this obsession. By now I was reading about the Indian history of Mexico. I had visited the ruins at Tenochtitlán, Cholula, and Monte Albán. I was discovering the grandeur of power which those ancient people had felt in their relationship to each other and to the mystery of the cosmos.

I was in Mexico City in the summer of 1974, when I received a call from the chairman of the English Department at the University of New Mexico. Would I come and teach creative writing for them? I left to take up my new position, but I would return to renew myself in my spiritual homeland.

Tortuga, A Trilogy Completed

The seventies were busy but rewarding years for me. I traveled extensively throughout the country, lecturing, reading from my work. Patricia and I traveled twice to Europe. Our world was growing, and we loved and appreciated it. At the university I worked hard to help develop the creative writing program, and I helped to found a state-wide writers association. Those were good years; the writers in the state and the region came together. We sponsored conferences and readings. We developed a summer writing workshop. The Rio Grande Writers grew. We looked seriously at the problem inherent in distributing small press works, and we began a distribution project.

In 1974 I was invited to serve on the board of the Coordinating Council of Literary Magazines (CCLM), whose office is in New York. It was an excellent opportunity to serve the community of writers I knew and had faith in, the small-press editors and writers of the country. I met a very important group of writers, writers like Ishmael Reed, Ron Sukenick, Toni Cade Bambara, many others. Twice a year the board held regional workshops around the country, so I not only got a good sense of the country, visited places I normally might not have known, but also got to know many writers and got a good feel for the grassroots writing of the country. From the Carolinas to Atlanta, from Seattle to Los Angeles, from Buffalo to Albuquerque, we took our show on the road and became a very active part of one of the most phenomenal literary movements in the country: the small-press revolution.

In retrospect, it seems I have been at the right place at the right time to see at least a few literary movements born. Certainly, the small-press movement of those years changed the course of publishing in this country. As more and more of the older, established publishers went under or were lost in the mega-worlds of the multinational corporations, the small presses established themselves as logical heirs to publish the serious first works of many of the country's young writers.

Before I joined the CCLM I had taken part in a conference held in Ellensburg, Washington. Frank Chin, Lawson Inada, Leslie Silko, Mei-Mei Berssenbrugge, Ishmael Reed, Victor Hernández Cruz, and others were there. We were there to discuss minority writing in America. The ever-growing number of writers in the Native American, Asian American, Black, and Chicano communities was a phenomenon destined to change the face of American literature. We were the vanguard of something new and exciting, as was the women-writers' movement. Many of us would remain friends for life.

During those years I was working on *Tortuga*, the third novel which I felt would complete my trilogy. *Tortuga* was my hospital story, and thus a very difficult novel for me to write. Yet I believe it to be one of my best works. The novel is loosely based on my experience in a hospital, but it quickly became more than that. The theme of healing still occupied my thoughts. How do people get well? I looked around and saw that we had created a society that was crushing and mutilating us. People were sick physically and spiritually. How could those people be helped? The hospital I created became an existential hell, symbolizing our own contemporary hell.

In *Tortuga* I took my characters to the depths of despair and human suffering, and they find in their hellish existence the faith they need to survive in the world. Perhaps I was finally bringing together my own foundations of faith, finally regrouping from an existential wasteland and giving form to my own credo.

Heirs to the Dream

My discipline as a writer evolved from early training. I would write every morning, and I still do. I traveled to explore the world and ventured out to do readings, but I would always return to home base. The old *Hispanos* and Indians of New Mexico knew that to be without a land base is to be cut away from the center of the universe. I feel the same about my home. In New Mexico I can connect to the people and the sustaining energy of the earth. We built an *adobe* home on the west *mesa* of the city in 1974. From there I can watch the Sandia and Manzano Mountains across the valley; I can watch the seasons change the character of the Rio Grande Valley below. I can watch as my city grows.

I embarked on a long novel, a novel about the city. In the meantime I had followed other threads. I had been writing short stories throughout; somewhere in between novels I squeezed out short stories. I also did translations of old Southwest Hispanic folktales, and these *cuentos* were published in 1980. Working with the old oral materials which had been collected by folklorists renewed my connection to that exciting and magical stream of the oral tradition. The magical realism, which the Hispanic writers of the region were weaving into the soul of their writings, was the historical inheritance which gave those *cuentos* life.

For those who had lived close to the oral tradition of the people, the literary inheritance was clear. From Spain, from the Mediterranean world of Catholics, Jews, and Arabs, from the borrowing of medieval Europe, from the dozens of waves which swept over the peninsula of Spain to evolve the characters of those groups, into the Mexico of the Americas with Cortez, to be enhanced with the serious magic of the pre-Columbian Indians, north into the heart of New Mexico, north up along the Rio Grande, a rich world view came to sustain the people. In the *cuentos*, in the oral tradition, the view of the world was kept alive, and it was fed to us with *atole* and *tortillas*, filling us with the wonder of creation. The old people respected the mystery of the universe, the awe it inspired in the individual, and they passed some of that wonder down to us.

But the inheritors of this fantastic world view and heritage were most often at the bottom of the socio-economic system. We resolved, in those years, always to fight to better the life of the Hispanics and Mexicans of the Southwest. That is why we called ourselves Chicanos. To be Chicano was a declaration of independence, to be free to create our destiny, to announce to the world that we would not live intimidated under injustice and prejudice. That movement we created is now a historic ripple in the stream of our time. Perhaps to declare to be Chicano, with that pride which we felt in the sixties and seventies, will pass away and the contemporary generation will move to join the mainstream culture of this country, but certainly the ideals of our movement will never be forgotten.

My interest with Mexican thought continues to grow. I will not rest until the people of Mexican heritage know the great cultures and civilizations they are heirs to from that country to the south. I've written a few stories with Mexico as the setting, and the story of *La Llorona* I also placed in Mexico. To write her story I went back to the Mexico of Cortez and the conquest of Mexico. The heroine becomes Malinche, a young Indian woman who befriends Cortez and is later betrayed by him. Using the scant details of legend, I wrote a novel about Quetzalcóatl, one of the most interesting deities of Mesoamerica. A redeemer and savior, Quetzalcóatl is the one who brings wisdom and the arts to pre-Columbian Mesoamerica. He represents the wise men and philosophers of Mexico, perhaps a new age of awareness, perhaps a god who walked among men, as Christ walked in Jerusalem.

And now, how do I summarize this short, autobiographical view into my life? How can one truly explore, in such short space, the details of sights and sounds and moments of poignant love and sadness? I wish I could acknowledge all the people who have helped me in my journey, those who have affected my life. The list would be long. I wish I could allow the reader into other corners of my heart, those darker niches where the view would be more profound and complex. Each of us is neither all good nor all bad. We share the natural human emotions. A writer is no different from the vast swarm of mankind, only in us, something is heightened; that vibration of creativity forces us to look closer into the lives of our brothers and sisters.

I am now spending more time writing plays, learning the techniques of writing drama. I also allow time to edit the work of other writers and to try to encourage and guide those young writers who are developing. I continue to read from my works and to lecture around the country; the public continues to be interested in my work and in Chicano literature. Quite recently my wife and I returned from a trip to West Germany, where we met the publisher who is publishing German editions of my novels.

I traveled for a month in China in 1984, and the University of New Mexico Press is publishing my journal, *A Chicano in China*. During the past few years, trips have taken me not only to Canada and Mexico but to China, Brazil, Israel, and to Peru where I visited the incredible Machu Picchu. My interest in exploring the world continues.

My writing is ongoing; it fills my life. I have many projects and planned novels, and teaching continues to be rewarding. I am forty-eight, and now time is the most valuable element; there is so much to do in life. Day-to-day relationships become more important, what one shares and gives is more important than the taking. One's autobiography does not end; it simply moves into a new, and, one hopes, exciting plane of living.

BIBLIOGRAPHY

Fiction:

Bless Me, Ultima. Berkeley: Tonatiuh-Quinto Sol Intl., 1972

Heart of Aztlán. Berkeley: Editorial Justa, 1976

Tortuga. Berkeley: Editorial Justa, 1979

The Silence of the Llano (short stories). Berkeley: Tonatiuh-Quinto Sol Intl., 1982.

Nonfiction:

A Chicano in China (travel journal). Albuquerque: University of New Mexico Press, 1986.

Plays--Selected Productions:

The Season of La Llorona, first produced in Albuquerque, 1979.

Screenplays:

Bilingualism: Promise for Tomorrow. Bilingual Educational Services, 1976.

Translator of:

Cuentos: Tales from the Hispanic Southwest. Santa Fe: Museum of New Mexico Press, 1980.

Editor of:

Cuentos Chicanos: A Short Story Anthology, with Antonio Márquez. Albuquerque: University of New Mexico Press, 1980.

A Ceremony of Brotherhood, 1680-1980, with Simon J. Ortiz. Albuquerque: Academia, 1981.

Blue Mesa Review. Creative Writing Center, University of New Mexico, 1989.

Aztlán: Essays on the Chicano Homeland, with Francisco Lomelí. Albuquerque: Academia/El Norte, 1989.

Tierra: Contemporary Short Fiction of New Mexico. El Paso: Cinco Puntos, 1989.

A Selected Bibliography of Works by and About
RUDOLFO A. ANAYA

María Teresa Huerta Márquez
University of New Mexico

WORKS BY RUDOLFO A. ANAYA:

The Adventures of Juan Chicaspatas. Houston: Arte Publico, 1985. Epic poem.

"An American Chicano in King Arthur's Court." *Old Southwest, New Southwest, Essays on a Region and Its Literature.* Ed. Judy Nolte Lensink. Tucson: Tucson Public Library, 1987.

"Antonio's First Day of School." *PACE* 1 (1983): 146-49. Short story.

"The Apple Orchard." *Hispanics in the United States, An Anthology of Creative Literature.* Eds. Gary D. Keller and Francisco Jiménez. Ypsilanti, MI: Bilingual/Editorial Bilingüe, 1980. Short story.

"At a Crossroads: Hispanos Struggle to Retain Values in the Face of Changing Lifestyles." *New Mexico Magazine* June 1987: 60-64.

"An Author's Reflections: *The Silence of the Llano.*" *Nuestro* April 1983: 14-17, 49.

Bilingualism: Promise for Tomorrow. (Film) Pasadena: Bilingual Educational Services, 1976.

Bless Me, Ultima. Berkeley: Tonatiuh-Quinto Sol, 1972.

Bless Me, Ultima. El Grito 5.3 (1972): 4-17. Excerpt.

Bless Me, Ultima. Southwest Fiction. Ed. Max Apple. New York: Bantam, 1981. Excerpt.

Bless Me, Ultima. Trans. Nuria Bustamante. *La comunidad, suplemento dominical de La Opinión* 21 Nov. 1982: 4-7. Excerpt.

"B. Traven está bueno y sano en Cuernavaca." Trans. Juan José Garcia. *La comunidad, suplemento dominical de La Opinión* 18 Sept. 1983: 3-5, 13.

"B. Traven is Alive and Well in Cuernavaca." *Escólios* 4.1-2 (1979): 1-12. Short story.

"The Captain." *A Decade of Hispanic Literature, An Anniversary Anthology. Revista Chicano-Riqueña* 10.1-2 (1982): 151-60. Short story.

"A Celebration of Grandfathers." *New Mexico Magazine* Mar. 1983: 35-40, 50-51. Rpt. in *Southwest Storyteller's Gazette* 1.1 (1986): 12-16. Essay.

A Ceremony of Brotherhood. Eds. Rudolfo A. Anaya and Simón Ortiz. Albuquerque: Academia de la Nueva Raza, 1981. Anthology of prose, poetry, and art work.

A Chicano in China. Albuquerque: U of New Mexico P, 1986. Travel journal.

"The Christmas Play." *Nuestro* Dec. 1984: 30-36. Short story.

"The Closing of Mack-Ellens." *Albuquerque News* 15 Feb. 1978: 1, 4. Short story.

"The Courage of Expression." *Century* 2.5 (1986): 16-18. Essay.

Cuentos Chicanos. Eds. Rudolfo Anaya and Antonio Márquez. Albuquerque: Department of American Studies, U of New Mexico P, 1980. Rev. ed. U of New Mexico P, 1984.

"Cuentos de los Antepasados: Spanning the Generations." *Agenda* 9.1 (1979): 11. Essay.

Cuentos: Tales from the Hispanic Southwest. Eds. José Griego y Maestas and Rudolfo Anaya. Santa Fe: Museum of New Mexico, 1980.

"Death in the Novel." Unpublished paper, 1986.

"Doña Sebastiana." Trans. Rudolfo A. Anaya. *Cuentos Chicanos.* Eds. Rudolfo A. Anaya and Antonio Márquez. Albuquerque: Department of American Studies, U of New Mexico P, 1980. Rev. ed. U of New Mexico P, 1984. Folk tale.

"El paisaje de mi imaginación." *Dal Mito Al Mito, La Cultura Di Espressione Chicana: Dal Mito Originario Al Mito Rigeneratore.* Ed. Lia Tessarolo Bondolfi. Bergamo: Jaca Books, 1988.

The Farolitos of Christmas: A New Mexico Christmas Story. Albuquerque: *New Mexico Magazine*, 1987. Children's story.

"The Farolitos of Christmas: A New Mexico Christmas Story." Dir. Irene Oliver-Lewis. KIMO Theatre, Albuquerque, New Mexico. 11-12 Dec., 1987. Play based on book by same title.

"The Four Elements." Trans. of "Los cuartro elementos " by Juan B. Rael. *River Styx* 9 (1981): 7-8. Folk tale.

"Freedom to Publish . . . Unless You're Chicano." *Monte Vista Journal* 10 Nov. 1982:

n. pag. Essay.

"From *Tortuga*." *River Styx* 9 (1981): 9-11. Excerpt.

"The Gift." *2 Plus 2* (198?): 38-49. Short story.

Heart of Aztlán. Berkeley: Justa, 1976.

"Iliana of the Pleasure Dreams." *ZYZZYVA* 1.4 (1985): 50-61. Rpt. in *VIAztlán* Feb./Mar. 1986: 16-21. Short story.

"In Commemoration: One Million Volumes." *A Million Stars: The Millionth Acquisition for the University of New Mexico General Library.* Ed. Connie Capers Thorson. Albuquerque: U of New Mexico General Library, 1981. Rpt. in *American Libraries* 14.5 (1983): 305-7.

Introduction. *A Ceremony of Brotherhood, 1680-1980.* Eds. Rudolfo Anaya and Simón Ortiz. Albuquerque: Academia de la Nueva Raza, 1981.

Introduction. *Los cumpleaños de doña Àgueda.* By Jim Sagel. Austin: Place of the Herons, 1984.

Introduction. *Mi Abuela Fumaba Puros, My Grandma Smoked Cigars.* By Sabine R. Ulibarrí. Berkeley: Tonatiuh-Quinto Sol, 1977.

"The Journal of a *Chicano in China*, New Mexico Novelist Rudolfo Anaya Searches for Symbols of His Native American Soul." *Impact Magazine* 16 April 1985: 4-9, 14-15.

The Legend of La Llorona. Berkeley: Tonatiuh-Quinto Sol, 1984.

"The Light Green Perspective: An Essay Concerning Multi-Cultural American Literature." *MELUS* 11.1 (1984): 27-32.

Lord of the Dawn, The Legend of Quetzalcóatl. Albuquerque: U of New Mexico P, 1987. Short novel.

"Man, the Burro, and the Dog/El hombre, el burro y el perro." Trans. *Cuentos-Tales from the Hispanic Southwest.* Eds. José Griego y Maestas and Rudolfo Anaya. Rpt. in *Ghost Ranch Journal* 1.2 (1986): 13.

"*Mexico Mystique*-Another View." Rev. of *Mexico Mystique*, by Frank Waters. *New Mexico Magazine* Nov. 1975: 37.

"The Myth of Quetzalcóatl in a Contemporary Setting: Mythical Dimensions/Political Reality." *Western American Literature* 23.3 (1988): 195-200. Essay.

"A New Mexico Christmas-Season of Renewal." *New Mexico Magazine* Dec. 1982: 39-43.

"The Place of the Swallows." *Voices from the Rio Grande: Selections from the First Rio Grande Writers Conference.* Albuquerque: Rio Grande Writers, 1976. Short story.

"The Publishing World." *Nuestro* Jan./Feb. 1983: 55. Essay.

"Pueblo on the Mesa." Address. The Centennial Convocation, University of New Mexico. Albuquerque 28 Oct. 1988.

"Reading Mostly Novels." *Rayas* May/June 1978: 4-5. Essay.

"Requiem for a Lowrider." *Albuquerque News* 28 June 1978: sec. A:1, 7. Rpt. in *La Confluencia: A Magazine of the Southwest* Oct. 1978: 2-6. Commencement address.

"Return to Spain." Address presented at Primer Encuentro Entre Nuevo Mexico y Estremadura. (Conference) Trujillo, Spain. Summer, 1988.

Rev. of *The Folklore of Spain in the America Southwest: Traditional Spanish Folk Literature in Northern New Mexico and Southern California.* By Aurelio M. Espinosa. Ed. J. Manuel Espinosa. *New Mexico Historical Review* 62.3 (1987): 313-14.

Rev. of *The Last of the Menu Girls.* By Denise Chávez. VISTA 5 July 1986. N. pag.

"The Road to Platero." *Rocky Mountain Magazine* Aug. 1982: 61-62, 84. Short story.

"Rudolfo Anaya." by Rudolfo A. Anaya *Contemporary Authors Autobiography Series* (vol. 4). Ed. Adele Sarkissian. Detroit: Gale Research, 1986. 15-28.

"The Season of La Llorona." Dir. José Rodríguez. Kimo Theatre, Albuquerque. 21-23 Dec. 1979.

Segne Mich, Ultima: Roman/Rudolfo A. Anaya. Horst Tonn. Trans. Frankfort: NEXUS Verlag, 1984.

"*The Silence of the Llano*: Notes from the Author." *MELUS* 11.4 (1984): 47-57. Essay.

Silence of the Llano, Short Stories. Berkeley: Tonatiuh-Quinto Sol, 1982.

"Southwest Christmas: A Mosaic of Rituals Celebrates Spiritual, Community Renewal." *Los Angeles Times* 27 Dec. 1981: sec. 4:3.

"Still Invisible, Lord, Still Invisible." *AMAE, Journal of the Association of Mexican-American Educators.* (1982-83): 35-41. Essay.

"A Story." *Grito del Sol* 3.4 (1978): 45-46.

Tortuga. Berkeley: Justa, 1979. Novel.

"The Village Which The Gods Painted Yellow." *Nuestro* Jan./Feb. 1983: 48-54. Short story.

Voces/Voices: An Anthology of Nuevo Mexicano Literature. Ed. Albuquerque: El Norte Publications, 1987.

"Who Killed Don José?" Dir. Jorge Huerta. Menaul High School Auditorium, Albuquerque, 24-25 July 1987.

"A Writer Discusses His Craft." *The CEA Critic: An Official Journal of the College English Association* 40.1 (1977): 39-43. Essay.

"The Writer's Landscape: Epiphany in Landscape." *Latin American Literary Review* 5.10 (1977): 98-102. Essay.

"The Writer's Landscape: Epiphany in Landscape." *Southwest. A Contemporary Anthology.* Eds. Karl and Jane Kopp. Albuquerque: Red Earth, 1977. Essay.

"The Writer's Sense of Place: A Symposium and Commentaries," Ed. John R. Milton. *South Dakota Review* 13.3 (1975): 66-67. Rpt. as "Writing from the Earth Pulse" in *La Confluencia* Mar. 1979: 3-4.

SECONDARY SOURCES:

Álves Pereira, Teresinha. Rev. of *Bless Me, Ultima. Hispamerica: revista de literatura* 4-5 (1973): 137-39.

"Anaya, Rudolfo A(lfonso)." *Contemporary Authors* (vol. 45-48). Ed. Clare D. Kinsman. Detroit: Gale Research, 1974. Short biographical sketch.

___. *Contemporary Authors: New Revision Series* (vol. 1). Ed. Ann Evory. Detroit: Gale Research, 1981. Expanded biographical and critical sources.

Anderson, Robert K. "Márez y Luna and the Masculine-Feminine Dialectic." *Critica Hispanica* 6.2 (1984): 97-105.

Arias, Ron. Rev. of *Bless Me, Ultima. The American Book Review* 1.6 (1979): 8.

Ármas, José. "Chicano Writing: The New Mexico Narrative." *De Colores* 5.1-2 (1989): 69-81.

Bamert, Pamela. "Farolitos Fable: An Ideal Gift." Rev. of *The Farolitos of Christmas*. *Las Cruces Bulletin* 16 Dec. 1987: sec. B.8.

"Barrio Life in Albuquerque." Rev. of *Heart of Aztlán*. *Albuquerque Journal* 13 Feb. 1977: sec. D.3.

Bauder, Thomas A. "The Triumph of White Magic in Rudolfo Anaya's *Bless Me, Ultima*." *Mester* 14.1 (1985): 41-54.

Beardsley, Charles. "Anaya's 10 Vivid Tales of New Mexico and Old." Rev. of *The Silence of the Llano*. *The Peninsula Times Tribune*. Feb. 1983: N. pag.

Black, Charlotte. "Albuquerque Author Hopes to Make it to Film." *The Albuquerque Tribune* 10 June 1983: sec. B.1. Article on Anaya.

___. "Fouled-up Yule Play Left Fond Memories." *The Albuquerque Tribune* 24 Dec. 1984: sec. B.1. Article on Anaya.

___. "Rudolfo Anaya--Fulfilling A Heritage." *The Albuquerque Tribune* 4 Nov. 1979: sec. D.3.

Blanco, Manuel. "Reseñas: An Outstanding Collection." Rev. of *Cuentos: Tales from the Hispanic Southwest*. *Revista Rio Bravo* 1.2 (1981): 12, 19.

Brauer Ramírez, Graciela. "An Existential Interpretation of *Bless Me, Ultima*." Thesis. California State U, Sacramento, 1986.

Brito, Aristeo, Jr. "Paraíso, caída y regeneración en tres novelas chicanas." Diss. U of Arizona, 1978. Includes chapter on *Bless Me, Ultima*.

Bruce-Novoa, (Juan). "The Author as Communal Hero: Musil, Mann, and Anaya." *Rudolfo A. Anaya: Focus on Criticism*. Ed. César A. González-T. La Jolla, CA: Lalo, 1990.

Bruce-Novoa. *Chicano Authors: Inquiry by Interview*. Austin: U of Texas P, 1980. Includes an interview with Rudolfo Anaya.

___. *La literatura chicana a través de sus autores*. México: Siglo Veintiuno Editores, 1983. Contains an interview with Rudolfo Anaya.

___. "Literatura chicana: De la revuelta a la madurez." *Quimera* 70/71 (1988): 108-11. Includes a short commentary on *Bless Me, Ultima*.

___. "Portraits of the Chicano Artist as a Young Man: The Making of the 'Author' in Three Chicano Novels." *Festival Floricanto II*. Albuquerque: Pajarito Publishers, 1977. 150-61. Includes an analysis of *Bless Me, Ultima*.

___. The Space of Chicano Literature." *De Colores* 1.4 (1975): 22-41. Contains brief discussion of *Bless Me, Ultima*.

___. "Two Views on *Heart of Aztlán*." Rev. of *Heart of Aztlán*. *La Confluencia* 1.3-4 (1977): 61-63.

Bucco, Martín. Rev. of *Bless Me, Ultima*. *Southwestern American Literature* 2.3 (1972): 153-54.

Burciaga, José Antonio. "Buzz of a Fly, Whine of a 747." Rev. of *The Silence of the Llano*. *San Francisco Chronicle* 24 Feb. 1983: 45.

___. "The Lost Link to China." Rev. of *A Chicano in China*. *San Francisco Chronicle Review* 18 Jan. 1987: 9.

Bus, Heiner. "Individual versus Collective Identity and the Leadership in Sherwood Anderson's *Marching Men* (1917) and Rudolfo Anaya's *Heart of Aztlán* (1976)." *Rudolfo A. Anaya: Focus on Criticism*. Ed. César A. González-T. La Jolla, CA: Lalo, 1990.

Calderón, Héctor. "Rudolfo A. Anaya's *Bless Me, Ultima*. A Chicano Romance of the Southwest." *Crítica*. 1.3 (1986): 21-47. Rpt. *Rudolfo A. Anaya: Focus on Criticism*. Ed. César A. González-T. La Jolla, CA: Lalo, 1990.

___. "To Read Chicano Narrative: Commentary and Metacommentary." *Mester* 11.2 (1983): 3-14. Includes brief analysis of *Bless Me, Ultima*.

Candelaria, Cordelia. "Furthering A Rich Tradition." *A History of the Mexican-American People*. Ed. Julian Samora and Patricia Vandel Simon. South Bend: Norte Dame UP, 1977. Mentions Anaya.

___. "Los Ancianos in Chicano Literature." *Agenda*. 9.6 (1979): 19-21. Contains a short discussion of characters in *Bless Me, Ultima* and *Heart of Aztlán*.

___. "The Old Ones in Literature." *Agenda* 9.6 (1979): 4-5, 33. Analysis of Ultima in *Bless Me, Ultima* and Crispín in *Heart of Aztlán*.

___. "On Rudolfo A. Anaya." *Chicano Literature: A Reference Guide*. Eds. Julio A. Martínez and Francisco A. Lomelí. Westport, CT: Greenwood, 1985.

___. "Problems and Promise in Anaya's *Llano*." Rev. of *The Silence of the Llano*. *The American Book Review* 5 (1983): 18-19.

___. Rev. of *The Silence of the Llano*. *MELUS* 10.2 (1983): 79-82.

___. Rev. of *Tortuga*. *La Palabra* 4.1-2 (1982-83): 167-69.

Cantú, Roberto. "Apocalypse as an Ideological Construct: The Storyteller's Art in *Bless Me, Ultima*." *Rudolfo A. Anaya: Focus on Criticism*. Ed. César A.

González-T. La Jolla, CA: Lalo, 1990.

___. "Degradación y regeneración en *Bless Me, Ultima*: El chicano y la vida nueva." *The Identification and Analysis of Chicano Literature*. Ed. Francisco Jiménez. New York: Bilingual/Editorial Bilingüe, 1979.

___. "Estructura y sentido de lo onírico en *Bless Me, Ultima*. *Mester* 5.1 (1974): 27-41.

___. Rev. of *Bless Me, Ultima*. *Mester* 4.1 (1973): 66-68.

___. "The Surname, the Corpus and the Body in Rudolfo A. Anaya's Narrative Triology." *Rudolfo A. Anaya: Focus on Criticism*. Ed. César A. González-T. La Jolla, CA: Lalo, 1990.

Cardenas Dwyer, Carlota. "Chicano Literature 1965-1975: The Flowering of the Southwest." Diss. State U of New York at Stony Brook, 1976. Includes a chapter on *Bless Me, Ultima*.

___. "Myth and Folk Culture in Contemporary Chicano Literature." *La Luz* Dec. 1974: 28-29. Includes a brief discussion of *Bless Me, Ultima*.

Carpenter, Lorene Hyde. *Maps for the Journey: Shamanic Patterns in Anaya, Asturias, and Castaneda*. Diss. U of Colorado at Boulder, 1981.

Carrasco, David. "A Perspective for a Study of Religious Dimensions in Chicano Experience: *Bless Me, Ultima* as a Religious text." *Aztlán* 13.1-2 (1982): 195-221.

Carrillo, Loretta. "The Search for Selfhood and Order in Contemporary Chicano Fiction." Diss. Michigan State U, 1979. Includes analysis of *Bless Me, Ultima* and *Heart of Aztlán*.

Catelli, Nora. "Los chicanos o la última cultura de frontera." *El Viejo Topo* 66 (1982): 52-55. Discusses the burning and banning of *Bless Me, Ultima*.

Cazemajou, Jean. "Mediators and Mediation in Rudolfo Anaya's Trilogy: *Bless Me, Ultima, Heart of Aztlán,* and *Tortuga*." U of Bordeaux. A paper presented at the Paris conference of March 12-14, 1986 on "The Cultural Expression of Hispanics in the United States."

___. "The Search for a Center: The Shamanic Journey of Mediators in Anaya's Trilogy, *Bless Me, Ultima, Heart of Aztlán,* and *Tortuga*." *Rudolfo A. Anaya: Focus on Criticism*. Ed. César A. González-T. La Jolla, CA: Lalo, 1990. This essay is the final development of the author's reflection on the theme of mediation in Anaya's trilogy, which began as a presentation made at the Paris Conference of March 12-14, 1986 on "The Cultural Expression of Hispanics in the United States."

Cervantes, Michael Anthony. "An Analysis of Rudolfo Anaya's Novels as Epics." Thesis. California State U, Los Angeles, 1985.

Cinader, Maud. "Rudolfo Anaya's *Bless Me, Ultima* as a Gesture of Trust." Unpublished paper, June, 1988.

Chase, Cida S. Rev. of *Cuentos: Tales From the Hispanic Southwest. Hispanic Journal* 5.1 (1983): 191-92.

Chávez, Fray Angélico. Rev. of *Bless Me, Ultima. New Mexico Magazine* Mar./April 1973: 46.

___. Rev. of *Heart of Aztlán. New Mexico Magazine* June 1977: 36.

Chávez, R. Martín. "Tierra de Encanto: An Essay on *Bless Me, Ultima*." Unpublished paper, 13 Dec. 1982.

Cheuse, Alan. "Anaya's Haunting Landscape, A New Mexico Writer's 'Anglo' Debut." Rev. of *The Silence of the Llano. Los Angeles Herald Examiner* 24 Oct. 1982: sec. F.5.

___. "The Voice of the Chicano: Letter from the Southwest." *New York Time Book Review* 11 Oct. 1981: 15, 36-37. Includes brief discussion of Anaya and *Bless Me, Ultima*.

Cinquemani, Frank. Rev. of *Bless Me, Ultima. Library Journal* 98.3 (1973): 433.

Clements, William M. "The Way to Individuation in Anaya's *Bless Me, Ultima. The Midwest Quarterly* 23.2 (1982): 131-43.

"The Cowboy in Western American Literature, A Discussion with Rudolfo Anaya, Lawrence Clayton, and James Folsom." Presentation at the Western Social Sciences Association Conference. Albuquerque, New Mexico, 1983.

Dasenbrock, Reed Way. "Intelligibility and Meaningfulness in Multicultural Literature in English." *PMLA* 102.1 (1987): 10-19. Includes a discussion of *Bless Me, Ultima*.

Dávila, Luis. Rev. of *Bless Me, Ultima. Revista Chicano-Riqueña* 1.2 (1973): 53-54.

De La Garza, Rudolfo O., and Rowena Rivera. "The Socio-Political World of the Chicano: A Comparative Analysis of Social Scientific and Literary Perspectives." *Minority Language and Literature*. Ed. Dexter Fisher. New York: MLA, 1977. Includes an analysis of *Bless Me, Ultima*.

Dolan, Maureen. "Aspects of Chicano Reality with Reference to the Novels of Rudolfo A. Anaya." Diss. Glasgow, Scotland, 1984.

Donaldson, Stephanie. Rev. of *The Magic of Words: Rudolfo Anaya and His Writings*. *Albuquerque Journal* 14 Nov. 1982: sec. D.1.

___. "Anaya's '*Silence of the Llano*' Complex Blend of Themes." Rev. *Albuquerque Journal* 14 Nov. 1982: sec. D.1.

Donnelly, Dyan. "Finding a Home in the World." Rev. of *Bless Me, Ultima*. *The Bilingual Review/La Revista Bilingüe* 1.1 (1974): 113-18.

Eckley, Grace. "Folklore and Faith in Anaya's Bless Me, Ultima." *English in Texas* 9.1 (1977): 11-13.

___. "The Process of Maturation in Anaya's *Bless Me, Ultima*." *English in Texas* 9.1 (1977): 8-10.

Eger, Ernestina. *A Bibliography of Criticism of Contemporary Chicano Literature*. Berkeley: Chicano Studies Library, U of California, 1981. Includes entries for Anaya's novels.

Elías, Edward. "*Tortuga*: A Novel of Archetypal Structure." *The Bilingual Review/La Revista Bilingüe* 9.1 (1982): 82-87.

Elizondo, Sergio. "Die Chicanos und ihre Literatur." *Iberoamericana* 2 (1977): 31-38. Contains a brief discussion of *Bless Me, Ultima*.

Farrell, Michael J. "Rudolfo Anaya's Literature of Liberation." *National Catholic Reporter* 22 Mar. 1985: 9, 20-21.

Fernández, José B. Rev. of *Heart of Aztlán*. *Latin American Literary Review* 7.13 (1978): 92-94.

García, Ignacio. Rev. of *Tortuga*. *Nuestro* Aug. 1980: 53.

García, Mario Trindad. "Chicano Writers and Chicanismo." Rev. of *Bless Me, Ultima*. *La Luz* May 1975: 43.

García, Reyes Roberto. "A Philosophy in Aztlán: Studies for Ethnometa-physics in the IndoHispanic (Chicano) Southwest." Diss. U of Colorado, 1988. Includes an analysis of *Bless Me, Ultima*.

___. "Politics of Flesh: Ethnicity and Political Viability." *CACR Review* 1.1 (1982): 102-30. Includes an analysis of *Bless Me, Ultima*.

Gard, Wayne. Rev. of *Bless Me, Ultima*. *Southwest Review* 43.2 (1973): 7.

Garza, Melita Marie. "Hispanic Arts Are Hot: Chicano Author Sees Great Cultural Opening in 'La Bamba.'" *The Milwaukee Journal* 22 Nov. 1987: 13 E. Interview.

Gerdes, Dick. "Cultural Values in Three Novels of New Mexico." *The Bilingual Review/La Revista Bilingüe* 8.3 (1980): 239-48.

___. Rev. of *Cuentos Chicanos*. *Hispania* 64.4 (1981): 642-43.

___, and Sabine R. Ulibarrí. "Una misma cultura, dos distintas literaturas: La mexicana y la chicana. *Grito del Sol* 3.4 (1978): 91-115.

Geuder, Patricia. "*A Chicano in China*: A Chronicle of Oneiric Dimensions." *La Confluencia* (Fall 1989): N. pag. Forthcoming.

Gibson, Daniel. "New Mexico Through Eyes of Novelist and Journalist." Rev. of *The Silence of the Llano*. *The New Mexico Sun* 20 Mar.1983: 16.

Gingerich, Willard. "Aspects of Prose Style in Three Chicano Novels: *Pocho, Bless Me, Ultima*, and *The Road to Tamazunchale*." *Form and Function in Chicano English*. Ed. Jacob Ornstein-Galicia. Rowley, MA: Newbury House, 1984.

Gish, Robert. "Calliope and Clio: Paul Horgan's River Muses." *Southwest Review* Winter 1984: 2-15. Brief discussion of Anaya's views on landscape.

___. "Curanderismo and Witchery in the Fiction of Rudolfo A. Anaya: The Novel as Magic" *New Mexico Humanities Review* 2.2 (1979): 5-12.

___. Rev. of *The Magic of Words: Rudolfo A. Anaya and His Writings*. *Western American Literature* 20.3 (1985): 265-66.

Gómez, Rudolfo. Rev. of *The Legend of La Llorona: A Short Novel. Nuestro* Aug. 1985: 53.

González-T., César A. Interview. 31 Mar. 1985. *Imagine* 2.2 (Winter 1985): 1-9.

___. Introduction. *Rudolfo A. Anaya: Focus on Criticism*. Ed. César A. González-T. La Jolla, CA: Lalo, 1990.

___, ed. *Rudolfo A. Anaya: Focus on Criticism*. La Jolla, CA: Lalo, 1990.

___. "Some Universal Dimensions of Evolving Chicano Myth: *Heart of Aztlán*." "Chicano Literature and Cultural Identity." National Endowment for the Humanities Summer Seminar. Dir. Luis Leal. University of California, Santa Barbara, 1984. Rpt., with modifications, in *Rudolfo A. Anaya: Focus on Criticism*. Ed. César A. González-T. La Jolla, CA: Lalo, 1990.

González, LaVerne. Rev. of *The Silence of the Llano*. *The Americas Review* 15.2 (1987): 109-11.

Gray Díaz, Nancy. Rev. of *Cuentos Chicanos: A Short Story Anthology. The Americas Review* 14.1 (1986): 83-84.

Greigo y Maestas, José and Rudolfo A. Anaya, eds. *Cuentos: Tales from the Hispanic Southwest.* Santa Fe: Museum of New Mexico, 1980.

Gutiérrez, Armando. "Politics in the Chicano Novel: A Critique." *Understanding the Chicano Experience Through Literature.* Mexican American Studies Monograph Series 2. Houston: Mexican American Studies, 1981. Includes an analysis of *Bless Me, Ultima.*

Haddox, John. Rev. of *Heart of Aztlán. Sundial* 15 May 1977: 20.

Hall, Rosanna. "Author Teaches Chicano Novel, Writes of Man's Violent Nature." *The El Paso Times* 22 Sept. 1979: sec. 2.C. Interview.

Hernández, Guillermo. "On the Theoretical Bases of Chicano Literature." *De Colores.* 5.1-2 (1980): 5-18. Mentions *Bless Me, Ultima.*

Herrera-Sobek, María. "Women as Metaphor in the Patiarchal Structure of *Heart of Aztlán.*" *Rudolfo A. Anaya: Focus on Criticism.* Ed. César A. González-T. La Jolla, CA: Lalo, 1990.

"Impresiones on Rudolfo Anaya, A Modern Day Cuentista." *Impresión* Dec. 1984: 12-15.

Jacobsen, Janet L. Study Guide for *Bless Me, Ultima.* Tempe: Department of Communication, Arizona State U, 1986.

Janowski, Jack. "New Novel Vividly Shows Albuquerque Barrio life." *Albuquerque Journal* 27 Feb. 1977: sec. D.3. Article on *Heart of Aztlán.*

___. "*Tortuga* Novel Completes Rudolfo Anaya's Trilogy." *Albuquerque Journal* 4 Nov. 1979: sec. D.3.

___. "22 Offerings in '*Cuentos*'." Rev. of *Cuentos Chicanos. Albuquerque Journal* 22 June 1980: sec. D.8.

Johnson, David. Rev. of *Heart of Aztlán. Puerto del Sol* 6 (1981): 121-23.

___, and David Apodaca. "Myth and the Writer: A Conversation With Rudolfo Anaya." *New America* 3.3 (1979): 76-85. Rpt. in *Rudolfo A. Anaya: Focus on Criticism.* Ed. César A. González-T. La Jolla, CA: Lalo, 1990.

Johnson, Elaine Dorough. "A Thematic Study of Three Chicano Narratives: *Estampas del valle y ortras obras, Bless Me, Ultima* and *Peregrinos de Aztlán.* Diss. U of Wisconsin, Madison, 1978.

Johnson, Richard S. "Rudolfo A. Anaya: A Vision of the Heroic." *Empire Magazine* 2 Mar. 1980: 25, 29.

Jung, Alfred. "Regionalist Motifs in Rudolfo A. Anaya's Fiction (1972-82)." *Missions in Conflict: Essays on U.S.-Mexican Relations and Chicano Culture.* Ed. Renate von Bardeleben. Tübingen: Gunter Narr Verlag, 1986.

Keuning, Patricia. Rev. of *Cuentos Chicanos. New Age Journal* July 1985: 67.

Killingsworth, M. Jimmie. Rev. of *Cuentos Chicanos. New Mexico Humanities Review* 5.1 (1982): 89-90.

___. Rev. of *Cuentos: Tales from the Hispanic Southwest. New Mexico Humanities Review* 5.1 (1982): 88-89.

Kopp, Karl. Rev. of *Heart of Aztlán. Pawn Review* 2.2 (1977): 80-83.

___. "Two Views on *Heart of Aztlán.*" Rev. of *Heart of Aztlán. La Confluencia* 1.3-4 (1977): 62-63.

Laird, W. David. Rev. of *Heart of Aztlán. Book of the Southwest* Nov. 1977: 1.

Lamadrid, Enrique R. "Myth as the Cognitive Process of Popular Culture in Rudolfo Anaya's *Bless Me, Ultima*: the Dialectic of Knowledge." *Hispania* 68.3 (1985): 496-501. Rpt. in *Rudolfo A. Anaya: Focus on Criticism.* Ed. César A. González-T. La Jolla, CA: Lalo, 1990.

Larson, Charles R. Rev. of *Heart of Aztlán. World Literature Today* 53 (1979): 246.

Lattin, Vernon E. "Chaos and Evil in Anaya's Trilogy." *Rudolfo A. Anaya: Focus on Criticism.* Ed. César A. González-T. La Jolla, CA: Lalo, 1990.

___. "Contemporary Chicano Novel, 1959-1979." *Chicano Literature: A Reference Guide.* Eds. Julio A. Martínez and Francisco A. Lomelí. Westport, CT.: Greenwood, 1985. Contains summaries of *Bless Me, Ultima, Heart of Aztlán,* and *Tortuga.*

___. "Ethnicity and Identity in the Contemporary Novel." *Minority Voices* 2.2 (1978): 37-44. Includes a brief summary and an analysis of *Bless Me, Ultima.*

___. "The Horror of Darkness: Meaning and Structure in Anaya's *Bless Me, Ultima.*" *Revista Chicano-Riqueña* 6.2 (1978): 51-57.

___. "The Quest for Mythic Vision in Contemporary Native American and Chicano Fiction." *American Literature* 50.4 (1979): 625-40. Includes a brief analysis of *Bless Me, Ultima.*

Leal, Luis, et al. *A Decade of Chicano Literature (1970-1979): Critical Essays and Bibliography*. Santa Barbara: La Causa, 1982. Includes a short commentary on *Bless Me, Ultima.*

___. "In Search of Aztlán." *Denver Quarterly* 16.3 (1981): 16-22. Includes a short discussion of *Heart of Aztlán.*

___. "Voices in the Wind: Anaya's Short Fiction." *Rudolfo A. Anaya: Focus on Criticism.* Ed. César A. González-T. La Jolla, CA: Lalo, 1990.

Lewis, Marvin A. *Introduction to the Chicano Novel.* Spanish Speaking Outreach Institute, College of Letters and Science. Milwaukee: U of Wisconsin-Milwaukee, 1982. Includes a chapter on *Bless Me, Ultima* and *Heart of Aztlán.*

___. Rev. of *Heart of Aztlán. Revista Chicano-Riqueña* 9.3 (1981): 74-76.

Lomelí, Francisco A. "Novel." *A Decade of Chicano Literature (1970-1979): Critical Essays and Bibliography.* Ed. Luis Leal. Santa Barbara: La Causa, 1982. Contains a brief commentary on *Bless Me, Ultima.*

Lomelí, Francisco A., and Donald W. Urioste. Rev. of *Bless Me, Ultima* and *Heart of Aztlán. Chicano Perspectives in Literature.* Albuquerque: Pajarito Publications, 1976.

___, Rev. of *Heart of Aztlán. De Colores* 3.4 (1977): 81-82.

López, María Elena. "Journey into the Heart of *Tortuga.*" *Rudolfo A. Anaya: Focus on Criticism.* Ed. César A. González-T. La Jolla, CA: Lalo, 1990.

López Hoffman, María (María Elena López). "Myth and Reality in *Heart of Aztlán.*" *De Colores.* 5.1-2 (1980): 111-14.

Lorbiecki, Marybeth C. "The Mystical Presence of the Earth: Two Significant Novels of the Contemporary Southwest--*House Made of Dawn* and *Bless Me, Ultima.*" Thesis. Mankato State U, 1985.

"Los farolitos de navidad: La compañia presenta nueva obra de Rudolfo Anaya." *El Hispano* 27 Nov. 1987: 10. Article on play, "*The Farolitos of Christmas: A New Mexico Story.*"

Lux, Guillermo and Maurilio E. Vigil. "Return to Aztlán: The Chicano Rediscovers His Indian Past." *The Chicanos as We See Ourselves.* Ed. Arnulfo D. Trejo. Tucson: U of Arizona P, 1971. Makes reference to *Bless Me, Ultima.*

Lyon, Fern. Rev. of A *Chicano in China. New Mexico Magazine* Jan. 1987: 19.

___. Review of *The Legend of La Llorona, A Short Novel*. *New Mexico Magazine* Dec. 1984: 24.

___. Rev. of *The Silence of the Llano*. *New Mexico Magazine* Feb. 1983: 14.

Lyon, Ted. "Loss of Innocence in Chicano Prose." *The Identification and Analysis of Chicano Literature*. Ed. Francisco Jiménez. New York: Bilingual/Editorial Bilingüe, 1979. Contains a brief discussion of *Bless Me, Ultima*.

___. "The Originality of Chicano Literature: A Comparison with Contemporary Mexican Writing." Paper presented at the Rocky Mountain Council for Latin American Studies Conference. Lubbock, Texas, Mar. 1974. ED 122 987. Contains a short discussion of *Bless Me, Ultima*.

Malpezzi, Frances. "A Study of the Female Protagonist in Frank Waters' *People of the Valley* and Rudolfo Anaya's *Bless Me, Ultima*." *South Dakota Review* 14.2 (1976): 102-110.

Márquez, Antonio. "The Achievement of Rudolfo Anaya." *Magic of Words, Rudolfo A. Anaya and His Writings*. Ed. Paul Vassallo. Albuquerque: U of New Mexico P, 1982.

Márquez, Benjamín. *Chicano Studies Bibliography: A Guide to the Resources of the Library at the University of Texas at El Paso*. El Paso: U of Texas P, 1977. Contains an annotated entry for *Bless Me, Ultima*.

Martín-Rodríquez, Manuel M. "El tema de la culpa en cuatro novelistas chicanos." *Hispania* 10.1 (1988): 133-42. Contains an analysis of *Bless Me, Ultima*.

Martínez, Douglas R. "China: Another Part of the Chicano Puzzle?" Rev. of *A Chicano in China*. Forthcoming in *Hispanic Link Weekly Report*.

___. Rev. of *The Silence of the Llano*. *Nuestro* Jan./Feb. 1983: 55.

___. "Sharing the Silence." Rev. of *The Silence of the Llano*. *Latino* May-June 1983: 28.

Martínez, Julio, ed. *Chicano Scholars and Writers: A Bio-Bibliographical Directory*. Metuchen, NJ: Scarecrow, 1979. Contains biographical notes and a short bibliography on Rudolfo Anaya.

___, and Francisco A. Lomelí, eds. *Chicano Literature: A Reference Guide*. Westport, CT: Greenwood, 1988. Includes a biographical essay on Anaya.

Martínez, Tomás O. Rev. of *Bless Me, Ultima*. *La Luz* Mar. 1973: 30, 43-44.

Mazur, Carole. "Compañia Production Rich in Warmth, Images." Rev. of "The Farolitos of Christmas." (Play) *Albuquerque Journal* 12 Dec. 1987: sec. A.15.

___. "Diversification Follows Intense Writing Decade." *Albuquerque Journal* 14 Nov. 1982: sec. D.1. Story on Rudolfo Anaya.

___. "New Mystery is Much More: Author, Director Say it Breaks Ground in Hispanic Fiction." *Albuquerque Journal* 19 July 1987: sec. G.1-G.2. Story on "Who Killed Don José?"

McAlpine, Dave. "The Occurrence of Beliefs and Legends in Selected Chicano Literature from 1959-1979." ED 211 294, 1981. Contains an analysis of *Bless Me, Ultima.*

McIlvoy, Kevin. "A Dialogue: Rudolfo Anaya/John Nichols." *Puerto del Sol* 17 (1982): 61-85.

McLachlan, Ross W. Rev. of *Cuentos Chicanos.* *Books of the Southwest.* Sept. 1980: 10.

Meier, Matt S. *Mexican American Biographies: A Historical Dictionary, 1836-1987.* Westport, CT: Greenwood, 1988. Contains a biographical sketch on Anaya.

___, and Feliciano Rivera. *Dictionary of Mexican American History.* Westport, CT: Greenwood, 1981. Contains an entry for Anaya.

Melville, Margarita B. "Family Values as Reflected in Mexican American Literature." *Understanding the Chicano Experience Through Literature.* Mexican American Studies Monograph Series 2 . Houston: Mexican American Studies, 1981. Includes an analysis of *Bless Me, Ultima.*

Mesa Redonda con Alurista, R. Anaya, M. Herrera-Sobek, A. Morales y H. Viramontes." [José Monleón, Chair.] *Maize: Notebooks of Xicano Art and Literature* 4.3-4 (1981): 6-23. Rpt. *Rudolfo A. Anaya: Focus on Criticism.* Ed. César A. González-T. La Jolla, CA: Lalo, 1990.

Michelson, Joel C. "The Chicano Novel Since World War II." *La Luz* April 1977: 22-29.

Miguélez, Armando. "Anaya's *Tortuga.*" Rev. of *Tortuga.* *Denver Quarterly* 16.3 (1981): 120-21.

Mindiola, Tatcho. "Politics and Chicano Literature: The Views of Chicano Writers." *Understanding the Chicano Experience Through Literature.* Mexican American Studies Monograph Series 2. Houston: Mexican American Studies, 1981. Includes an analysis of Anaya's interview in *Chicano Authors: Inquiry by Interview.*

Mitchell, Carol. "Rudolfo Anaya's *Bless Me, Ultima*: Folk Culture in Literature." *Critique* 22.1 (1980): 55-64.

Mondín, Sandra. "The Depiction of the Chicana in *Bless Me, Ultima* and *The Milagro Beanfield War*: A Study in Contrasts." *Mexico and the United States: Intercultural Relations in the Humanities.* Ed. Juanita Luna Lawhn, et. al. San Antonio: San Antonio College, 1984.

Monleón, José. "Ilusión y Realidad en la Obra de Rudolfo Anaya." *Contemporary Chicano Fiction.* Ed. Vernon E. Lattin. Binghamton, NY: Bilingual/Editorial Bilingüe, 1986.

Montes de Oca Ricks, María. Rev. of *The Legend of La Llorona. The Américas Review* 24.1 (1986): 85-86.

Montini, Ed. "Short Stories Wring Emotion From Catastrophes." Rev. of *The Silence of the Llano. The Arizona Republic* 21 Nov. 1982: n.p.

Moody, Michael. "Plática con Rudy Anaya." *Caracol* Mar. 1975: 3-4. Interview.

Myers, Carol. Rev. of *Cuentos Chicanos. Book Talk* 9.4 (1980): 2.

___. Rev. of *The Magic of Words: Rudolfo Anaya and His Writings. Book Talk* 11.5 (1982): 6.

___. Rev. of *The Silence of the Llano. Book Talk* 11.5 (1982): 6.

Neiderman, Sharon. Rev. of *Voces: An Anthology of Nuevo Mexicano Writers. Route Sixty-Six* Dec. 1987: 18.

Nelson, John D. "The Archetypal Image in Rudolfo Anaya's Trilogy of *Bless Me, Ultima, Heart of Aztlán* and *Tortuga.*" Thesis. Northern Arizona U, 1982.

Newman, Katharine. "An Ethnic Literary Scholar Views American Literature." *MELUS* 7.1 (1980): 3-19. Includes brief comments on *Bless Me, Ultima.*

Nieto, Margarita. "The Writer as Shaman: A Reading of the Works of Rudolfo A. Anaya Through the Works of Carlos Castaneda." *Rudolfo A. Anaya: Focus on Criticism.* Ed. César A. González-T. La Jolla, CA: Lalo, 1990.

Orodenker, Richard. Rev. of *The Silence of the Llano. The North American Review* 268.3 (1983): 69-70.

Ortiz Pinchetti, Francisco. "La cultura chicana, amenazada por la brutalidad anglosajona: Rudolfo Anaya." *Proceso: Seminario de información y análisis* 16 Nov. 1981: 46-47. Article on Anaya and his writing.

Pacheco, Javier. Rev. of *Heart of Aztlán. Rayas* Jan./Feb. 1978: 10-11.

Padilla, Ernesto. "*Tortuga*: The Black Sun of Salomón's Wards." *Rudolfo A. Anaya: Focus on Criticism.* Ed. César A. González-T. La Jolla, CA: Lalo, 1990.

Paredes, Raymond. Rev. of *Cuentos Chicanos*. *Western American Literature* 21.3 (1986): 270.

Parker, Kerry. Rev. of *The Silence of the Llano*. *Grito del Sol Collection: Views* Summer 1984: 4.

Paul Phillips, Aileen. "Collection of Chicano Short Stories; Good Reading." Rev. of *Cuentos Chicanos*. *The New Mexican* 20 Nov.1980: sec. D.8.

Pickett, Rebecca. "*Bless Me, Ultima*: A Chicano Novel for Young Adults." Southwest Texas State U, n.d.

Pino, Frank. *Mexican Americans: A Research Bibliography*. East Lansing: Michigan State U, 1974. Contains brief entries for *Bless Me, Ultima*.

Portales, Marco. "Rudolfo Anaya" *Contemporary Novelists*. Ed. D. L. Kirkpatrick. London: St. James, 1986.

Portillo-Orozco, Febe. "A Bibliography of Hispanic Literature." *English Journal* 71.7 (1982): 60. Includes entries for *Bless Me, Ultima* and *Heart of Aztlán*.

___. "Rudolfo Anaya's Use of History, and Myth and Legend in His Novels: *Bless Me, Ultima* and *Heart of Aztlán*. M.A. thesis. San Francisco State U, 1981.

Pries, Carla. "La función de los sueños en la novela *Tortuga* de Rudolfo Anaya." Unpublished paper, n.d.

___. "Rudolfo A. Anaya's Roman *Tortuga* als Gothie Novel." Thesis. Johannes Gutenberg Universität, Mainz, 1988.

Quackenbush, L. Howard. "El dualismo conflictivo en *Bless Me, Ultima*." *Perspectives on Contemporary Literature* 9 (1983): 27-35.

Ray, J. Karen. "Cultural and Mythical Archetypes in Rudolfo Anaya's *Bless Me, Ultima*." *New Mexico Humanities Review* 1.3 (1978): 23-28.

Reed, Ishmael. "An Interview With Rudolfo Anaya." *San Francisco Review of Books* 4.2 (1978): 9-12, 34.

Restivo, Angelo. Rev. of *Tortuga*. *Fiction International* 12 (1980): 283-4.

Rev. of "Bilingualism: Promise for Tomorrow." (Film) *Hispania* 60.4 (1977): 1045.

Rev. of *Bless Me, Ultima*. *El Renacimiento* 8 April 1974: 5.

Rev. of *A Ceremony of Brotherhood*, 1680-1980. *Agenda* 11.4 (1981): 57.

Rev. of *Cuentos Chicanos*. *Books of the Southwest* 262 (1980): 10.

Rev. of *Cuentos: Tales from the Hispanic Southwest*. *The American West* 28.3 (1981): 72.

Rev. of *Heart of Aztlán*. *Multi-Ethnicity in American Publishing* 6.3 (1978): 2.

Robinson, Cecil. "Chicano Literature." *Mexico and the Hispanic Southwest in American Literature*. Revised from *With Ears of Strangers*. Tucson: U of Arizona P, 1977. Includes summary of *Bless Me, Ultima*.

___."Rudolfo Anaya: An Overview." *Puerto del Sol* 19 (1983): 125-33.

Rodrígues, Raymond. "*Bless Me, Ultima*" *English Journal* 65.1 (1976): 63-64. Brief summary of novel.

Rodríguez, Juan. "La búsqueda de identidad y sus motivos en la literatura chicana." *The Identification and Analysis of Chicano Literature*. Ed. Francisco Jiménez. New York: Bilingual/Editorial Bilingüe, 1979. Rpt. in *Chicanos, antología histórica y literaria*. Ed. Tino Villanueva. México: Fondo de Cultura Económica, 1980. Brief comments on *Bless Me, Ultima*.

___. Rev. of *Heart of Aztlán*. *Carta Abierta* Feb. 1977: 3-4.

___. "Temas y motivos de la literatura chicana." *Festival flor y canto II: An Anthology of Chicano Literature*. Ed. Arnold C. Vento, et. al. Albuquerque: Pajarito, 1975. Short comments on *Bless Me, Ultima*.

Rodríguez del Pino, Salvador. Interview With Rudolfo Anaya. *Encuentro With Chicano Writers Series*. Santa Barbara: Center for Chicano Studies. U of California, 1977.

Rogers, Jane. "The Function of the La Llorona Motif in Rudolfo Anaya's *Bless Me, Ultima*." *Latin American Literary Review* 5.10 (1977): 64-69.

___. Rev. of *Heart of Aztlán*. *Latin American Literary Review* 5.10 (1977): 143-45.

"Rudolfo A(lfonso) Anaya." *Contemporary Literary Criticism* (vol. 23). Eds. Sharon R. Gunton and Jean C. Stine. Detroit: Gale Research, 1983. Includes a biography and excerpted criticism.

"Rudolfo Anaya trata de sobrevivir y ayudar a sobrevivir a una minoría." *Cambio* Sept. 1984: 8.

Sagel, Jim. Reseña de *Cuentos Chicanos*." n.d., n.p.

Salazar Parr, Carmen. "Current Trends in Chicano Literary Criticism." *The Identification and Analysis of Chicano Literature*. Ed. Francisco Jiménez. New York: Bilingual/Editorial Bilingüe, 1979. Includes brief comments on

Bless Me, Ultima.

___. "Literary Criticism." *A Decade of Chicano Literature (1970-1979): Critical Essays and Bibliography.* Ed. Luis Leal, et., al. Santa Barbara: La Causa. Includes brief comments on *Bless Me, Ultima.*

___, and Genevieve M. Ramírez. "La Chicana in Chicano Literature." *Chicano Literature: A Reference Guide.* Eds. Julio A. Martínez and Francisco A. Lomelí. Westport, CT: Greenwood, 1985. Makes references to *Bless Me, Ultima.*

Salinas, Judy. "The Chicana Image." Paper presented at the Popular Culture Association Conference. Mar. 1975. ED 106 032. Includes discussion of *Bless Me, Ultima.*

Salmon, Roberto M. Rev. of *Cuentos Chicanos. New Mexico Historical Review* 56.1 (1980): 111-12.

Schiavone, Sister James David. "Distinct Voices in the Chicano Short Story: Anaya's Outreach, Portillo Trambley's Outcry, Rosaura Sanchez's Outrage." *The Américas Review* 16.2 (1988): 68-81.

Sebold, Jane. "Voyage of Discovery Takes a Chicano to China's Heart." Rev. of *A Chicano in China. Sunday Local News* 25 Jan. 1987: sec. A.18-19.

Segade, Gustavo V. "Una panorama conceptual de la novela chicana." *Fomento literario* 3 (1973): 5-17. Includes a short discussion of *Bless Me, Ultima.*

Shirley, Carl R. Rev. of *A Chicano in China. MELUS.* 14.1 (1987): 95-97.

Skenazy, Paul. Rev. of *The Silence of the Llano. Western American Literature* 18 (1984): 351-52.

Smith, Larry. "Rudolfo Anaya: Storyteller of the Southwest." *New Mexico Daily Lobo* 21 Mar. 1988: 9. Interview.

Smith, Roger. "Modern Chicano Culture." *Journal Review* 2 Mar. 1979 n. pag. Article on Anaya's lecture in Reno, Nevada.

Sommers, Joseph. "Critical Approaches to Chicano Literature." *The Identification and Analysis of Chicano Literature.* Ed. Francisco Jiménez. New York: Bilingual/Editorial Bilingüe, 1979. Rpt. in *Modern Chicano Writers: A Collection of Critical Essays.* Eds. Joseph Sommers and Tomás Ybarra-Frausto. Englewood Cliffs, NJ: Prentice-Hall, 1979. Includes brief comments on *Bless Me, Ultima.*

Somoza, Oscar U. "Introducción a la nueva narrativa chicana." *Nueva narrativa chicana.* Ed. Oscar U. Somoza. México: Diógenes, 1983. Briefly mentions

Bless Me, Ultima.

___. *Narrativa chicana contemporanea: Principos fundamentales.* México: Signos, 1979. Includes an analysis of *Bless Me, Ultima.*

___. Rev. of *Mexico and The United States: International Relations in the Humanities.* Ed. Juanita Luna Lawhn, et. al. *The Américas Review* 14.2 (1986): 1-94. Briefly discusses Sandra Mondín's essay on *Bless Me, Ultima.*

___. "Vision axiológica en la narrativa chicana." Diss. U of Arizona, 1977. Includes an analysis of *Bless Me, Ultima.*

Steinberg, David. "N.M. Anthology Stars Hispanics." *Albuquerque Journal* 17 July 1987: sec. C.1, C.7. Article on *Voces.*

Sullivan, Carol. "Anaya Encourages Young Writers During Visit to UNM-Gallup Branch." *The Gallup NM Independent* 27 April 1982: 12.

Tatum, Charles M. "Contemporary Chicano Novel." *Chicano Literature.* Boston: Twayne Publishers, 1982. Includes summaries of *Bless Me, Ultima, Heart of Aztlán,* and *Tortuga.*

___. *A Selected and Annotated Bibliography of Chicano Studies.* 2nd ed. Lincoln, Neb.: Society of Spanish and Spanish-American Studies, 1979. Contains entries for Anaya's work.

Taylor, Paul Beekman. "The Strands of the Web: Mythic Matrix of Anaya's *Heart of Aztlán.*" Unpublished essay, Université de Genève, 1989.

Tenorio, Marta. "Rudolfo Anaya, un escritor chicano." *Universidad De México* 40.418-14 (1985): 29-33. Interview.

Tessarolo Bondolfi, Lia. *Dal Mito Al Mito, La Cultura De Espressione Chicana: Dal Mito Originario Al Mito Regeneratore. Con Test di Rudolfo Anaya, Lucha Corpi, Sergio Elizondo, Rosa M. Fernández, Erlinda Gonzáles-Berry, Francisco Lomelí.* Bergamo: Jaca Books, 1988. Contains an essay by Anaya.

Testa, Daniel. "Extensive/Intensive Dimensionality in Anaya's *Bless Me, Ultima.*" *Latin American Literary Review* 5.10 (1977): 70-78.

Todd Hopper, Glenda. Rev. of *Bless Me, Ultima. The Booklist* 15 Dec. 1975: 557.

Tonn, Horst. "*Bless Me, Ultima*: Fictional Response to Times of Transition." *Rudolfo A. Anaya: Focus on Criticism.* Ed. César A. González-T. La Jolla, CA: Lalo, 1990.

___. "Interpretations of the Chicano Novel Written in English: E. Galarza, *Barrio Boy,* O. Acosta, *The Revolt of the Cockroach People,* R. Anaya, *Bless Me, Ultima.*" Diss. Free University Berlin, 1986.

___. "Themen und Erzähltechniken der Chicano Literatur: Rudolfo A. Anaya, *Bless Me, Ultima*, Tomás Rivera . . . *Y no se lo tragó la tierra*. Thesis. Free University of Berlin, 1981.

Tórrez, Juliette. "Anaya Writes New Mexican Literature." *New Mexico Daily Lobo* 20 Sept. 1984: 3. Interview.

Trejo, Arnulfo D. "As We See Ourselves in Chicano Literature." *The Chicanos as We See Ourselves*. Ed. Arnulfo D. Trejo. Tucson: U of Arizona P, 1979. Contains a short biographical sketch on Anaya.

___. *Bibliografía Chicana: A Guide to Information Sources*. Detroit: Gale Research, 1975. Contains an entry for *Bless Me, Ultima*.

___. Rev. of *Bless Me, Ultima*. *Arizona Quarterly* 29.1(1973): 95-96.

Treviño, Albert D. "*Bless Me, Ultima*: A Critical Interpretation." *De Colores* 3.4 (1977): 30-33.44

Trujillo, Roberto G., and Andrés Rodríguez. *Literatura Chicana: Creative and Critical Writings Through 1984*. Oakland: Floricanto, 1985. Contains entries for Anaya's work.

Trujillo, Lorenzo A. "The Last Word." Rev. of *Tortuga*. *Kappan Connection* 1.1 (1977): 2

Turner, Alice. Rev. of *Bless Me, Ultima*. *Publisher's Weekly* 18 Mar. 1974: 54.

Urioste, Donaldo. "The Child Protagonist in Chicano Fiction." Diss. U of New Mexico, 1985. Contains a chapter on *Bless Me, Ultima*.

___. "Literary Scope of the Rites of Passage in *Bless Me, Ultima*." The Pacific Coast Council on Latin American Studies 26th Annual Conference, Laguna Beach, Oct. 1980.

___. Rev. of *Cuentos Chicanos*. *La palabra* 4.1-2 (1982-83): 175-77.

Urrea, Luis Alberto. Rev. of *The Legend of La Llorona*. *Imagine* 1.2 (1986): 193.

___. Rev. of *Rudolfo A. Anaya: Focus on Criticism*. *Erato: Harvard Book Review* Fall 1989.

Valdés, Guadalupe. "Metaphysical Anxiety and the Existence of God in Contemporary Chicano Fiction." *Revista Chicano-Riqueña* 3.1(1975): 26-33. Includes an analysis of *Bless Me, Ultima*.

Valdés, Ricardo. "Defining Chicano Literature, or The Perimeters of Literary Space."

Latin American Literary Review 5.10 (1977): 16-22. Mentions *Bless Me, Ultima*.

Vallejos, Thomas. "Mestizaje: The Transformation of Ancient Indian Religious Thought in Contemporary Chicano Fiction." Diss. U of Colorado, Boulder, 1980.

___. "Ritual Process and the Family in the Chicano Novel." *MELUS* 10.4 (1983): 5-16. Includes an analysis of *Bless Me, Ultima*.

Van Hook, Beverly. "Noted Author Draws on Subconscious." *Quad-City Times* 8 Oct. 1983: 21 Article on Anaya's lecture at Marycrest College.

Vargas, Jutta. "Rudolfo Anaya: Mexikaniscche Mythologie Und Amerikanische Realität." Unpublished paper. Universität Stuttgart, 1987.

Vassallo, Paul, "Interview with Anaya." 4 Dec. 1985.

___. "Preface: Un hombre con ánima." *American Libraries* 14.5 (1983): 304. Introduction to *The Magic of Words*.

___. Vassallo, Paul, ed. *The Magic of Words: Rudolfo Anaya and His Writings*. Albuquerque: U of New Mexico P, 1982.

Vowell, Faye Nell. "The Chicano Novel: A Study in Self-Definition." Diss. U of Cincinnati, 1979. Includes discussion of *Bless Me, Ultima*.

Waggoner, Amy. "Tony's Dreams-An Important Dimension in *Bless Me, Ultima*." *Southwestern American Literature* 4 (1974): 74-79.

Walker, Dale. "Book is Story of How 'Farolitas' came to be." Rev. of *The Farolitos of Christmas*. *El Paso Herald Post* 21 Dec. 1987: n. pag.

Warshall, Peter. Rev. of *Bless Me, Ultima*. *Community* 98, n.d.

Weller, Ines. "Los chicanos: Mexicanos-norteamericanos bregando por la convivencia cultural." *Aurora, decano de la prensa Israelí en castellano* 30 Enero 1986: 15. Interview with Anaya.

Wilson, Carter. "Magical Strength in the Human Heart." Rev. of *Bless Me, Ultima*. *Ploughshares* 4.3 (1978): 190-97.

Wood, Scott. Rev. of *Bless Me, Ultima*. *America* 27 June 1973: 72-74.

Woodford, Bruce. Rev. of *Cuentos Chicanos*. *The Santa Fe Reporter* 3 July 1980: 32.

"Writer to Lecture on Chicano Literature." *El Paso Times* 22 Sept. 1979: sec. 2.C. Article on Anaya's visit to El Paso Community College.

Wylder, Delbert E. Rev. of *The Magic of Words: Rudolfo A. Anaya and His Writings. Fiction Studies* 29.4 (1983): 721-22.

Zimmerman, Enid. "An Annotated Bibliography of Chicano Literature: Novels, Short Fiction, Poetry, and Drama, 1970-1980." *The Bilingual Review/Revista Bilingüe* 9.3 (1982): 231-32. Contains annotated entries for *Bless Me, Ultima, Heart of Aztlán,* and *Tortuga.*

Myth and the Writer:
A Conversation with Rudolfo Anaya*

David Johnson and David Apodaca

APODACA: First we wanted to ask you about your personal background. Are the characters in both *Bless Me, Ultima* and *Heart of Aztlán* family people, or are they people that you really know?

ANAYA: I was born in a small pueblo--the small pueblo of Las Pasturas right outside of Santa Rosa--which is a pueblo on the Llano. I have a lot of very basic types, primal types of memories and images somehow burned into my mind about it--because I lived there only the first year of my life. Then we moved to Santa Rosa. The interesting thing about Pasturas and the Llano is that it was a kind of place where I first became aware of the elements. There was space, there was sun, there was wind, there was sky, and there were these people marching across this kind of barren landscape. Very earthy, down-to-earth people, and it seems to me that somehow that got imprinted on my mind. When I did *Bless Me, Ultima* I kept going back to those people that I could first recall as a very, very young child. I was trying to think of them in terms of when I was a year old, what they did to me when I was born, how they affected me when I was in my mother's womb. There were conversations in which I could hear something--or was privileged to [hear] in some kind of way. In fact, the more I write, the more I keep going back to developing a landscape that is like that--which is very stark and very bare. It's almost like setting up the barest stage, and people walk across it and they play out their lives, their joys and their tragedies, on it.

* Reprinted from *New America*, 3.3 (Spring 1979): 76-85.

JOHNSON: Are there then actual characters that come out of an early landscape?

ANAYA: To me all writing is biographical. It comes out of experience. It comes out of things that you have felt, that you have seen, that you have been involved in; people that you have met, that you have bumped into on this bare stage of life or that you have heard about in stories. And all that became the material for *Bless Me, Ultima.*

APODACA: How old were you when you moved into Santa Rosa?

ANAYA: I don't know specifically. I must have been just a year old--two years.

APODACA: Why did your family move? Do you know?

ANAYA: Pasturas used to be, for some of the reasons I state in *Bless Me, Ultima*, a very thriving, central pueblo in terms of the ranching that went on there. There were families that lived there. There was a *cantina*. There was a big general store that used to be called The General Store where you could buy everything you needed. And then the railroad came in and set up, I think, a water tank. It might also have been a refueling place. So you have the introduction of the railroad. And then, I think, it began to die--because the big ranches came in. You set up bigger and bigger ranches, and the pueblo dies by a kind of natural process of attrition. My father used to work on ranches all his life. And I guess one day he looked around and there wasn't any future in staying in that place, and so he moved. The next step would have been Vaughn or Santa Rosa. We moved to Santa Rosa.

JOHNSON: We hear about the dichotomy between the people--the Lunas of the valley and the people of the Llano. Was that in that area then? A conflict of lifestyles? People who farmed as opposed to the people who ranched?

ANAYA: There's a definite difference in lifestyle. In *Bless Me, Ultima* I happened to attribute the lifestyle of the *jinete*, the *vaqueros*, to the *llanero*, which are the Marezes, who are tied to the restless sea, the ocean; and the lifestyle of the more passive, more settled Luna to the lifestyle that goes on along the river valley. The dichotomy of a nomadic versus a civilized, settled people.

JOHNSON: And then the contrast between the sun and the moon comes in at that point--the sun of the Llano?

ANAYA: The sun is in a sense more restless than the moon, although it has its own cycles. The moon is tied in more to the psyche of the settled farmer.

JOHNSON: Is Ultima, then, drawn from a real character?

ANAYA: Ultima is a character that I never discuss because she can actually be traced. There were women like this; specifically one woman in Pastura, who I think was even related to our family. The interesting thing for me is that I didn't know her at a conscious level when I was old enough to say, "I know this person." But people have since told me, "Well, you wrote about this person," and I say, "No, I didn't remember her, I was too young." And that's where my interest comes in. How soon are we aware of people and the impressions they leave us with? Even when we are not at that very conscious stage of knowing people, but rather the kind of swirl that takes place all around us. People live and die, and the tragedies happen. I heard music and the coming together of dances and stories--and then I picked from those. My writing is biographical; I'm not concerned about its being true to reality.

JOHNSON: Ultima rides a thin line. Although she seems to be on the helpful side as the *curandera*, nevertheless, she has the kinds of powers that are associated with the *bruja*, or the black magic. And that line is thin, isn't it, through the novel? Because the people know that she has powers, and they are powers almost outside of the church? Their roots are deeper, aren't they? Almost pagan roots.

ANAYA: Well I think all people are like this. We respond to people of power--in one sense--as the characters in the novel respond to Ultima--with some kind of awe. Sometimes admiration. Sometimes they're thankful for the fact that she can heal them with her remedies, her herbs, her wisdom, her folk psychology if you wish. But the minute that people have power, you also bring another element of response to them. You don't necessarily fear them, but you watch them, create a distance between them. Because if they have the power to do wise and good things in terms of healing--physical, mental or spiritual illnesses--you also wonder, do they have the power to create the opposite effect? That's the line that Ultima rides, I think. And she also creates her own distance from people for that reason. She's aware enough to know that happens to people like her. And so she has no truck with people. If they come to her for help, she'll help, but she also knows that they're a little leary of her.

APODACA: Then you would say that people who reach that kind of power--in New Mexico to be specific--don't very often get involved politically in their communities. They're more or less isolated. Or do they, at times, become involved politically?

ANAYA: They might. But, see, we're talking about different types of power. If the ego generates a power that leads a person into the realm or the arena of mixing with people politically and socially, that's a different power. That's charisma. That is more identifiable with the Western ego. The kind of power that I think I'm alluding to is different. It's a power that is generated more from the soul or from the sense of being, the sense that you realize that you take your power not from an ego-type of charisma, but a power from what you have learned from the earth, your identification with the earth--what you have learned about people and the nature of mankind. That's not specific to New Mexico, because I have met people from many different places like that.

APODACA: I was thinking of Frank Waters' old woman, Maria, in *The People of the Valley*. She is very much like Ultima in some ways, but yet she has a very large political power it seems. The people don't go to her just for spiritual healing, or physical healing, but when it comes to points of politics or counseling even--which often involves politics in their case--they would go to Maria. That might seem to be more Western, or not--but it's almost from the outside that Frank Waters develops Maria.

ANAYA: When you study the process of self-actualization, you can study it in various ways. Two ways come to mind. One is you are so conscious and so aware of yourself--and self-actualized in a psychological sense--that you're totally aware of yourself in a social situation. You're not paranoid, you're always yourself and that is often described in terms of social behavior. But what interests me most in my own life, and in the life of the characters, is to study that process of isolation of the character. The character being able to live almost without people, without social setting. Ultima can go and interact. She understands what that social setting is like. But she doesn't need it. She self-actualizes another way.

APODACA: What about the other women in your novels? Now you can also bring in *Heart of Aztlán* if you want. The other women in your novels, compared to Ultima, seem to be very typical women characters. In other words they're not nearly as strong, or they don't play nearly the kind of roles that Ultima plays, or the men in *Heart of Aztlán* play. Was this fabricated to be that way?

ANAYA: When I have to develop a woman character, I have a very difficult time. I look at the earth, I look at life from the male principle. People can argue that this has been imposed on me socially, but I think that there is such a thing as a male and a female perspective, a perspective from which you view the universe, the world. The optimum, or the self-actualized stage, is to have the male principle and the female principle working in harmony, like the yin and the yang. And we have that happening in *Bless Me, Ultima*. Antonio, when we discover him, is both. He's complete. He hasn't broken up that harmony. One of the things that happens during the novel is that he is taught more and more about the male character and imbued with that, so that eventually he acquires more of a sense of the male principle.

APODACA: So it's more balanced when you're a child?

ANAYA: It's more balanced when you're a child, and it should be balanced all along, but the way we're taught to grow up, it's unbalanced. And it only begins to be balanced again when you reach an age of conscious reasoning, when you can start looking at this all over again and say, "It really shouldn't be that way." Some psychologists, or even some novelists, would say that you're thirty or forty when you begin to try to re-establish your own harmony. It seems to me that I haven't been able to develop, or haven't been interested in really developing, strong female characters because that is *such* a difficult thing to do from my specific given time and male perspective. I'd like to get into it in the future. It would require for me a time of maturation, in order to be able honestly to look at what the female principle is like.

JOHNSON: How much is it related to the role of the woman in the movement? When we begin to talk about the possibilities for the male character to grow up and look at what he is able to do in terms of his life, is the woman's possibility still more limited and therefore more difficult as a character? Adelita, for instance, in *Heart of Aztlán* doesn't really have the opportunity to do what Clemente does. She really couldn't realistically lead the strike, for example.

ANAYA: Right. She couldn't lead it simply because of the kind of social and cultural behavioral patterns that are put on male-female, but that's not what I'm talking about. It's only one step to say, "Well, a woman can lead a strike," but it's another role to say, "Why don't we look at people as having a kind of inherent knowledge of both principles to begin with, and never screw them up, never mess them up, so that we only think one way." That's a broader way of looking at an enlightened picture of mankind of the future--when we don't need to worry so much about roles, or even define our individuality in terms of roles. Roles are prescribed by whomever wants you to act in a certain way. Roles are prescribed by forces, by systems. The church and the educational system prescribe roles. Many times they never ask if these roles are good for a person or not. They ask are they good for what we want to do with you. So it becomes a kind of pressure. And it seems that the Chicana and the woman outside the ethnic thing are still very, very much hampered by those kinds of roles that have been assigned.

APODACA: You use the term self-actualization. And in *Bless Me, Ultima* and *Heart of Aztlán* you often talk about the land. And also in a sense about "roots," although I don't know if you use that word. Would "roots," land, and self-actualization be synonymous?

ANAYA: Yes, because the way in which you self-actualize is by discovering your total environment. Again, we very often talk in modern terms only of being self-actualized with other people. That is, to be congruent with other people. What I am talking about is that there are many more ways which complete the person. A person to me is the pole of a metaphor. Always searching for the other pole. Usually in tension with it. Male in tension with female. You complete the metaphor by dissolving the tension with the other pole, social or communal, finding some kind of a meeting ground. You also complete that by rediscovering the naturalness of the poles and metaphor of man in his environment. So that if we have been alienated or disassociated or torn apart from the earth itself, to self-actualize you have to rediscover that. You also have to rediscover people, and the female as a principle, the female as a woman.

JOHNSON: There's this thing of moving into the city, the migration into the city, in *Heart of Aztlán*. And what happens to people who have moved into the city, the sense of losing those kinds of ties to the land, that also tend to lead to the breakdown of the family and to a loss of identity? Is there anything you want to say about what that means? Does it mean moving out of the city, for example?

ANAYA: No. Most of the recent statistics I've seen say something like 85 percent of Chicanos are now urban dwellers as opposed to rural dwellers. I don't know if it's only romantic to think about going back and reconstituting the ranchos, the pueblos, but it seems to me that's a most interesting, intriguing question that the novel raises. I say that in modesty because it's already been asked of me; I was in California recently and some of the Chicanos there said, "well, look, you know you're saying we're a lost generation; we've lost the contact. What do we do?" They were asking the question not only of me, but of themselves. Partly the novel doesn't answer that question, but it's a very important question because it's not just the Chicano, it's all of us.

JOHNSON: All of us--urban dwellers.

ANAYA: Every urban dweller. If he has severed one of those primal connections, that meta-point, and is only one pole of a duality of the metaphor, he is not complete. And how do you complete it? Well, you go around looking for the other pole, and probably there're a lot of answers. One way of answering it is that we must transfer the need for a relation to the earth to a person-to-person relationship. And that means a complete change in the way we look at each other: understanding, first of all, what the relationship meant, and how we can rediscover it. And if not, *then* we're really damned, because then it's every individual to himself, alienated--not only from roots, a connection to the earth, but from fellow human beings.

APODACA: So in other words, rather than going back to the land in that very direct, literal sense, what you're saying is, recreate a myth and live it or become self-actualized as a substitute.

ANAYA: That's the question that I would like the novel, say, to raise, and spark some kind of dialogue.

JOHNSON: When the characters in *Aztlán* talk about the land, it's almost a mystical use of the land. Where did this come from? It's a religious feeling, isn't it?

ANAYA: It's more religious than mystical, I think. Original man was in harmony with his metaphoric setup. And by original I mean a kind of primal sense of understanding the earth without its being mythological or religious or spiritual. You just understood it. You were in touch with it. You gave to it, and it gave to you. There was harmony. Now we call it mythical, because we're so separated from it. It shouldn't be mythical. It's not out there. It's not an abstraction. It's right outside my door. It's in the floor of this room. And if I don't have the sense of harmony to understand myself in relationship to it, then I make it mythical and I separate myself from it, but I don't think that's the way it should be.

JOHNSON: Do you see that certain people--I'm asking now about the Indians--preserved this relationship in a way, for example, that the Anglo has not? The Anglo in some sense conquered the land, but was not *one* with the land. Is that part of the tension that goes on in the Llano for example? When the big rancher comes in, he doesn't have that feeling for the land. Is there that kind of distinction?

ANAYA: I suppose there is. My sense of trying to deal with the earth or the land is not to put that distinction, though, on people. It's more a kind of thing that we should all rediscover about ourselves. Rediscover if we need to. Some people don't need to, you know. Some people have throughout their historic time been very much in touch with the earth, and have never lost it. The empirical reality can be just as screwed up for the Indian, or the Chicano, or the Anglo, as anyone. There's no secret attachment, there's no secret mythology for anyone. I think it's equal for everyone.

JOHNSON: How does the Indian motif fit into these novels? You invoke it; it's there, but not explained.

ANAYA: It's not Indian. It's indigenous. All people at one time are an indigenous people. One way I have of looking at my own work, not so much in process but in retrospect, is through a sense that I have about primal images, primal imageries. A sense that I have about the archetypal, about what we once must have known collectively. What we all share is a kind of collective memory. There was harmony there. It didn't mean it was all Eden. It wasn't like that. The earth is indifferent. It doesn't create an Eden for you, and it doesn't say that collective memory at one time was Eden. It simply says that there was more harmony, there was more a sense that we knew we are dust. That we had been created from it, that we were in touch with it, that we danced on it, and the dust swirled around us, and it grew the very basic stuff that we need to exist. That's what I'm after. My relationship to it. Whatever I am searching for to give more complete meaning to me as a person comes from that sense that part of me in my mestizo nature is Indian or indigenous.

APODACA: By mestizo, you mean what?

ANAYA: Primarily, because I like to deal in dichotomies, because I like to deal in polarities that have to be reconstituted, I mean European Spaniard and American Native. Those two poles trying to come to a kind of harmony in themselves.

JOHNSON: This leads us then to Chicano, and where that fits in. Is this part of how you see your role as a writer? That is, rediscovering that tension, that body of belief for the Chicano?

ANAYA: Not for the Chicano. For myself.

JOHNSON: Is there a larger role for these works in terms of a people or a region? Or isn't this part of your consideration?

ANAYA: I don't know how much of a consideration it can be when you're writing, when you're creating any work of art. I don't think that most artists think in terms of the overall, the world view. It flows from within, it flows from the individual, and it flows into whatever particular work of art you are into.

JOHNSON: But outside the actual process of creating the work, aren't you somehow asked by the community to be something more? As the author of *Bless Me, Ultima*, doesn't the movement itself make demands, ask you to play a *role as a writer*, not just as a creator?

ANAYA: It's true that the Chicano literary movement of the '60's and '70's has looked at its writers, and the artists in the plastic and visual arts, to begin to give a picture, or to present the sense of the overview. What are we as a people? I don't think the artist should get caught up in that. I think any kind of description or dictation to the artist as a creative person will ruin his creative impulse.

APODACA: Then you don't have any feeling of responsibility towards the people--the Chicano people, or the Chicano movement. One critic said that he felt that *Heart of Aztlán* really failed in a certain sense, because that responsibility was not there on your part. Because there were things in the novel that were not of the times or of the Chicano movement, and therefore they didn't contribute to that movement, or to bettering the life of the people in any way.

ANAYA: You have to reword that, because for one thing I'm not concerned with what critics say, or with their response to my work. If I get concerned with a critic, then what should I do, write for that critic? That's just like being prescribed to by anyone else. Your responsibility in the end is totally your own. If somebody says you failed in it, that's the way he sees it.

APODACA: I was just stating that someone had felt that you should have some responsibility in your work towards the people of the Chicano movement. Of course, you said that you don't feel that way.

ANAYA: I can't say that I'm totally unaware of a responsibility that I might have towards the movement, towards my people, towards myself as a part of an ethnic group. Of course, I'm aware of it. The writers are the ones that usually get asked the question, "why don't you be responsible, why don't you write about the people and the real settings?" and so on. "Why mess around with the magical realism trip that you get into with *Ultima*?" I'd like to see the same question asked of Chicano leaders, Chicano musicians, Chicano middle class people, Chicano scientists, Chicano doctors, Chicano lawyers.

Nobody ever gets tagged with that really heavy question except the writers.

APODACA: Maybe it's because writers are published, and their creations are spread out so far.

ANAYA: But, you see the kind of pressure that it puts on the writer. It's a very, very difficult type of pressure to deal with, and it's especially difficult for writers who are beginning, who are really young, who want to say, "I want to express myself from my viewpoint, from wherever I'm coming from, from what is important to me, as opposed to that responsibility someone puts on me from out there." I think it can ruin a writer. The best writers will deal with social responsibility and the welfare of the people indirectly--as opposed to a direct political statement or dogma.

APODACA: Both of these novels, *Bless Me, Ultima* and *Heart of Aztlán*, are the kind of work that after I have read them I immediately wanted to turn around and give them to somebody in La Raza, say my father or my aunt--and they aren't necessarily people who read books. They read newspapers, they read very little, but I had the feeling that they would pick up this book and get a tremendous amount out of it. And on the opposite side, of course, you have the literary critics, the educated who are reading the novel maybe for an entirely different reason. But it does seem that your novels reach out further than many literary works do. There are a large number of people in the barrios, and so on, who don't normally read, but they hear about the novels and will pick them up. In that way the work is influencing the movement or the people.

ANAYA: But where I part company is that . . .

APODACA: You won't tailor the work?

ANAYA: I won't tailor the work, and I can't be responsible for the influence. The responsibility is there because we all share this planet. The paradox is this: if I say I take responsibility only for myself and for my actions, it sounds selfish, it sounds egotistical. I'm willing to stretch that and say that in taking ultimate responsibility for my own actions and my own creation, I therefore take responsibility for everyone in all of the universe. Do you see what I mean? People don't get past that paradox. When you say you're only responsible and interested in your own creation, they immediately stop there and they say, "Aha! you're creating art for art's sake." What a limited view! Every action, everything I do, not only affects the universe, but I'll take it a little bit further and say with every moment that I live I am creating a universe. If there is morality or immorality, or good and evil in the universe, I am creating it.

APODACA: In your dealing with myth--whether it's with Ultima or with the Aztec myth in *Heart of Aztlán*, do you see yourself as creating, re-creating, the myth? Or as simply using myths and symbols that are already there?

ANAYA: I see myself more in the process of re-creation. Because I'm not interested in telling or adhering to any myth and being truthful--in the sense that you research and really try to understand the myth. Man is a myth-making animal and this is one of our failures as modern man. We're not making myths anymore, and it interests me in writers that I read and in my own work to make myths; and not only to retell a myth, but to take bits and pieces and remake it with a modern meaning that says something to our lives now. So the myth of the migration of the tribes that passed through this country--then travelled in Meso-America and the Valley of Mexico and its environs--interests me only because of the bits and pieces that strike a chord in that kind of memory that I have about what happened. Then I take bits and pieces and re-create them as I did in *Heart of Aztlán*. The merging of the eagle and the serpent in the mythology of the Aztecs became Quetzalcóatl, the plumed serpent. It became the merging of polarities; it became the drawing down of the highest power that there is, that is closest to God, that aspires to the heaven, with that power that is closest to earth. You merge the two. What if we then create a snake that is like the train, that is the snake of steel? And then Clemente takes on the aspects of the new bird, the man who can fly, and he must come down and wed those principles again. If you leave them separated, if you leave a polarity or dichotomy, then the world is going to destruction. So it seems to me that we have to look at that principle that is throughout all cultures and throughout all mythology, and say, what does it mean to us?

JOHNSON: So it's not so much that the myth is a myth that has to be in some sense true outside the novel, but the primary thing is this wedding of tensions. That can happen outside the novel even though the actual myth might be slightly different.

ANAYA: Right.

JOHNSON: When you think, for example, of asking where is Aztlán? Aztlán becomes the person who weds them, is that it?

ANAYA: It's an attempt to give a modern sense of ourselves as myth-makers, as opposed to people who only hear ancient myths and wonder what the hell they're about. You see, if we look at all the ancient myths of the world and we assume that only at one phase of mankind we made myths, then we're in trouble. But if we say, we too are myth-makers, because the myth has at its core a very basic type of human imprint, or symbol. . . .

APODACA: But isn't it necessary actually to live the myth, rather than just to write it and read it?

ANAYA: In writing it, I live it. I encounter myself in the myth, and for me it's a tremendous process in terms of learning about myself. The reader also takes from the arts, or from whatever sources are available, and uses the myths. The myths are a way of getting in touch with yourself, your real essence, what you really think of your nature.

JOHNSON: One of the things that's interesting about the Aztec, and use of that material, is the tremendous amount of violence that was associated with those original materials. Doesn't it relate to motifs in the barrio? We see Clemente pounding on the steel. What about violence?

ANAYA: In terms of mythology, we also see Beowulf pounding on Grendel, and savagely and violently destroying a part of his own reflection. We can go on and on. I think we have to separate the two. It is not the violence of the myth that gets translated, necessarily, into a modern setting in which we live. The violence of the barrio is a reaction towards oppression. When you are shut off from being who you can most completely be, you strike out. When you can't be a doctor; when you can't be a scholar; when you are trapped by forces that tell you you have a limited way of expressing yourself, a limited way of being, you have a limited essence. Everything that is natural to you as a person, as a human being, rebels against it; you strike out.

APODACA: Why did you pick the Quetzalcóatl myth for *Heart of Aztlán.* Is it because of what you mentioned before, the unity that you're trying to establish? There could have been other myths, I'm sure.

ANAYA: The Quetzalcóatl myth is the most basic one to the mythology of Meso-America. It's the primal, the overriding myth. How do you wed the highest aspirations of man with the earth? How do you wed God and the snake? The eagle that represents the aspirations toward the sky-head--and the understanding of that kind of unity--with the unity that the earth itself gives you? Knowing that you are part of both, both polarities again.

APODACA: Do you think you have to have any justification for this myth sort of popping up in the middle of the barrio, and becoming so important? For Clemente, who came from some place else entirely, and obviously all these people in the barrio. Did they know anything about Quetzalcóatl as such, in a historical sense, or in an educated sense?

ANAYA: It's important to know it in an historical sense; it's important that people are literate about their own literature, their own historical background, but myth is a level beneath the literate level. It operates all the time, and you can be separated for a hundred years, for two hundred, for four hundred, for a thousand years, from what is essentially your mythology, but the separation is a veneer. The myth will always emerge. It has to surge out and be known, because you carry it with you.

APODACA: Is that true for the Anglo as well? This particular myth?

ANAYA: Yes, because this particular myth is universal. It's Christ the man also being Christ the God, the plumed serpent. It's having all the powers of godhead and yet being composed of the clay of the earth, of the dust. And how do you reconcile them?

JOHNSON: There are almost magic elements in the *Heart of Aztlán*, Crispín and the guitar, the woman with the *piedra mala*. Can you talk about those supernatural elements?

ANAYA: The blue guitar is not supernatural; the blue guitar is a symbol in a sense, or an emblem, or a voice of the poet. The poet will sing, the poet will speak. The priest or the philosopher will speak. It's interesting that in the third manuscript the blue guitar gets passed on. You have to have a poet that will dig to the level of myth and speak the truth, not only of that substratum level of myth but about his reality, and then tie the two together.

JOHNSON: But that person is not necessarily the leader. That merely is passing on the tradition.

ANAYA: Passing on the tradition. It could be the *cuento*, the oral tradition, the stories, the myths. The other part you asked about was the rocks. That's something else that I really worked with. The power of Quetzalcóatl is the power of the blending or the merging of the dichotomies. These polarities of God and earth, of spirit and flesh, cooled off, cooled and congealed into rocks. *La piedra mala* is the congealing of this force into a rock which the poet, or the writer, has to reinfuse with life and mythology for the sake of mankind, for the sake of people. Rocks contain our history; they're almost a way of going back to my collective memory--if you want to know what happened in this land 20,000, 40,000 years ago. If we can decipher the story in the rock, we can decipher our own memory, our own history. There's even a scientific explanation for that, if you want to carry it a little bit further. Given a certain amount of radiation and energy that rocks give off, some day we'll be smart enough to put a machine next to a rock and decipher the history of the earth.

JOHNSON: Is there anything you have to say about the problems that the writer has when he tries to deal with that kind of material?

ANAYA: For me it has been a very enlightening process. Writing for me has revealed more and more of who I am. And at the same time, it's psychologically and physically very difficult. Any time we engage in the process of knowing who we are as completely as we can--given our limited apparatus--and really dive into the rock, we run into all sorts of edges where we might step off and never come back. I run into that sense of, how far can I go? How do I separate the reality of myself vis-á-vis the rock over there as opposed to this complete blending?

JOHNSON: Are there influences--books, writers--that feed into this growing process, that have been important to you in terms of the process of incorporating these kinds of materials and ideas?

ANAYA: There're just too many to talk about a specific literary influence. It's more the kind of influence where you take all of life, not only writers, but back to that stage I talked about earlier where you think about people you have known, the people that came across the Llano and stopped at our home and visited and gathered me in their arms when I was a child and kissed me and held me and told me their stories. The influence is so broad.

APODACA: Did you do any research for either of the novels?

ANAYA: I don't like research. I think research is harmful to the writer. It's not harmful to a presentation like a Michener makes. He can go out and research material and then put it in his own words and incorporate it in a story, but for my search for who I am and the story that I want to tell about those findings, I don't think research is needed. In research you wind up telling somebody else's story or somebody else's idea.

APODACA: You explained about your background, the movement from Las Pasturas to Santa Rosa; how did you get there? Did your family make another move or was that on your own?

ANAYA: Yes, we moved from Santa Rosa to Albuquerque.

APODACA: How old were you then?

ANAYA: I guess about 14, 15.

APODACA: Did your dad come to work on the railroads?

ANAYA: Writing is biographical but it's not autobiographical. The kind of translating that you do from your history to the page is not exactly as it happened. It can't be.

JOHNSON: What about Clemente and his awakening? That's a difficult part of the novel in terms of making it believable.

ANAYA: It's the most difficult because he's caught up in a very realistic setting, and then how in hell do you take him into this visionary trip that I attempted to do with Clemente? It's very difficult, especially the way I did it. I suppose I could have done it in a dream, I could have done it in some kind of revelation, and I chose to do it instead through Crispín and the old woman, the keeper of the rock.

APODACA: Do you think the revelation that Clemente comes to, works in the novel?

ANAYA: I'm no longer concerned with whether it worked or not. It worked for me while I was doing it. And I had a final manuscript and that was it. If I look back at it now, or if I look back at it in 20 years and I say, by god, it didn't work, it's of small importance as long as I go on and do another work which might work better.

JOHNSON: Do you want to say something about the act of writing? Are there things that a young writer needs in order to go about the process?

ANAYA: I think anybody who writes should just write the hell out of everything, and not be concerned with the other things we get concerned with. When writers begin to write they often get concerned with publishing, things like that. I don't think that's a concern of the writer. What do other people think of it? That's not the concern of the writer. He or she can get help from other people. It's very important to get good editorial help, somebody that'll really take a heavy look at what you're doing and give you a lot of constructive, hard criticism.

APODACA: Who did this for you?

ANAYA: My wife.

JOHNSON: What about your publishers?

ANAYA: My publishers, the two that I have worked with, have done very, very little editing of my work. I've had to present it as it is. In other words, *Bless Me, Ultima* and *Heart of Aztlán* are as is, the way they were when I did them. Herminio Rios helped me with my Spanish, which is rusty. But in terms of major editing, like here you should develop another character, or this character needs this real hard core editing--it was already complete when I sent it in. Someone who submits a first manuscript should get an editor that takes an interest in it. If you have to spend another year or two on it, spend it, because usually if you're working with people who know the business, it's for the best.

APODACA: The kind of editing you're talking about, I tend to associate with the larger publishing houses. Would you classify the publishers of your two novels as small press publishers?

ANAYA: Yes. Definitely.

JOHNSON: Do you have feelings about how you would like to see your work published in the future? Would you like to see your work in a larger house?

ANAYA: Yes and no. Quality will eventually be known. While I know that poorly written work can be sold to the American reading public because of the media and the kind of money that publishers can put into selling, I still have a gut feeling that people who really create and are interested in literature will eventually look for the best, the quality.

JOHNSON: But isn't there the problem of distribution and promotion that the larger publisher takes for granted?

ANAYA: Yes and no. Some big commercial publishers will take a work and do a 2,000, 3,000, 5,000 edition and do nothing at all for it.

JOHNSON: You've mentioned at various times that there's something positive about supporting the publisher that backed you earlier by saying, "This is something we believe in." Is that still part of your thinking?

ANAYA: Yes, especially because Chicano publishing houses in my case began to publish Chicano writers and that's how many of us got published. I think we have felt loyalty because they helped us. The next step, which is already here because there're Chicano writers publishing with all sorts of publishers now--the next step is that the Chicano publishers will establish themselves well enough so that we don't need that kind of relationship forever.

APODACA: So that you can break away from the Chicano publishers?

ANAYA: So you don't have to feel that sense of staying in one place. And I would hope that that would come very quickly, because Chicano publishers cannot publish all that's being written. The new writers will have to go to other publishers elsewhere.

APODACA: What about what other Chicano writers are doing? What do you think of their work?

ANAYA: I'd rather not get into that. There's just too much work; there's damn good work. Whatever started in terms of a literary movement is still very much alive and it's producing new works all the time. You know some of the works that have come out, Ron Arias' *Road to Tamazunchale*, Orlando Romero's *Nambe Year 1*. Whether or not writers like that see themselves as Chicanos or in the movement somehow doesn't matter. The work is coming out. Tomás Rivera has a new book; Rolando Hinojosa has a new book; Joseph Torres-Metzgar has a new book, *Below the Summit*.

JOHNSON: What about techniques in your writing? Is there anything you want to say about that? Either the procedure that you go through or from the standpoint of what you've studied?

ANAYA: I'm very interested in setting up a kind of universe of people and characters and place around which I could do all of my writing. I'm very interested, obviously, in myth; I'm very interested in symbol and how it works. I'm very conscious about plotting symbol, of using it. I get a kick out of doing things that I know people will respond to, especially critics. In *Heart of Aztlán* I did something that was really maybe too cutesy. Here, I'll read it. It starts with the italic which is the extra-reality type of story that's going on in this book, as opposed to being told in dreams and mythology as in *Bless Me, Ultima*. This is done with a sense of you don't know who the narrator is that's dropping this:

> *The sun sucked the holy waters of the river, and the turtle-bowl sky ripped open with dark thunder and fell upon the land. South of Aztlán the golden bear drank his fill and tasted the sweet fragrance of the drowned man's blood. That evening he bedded down with the turtle's sisters and streaked their virgin robes with virgin blood.*

> *Oh, wash my song into the dead man's soul, he cried, and soak his*

> *marrow dry.*

That's part of that. I get carried away.

> *Let his eyes burst like drying suns and let his blood sweeten my fields*
> *of corn . . .* (112)

I'm very interested in the resolution of the body and soul, the body into becoming the things that we eat again and the soul into the winds of the universe, which is the sense I have of the oversoul or what we go to.

> The deep water of the canal had dumped Henry in the river and the
> muddy current of the fish-thumping river sang as it enveloped its
> burden. It was a high river that bore the body southward--

So that if he drowns in Albuquerque it's going to take him south, right?

> --toward the land of the sun, beyond succor, past the blessing of las
> cruces, into the desolation that lay beyond el paso de la muerte. (112)

I planted it, right? Socorro, Las Cruces, El Paso. That's what we're talking about. I like to play around with names of characters; for example, Ultima, the last, the last one. But earlier you mentioned something that I wanted to talk to you about. We were talking about the axes, the North-South, East-West axis. I'm very interested in the sense of direction in *Bless Me, Ultima* and that it's obviously an archetype--you pointed that out to me. But did you ever carry it to this? The East-West axis is a Western axis; that is, it starts on the East coast from a European source, and comes . . .

JOHNSON: The westward movement.

ANAYA: And the North-South is the other migration, the Asiatic migration through the Americas down south. But in terms of psychologies or world views again, can we attach a psychological frame of reference to the two axes?

Is the East-West axis fundamentally a Freudian axis, and a way of explaining everything that we do as human beings through sexual impulses, as opposed to a North-South axis that always is looking for a reconciliation of what we talked about earlier, the eagle and the serpent? It sees a polarity but it also see a unity which the East-West axis doesn't provide us.

JOHNSON: I see the East-West axis--and this fits in with Freud--as being the problem of the individual.

ANAYA: And you also have individual--communal.

JOHNSON: Exactly. So you go to the East if you want to save yourself. In other words, having gone as far west now as we can, we now look back to the East, but it's the East for individuals, to save their own souls. You take up Zen, or whatever. And it's the North-South axis that is beginning to talk about the sense of the community being healed.

ANAYA: Well, all of Chicano literature, or a great deal of it, is talking about the reconciliation of self within the community, with the communal self, which is exactly what Jung says. You rediscover who are individually in your collective memory, not in your individual memory. It's Freud who hung us up with the individual memory.

JOHNSON: You're not whole until the community is whole.

ANAYA: And not only that but, take it further, diagram it; you have a graph, and you come up with . . .

JOHNSON: The cross.

ANAYA: Or the tree of life, and the question is, can these two meet, and you not only have what each one presents as a world view, but you have again two polarities that can be reconciled and point to a new kind of way.

JOHNSON: And when you take that North-South axis seriously, then we are in Aztlán; we are the borderline between the two, the meeting place, the cusp. That is, this whole region.

APODACA: Where do you feel your roots are? Are they in the mythology you're talking about, in Las Pasturas, in the mestizo, or are they just in the land?

ANAYA: Well, I think they're primarily in the land, and in the collective memory; in the collective sense of who I am, with both of the axes. Because if I am mestizo, I share in the East-West axis. But I'm more aligned on the North-South axis; for the total sense of me as a communal person, I have to find the point where they meet. They almost become the eagle and the serpent again. East-West-North-South: how do we wed them together?

JOHNSON: Where does your work go from here? David thinks there's a trilogy.

APODACA: I see Antonio in Jason. As Jason is an older Antonio, and then the third part of the trilogy I want to see an older Jason. Could you say something about the third part of the trilogy?

ANAYA: The manuscript that I'm working on now, which will be the third part, will take one of the characters from *Heart of Aztlán* into an environment that is as bleak and as stark as this little village on the llano. And it will deal with the kind of crippling of life that we have created in our society, where love is no longer the predominant feeling that we have for one another. Once love is not the feeling that dictates our social interaction with each other, then we cripple people, and create outcasts, aliens, and that's what I'll be looking at in the third work.

APODACA: Do the myths play a large part in the third book?

ANAYA: A different kind of mythology. It won't be like the golden carp or like the myth that Crispín tells Clemente.

JOHNSON: What did you say at the beginning about creating a place?

APODACA: That you would create an environment, essentially, where all of your work would move in that same environment, all of the characters?

ANAYA: Somehow it's coming that I'm working not only my way out of words into silence, but my way out of complex environment or place into the most essential element. I would like to go back and do some dramatic work that is set in nothing but an horizon where there are little adobe houses. All the tradegies that we know can take place there.

JOHNSON: That's interesting, stripping away some things . . .

ANAYA: Stripping away everything. And as you strip away everything, you go back to that kind of thing I was talking about earlier. What did these people say when I was a child, what did they tell me about their lives and in their stories? The *cuentos* they told mother and father. And you strip away everything and get a different kind of environment to come from.

Mesa redonda con ALURISTA, R. ANAYA, M. HERRERA-SOBEK, A. MORALES y H. VIRAMONTES*

A principios de este año, coincidieron en la Universidad de California, Irvine, un grupo de escritores y escritoras chicanos. Aprovechando la ocasión, se decidió hacer una mesa redonda abierta y un tanto espontánea. Nadie había preparado niguna ponencia, y la idea era platicar, cambiar impresiones. . . . La discusión giró en torno a la función del mito en la literatura chicana desde los 60, y más en concreto sobre Aztlán. El tema parece estar latente en los círculos literarios, pues, con posterioridad, en el NACS, volvió a discutirse en distintos paneles. Por ahora, quedan muchas cosas por aclarar. Pero lo que ya asoma como necesario es un balance, un análisis sistemático de estos últimos quince años de producción literaria chicana. Estudios que deben abordarse con rigurosidad tanto en los planos genéricos como en los concretos. Es hora de abandonar las refelexiones sobre lo que diferencia a la literatura chicana de otras, y entrar de lleno en ella. Agarrar el toro por los cuernos. Todo esto dicho sin desmerecer la labor de algunos críticos que sí han tratado de insertarla en su contexto.

El enfoque principal por el que queríamos llevar la discusión quedó, en gran parte, fuera de la mesa redonda o tocado marginalmente: ¿para qué sirve un mito?; ¿cuál es su función social y política?; ¿de qué manera ha influido en el desarrollo de la "conciencia chicana"?

* **Reprinted from** *Maize: Xicano Art and Literature Notebooks,* **4.3-4 (Spring-Summer 1981), 6-23. [Note: José Monleón chaired the *Mesa redonda*.]**

Si creemos en el mito como una realidad objetiva y no como una proyección ideológica, no queda más remedio que aceptar, en última instancia, la inmovilidad o la condición cíclica del paso del tiempo. Porque, ¿no es acaso lo mítico esa esencia "vertical", permanente por los siglos de los siglos? De ser así, poco o nada nuevo se habría dicho desde los clásicos. Por el contrario, si se toma como referencia de juicio la historicidad y la evolución social, la adherencia a lo mítico no pasa de ser una postura política, una afirmación ideológica que mixtifica la realidad.

Dada la espontaneidad de la mesa redona, hemos preferido transcribiria lo más fielmente posible, guardando las "imperfecciones literarias" propias de un diálogo.

José Monleón

Monleón: In general terms, myth is defined along two lines. On the one hand, it would be a sort of universal subconsciousness, a universal way of thinking that all cultures of the world would share. On the other hand, it would seem to apply to very concrete experiences. In the case of Chicano literature, there is a spread belief that the Chicano cultural world is set within two worlds, following a pattern that would include pre-Columbian, Hispanic, pagan, Catholic values. So what strikes me about these two ways of putting together the same argument is the dualistic value of myth itself. The first argument seems to project universal values, and one would have the tendency to believe that Chicano literature has a direct connection with the Anglo world, since it would share the same mythical, universal subconsciousness. The second argument seems to provide a very concrete frame of reference, that would be particular to the Chicano world. How can this contradiction be resolved? To my understanding, the only way to approach an abstract problem like that is to see it in a specific and concrete way, which is to set it down in its particular manifestation which is Chicano literature, and more concretely, on its function within such literary production. So the first general question is: what has myth been in Chicano literature, and specifically since the '60s and the '70s? (I'm talking about modern Chicano literature) and what has been the purpose of the authors' use of Chicano myth? There are many different aspects of what a myth is, and I'm not going to start discussing them, I guess there is a consensus, we all understand what we're talking about. Then, what is the function of myth in Chicano literature?

Sobek: The political scene was very intense during the '60s and '70s, and there was a general introspection of the Chicano as to what he is and what he was. Myth provided an excellent vehicle to try to discover these origins, personal and group identity. They took also from the European tradition, of course, knowing that Europeans had been using myth, and of course, the United States too, but it seemed that with our Indian and pre-Hispanic origins, with all the mythology of the Aztecs, for example, surfaced an excellent vehicle to strive to discover our identity, who we are. I think that's one of the things that prompted or stimulated Chicano authors to seek in myth a personal identity.

Monleón: Well, probably, the search for identity is also represented mythically. So specifically, we should start with some of the typical Chicano myths. For instance, Aztlán, or the Aztec past functions especially at the beginning of the '60s, as a catalyst for identification. Alurista was one of the poets most responsible for putting through the Aztlán idea. What is Aztlán?

Alurista: El mito de Aztlán no es una cuestión así, digamos, metafísica en el sentido de que uno buscaba un retorno a unas raíces indígenas que nos llevaran al taparrabos, a las plmas, arriba a las montañas, playing hippy, you know? There was a real need for us--when I say us, I'm talking about all the Chicanos throughout, specifically the Southwest, even though we are fully aware of the fact that there are Chicanos all over the land; wherever there are industrial centers, or agricultural centers, there is a raza that lives across the tracks. There was a real need for all of us to find a way, a metaphor, let me put it that way--and at this level I think I'm equating metaphor with myth--a metaphor that would serve as a unifying tool to look at each other as brothers and sisters. There has been an antagonistic relationship between, specifically California and Texas, that I think in order to wage and to forge a national consciousness, we must overcome. Our unity is not bound to, let us say homogeneity. I mean we aren't all the same, and because we recognize that, we looked for something older than us and that had more future than us, that was based on the present. The myth of Aztlán, as I saw it, in the '60s was just a way to identify a people, a land, and a consciousness that said, "Struggle, do not be afraid." I did not see myth, and I do not see myth, as a way to returń to the past or as a way to project oneself in the future without bearing and confronting your present. So when that myth surfaced again, I think the intent was to deal with our present, not to retreat to the past, or to flee to the future.

Audience: This is a question that is asked in retrospect; why do you think that this search for identity, which is a regressive movement, was placed so far in the past?

Alurista: First of all, I disagree that a search for identity is a regressive step. When your identity has been taken away from you, when you have been told you are naught, when you are told you have to be something or someone that you are not, I don't think it's a regressive step to reassert your identity, your history and your heritage.

Audience: Well why don't you do it in the present, as what it is; in other words what I am saying is that the Chicano in this country has a path that is . . .

Alurista: I think I did. I think I did. When I talked about the Llorona I wasn't talking about the Llorona in the river, I was talking about the factory.

Audience: You were talking about the factory of Quetzalcóatl or whatever, what I am asking you . . .

Alurista: Factory of Quetzalcóatl?

Audience: I'm putting that metaphor together, as you would; in other words, the only thing I'm asking you is why did you think that myth, in that particular moment in history did not grow on the most present let's say literary, historical and political conditions; why did it go that far into the past? And I just want to know if you can give me some ideas, in terms of your contact with other poets; what it meant for them going that far back historically; that's my only question. I'm not saying that the search for identity as a means of affirmation of an identity is necessarily wrong, what I'm asking is why it went back so far in history.

Morales: I've asked myself the same question several times, and I ask it in classes, and so forth, and I really think that in 1966 there was a definite need to create a particular literature. In other words, in 1966, there weren't any heroes, literary heroes, that were known, so we couldn't necessarily turn to existing heroes. Chicano literature was not like the literature of Norteamérica that was being published and pushed by major publishing houses, we didn't feel comfortable turning to, necessarily Norteamericano writers. Now, I think that at that time we found ourselves too, we found that we needed to recreate a past. At that time, also for political reasons, we needed to choose a literary past, that marked resistance against a repressive society. So who did we choose for heroes? For literary heroes we went to the Aztec world. We chose the literary traditions of the Aztec to begin to recreate this, you might say, new tradition. For political heroes who did we choose? We chose Francisco Villa, Emiliano Zapata, we chose Ché Guevara, or we chose political heroes that had fought against oppression through peaceful means. So I think that what you're asking is a question that everybody asks, and I think that you have to look at the political situation at the time. I think that that's why we went back. Another thing is that the Chicano movement politically--or I'd say philosophically--was an incomplete movement, because we went all the way back to the Aztec ideology, and we forgot the whole Colonial Period of Mexico, and we forgot that people like Sor Juana Inez de la Cruz, and other Mexican intellectuals, existed. We could have chosen them, but we didn't. We went back to create, you might say a tradition of resistance, and from that point there was a literature that was more or less established, and we could move on to market a literary creation.

Sobek: I was just going to say that Chicanos followed the pattern that Mexico had established when they had their social revolution. Mexico also went back to the past, to the Indians, and they revived this past, to the Indians, and they revived this past in a mythological sense, also, with the painters, Orozco and Siqueiros . . . muralistas. And the other factor, I think, that contributed to this mythical consciousness coming to being was the social experience of the Chicano, in the sense that we were always denied our Indian heritage. I grew up in Arizona and Texas. We were always told we were Spanish, Españoles, not Mexicanos; the word Mexicanos was not used, and as for Indians, forget it, Indians were savages. You didn't want to identify with that. Well, when we started to question what we were, and we found out from our parents that we are indios, that we have Indian blood in us, then we said OK, so we are indios, what kind of indios were they? And then we began to find out that they weren't the savages that they had told us in first, second, and third grade, but that there was a great civilization. I think we started to nourish our souls from that. . . .

Anaya: I define myth as the truth in the heart. I do have a definition. We're not looking at myth in the right context, or not defining it correctly. There is no reason why we had to go back to the Aztecas for symbols, or for heroes, or for archetypes, if myth is the truth in the heart. It is the truth that you have carried, that we as human beings have carried all of our history, going back to the cave, pushing it back to the sea. It seems to me that what happens at a certain time with peoples, is that, in order to come to a new conscious awareness they need to separate necessarily from a social, political context. The context, which is social and political, may or may not be there. But we go through cycles, and we return to the unconscious to make one step forward. When you return to the unconscious is when you come up with your mythic, archetypal symbols, your imagery. When we return to the myth of Aztlán, it is not because we are going back to make Aztecas our heroes . . . I am more Pueblo and Navajo and Apache than any Azteca I ever knew. How the hell do I tie in to the Aztecas? No way. I'm New Mexican Indian. When I return to the myth of Aztlán, what I have found there is not necessarily only the symbol of a particular people, but an archaic symbol which I don't think we have understood completely. It seems to me that the symbols that the people found who wandered in through Anahuac and that valley, is a symbol of archaic man, first man, and woman, primal man and woman, if you will, and that is a symbol for the tree of life, the cosmic tree. Now that symbol is not available only to Chicanos. That's where I think, in talking about it, we leave out other cultures. The tree of life, the cosmic tree, is available to all peoples, and all peoples will eventually return to it, and find it in their way, and clothe it in the name they want. The step into the unconscious to discover symbology, is not retrogressive. It is a step forward, because what you bring from the unconscious will serve you in the step that you are going to take in your profane reality. A nopal is the tree of life. What is sitting on top of that nopal? An eagle. The eagle is the bird of the heavens, the bird of the gods of the heavens. What does the eagle have in its beak, or in its claws? The snake. The snake is the symbol of the mother earth, the symbol of the gods of the underworld. What did archaic men do that we cannot do? Archaic man could communicate with both worlds. Where does dualism and polarity come from? We can say it comes from our social reality and the dialectic. I disagree. I say it comes from our spiritual self, a disharmonizing force. Our civilizing and socializing influence has made us not as unified, not as harmonious, as archaic man. To go back and get in touch, and to become more harmonious, we go back to the unconscious and we bring out all of the symbols and archetypals that are available to all people. We just give them the cultural setting we happen to be tied into. We give it the nopal, instead of the shamanistic tree . . . My Indian brothers in the pueblo use the tree, they don't use the nopal. We communicate perfectly well. We both use the eagle; in particular, I use the owl. We communicate perfectly well. We both use the serpent. We know where that symbol comes from--the underworld, the mother earth. We look for spiritual unity, to move one step forward. Now whether those pressures are brought about by social and political reality, I don't know. Perhaps the case may be made that you search them out in times of tension, of oppression, of meaning; it may be true. I can't speak for that. It makes sense, doesn't it? But the symbol and the archetypal, I think, is available to all peoples.

Morales: I think that that takes us back to the original statement José made, when he said that myth can be basic general structures, that are found in all cultures and all societies. And those basic general structures, I think, are translated into what is myth, into what is legend, into what is proverb, into what is el cuento, that have been, that have evolved, as you might say culture has evolved. All those forms are simple literary forms which the writer, through his cultural baggage, is aware of. Now the writer can draw from those particular forms. Another statement that José made was, for example, that myth is not only a basic general structure that is common to all cultures, all humanity, and is simply manifested in different ways in different cultures, but also that the Chicano myth, is found or set within two worlds. I don't necessarily see that as a contradiction. I see that as perhaps co-existing together. For example, La Llorona is an ancient, you might say legend, that some people say has its origins back in Aztec times. It has many versions throughout the Southwest. But some writers . . . and I have to say myself, at this particular time, that in my first book, La Llorona is that ancient voice, but it is also translated or manifested, in a police car. So that, in a sense, it is an ancient myth that has been modernized, or a new myth that has been created. I think that Chicanos in general and its writers are very lucky people, because they can draw from indigenous myth, they can draw from myths or basic structures that are found in the Southwest, and they are also drawing from Norteamericano myths, or modern myths. It is a simple literary form among many simple literary forms that a writer can draw from and use to create.

Anaya: If I may insert, interject and interrupt, let me suggest that perhaps one reason why Chicano literature is so alive and interesting, and why we are sitting around discussing its mythic elements, is because North America, what we call Anglo American literature, doesn't have it. You go back and try and look at some of the early writers--Melville is the one that gets closest to it. So, what happened to the Anglo-American people that lost touch? I'm not a scholar of this, but perhaps it was the puritan influence of the church. There is no great American novel. They never produced any. And the mythic element in Anglo American literature is just not there. It is so hidden, that it might have been a process of religion. And indeed people are finding our literature interesting because we're dealing with it. We go back and pick it up. We are in touch. I think that that's saving grace. Five years ago I would have sat here at this campus, or anywhere else . . . in fact I've sat in a few campuses where they told me "You're crazy, because you're writing a myth that is not useful socially, in a social context!" I say it is because it's a regenerating thing, it makes a person more and more whole, or complete.

Audience: It seems to me that you are pushing that myth construction very far back. You had mentioned the unconscious, but I was intrigued more by what you said about myth being the truth in the heart. Now, I interpreted it as something that can be dynamic and always being created. As a matter of speaking, I was also thinking about current mythology, how that would fit in, and I think that there is a good deal of current mythology being created. It's very different than the kind of general frame of reference that people had in the Middle Ages when they were all surrounded by Christianity, and all you had to say were a few words and they all knew what you were speaking about. This kind of thing doesn't exist, but what we have today are other myths and symbols being created from the television and the material world, and so there is a regenerating, ongoing, dynamic mythology, which is quite different. So what I'm wondering about is, are you speaking about two different kinds of mythology? Am I correct in interpreting your truth in the heart definition as a dynamic, ongoing thing? or does it only refer to something . . .

Anaya: It's dynamic, it's dynamic, but it's part of our evolutionary history. I'm not sure that anybody can defend the imprinting of the making of the modern myth in the last generation or two in the human heart. You see? If you go to an aboriginal tribe in Australia that has never seen cars and has never seen televisions, are we indeed making myth as primal man did? Primal man made myth out of given archetypes, and there's just so many of them, they're limited, and they're in all the hearts. That's what I'm saying. Yes, they're dynamic, and because they're dynamic we use them, and they do surface, but I wouldn't push it so far as to say that we're making myth, although some people have alluded to the making of modern archetypal and have said that the atomic bomb is a modern archetype that will eventually become embedded and imprinted in our souls and our cells.

Alurista: I would like to go back to the definition of myth. Where does myth come from? Myth can be enunciated by a person, by an individual, but I don't think that myth is the kind of thing that becomes myth unless it is accepted, and certified and legitimized by a mass of people. It's the kind of thing that other people accept as what reality is collectively . . . it may surface out of a need to join individual reality versus collective historical reality--individual psychological reality versus collective historical reality--whatever the need may be. I think Chicanos for a long time, ever since 1848, were subjected to a number of modern myths, such as the Christian myth, which said the kingdom of heaven is for the poor and the meek; or the American dream, the notion that America and its thirteen colonies are the future of the world and whoever wants to join it, join it; whoever doesn't like it, leave it. Manifest Destiny, the notion that the United States was the savior, not only of this continent, but of the world, the notion that the individual could make it on his own, and by himself, and be a rich and happy man. And now we find the modern myth, the myth of the urban cowboy, exemplified by, or epitomized by Mr. Reagan, the Fascist Gun in the West. So these are myths that I think Chicano people have been trying to fight back against, and I don't think that Christian mythology helped us any. I mean I don't think that Catholic mythology assisted us in coming up with a myth of resistance. The myth that we came up with in the '60s was a myth that said hey, you know, we're not foreigners in this land--yes, some of us may be immigrants in the United States of America. That's one. Two: Spanish is really not that bad of a language. Three: We may have our vision of the world. Four: We may not be as materialistic as these people want us to be; the measure of success is measured in terms of a goal-oriented society, whereas, by and large I think, given our history and our heritage, we are more process oriented. We are more interested in living life than finding the goal at the end of life which is ultimately death. So mythology, in a contemporary sense, serves the purpose of unifying people, but it should not be the kind of thing that becomes an opiate--a new faith to kneel down to, and to pound your chest at, and say Aztlán, Aztlán, Aztlán, Viva la raza, Chicano power, Chicano power--that's not going to do it. I think we're talking about rediscovering ourselves, looking at the world with our own eyes, and making sense out of it, with our own eyes, and facing reality honestly. With all of the sex, the violence, the stupor, the exploitation--the worst of it and the best of it. The moments of solitude when a person says, hey, there is hope, and there is brotherhood, and there is sisterhood, and we will not give up, we're here to stay. Myth serves a purpose there. But there's a danger to think of going that far back into the past and saying, well, we had a great past and therefore we should have a great future. If we don't face our present, no myth will do.

Audience: How does the Chicano movement compare with other movements of liberation in Third World countries? In other words we're talking about self affirmation in terms of oppression . . .

Alurista: Well, you know, when a person and a people have been denied the opportunity to look at themselves in a historical way, when a people have been isolated to individuals that are only numbers, or wage earners, then that people see the need to realize themselves historically, to see a past, and reaffirm themselves. I don't think the myth will make you free. I think the myth can give you a sense of unity, but again that unity must be realized in the present.

Audience: Chicanos are really involved in the urban phenomena and somehow, if you're going to deal with the Chicano community you have to put it into a suburban context. Most of us here are going to get on a freeway, and it's made out of cement, you see, and we're going home to a nice little home in the suburbs; OK, some of us live in a barrio, granted, but we're lastly moving into an urban phenomena and we have to deal with it and somehow, I have the feeling that Chicano literature is not dealing with the modern world--the suburban peoples. I'd like to see the Chicano writing about the conflicts in suburbia. I guess I'm playing the devil's advocate. You say that Chicanos are all spiritual, and the Anglo world is all materialistic. I know a lot of Chicanos that own condominiums, you know . . . A steady paycheck would do great for my psyche . . . I hate to be a devil's advocate, but . . .

Morales: I can see what you're saying. There are some writers that have dealt with urban problems, and they have dealt with barrio life, and they have painted the barrio in a very negative way, or they were seen as painting a vision that was threatening. I agree with you as far as saying that what you say really reflects a diverse society, and I think that in this diverse society that we live in, you find Chicanos that are not only workers in the fields, but nowadays people who are professionals, people who are blue collar workers and very much involved in the American way of life. And I think in the future there will be those writers. We have to understand the first manifestations of Chicano literature within a historical context. How did they serve? What is the importance of them? How did they function? etc., etc. It's not to say that that is going to continue. Chicano literature is a dynamic thing. It's going to change. Just as myth is also dynamic. The same basic structures may be there, but as we move on you're going to have different manifestations, or different uses of those basic structures. At one time there was perhaps a fear that Chicano literature would be very limited to particular themes, or almost a literature of formulas. I think that in general you're going to find writers--I think you have them in this room here; I can point to David Monreal, for example--who deal with a, to a certain extent, non-Chicano theme, but a theme that would interest everyone. Not that Chicano themes do not interest everyone. So I think that even in the writers that we have and poets that we have--poets that were very political at the very beginning--if you read their works today you're going to see a tremendous change. In other words, those writers evolved. If you look at the other writers they also evolved from a very political stance on to other things. I think that from the very beginning there were some very, very important writers: Rivera, Hinojosa, Anaya, Alurista, Méndez, and many more of that generation. They established a particular literary tradition, and that tradition se establece para que sea . . . para romperla . . . to break away from it, it forms un paso adelante, becomes a stepping stone to move on. I think that younger writers, and people who are very much involved with American society are going to be writing about different things. We see that in Black literature or Japanese Americans or Chinese, writers write about their ancestors but they also deal with problems of alienation, etc. I think you'll find that in the future. Writers are doing that today.

Viramontes: If you really take a good look at some of the Chicanos that are writing today, I think that there's a voice of urgency going on, and what they're doing is addressing what is most familiar to them, which is the everyday and comparing their past myth with the present reality and looking at the two of them, exploring politically and culturally the two contradictions, and then from that expressing themselves.

Audience: I think that we're dealing with two definitions of myth, and we're mixing them up.

Anaya: Yes, I would like to clarify it because Alurista alluded to myth and I would suggest he's alluding to religious schema and political and social movements. That is, he talked about Manifest [Destiny] and Catholic or Christian myth--that's a way to use myth in a modern context. I could say, the myth of Madison Ave. And what you just finishing saying, you said that women have dealt with myth, i.e., the myth of the role of the stereotyped woman. That's not the way I'm using myth, when I define it, and I don't think that that's the way it should be properly used if we attempt a definition. Because that gets us into trouble: we say, myth is not valuable anymore. What I'm going to suggest to our devil's advocate is that it doesn't matter where we go to write or create our art. It doesn't matter if we stay in the villages of Nuevo Mexico, in Texas or come to L.A. The content will merely shape part of the characters and conflicts in the background. What I would suggest to you is that when you get on the freeway and go to your home, you take the same problems that archaic man took to his cave. You take the same myth element with you. You're not that different. I only say that, of course, out of my personal orientation towards life. I'm suggesting that we can strip everyone down in this room and make you archaic persons so fast that it would surprise you. So there's not that much difference when we talk about the ranchero that goes to the rancho, the man who goes to suburbia, if it's L.A. or the Valle. The mythic element is the unifying element.

Morales: If I may ask you a question. You would agree then that man does inherit certain very basic psychological mythic structures?

Anaya: that we share with archaic men . . .

Morales: OK, I think that that's one way that myth was presented . . .

Alurista: O sea que ha llegado la linea de diferencias entre lo que es un mito y lo que es una fantasia, en el sentido de que, when we're talking about the American Dream, Manifest Destiny, Horatio Alger, the Urban Cowboy, those are fantasies. And when you're talking about myth, you're talking about primal man, you're talking about the fact that the human species remains human species. Well fine. I agree. The human species remains the human species. We still have the same basically biological functions that we used to have probably 10,000 years ago. Nonetheless, the conditions of production that we have to face today are totally different, and I postulate that religion, that a structural set of notions that are based on faith without knowledge of what is to come, are no longer functional because we did not have the power a thousand years ago, ten thousand years ago or 50,000 years ago to destroy the earth. We now do. So we can no longer live under the affectation that faith will make us free. I do not believe that. And I have faith. I think that there is a definite amount of clarity, rationality that has to come into being. We have to face the conditions of the world in which we live. The system of production that has reached the highest peak in this world today has to be faced, and it will not be easily dismissed by saying we are all members of the human species, let us be brothers. I wish that would work. I don't think it will, so we have to live up to the new conditions of production which the human species has created. We have to face it and facing it . . .

Audience: Maybe I can answer what you're saying . . . I think there is in this day and time in literature itself--not only in Chicano literature, but in Black literature and Asian literature, gay literature--a return to the myth to substantiate ourselves as people. And not just using it to step back, and be archaic man, but I have to agree with Anaya from the standpoint that we all are archaic, or archetype . . . and it's not refusing being in this world itself; it's a means of balancing. This world doesn't balance itself at all; as far as what's going on right now, there's too much discord. We need to return to a humanistic level, where man is in touch with nature, the spirit. I think that returning to the archetype is important because modern man right now is computerized. He has no sense of touching his own skin, he doesn't know what his skin feels like. I think that one of the means of getting back is using archetypes, because I myself go back to my African heritage and deal with that to live in this modern world.

Audience: Yes, but I think you have to express them in these old terms. Why can't we use modern ingredients of this world to express these same archetypes? It's done constantly . . .

Monleón: Maybe at this point it would be a good idea to get back together all the discussion. And I think the basic difference is that Anaya has been talking about the myth as the truth in the heart, that is the ultimate essence of something, and probably what I was suggesting at the beginning of the discussion, and what Alurista has picked up, is how this shows, how this is expressed. What makes the 1960s and 1970s call to Aztlán, and not the 1950s, or why Rudolfo Anaya writes his novel in the late 1960s, and not the 1950s. That is, what is the function of myth, why do we call on myths, what purpose it has in coming about in our society? In that sense I would just like to add, retaking Aztlán, that I think, in a sense, it was a good way of creating a sense of unity, actual political unity, at a moment when that unity was needed. Mexico has its boundaries, as El Salvador does, or Chile . . . the Chicano people do not have those boundaries, and it was a good symbol, a good myth, a good essence to call upon, and give it a form. Now as we can see in this discussion, the unity does not really exist. So to call upon a myth does not really mean that the essence of the myth does exist for everybody.

Morales: I really think that if you believe that man has inherited basic psychological structures, as Jung says, then those structures are repeated over and over and over again throughout the history of man.

Alurista: With different social contexts . . .

Morales: With different manifestations of the structures. I think that this idea of truth in the heart is to me, to be devil's advocate, very, very abstract; it's very difficult to understand, and perhaps every single one has a definition of what truth in the heart is. For me, myths are structures, literary structures, that have been repeated over and over again. One of those structures is voyage, for example. Another structure is the return to the origin. Another one is initiation of a child going into manhood. The hero, you know, the structure of the hero, and so forth. I really think that that is the essence of myth.

Monleón: You had a question?

Anaya: I think Marxist analogy . . .

Alurista: No, no, no, no. It's not ideology, man. I'm talking about at a primal level, the species, you know? When I want a torta, I go to a tortera . . . necesitamos un mito más racional que confronte las necesidades contemporaneas, y que confronte el enemigo del espíritu del hombre.

Anaya: ¿Que es qué?

Alurista: No el diablo, eso dalo por seguro . . . porque si voy a buscar al diablo tendré que encontrar el infierno primero, you know? I'm not sure I want to go there. I think he's around, you know, and he has no horns, but he's got a lot of guns and a lot of money.

Audience: I just want to ask Mr. Anaya if I understand correctly what he's been saying. It seems to me that he's been suggesting that there's some kind of innate incompatibility between the archetypes--which man carried within himself, all of us--I know I carry it within myself, I'm not a Chicano--and the modern world, that is this modern technological world which we've created for ourselves and by ourselves, and I don't quite understand how that's possible. Why can't we express these archetypes, these mythical structures that we carry inside of us in terms of this modern world? And if we carry them inside of us, then we must express them in terms of this modern world? I would disagree with you strongly that these myths are not in American literature, Anglo American literature, because I think they are, because I think they have to be. People express themselves in a creative way. Expressing themselves from the heart will automatically bring these archetypes, and in their contemporary setting if that's what they choose to do. I think they permeate and penetrate Anglo American literature through and through.

Anaya: You find very little study of it, or reflection of it. I mean I'm not that well read, but I've read some, and I guess even in that little reading, I find very little interest in it. There's a renewed interest now. Yes I would say that the archetypes surface today, they come out, that's what this panel is all about. All of the writers here I think in one way or another use them. Why there is a wrenching in contemporary, modern man is probably because we lost touch with the original unity and harmony. And you can decide why. Probably because we decided not to talk to the gods, or the gods got so mad at us, they decided not to talk to us. . . . Either way we cut off the communication. And then we get to the step that Alurista said, and now we have grown so perverse that we are now possibly deciding on destroying what the gods created for us, you know? We have arrived at the point where we can destroy the earth. That is mind boggling, that really wrenches whatever unity anyone may have inside of him.

Audience: Yes, but isn't this rift also due to your kind of refusal to accept this new modern world and insist upon the myths expressed in ancient terms?

Anaya: I live in this modern world, I accept it.

Audience: But expressing the old archetypes in terms of the eagle, and a snake, they don't work anymore . . .

Anaya: They're not old, you see, that's what I'm trying to say. When you cut through, when you get to the heart, it's not old. What it carries with it, it's not old. And as Alurista said, we need something that's real, that deals with reality. Well, it deals with reality. We wouldn't be here if archaic men had not survived. We carry that same survival, that same stuff . . . with us.

Audience: Yes, I'm just very interested in our discussion. I think a lot of things we touched on are very, very important. There was a lot of lack of definitions of a lot of concepts that came forward, and I think it would be important if we could have a second discussion somewhere down the line. And to me it is very important to understand what is the goal of the myth in Chicano literature, why it has been so dominant, in early Chicano literature. I think Alurista is right when he alludes to the fact that the creation of the myth of Aztlán--and that we were going to conquer the Southwest, and make all the Anglos Mexican citizens--the kind of ideology that guided us at a time was essential. It was essential because we did not interrelate directly; from California to the Valle de Texas, there's a different reality. Aztlán was an essential part of our vision. But what also happened is that once we established that unity we began to work together, we began to see that looking to the past for the ultimate aspect of the communalism that the Indians put forward, did not resolve our problems. We began to drop these myths. They were important, not that we ignored them, but we began to see a much broader reality. That is where the problem lies. I guess I do have a difference with Compañero Anaya here, with respect to that. For example, for me, when I read *Heart of Aztlán*, I thought it was a very, very good book, and I thoroughly enjoyed it, but to me it really shows the kind of confusion that existed within our movement. Where we began to change, sí when we saw a strike of the workers, a strike trying to deal with the physical reality that was there trying to crush it. Looking back to the man with the ultimate wisdom, and fighting the ultimate myth, that won't answer the problem that's facing us directly and that's never answered. I've been a political activist for 10 years, and I really cannot see that studying the ancient Indian myths will really aid us. To me the myth is dropping out slowly, but surely, and what you're going to see is a whole new era, as Alejandro was pointing out, of writers that are really more directed to reality than to myths. Of course, they will incorporate mythical elements because I'm asserting that they're really part of the culture.

Anaya: But dealing with the reality doesn't exclude the other. I haven't made the statement that dealing with myth somehow makes you a person who doesn't live in reality. Maybe if I did I would have to come back and say, redefine it. I said we survive, and we've always dealt, primal man and us, with reality. But we carry along with us the myth. And I think you don't separate yourself and say today I'm going to take on the system, you know. Or if I'm a Hopi I'm going to take on the coal companies that are destroying my sacred mother earth, or I'm going to take on the developers that want to buy me out of my barrio and put in a big development, and I'm not going to have a home. And then after I get that done I'm going to deal with myth. I say that whatever that content is of myth, it's spiritual, and there's nothing wrong with carrying it into your everyday world. I would say that you do not become a Hopi corporation, and that that's the way you solve the problems of reality. I say that's a way you destroy yourself. As Alurista suggested, we do have the capability to destroy this earth. The only people that are going to survive the catastrophe are going to be the indigenous people. They have something that we have forgotten. And a great deal of that is their spiritual response to the universe. If they go corporation, forget it. Se acabó todo.

Monleón: We have to finish up the round table, la mesa redonda, and I guess the general feeling is that probably it's time to make a balance of the '60s and '70s production of Chicano literature and the mythical aspect is probably one of them. We didn't touch many of the things that probably should have been touched, but hopefully there will be more mesas redondas. I wanted to talk about the act of writing as a myth also, and I wanted to talk of more of the functions of the myth in our society, and not as much of the essence of myth. Hopefully we will continue having more discussions. So, thank you very much.

An Interview With Rudolfo A. Anaya*

César A. González-T.
San Diego Mesa College

On the occasion of Rudolfo Anaya's visit to San Diego, California (March 29-31, 1985), to participate in the 5th Annual Xochicuicatl "Flor y Canto," poetry readings by the community, *al aire libre*, at Chicano Park under the Coronado Bridge. Organized by León Aztleca. The program included the following: Aztec ceremony for Mother Earth, offering of flowers, Aztec prayer for the spring equinox, words by Rudolfo Anaya, poetry recital, and health ceremony.

Some Questions--*Atinadas y Desafinadas*

César González: First of all, Rudy, would you please recount the story you told me yesterday of the gift of the turquoise that you are wearing and about Cruz at Taos Pueblo. You mentioned three dreams in your forthcoming China journal, with their verisimilitudes in experience when you returned home. You spoke of your grandfather and Cruz as guides.

Rudolfo Anaya: In the summer of 1984, May and June, I spent the month traveling throughout China from Beijin, the capital, down in Central China, Chengdu, Chungking, and on the Yangtze. I thought it was a very important trip, a very incredible pilgrimage for me to take the Asiatic sources of the migrations of the Native Americans into the Americas. I also felt a strange trepidation, almost a sense of fear to enter a country that has a billion people. And so as I was entering, I kept remembering my grandfather who was a farmer in Puerto de Luna in a river valley in Nuevo Mexico. For some

* **Reprinted from** *Imagine: International Chicano Poetry Journal,* **2.2 (Winter 1985): 1-9.**

reason I kept using him as a guide, as a mentor, who was lending me his strength to go into that country, strange and foreboding, and a new country for me in many ways. And so my grandfather became the guide because he is in many ways like the Chinese rural peasant who is very much like our Hispanic peasant who worked on the land in the small *ranchos* and *pueblos*. They look the same--small, feisty, withered old men working the land. Also I had a friend, Cruz, from Taos Pueblo from New Mexico. I had visited with him a lot and hunted with him years ago when I was a young man.

During my trip to China, I had a lot of dreams. In many ways they revealed interesting symbols to me and answers I was searching for. One of the first dreams I had was that Cruz came to speak to me and also to serve as a guide like my grandfather. And this gave me the courage that I needed to approach the country and the people, and to look for the symbols and those little secrets that I seemed to be searching for in the culture and in the people and in the land.

When I came back from China a month later, I went up to Taos Pueblo to visit Cruz. I drove up to the pueblo to his home, and Tonito, his wife, answered the door. Right away she told me that Cruz had died. He had been sick, and we had all expected it. But it was a shock. We started to talk and got around to, when did he die? And she told me that he died the exact day that I had my dream of him in China. So he had gone to China. My sense is that the dream is the flight of the soul, and who knows, but it may be more than that. It was just interesting to me that in his last moments on earth before the transformation of his body, he visited me; he spoke to me again, and lent me his courage as a guide.

The turquoise bolo tie that you refer to that I am wearing is his. He had given it to me a year earlier, before his death. I had been up there in the summer and taken him--it's very common in the Indian culture as it is with the *Mexicanos*, to always take a little regalito or gift, *o lo que sea, verdad?*-- and so I had taken him a couple of shirts, beautiful shirts to wear, and he gave me this bolo tie which I wear.

CG: You said also there was a dream of a truck, and also about a wall and bricks. I would like to hear them recounted briefly.

RA: I had another very important dream. And these are dreams that I record, that actually, in a way, I say came true. One of my dreams in China was that I thought I had bought a new, blue truck. Very merrily I came down the street, and I was traveling with a group of nineteen [Kellog Foundation] Fellows, and I told them, "if you really want to see"--with an emphasis on *see*--"if you really want to see into the heart of China, what the people are really like, jump on my truck, and I'll take you and show you." So I guess I was becoming, or thought I could become, a guide for my tour group. I say that modestly, but I think that was what the dream was saying. And some of them jumped on, and I remember in the dream just smiles. They were very happy, those who were willing to see China my way--a different way--not statistically, not how many people are there, not how many crimes are committed during a year, not numbers, but a different kind of seeing, a different kind of understanding. When I came home, I hadn't planned to buy a truck. I bought one that summer and the blue truck that I bought was identical to the truck that I was driving in the dream.

CG: A very short interruption here. You speak of the blue truck and the blue guitar in *Heart of Aztlán*. Is this in any way an allusion to Picasso's blue guitar that inspired Wallace Stevens' poem? Because, in that poem, Wallace Stevens says, "I am the blue guitar," somewhere in the middle.

RA: I read Wallace Stevens a lot when I was a student. I think he is one of the major poets of the imagination, let's say during our generation and the generation preceding that. Our time, let's say. So there is obviously, in *Heart of Aztlán*, an interplay with *The Man With The Blue Guitar*. And the blue guitar is an instrument of poetry and the imagination. More than that, I think the color blue in the blue guitar is symbolic of other things: The blue Mexican sky, the heavens, and also the realm of imagination.

CG: May I bring you to your third dream in China--of the great wall.

RA: Oh, the third dream! My wife and I had been talking a lot about building a fence around the front of our home in Albuquerque, and one of the dreams I had in China was that I met the contractor who helped me build our adobe home there about ten years ago. I said, "I want to build this fence." And he said, "Fine, let's do it." But the brick we saw in my dream were bricks that were made of Chinese, they were incomprehensible. He said, "I can't do this; I can't build a wall with Chinese character blocks." *¡Ni modo!* So we didn't get the wall built. The deal fell through.

I came back to Albuquerque in the summer and thought more and more about the wall. I finally got, not my original contractor, but a guy that happened to come through the neighborhood and gave me a good deal on the wall. We got to work on it. And he designed an unusual wall in tiers, that has a sculptured effect of a Mayan pyramid temple. Very strangely, people remarked about it. It's stucco, adobe-colored so it looks like an adobe wall. People came by and first remarks were--I remember them precisely because I had such a laugh out of them--people would say, "You know, that looks like an Egyptian wall." And the second remark was, "You know, that looks like an Aztec wall from Mexico." None of them were saying it's a typical New Mexico wall. And it isn't. My old contractor came by, looked at it, and he said, "Is that your Chinese wall?" So somehow he had also worked his way into my dream, and there was a relationship.

CG: *Pregunta*, What is the relevance and relationship of archetypes in dreams and archetypes in myths to personal and social integration? Is there a focus, so that dreams relate more to personal integration and myth more to social integration? You seem to relate personal with social integration; what is the relationship between archetypes in dreams and archetypes in myths?

RA: The nature of the question is one that would require a great deal of time and thought to put your ideas in order and respond to it. But I really think that my answer to the first question would somehow be, "Yes, dreams have a greater relevance to personal integration because the dream is more personal." Although having given you just those three examples of dreams already, I don't know if dreams are that much personal because there is what I call the flight of the soul. If another soul can come in to me or visit me, then how personal is it really? . . . and then if there is some later kind of a correlation of that dream and another reality.

CG: We are our relationships. We define ourselves in terms of relationships.

RA: What will happen, I think, is that the myth will feed the dream and the dream will feed the myth in terms of energy and re-creation. But clearly in your question, I would also say that the myth has to do with that social, communal integration because the myth belongs to the community. It belongs to *the* people in any way you choose to define that communal group.

CG: Besides dream and myth, where else is archetype found in literature and experience?

RA: I think it depends on how you define the archetype. My sense has always been to define the archetype as a primal symbol. And that primal symbol would be available to all of us throughout mankind's history on earth. It is in the creation of art that we take those primal symbols or those archetypal symbols and infuse them into art. So that, I guess, what they become is a reflection that then speaks back to us because so many of those come from the subconscious. Sometimes we are not clearly aware of the use of archetypal symbols on other planes, or conscious planes.

CG: Luis Leal tells us that we must create myth to enter into universalism. ["The problem of Identifying Chicano Literature." *The Identification and Analysis of Chicano Literature.* Ed. Francisco Jiménez. New York: Bilingual, 1979. 4.] You have often spoken of the need to create myth. What do you mean when you say that we must create myth? Make up stories of gods and people in fairy tales? Or should we study world mythology, especially Native American mythology to which we may relate, and then open ourselves to our collective consciousness in order to focus on archetypal symbol? It sounds pretty abstract. What do you mean when you say we must create myth? How do you create myth?

RA: I think the key here is that, really, all of these would fit. We should all engage in the study of world mythology because that has an integrating sense to it. When we discover that there are points of contact to other world myths, we become sure of ourselves and say, "well because our particular mythology comes clothed in a certain garment, it's not so strange because it will have points of reference in contact to other mythologies." The key, when we say we have to create myth, has to do with a collective memory. If we all share a collective memory that has a biological base to it, then we share with everyone on earth and everyone who has preceded us, those points of contact, points of reference, and we also share that archetypal pool. So it is very important--given my particular bias or opinion or how I am--to understand that collective reservoir, that collective memory and to find in it those pure symbols, those archetypal symbols.

CG: How do you get in touch with this common reservoir of the collective unconscious?

RA: Well, there are many ways to do it. I guess, the most popular way would be to meditate. To pray. To fast. To think. Also, in an artistic way, I think here is where I get a big kick out of being a writer, being an artist, because it is my process of writing that becomes a kind of meditation in which I begin to tap myself. The archetypes reside in me, and in that process of writing and thinking the story and energizing myself and using the energy of the story, I begin to find those archetypals in me and, as I said earlier, infuse them into the story. When I say we must create myth, I think that what I mean by that is that we often look at mythology as if it happened in the distant past. We say: "The Greeks had their mythology, and the Toltecs and Aztecs of meso-America had their mythology. Isn't that interesting? It's all in the past; it's gone." We tend to view myth as static. What I am saying is that it is not static. It's working in us even now. Because those same archetypals that were discovered by the ancient people are in us today. And it is the creation of myth and that reference to that collective pool that we all carry inside of us that re-energizes us and makes us more authentic. If part of the search is for the authentic self in us, then those archetypals and symbols are clear messages that begin to define the authentic self.

CG: Luis Leal told me that, in his opinion, you, Miguel Méndez-M., Ron Arias, and Tomás Rivera are the leaders in creation of myth (especially you and Méndez). How do you understand this? . . . And you say that you've never seen Rivera as particularly working in myth?

RA: I've taught Rivera's work, and I admire it. I teach it every semester: ". . . *y no se tragó la tierra*." I teach it more from an existentialist point of view.

CG: Yes . . . defining himself. The little boy is under the house, at the end. Other children say they see "a man under the house." This perhaps could be understood as his having gone back into himself to find freedom and break with former structures . . . that he finally integrated himself at the point of transcendence. That may be what Luis Leal is referring to. Just as Arias is dealing with a point of transcendence, at the point of approaching death. The old man reconciled himself and came to peace and terms with reality. You have here this young man on a quest. Here he is trapped with the old institutions and forms and is breaking away from them. I don't know if that is necessarily mythical, but at any rate, it is interesting that you have not seen Rivera from that point of view.

RA: I haven't seen him . . . I haven't seen ". . . *y no se lo tragó la tierra*" as a work that actively engages the presentation of a myth that we all know and understand--or say, the work gropes to understand--infused again into the story he tells. Certainly the house is an archetypal symbol. But just to have archetypal symbols and to use them and to know how to use them doesn't make the writer an active participant in the creation of myth.

CG: How about Méndez and Arias? Do you see them as active in this development of myth?

RA: I can't speak well to Méndez's work because I haven't studied it enough to say something useful. Arias, I see very clearly in the stream of what we call magical realism which has a tremendous sense of playfulness with myth, but is concerned also with presentations of realities.

CG: Do you see your approach to myth as eclectic, drawing from Jung, Freud, Lévi-Strauss, Cassirer, and others, or is there a focus and preference for one of these approaches to myth?

RA: I think my approach is eclectic. I have probably read, at one time or another, these philosophers, psychologists, cultural anthropologists, but I have never found myself following any particular school of thought. Although, of course, if you have read my work and you know anything about the work of these thinkers, you would put me in Jung's camp immediately. And you would say, "Your work is Jungian," which is fine with me. But I don't read Jung as a bible every night. So it is eclectic, and, so, much of it has a basis in the thought of men like these--thinkers. But I am also very much interested in just allowing myself to see things and to learn things. I like to go to different cultures, to different people, and look at their dance, their art work, the little things in their homes, and their stories . . . their *cuentos.* How do those describe their world view in the use of archetypal symbols. I guess I'm eclectic in the sense that I like to open myself up to experience. It's like opening myself up to that collective memory, and letting the impressions affect me, then I reflect on them and see. And then I also use them some times not only for thinking but also for my work, for literature. I don't care very much if I am doing it correctly or incorrectly depending on Jung or Freud or Lévi-Strauss.

CG: Do you use Northrop Frye's "Structure of Literary types" as a map, as it were, for developing your novels sometimes?

RA: No, never.

CG: A question from a student (R.M.). I am Catholic. I read you and other Chicano writers caricaturing the church. For example, your character of Father Cayo in *Heart of Aztlán*. And these writers point out how much the church has collaborated with other institutions to exploit the people. Are you asking me to reject the church and/or my faith? Is this rejection of the Catholic church/faith essential to finding and defining my freedom? I'm thinking in part of the young man in ". . . *y no se lo tragó la tierra*." Are you asking me to search for some kind of natural religion based on myths and nature?

RA: Well, I would start first of all by saying I am not asking this student to do anything. Certainly, I am not asking him to reject his religion or to embark on a new search for a natural religion. I think the nature of his question might suggest that he is asking himself whether he should do that. As to the church, it would take a long time to describe my personal crisis of faith that I went through as a young man after having been raised a Catholic and in the church and having to come to my own view of the world and the integration that I wanted in terms of the authentic self. I didn't think the church was providing me everything that I needed. I also think that in many respects the church has been an institution that, to be quite blunt, has been repressive in the lives of people. I meet many people who talk about having a sense of this institution that is very important and intricately tied in with faith, being a force that, rather than liberating self, represses self. And since I think that's part of my job as a writer--to liberate myself and to search out what is the most authentic in me--I did for years question the basis of this very fixed and dogmatic religion and then embarked on my own path. But I don't really proselytize for everybody to do that because religion is, I think, a question bound up with what you believe with faith.

CG: And that is ultimately the person. However, you would be saying, if I understand you, don't let the church or any other institution so lock you in, that your freedom, your autonomy, your self-definition, ends up in constraints.

RA: Yes, I think so. It is like we live under a set of laws and governments--national, state, and local governments--and we accept the rule of law, but that doesn't mean we are not constantly critical of it, or shouldn't be critical of it.

CG: Or that the only alternative is anarchy.

RA: Yes, or that the only alternative is anarchy. In search of a better world for everyone, we keep being critical of those laws that we impose on ourselves. And so, if the church is, indeed for me one more institution that imposes a set of laws, I feel that I have the right also to be critical of that set of laws.

CG: A woman whom I knew in the movimiento years ago in L.A. asked last night about women in Chicano literature and your role. I understand that women once walked out on you during one of your presentations.

RA: No. I think women have never walked out on one of my presentations.

CG: That must have been a misapprehension on her part. I thank you for your clarification. Setting that aside, do you think of your writing as being concerned with women? Are you explicitly conscious and looking out for how women are portrayed in your writings in the evolving Chicano culture and the dynamics of their growth?

RA: I think so. Very obviously. In fact, I open myself to more critical thought on the subject because I don't think there is any other Chicano writer who has created as many strong women characters as I have. I think there were reservations with Ultima in *Bless Me, Ultima* for awhile. The Chicana in pursuing fulfillment of her own authentic self looked at Ultima and said: "I somehow don't seem to find a model that fits me if I want to be a doctor, attorney, or professional woman." And the only thing I can say to that is--in a sense it is a limited view, because I was writing about a certain time in our culture, in a very rural New Mexican setting which had a very traditional role for both the men and the women, and I was trying to reflect that. So I could not make Ultima an aspiring Chicana attorney and have any kind of a novel that I was writing of that time. On the other hand, in her own time, she acts with tremendous power in the world of men, so I think it's fair to remember that.

CG: You spoke of creating other powerful women characters.

RA: Well, I just finished the novel, *The legend of La Llorona* which has to do with Malinche, in which I suggest a new motivation for Malinche. That is, that she did not act out of impulse, rage, and jealously when Cortez jilts her, and then she has to make a decision about whether she gives up her son. In this case, I describe two boys that she has. (I play around with whatever the facts are.) She had to decide whether she would give them up to Cortez, who will take them to the court of Spain where they will be held up to ridicule, or to sacrifice them as warriors of a new resistance. And so the motivations I ascribe to Malinche are, I think, much more noble in the sense of how we describe classical tragedy. I have also done a screen play, that hasn't been produced, which has as the central character a young girl, Rosalinda. So I continue, I think, to attack the portrayal [of stereotypes] as best I can.

CG: A quick question, just to satisfy my curiosity. What is the symbolism of the steel pins in *Heart of Aztlán*?

RA: It comes out of part of the folk belief that you ward off a *bruja*, or a witch, by making the cross of the *fileres* or little pins that have been blessed at the church. And to me it was just a common part of some of the belief that I grew up with, and thought it would be very clear for most Chicanos that grew up with that body of what we call folklore and I call a system of belief. The way you trap a witch in your house is by inviting her in and then putting a *crucita* of *los* pins on the door, and then she cannot pass because they symbolize, of course, the cross of Christ. Whatever evil the *bruja* has that has come to your home cannot pass against the cross.

CG: One closing question. You came here to Floricanto Cinco organized by Aztleca. The academic part of the program organized by the university did not take place on Friday. You knew ahead of time that it would not take place, and yet you came. Why did you come?

RA: I think I came because, since I began writing--and since I first published in 1972, which is a number of years ago--I have been very much in tune with this world that we had to discover which was that second part of our nature for those of us who relate to our Indian heritage. There were, in the beginning, some people who opposed it because they thought it was too much of that fairy tale mythology, you see, that had no relevance to our life. Now it pleases me to see the young people, community people, and other people, continuing that kind of search and carrying it forward and re-establishing their roots in that very important other part of ourselves. The search for that authentic self again can't take place in only one *campo*, in one camp. It has to be eclectic. It has to begin to draw in all sources that have fed our history.

CONTRIBUTORS

Bruce-Novoa

Born in Denver, Colorado, Professor Bruce-Novoa went on to study at the University of Colorado in Boulder, where he received his Ph.D. in contemporary Mexican narrative (1974). He has taught at Yale ('74-'83), the University of California, Santa Barbara ('83-'85), and Trinity University ('85-'89), as well as at the Universität Mainz, West Germany. His articles have appeared in the U.S., Mexico, France, Germany, England, and Spain. He has authored a book of poetry, *Inocencia perversa/Perverse Innocence*, another of interviews, *Chicano Authors: Inquiry by Interview*, and one of critical analysis, *Chicano Poetry: A Response to Chaos*, as well as edited six others. His most recent title is *Antología restropectiva del cuento chicano*. Juan organized the series of European conferences on U.S. Latino cultures, now going into its sixth year. Presently he is founding an association of critics of Mexican literature.

Heiner Bus

Professor of American Studies at the Johannes Gutenberg-Universität at Mainz (Germany), Heiner has also held assignments at the universities of Trier and Bamberg and was an ACLS postgraduate Fellow at Yale University. He has a special interest in American literature, focusing on our literatures of cultural diversity from a comparative point of view. He has published books on Saul Bellow and Washington Irving, articles on the impact of American English on German, Jewish-American literature, Black autobiography, Jean Toomer's *Cane*, Canadian theatre, Native American literture, and studies in Chicano Literature, including the works of Sandra Cisneros and Gary Soto.

Héctor Calderón

A native of Calexico, California, Professor Calderón received his Ph.D. in Latin American Literature, with a Minor in Comparative Literature, from Yale. He attended the National School of Criticism and Theory (1978) and was a Ford Fellow at the Stanford Humanities Center (1987). He is Associate Professor of Hispanic Studies and Chicano Studies at Scripps College. Héctor is the author of numerous articles on Latin American and Chicano literature. A recent book is *Conciencia y lenguaje en el "Quijote" y "El obsceno Pájaro de la noche"* (Madrid: Editorial Pliegos, 1987). He is also co-editor of *Chicano Literary Criticism: New Essays in Cultural Studies and Ideology* and is currently completing a book-length study of Chicano narrative genres, *Contemporary Chicano Narrative: A Tradition and Its Forms.*

Roberto Cantú

Roberto is a Professor of Chicano Studies at California State University, Los Angeles, and currently editor of *Campo Libre: Journal of Chicano Studies*, and *Escolios: Journal of Literature and Criticism.* From 1972 through 1975, he was editor of *Mester.* A prolific writer, he has published articles on Mexican and Chicano literature, as well as on Mexican intellectual history, in *Hipótesis* (Bolivia), *Cuadernos Hispanoamericanos* (Spain), *Caribe* (Hawaii), *Los Ensayistas* (Georiga), and in journals under his editorship. Currently his research interests are mainly in the area of theory and Chicano studies.

Jean Cazemajou

Professor Cazemajou was born in 1924 near Bordeaux, France. After receiving his master's degree from the University of Toulouse (1947), he obtained a "Doctorat d'Etat" from the University of Paris in 1970. He currently holds the position of Professor in the English Department of the University of Bordeaux III, and has taught in a number of French and American Universities, including the University of West Virginia (1957-58), the University of Toulouse (1962-68), and at the University of California (1973-74) on the Davis campus. Recent works which reflect Jean's interest in Hispanos in the U.S., include *La crise du melting-pot* (Paris: Aubier, 1983) written with Prof. J. P. Martin; a casebook *Les Minorités hispaniques en Amérique du Nord 1960-80* (Bordeaux: PUB, 1985); and *American Expansionism and Foreign Policy 1885-1908* (Paris: A. Colin, 1988).

César A. González-Trujillo

A native of Los Angeles, California, César's studies at Gonzaga Univerity, the University of Santa Clara, and the University of California, Los Angeles were in the fields of philosophy, Spanish literature, theology, and sociology. He was a member of the first National Endowment for the Humanities fellowships in Chicano studies, with Don Luis Leal (1984). A poet and writer, he published *Unwinding the Silence* (Lalo Press 1987). María Teresa Huerta Márquez and he are preparing *Rudolfo A. Anaya: A Bio-Bibliography* as a title in the Series Bio-Bibliographies in American Literature (Greenwood Press). César is currently Professor and Chairperson of the Chicano Studies Department at San Diego Mesa College.

María Herrera-Sobek

Professor Herrera-Sobek grew up in Texas, moving to Gilbert, Arizona in the '50s. She received her B.A. in chemistry from Arizona State University, Tempe in 1965. After working at a biochemistry laboratory at the University of California, Los Angeles, she went on to receive her M.A. in Latin American Studies (1971) and her Ph.D. in Hispanic Languages and literature (1975) at that institution. Aside from her remarkable record of publishing in professional journals, María has edited two books on Chicana writers: *Beyond Stereotypes: The Critical Analysis of Chicana Literature* (1985) and *Chicana Creativity and Criticism: Charting New Frontiers in American Literature*

(1987). She recently completed two book-length manuscripts: *Mothers, Lovers, and Soldiers: Archetypal Representation of Women in the Corrido* and *Northward Bound: The Mexican Immigrant Experience in Corridos and Canciones.*

Enrique R. Lamadrid

Critic and folklorist Enrique R. Lamadrid teaches at the University of New Mexico in Albuquerque and in Morelia, Michoacán where he directs the CONEXIONES Institute. His research and field work in 19th century *indita* ballads and other New Mexican folk music charts the influence of indigenous cultures on the Spanish language and imagination. His literary writings explore the borderlands between cultures and between the orality of popular traditions and the inter-textuality of literary expression. Recent projects include two anthologies of Mexican poetry in translation, *Un ojo en el muro: Mexican Poetry 1970-1985,* and *En breve: Minimalism in Mexican Poetry 1900-1985* (Santa Fe: Tooth of Time, 1986 and 1988). He recently produced a three-hour sound track "Tesoros del Espíritu" for the permanent exhibit on New Mexican folk culture at the Museum of International Folk Art in Santa Fe.

Vernon E. Lattin

Professor Vernon E. Lattin received his bachelors and masters degrees at the University of New Mexico. His field of specialization for the Ph.D. in English, at the University of Colorado, was British Romantic Literture. His academic career has included faculty positions at the University of Tennessee, Northern Illinois University, and the University of Wisconsin-Madison. Publications include edited books on the Chicano Novel (*Contemporary Chicano Fiction: A Critical Survey*; Bilingual Press, 1986) and on Tomás Rivera, as well as over two dozen articles and reviews. Vernon has written articles and reviews on Arias, Anaya, Rivera, Trambley, Morales, and other Chicano writers. Among his recent works is a Modern Language Association publication on teaching S. Momaday's *The Way to Rainy Mountain.* He is current CEO and Provost at Arizona State University West Campus, Phoenix, Arizona.

Mária Elena López

Professor López is a distinguished member of the faculty of the University of Northern Colorado.

Luis Leal

Professor Luis Leal, born in Mexico, studied at Northwestern University (B.S.) and the University of Chicago (M.A., Ph.D.). He has taught at the University of Chicago, the University of Mississippi, Emory University, and the University of Illinois (Champaign-Urbana), from where he retired in 1976 as Professor Emeritus. He has published numerous articles and several books, among them *Historia del cuento hispanoamericano* (1966; 2nd rev. ed., 1971), *Mariano Azuela* (Twayne, 1971), *Juan Rulfo* (Twayne, 1983), *Aztlán y México* (Bilingual Press, 1985). In 1988 the Chicano Studies Library, University of California, Berkeley, published *Luis Leal: A Bibliography with Interpretative and Critical Essays*. In 1987, Don Luis was honored with the Distinguished Scholar Award by the National Association of Chicano Studies (NACS). He is now Visiting Professor in the Department of Chicano Studies, University of California, Santa Barbara.

María Teresa Huerta Márquez

Professor Márquez is Assistant Department Head of the Government Publications Department at the University of New Mexico General Library. She is Vice-President of El Norte Publications, Vice-Chair of the New Mexico Endowment for the Humanities, and a member of the Women's Studies Advisory Board. Teresa is co-editor of *Las Mujeres Hablan: An Anthology of Nuevo Mexicana Writers.*

Margarita Nieto

An Associate Professor in Chicano Studies at California State University, Northridge, Professor Nieto has published numerous articles on Mexican, Chicano, and Latin American literature, as well as on Latino and Latin American visual art. She has written on Carlos Castaneda, Octavio Paz, Carlos Fuentes, and Ron Arias. She has also devoted her attention to Rufino Tamayo, Carlos Almaraz, and to the history of the Latino art movement. Margarita is a reviewer for the *Los Angeles Times Book Review* and *ARTWEEK*. Her Ph.D. in Hispanic Languages and Literatures was earned at the University of California, Los Angeles.

Ernesto Padilla

Professor Padilla (born in Las Cruces, New Mexico and raised in Tulare, California) received his Ph.D. in Victorian literature from the University of California at San Diego. He writes both poetry and fiction and is currently finishing a collection of short stories entitled *The Emperor of Ice-cream*, stories of his boyhood Barrio in Tulare. In addition, he is the editor and publisher of Lalo Press. Ernesto is currently with the English Department at California State University, Bakersfield where he teaches Nineteenth Century literature (British and American), creative writing and American Ethnic literature.

Horst Tonn

Professor Tonn was born in Oldenburg, West-Germany, in 1953. He completed his Ph.D. at the Free University Berlin in 1986 and is currently Assistant Professor of American Studies at the University of Duisburg. He is the co-author of a book on the farmworker movement in the United States, and the German translator of Rudolfo A. Anaya's *Bless Me, Ultima*, which was published in the Federal Republic in 1984. His dissertation on the contemporary Chicano novel and autobiography was recently published (Frankfurt/M., 1988).

INDEX OF AUTHORS*

*This index does not include names appearing in the appendices nor in the
bibliography by María Teresa Huerta Márquez.